Emergency Medicine Maltreatment & Syndromes

SECTION EDITORS

Ilene Claudius, MD
Associate Professor
David Geffen School of Medicine at UCLA
Director of Quality Improvement
Harbor-UCLA Department of Emergency Medicine
Torrance, CA

Erik Langenau, DO, MS
Professor, Pediatrics
Chief Academic Technology Officer,
Department of Professional Development and Online Learning
Philadelphia College of Osteopathic Medicine
Philadelphia, PA

MEDICAL EDITOR

Lynn Bullock, MD
Colorado Springs, CO

Table of Contents

TOXICOLOGY

POISONINGS 7-1
  OVERVIEW 7-1
  INITIAL MANAGEMENT 7-1
    History 7-1
    Physical Examination 7-1
    Toxidromes 7-2
    Laboratory Findings 7-3
    Decontamination 7-3
  ACETAMINOPHEN INGESTION 7-4
  SALICYLATE INGESTION 7-4
  IBUPROFEN INGESTION 7-5
  OPIATE / OPIOID POISONING 7-5
  ANTIHYPERTENSIVE INGESTION 7-5
  IRON INGESTION 7-6
  ANTICHOLINERGIC INGESTION 7-7
  TRICYCLIC ANTIDEPRESSANT (TCA)
    INGESTION 7-7
  SEROTONIN SYNDROME AND NEUROLEPTIC
    MALIGNANT SYNDROME 7-7
  ORAL HYPOGLYCEMIC AGENTS 7-7
  METHEMOGLOBINEMIA 7-8

ENVIRONMENTAL INGESTIONS AND
  EXPOSURES 7-8
  LEAD 7-8
  CARBON MONOXIDE (CO) 7-9
  CYANIDE 7-9
  CAUSTIC SUBSTANCE INGESTION 7-10
  HYDROCARBON POISONING 7-10
  ETHANOL INGESTION 7-11
  METHANOL INGESTION 7-11
  ETHYLENE GLYCOL INGESTION 7-11
  ORGANOPHOSPHATE POISONING 7-12
  PLANT EXPOSURES 7-12
  ESOPHAGEAL FOREIGN BODIES 7-12

ENVENOMATION AND TRAUMA

BITES 7-13
  DOG / CAT BITES 7-13
  HUMAN BITES 7-14
  SNAKE BITES 7-14
  SPIDER BITES 7-15

LACERATIONS AND PUNCTURES 7-16

BURNS 7-16
  OVERVIEW 7-16
  MINOR BURN CARE 7-17
  MAJOR BURN CARE 7-17

SUBMERSION INJURY 7-18

HEAD INJURY 7-18
  OVERVIEW 7-18
  NEUROIMAGING 7-20
  MILD TRAUMATIC BRAIN INJURY (mTBI;
    CONCUSSION) 7-20

ELECTRICAL BURNS 7-21
OCULAR CHEMICAL BURNS 7-22
CHEST WALL TRAUMA 7-22
BLUNT ABDOMINAL TRAUMA 7-22
FRACTURES 7-23
  OVERVIEW 7-23
  GREENSTICK FRACTURE 7-24
  TORUS (BUCKLE) FRACTURE 7-24
  SPIRAL FRACTURE 7-24
  CLAVICLE FRACTURE 7-24
  DISTAL HUMERUS (ELBOW) FRACTURE 7-25
  FRACTURE COMPLICATIONS 7-25

SUBLUXATION OF THE RADIAL HEAD 7-26
SHOULDER INJURIES 7-26
SPRAINS 7-26

OTHER EMERGENT EVENTS

BRIEF RESOLVED UNEXPLAINED EVENT (BRUE) ..7-27
SHOCK 7-28
PEDIATRIC ADVANCED LIFE SUPPORT (PALS) 7-29
  OVERVIEW 7-29
  CIRCULATION 7-30
    Tachycardia 7-30
    Bradycardia 7-30
    Pulseless Algorithm 7-31

CHILD MALTREATMENT

CHILD MALTREATMENT SYNDROMES 7-31
  OVERVIEW 7-32
  NEGLECT 7-32
  PHYSICAL ABUSE 7-32
    Common Presentations 7-32
    Evaluation 7-34
  SEXUAL ABUSE 7-34
  PSYCHOLOGICAL MALTREATMENT 7-35
    Long-Term Psychological Effects of
    Maltreatment 7-35

MANAGEMENT OF MALTREATMENT 7-36

THE MEDSTUDY HUB: YOUR GUIDELINES
  AND REVIEW ARTICLES RESOURCE 7-36

FIGURE SOURCES 7-37

TOXICOLOGY

POISONINGS

PREVIEW | REVIEW

- What ingestions cause miosis?
- What ingestions cause mydriasis?
- What are the symptoms of an anticholinergic ingestion?
- What are the symptoms of cholinergic poisoning?
- Name some toxins for which activated charcoal would not be a useful treatment.
- Is ipecac routinely recommended for use?
- Know the stages of acetaminophen poisoning!
- What are the lab findings of salicylate poisoning?
- Why is sodium bicarbonate given for treatment of salicylate poisoning?
- What are the classic symptoms of opiate poisoning? Treatment?
- What toxicity can clonidine exposure mimic in children?
- A child presents with nausea, hematemesis, and abdominal pain shortly after getting into the mother's vitamins. What specific ingestion should you be worried about?
- Know the stages of iron poisoning!
- Name the key cardiac findings seen with tricyclic antidepressant ingestion.
- What agent is used in tricyclic antidepressant overdose to prevent or treat dysrhythmias?
- What drugs are commonly involved in serotonin syndrome?

OVERVIEW

In the U.S., > 2 million poisoning events are recorded annually, and about half of these occur in children < 6 years of age. The peak age for unintentional ingestions is 18 months to 3 years. Over 90% of these events occur in the home, and most involve only 1 substance. Fortunately, the majority can be managed safely at home.

The majority of poisonings in young children are unintentional; intentional exposures predominate in 13- to 19-year-olds. The majority of exposures in young children involve nonpharmaceuticals—the most common being foreign bodies, cosmetics, cleaning products, and pesticides. The most common unintentional pharmaceutical ingestions are analgesics, antihistamines, topical preparations, vitamins, and dietary supplements/herbals.

Of the 18% of poisonings that are intentional, most occur in adolescents and adults. About 2/3 of poisonings are due to suicidal intent, with about 1/3 due to intentional misuse. Intentional exposures account for > 90% of poisoning deaths. Misuse and overdose of prescription opioid painkillers have increased markedly in recent years.

Poison control centers and medical toxicologists are invaluable resources for information on the prevention and management of poisonings. Encourage families to keep the poison control phone number (American Association of Poison Control Centers: 1-800-222-1222) available at all times to call for advice in the event of a possible poisoning.

INITIAL MANAGEMENT

Initial evaluation and stabilization for all poisonings follows the **ABCD**s: **a**irway/**a**ntidotes, **b**reathing, **c**irculation, and **d**isability/**d**econtamination. Most substances do not have specific antidotes; thus, supportive care is the mainstay of treatment. In any child with altered mental status, obtain a bedside glucose. Order an electrocardiogram (ECG) with cardiotoxic or unknown ingestion, and look for changes suggestive of a drug poisoning that needs specific intervention (e.g., wide QRS complexes in tricyclic antidepressant overdose). Routine urine drug screening is often not helpful; many substances are not detected by standard urine drug screens, including cyanide, clonidine, organophosphates, β-blockers, calcium channel blockers, and iron. Blood levels are useful for specific poisonings (e.g., acetaminophen, salicylates, iron). If the history is unknown, or in the case of polypharmacy or potential suicidal ingestions, always obtain acetaminophen and salicylate levels and an ECG, and consider ethanol levels.

History

Obtain a careful history, including substance(s) ingested, time of ingestion/exposure, quantity, and other circumstances such as suicidal intent. It is not uncommon for a child to present with altered mental status or other signs of poisoning without any known history of exposure. Ask about substances available in the home, including adult/pediatric medications, illicit drugs, and household products. In addition, ask about over-the-counter (OTC) and complementary/alternative medicines taken by or available to the child.

Physical Examination

For unknown ingestions, the physical exam often offers clues as to what the toxin is. Pay attention to vital signs, neurologic status, pupil size (mi**O**sis = pinp**O**int; **D**ilated = my**D**riasis), breath odor, and skin findings (temperature, color, and diaphoresis). Refer to Table 7-1 on page 7-2 as you review this information.

Table 7-1: Physical Exam in Toxic Ingestions		
Physical Exam	**Category**	**Examples**
"Excited": • Agitation • Restlessness • Hypertension • Tachycardia • Hyperventilation • Hyperthermia • Mydriasis (usually)	Anticholinergics	Antihistamines Neuroleptics (e.g., chlorpromazine, quetiapine) Tricyclic antidepressants Atropine Antispasmodics (e.g., hyoscyamine) Plants: nightshade (belladonna) and jimson weed
	Sympathomimetics	Ephedrine Dextromethorphan (5–10× therapeutic dose) Cocaine Amphetamine Methamphetamine MDMA (Ecstasy) 4-Bromo-2,5-dimethoxyphenethylamine (2C-B, Nexus, 2s) 2,5-Dimethoxy-4-n-propylthiophenethylamine (Blue Mystic, 2C-T-7) Phencyclidine (PCP; Angel Dust; is also a hallucinogen; causes miosis, not mydriasis)
	Hallucinogens	Lysergic acid diethylamide (LSD; also has weak sympathomimetic effects) Mescaline (peyote) Phencyclidine Psilocybin (found in certain mushrooms)
"Depressed": • Obtundation • Hypotension • Bradycardia • Hypoventilation • Hypothermia • Miosis (usually)	Cholinergics	Organophosphate and carbamate insecticides
	Sympatholytics	Clonidine
	Opiates	Oxycodone (frequently combined with acetaminophen; has extended-release formulations) Hydrocodone (frequently combined with acetaminophen; has extended-release formulations)
	Sedative-hypnotics	Benzodiazepines Barbiturates

Heart rate clues:

• **FAST** heart rate
  ◦ **F**reebase cocaine (or any form cocaine)
  ◦ **A**nticholinergics, **A**SA (acetylsalicylic acid)
  ◦ **S**ympathomimetics
  ◦ **T**heophylline

• Slow-**PACED** heart rate
  ◦ **P**ropranolol (β-blockers)
  ◦ **A**nticholinesterases
  ◦ **C**lonidine, **c**alcium channel blockers
  ◦ **E**thanol
  ◦ **D**igoxin

Common causes of **miosis** include (**COPS**):

• **C**holinergics, clonidine
• **O**piates, organophosphates
• **P**hencyclidine, **p**henothiazines, **p**ilocarpine
• **S**edatives (barbiturates)

Common causes of **mydriasis** include (**AAS**):

• **A**nticholinergics (e.g., atropine)
• **A**ntihistamines
• **S**ympathomimetics (e.g., amphetamine, cocaine, lysergic acid diethylamide [LSD])

Skin discoloration can be another clue in carbon monoxide poisoning; "cherry-red" skin is classically described (although rarely seen). Cyanosis can indicate hypoxemia or methemoglobinemia.

Toxidromes

There are classic sets of signs and symptoms, called **toxidromes**, that can help identify unknown poisonings. We will discuss some of the well-known toxidromes here.

Anticholinergic toxidrome—"dry as a bone, red as a beet, hot as a hare, blind as a bat, mad as a hatter, full as a flask":

• Dry, flushed skin and dry mucous membranes
• Hyperthermia
• Mydriasis
• Agitation, delirium, hallucinations
• Urinary retention, decreased bowel sounds
• Tachycardia, hypertension
• Coma, seizures (rare)

Examples of drugs that can cause an anticholinergic toxidrome include atropine and antihistamines. Tricyclic antidepressants (TCAs) have anticholinergic effects, but the pupillary findings can be offset by antagonism of α receptors. Some medications used for urinary incontinence, such as oxybutynin, also have anticholinergic properties, capitalizing on the side effect of urinary retention.

Cholinergic toxidrome—produces muscarinic and/or nicotinic signs and/or central nervous system (CNS) effects. A possible scenario is a child who presents with confusion, wheezing, and increased secretions after playing unsupervised in the backyard.

Remember **DUMBELS** for muscarinic effects:

- **D**iarrhea
- **U**rination
- **M**iosis
- **B**ronchorrhea, bronchospasm, bradycardia
- **E**mesis
- **L**acrimation
- **S**alivation

Nicotinic effects include muscle weakness, fasciculations, and paralysis, as well as CNS effects, including respiratory depression, seizures, lethargy, and coma. Bradycardia is classic, but tachycardia can be seen, too. Classic agents include insecticides (organophosphate/carbamate) and nicotine.

Opioid toxidrome—effects include CNS depression, miosis, respiratory depression/apnea, bradycardia, and hypotension. Clonidine can produce a similar picture.

Sympathomimetic toxidrome—findings include agitation, tremors, hallucinations, seizures, tachycardia, hypertension, mydriasis, and diaphoresis. Examples include decongestants such as pseudoephedrine, cocaine, amphetamines, and psychostimulants. Some sympathomimetics have specific associated findings to know—like nystagmus (typically vertical or rotary) and miosis with phencyclidine (PCP). Both the use of the sympathomimetics and the resultant agitation can contribute to rhabdomyolysis.

Laboratory Findings

Some classic lab findings can also be clues to the cause of the poisoning:

- ECG: prolonged QRS in tricyclic poisoning
- Elevated serum osmolal gap: methanol, ethylene glycol, isopropyl alcohol (See the Nephrology & Urology section for the formula.)
- High anion gap: **MUDPILES** (**m**ethanol, **u**remia, **d**iabetic ketoacidosis [DKA], **p**ropylene glycol, **i**ron/isonicotinic acid hydrazide [INH], **l**actate, **e**thanol/ethylene glycol, and **s**alicylates); cyanide; carbon monoxide
- X-rays: radiopaque substances, including **CHIPES** (**c**hloral hydrate, **c**alcium, **h**eavy metals, **i**ron, **p**henothiazines, **e**nteric-coated preparations, **s**alicylates, **s**ustained-release tablets)

Decontamination

Many ingestions/exposures are nontoxic, in which case no therapy is needed besides reassurance and anticipatory guidance. For children with potentially toxic exposures, preventing agents from being further absorbed is important, depending on the type of exposure:

- **Dermal**—remove clothing, wash skin with water and then with soap and water (1st priority for organophosphate poisoning). Wear protective gear to avoid self-contamination.
- **Ocular**—remove fragments and irrigate eyes with copious normal saline (goal—normalization of ocular pH).
- **Respiratory**—move the patient to fresh air. Protect self from exposure.
- **GI**—most liquids are absorbed within 30 minutes and most solids within 1–2 hours. Many ingestions present outside of this time window for effective decontamination. Poison control centers and/or toxicology specialists can help determine if GI decontamination is needed.

Activated charcoal (AC) is the most commonly used method of GI decontamination, though use is declining. Never administer AC in a patient at risk of aspiration, especially those with depressed mental status or seizure who cannot protect their airway. Additional contraindications include GI obstruction or perforation and ingestion of hydrocarbons or caustic substances. AC is generally used in the 1st hour after ingestion to absorb substances and decrease bioavailability. It can be useful even after 1–2 hours for certain drugs with ongoing enterohepatic circulation (e.g., carbamazepine). Repeated doses of activated charcoal may be helpful to continue the absorption of some drugs, such as drugs with significant enterohepatic recirculation. Potential complications of AC therapy include pulmonary aspiration, emesis, and constipation.

Activated charcoal is ineffective or contraindicated in the following. Think **CHEMICAL CamP**:

- **C**austics
- **H**ydrocarbons (and most water-soluble compounds)
- **E**lectrolytes
- **M**etals
- **I**ron
- **C**yanide
- **A**lcohols
- **L**ithium
- **Cam**phor
- **P**hosphorus

Gastric lavage is seldom indicated; the risks generally outweigh any potential benefit. It can be considered within 30–60 minutes of a life-threatening ingestion with no other potential treatment, once airway protection is ensured. A large-bore tube is needed for most substances, limiting usefulness in younger children. One worrisome complication is pulmonary aspiration. Contraindications for gastric lavage include caustic, hydrocarbon, and sharp-item ingestions. The absence of pill fragments seen on lavage does not rule out toxic ingestion.

Whole bowel irrigation (WBI) involves flushing the entire GI tract with polyethylene glycol solution until the rectal effluent turns clear. Clinical studies have not shown clear benefit. Patients often experience nausea/vomiting and GI discomfort. A nasogastric nasojejunal tube is often needed. WBI is used in significant ingestions in which activated charcoal is expected to be ineffective or extended release of the toxin is anticipated (e.g., heavy metals, sustained-release medications, patches, "packers and stuffers" [patients smuggling illicit substances inside of a swallowed or inserted condom or balloon]). Contraindications include airway compromise, ileus, bowel obstruction, intestinal perforation, GI hemorrhage, hemodynamic instability, and recalcitrant vomiting.

Cathartics (which decrease GI transit time) and ipecac (an OTC agent that induces vomiting) are no longer recommended for use.

ACETAMINOPHEN INGESTION

Know this topic well! Acetaminophen is the most frequently used analgesic in the U.S., leading to many overdoses in children. In subtoxic doses, acetaminophen is rapidly absorbed, and some of it is metabolized in the liver to nontoxic metabolites using glutathione. In an overdose, glutathione stores are overwhelmed and the toxic metabolite *N*-acetyl-*p*-benzoquinone imine (NAPQI) accumulates, causing liver damage. Mortality is rare in children, especially if treated within 8–10 hours, and young children seem less susceptible to hepatotoxicity than teenagers and adults.

The minimal toxic dose in a child < 12 years of age is 150 mg/kg; in adolescents and adults, it is 7.5 g. Note: Repeated supratherapeutic doses can lead to severe toxicity as well. This can occur through dosing errors, use of adult formulations, or when multiple acetaminophen-containing products are simultaneously administered.

Progression of acetaminophen toxicity occurs as follows:

- **Stage I** (0–24 hours): nausea/vomiting; can be asymptomatic; normal liver transaminase levels
- **Stage II** (24–72 hours): RUQ pain; liver transaminase levels begin to increase; prolongation of prothrombin time (PT); and elevated international normalized ratio (INR)
- **Stage III** (72–96 hours): peak of symptoms; fulminant hepatic failure; coagulopathy; and in severe cases, multisystem organ failure
- **Stage IV** (4–14 days): recovery or death; symptoms resolve in survivors

Most patients are asymptomatic, unless they present late in the progression. When a patient presents within 1 hour of an acetaminophen ingestion of ≥ 150 mg/kg (for those < 12 years of age) or ≥ 7.5 g (≥ 12 years of age), give activated charcoal if there are no contraindications. Next, check the acetaminophen level 4 hours after an acute ingestion, and use the Rumack-Matthew nomogram (Figure 7-1) to determine likely toxicity. If toxicity is possible or probable based on the nomogram, start oral or IV *N*-acetylcysteine (NAC). The benefit is greatest within 8 hours of ingestion, and NAC can even be started before the acetaminophen level is drawn if concern for toxicity is high. The IV form is as effective as the oral form. Although acetaminophen levels are useful in determining appropriate treatment for a single overdose, do not use the nomogram to determine toxicity if multiple doses were ingested over a period of time. In addition, an undetectable level > 24 hours after ingestion does not exclude toxicity and the nomogram cannot be used at this point. Any elevation of acetaminophen, abnormal liver enzymes, or an elevated prothrombin time should prompt treatment with NAC in a patient tested 24 hours or longer after ingestion. Do not delay treatment while awaiting levels in patients with delayed presentation. Do not forget to consider coingestions, such as opioids in prescription pain relievers. After acute ingestion and once toxicity has been determined, there is no need to follow acetaminophen levels, keeping in mind NAC does not directly decrease acetaminophen levels. However, you do need to follow aspartate aminotransferase (AST), alanine aminotransferase (ALT), and PT/INR levels. Toxicology consultation is highly recommended if you are considering antidotal treatment.

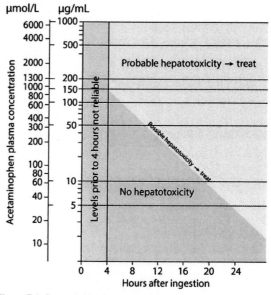

Figure 7-1: Rumack-Matthew nomogram

SALICYLATE INGESTION

Salicylates are found in aspirin, OTC cold medications, antidiarrheal medications, herbal preparations, bismuth subsalicylate, and oil of wintergreen. Overdose can be acute or chronic. Ingestion of > 150 mg/kg puts the patient at risk of toxicity. Significant toxicity is typically seen with ingestions > 300 mg/kg, and ingestions > 500 mg/kg can be fatal. Early symptoms include **tinnitus** (the most specific finding), fever, nausea, vomiting, and vertigo. Major systems affected include:

- GI (i.e., nausea, vomiting)
- Respiratory (i.e., hyperpnea and tachypnea leading to respiratory alkalosis, pulmonary edema)
- Metabolic (e.g., acidosis, fluid loss and resultant tachycardia, hypo- or hyperglycemia)
- CNS (with severe poisoning—agitation, confusion, and coma)

Ironically, severe overdoses can cause fever. Death occurs from pulmonary or cerebral edema, electrolyte imbalances, and cardiovascular collapse. Because salicylates are weak acids that uncouple oxidative phosphorylation, they cause an anion gap metabolic acidosis. Lab findings include:

- Blood gas: Classic pattern is a mixed acid-base disturbance with **respiratory alkalosis plus metabolic acidosis**; other patterns are also seen. The acidosis is a gap and nongap acidosis with elevated lactate and ketone levels.
- Electrolytes: Hypokalemia, acidosis, and high or low glucose may be observed (usually high early, followed by low). Glucose can be low in the cerebrospinal fluid (CSF) even if it is normal in the blood.
- Salicylate level in serum:
  - > 30–50 mg/dL is potentially toxic.
  - > 50–100 mg/dL is typically symptomatic.
  - > 100 mg/dL indicates serious toxicity.
  - Should be checked initially and approximately every 2 hours until improvement

Provide supportive care, including activated charcoal within the 1st hour after ingestion if applicable. Be aware that salicylate tablets can form a bezoar in the stomach that may even require endoscopic removal. Carefully rehydrate (avoid pulmonary edema) and replace electrolytes. Monitor levels every 1–2 hours. Follow blood gases, electrolytes, and coagulation studies, as well as serial salicylate levels.

Alkalinization with sodium bicarbonate traps salicylates in the blood (away from brain tissue) and renal tubules (enhancing elimination). Aim for a urine pH > 8.50, with a serum pH no higher than 7.55. Alkalinization should be used in any patient with a level > 30 mg/dL or with clear clinical evidence of toxicity. Hemodialysis can be helpful in severe cases. Maintain potassium levels > 4 mEq/L, because lower levels cause excretion of H^+ ions (in an attempt to resorb potassium via the kidney K^+/H^+ transporter), making it difficult to alkalinize the urine.

Exam tip: Ferric chloride turns urine purple or brown if salicylates are present.

IBUPROFEN INGESTION

Ibuprofen inhibits prostaglandin synthesis and can result in GI irritation, reduced renal blood flow, and platelet dysfunction. A dose of < 200 mg/kg usually does not cause toxicity, whereas a dose of > 400 mg/kg can cause severe toxicity. Symptoms generally occur within 4 hours of ingestion and resolve in 24 hours. Nausea, vomiting, and epigastric pain can occur. Serious complications are rare but can include anion gap metabolic acidosis, renal failure, and coma. Monitor renal function and acid-base status. Use activated charcoal and supportive care.

OPIATE / OPIOID POISONING

Common opiates/opioids include morphine, heroin, methadone, oxycodone, hydrocodone, fentanyl, codeine, and meperidine. Most cases of toxicity present after intentional drug use/misuse. Of course, young children can accidentally ingest oral formulations or discarded patches, which contain a large dose of medication, but misuse of prescription analgesics is a growing cause of poisoning morbidity and mortality.

The classic triad of coma, respiratory depression, and **pinpoint pupils** (miosis—recall COPS) suggests opioid poisoning.

Treatment consists of ABCs, naloxone if needed, intubation if necessary, and activated charcoal (for large oral overdoses). Patients responding to naloxone must be monitored for recurrence of symptoms because the duration of action of naloxone can be shorter than the culprit drug. **Naloxone** is likely to precipitate withdrawal syndrome (e.g., agitation, anxiety, nausea, vomiting) if the patient is opioid dependent (think teens and infants of opioid-abusing mothers). It typically is only used to reverse severe respiratory depression or apnea, not just sedation. Naloxone is now available to at-risk patients to be delivered by a friend in the event of an overdose and prior to the arrival of emergency medical services.

ANTIHYPERTENSIVE INGESTION

Ingestion of medications used to treat hypertension—such as β-adrenergic blockers, calcium channel antagonists, and clonidine—can cause serious toxicity. Ingestion of most other antihypertensive medication classes (e.g., angiotensin-converting enzyme [ACE] inhibitors, angiotensin II receptor blockers [ARBs], α-adrenergic blockers) can cause hypotension, but they are less likely to cause severe symptoms. Many antihypertensives are supplied in extended-release preparations, which can cause prolonged toxicity.

Symptoms due to **β-blocker** ingestion vary, depending on factors such as receptor selectivity, membrane stabilizing activity, and lipid solubility. Highly lipid-soluble agents (e.g., propranolol) can cause CNS symptoms in addition to cardiac toxicity. Sotalol can cause severe dysrhythmias, including torsades de pointes. Most children ingesting β-blockers become symptomatic within 2–6 hours, unless sustained-release forms or sotalol is involved. Bradycardia and hypotension are typical; watch for ventricular dysrhythmias. Children are frequently hypoglycemic.

Treatment involves the following measures, tailored to the severity of symptoms:

- Cardiopulmonary monitoring
- Activated charcoal if appropriate
- Stabilization of the airway if required
- IV boluses of crystalloid
- IV dextrose if hypoglycemic
- Toxicology or poison control center consultation
- IV glucagon (helps increase HR by increasingly intracellular levels of cyclic adenosine monophosphate [cAMP])
- IV vasopressor (epinephrine or norepinephrine)
- Cutting-edge therapies: IV lipid emulsion and high-dose insulin and glucose
- Intense temporary support: including cardiac pacing, intraaortic balloon pump, and cardiopulmonary bypass

Calcium channel blockers also commonly produce hypotension and bradycardia; patients ingesting these agents can deteriorate quickly. Unlike β-blockers, they can cause hyperglycemia. Diltiazem and verapamil are the most cardiotoxic. Treatment is the same as for β-blockers with the addition of IV calcium gluconate or chloride (if central line is present). Glucagon is less helpful for calcium channel blockers.

Clonidine is used to treat a wide array of problems, including hypertension, attention deficit hyperactivity disorder (ADHD), and nicotine withdrawal. It is an α₂-adrenergic agonist. In children, even 1 pill can cause toxicity. Dermal patches contain a high dose, and up to 75% of the medication remains in the patch even after a week of use. Symptoms occur within 1 hour of ingestion (except for patches, which may result in symptoms beyond 4 hours) and mimic opioid toxicity: CNS and respiratory depression, pinpoint pupils, bradycardia, and hypotension. Occasionally, there is early, transient paradoxical hypertension. Ingestion of imidazole drugs, such as those found in OTC eye drops (i.e., tetrahydrozoline, naphazoline, oxymetazoline), can produce similar toxicity.

Most patients recover with supportive care. Many children respond to vigorous tactile stimulation (sternal rub), though intubation is needed for persistent apnea. Monitor ECGs and vital signs closely. Give atropine or dopamine for bradycardia that is unresponsive to stimulation, and give IV fluids for hypotension. Use vasopressors for hypotension unresponsive to fluids. Activated charcoal is recommended, and whole bowel irrigation is considered, for children who ingest a patch. Naloxone sometimes reverses clonidine toxicity; consider it for severe symptoms such as apnea. If effective, either repeat doses or give continuous infusion. Toxicity usually resolves within 24 hours.

IRON INGESTION

Know: Iron ingestion is a common pediatric concern. Most exposures involve children's multivitamins with iron, which are unlikely to cause problems. More serious poisonings involve adult iron pills, especially prenatal vitamins. Fortunately, due to changes in packaging, severe iron poisoning is now relatively uncommon. The severity of iron poisoning correlates with the amount of elemental iron ingested: < 20 mg/kg is mild/asymptomatic; 20–60 mg/kg can cause moderate toxicity; and > 60 mg/kg is potentially severe.

There are 5 overlapping phases of iron toxicity:

1) **GI phase** (30 minutes–6 hours): symptoms due to direct corrosive damage to gastric/intestinal mucosa
   - Nausea, vomiting, diarrhea, and abdominal pain
   - Hematemesis and bloody diarrhea in severe cases
2) **Relative stability phase** (6–24 hours): can be asymptomatic or with subtle signs, such as poor perfusion and hyperventilation
3) **Systemic toxicity phase** (6–72 hours):
   - Hypovolemic shock and cardiovascular collapse
   - Severe metabolic acidosis (positive anion gap)
   - Hepatic failure and jaundice
   - Worsened GI bleeding from coagulation disruption
   - Coma
4) **Hepatic toxicity/failure** (usually within 48 hours)
5) **GI/Pyloric scarring** (2–6 weeks)
   - Bowel obstruction

X-rays may show pill fragments, but liquid preparations and chewables are not generally visible. Obtain a serum iron level at 4–6 hours after ingestion (8 hours for sustained-release formulations) for children ingesting > 40 mg/kg. Serum iron levels do not always correlate with clinical severity because it is the intracellular iron that causes toxicity. Generally, a nontoxic iron level is < 350 µg/dL; 350–500 µg/dL produces mild-to-moderate symptoms; a level > 500 µg/dL produces serious toxicity. Total iron-binding capacity (TIBC) measurements are not helpful. Children often have elevated WBC counts and hyperglycemia, but these are nonspecific.

Treatment includes supportive care such as IV fluids. Chelation with IV deferoxamine is recommended in the presence of moderate-to-severe symptoms or if the serum iron level is > 500 µg/dL. Accomplish volume resuscitation before using deferoxamine to minimize risk of hypotension and renal impairment. Although a benefit has not been established, some clinicians will consider whole bowel irrigation if a large number of pills remain in the GI tract. Do not use gastric lavage, ipecac, activated charcoal (does not bind iron), oral bicarbonate, magnesium hydroxide, or oral deferoxamine.

ANTICHOLINERGIC INGESTION

Anticholinergic agents include antihistamines (e.g., diphenhydramine), TCAs (e.g., amitriptyline, imipramine), antispasmodics, some anti-Parkinson agents, atropine, some OTC sleep medications, and toxic plants (e.g., certain mushrooms, jimson weed, deadly nightshade). See the anticholinergic toxidrome under Toxidromes on page 7-2 for typical signs and symptoms.

Treatment is primarily supportive, including activated charcoal. The "antidote" is physostigmine, but because of its short duration, it is used mainly for diagnosis or short-term treatment of acute agitation. Definitely do not give physostigmine for TCA poisoning because of the high risk of seizures and serious arrhythmias.

TRICYCLIC ANTIDEPRESSANT (TCA) INGESTION

TCAs have anticholinergic activity, and they inhibit cardiac fast sodium channels. Some common TCAs used in the United States include imipramine, amitriptyline, nortriptyline, desipramine, clomipramine, and doxepin. On the exam, be suspicious of a younger child who "got into" the medications of a relative with depression. Overdose symptoms occur within 30 minutes to 6 hours. Ingestion of 5–20 mg/kg is potentially toxic, depending on the specific tricyclic. Patients can initially appear to be well but then deteriorate rapidly. Death most commonly results from intractable hypotension. In children, CNS effects are more prominent and include drowsiness, lethargy, seizures, and coma. Cardiac effects include:

- Tachycardia, including sinus and ventricular
- Hypotension (sometimes mild hypertension early in the progression)
- Widened QRS (> 100 ms)
- Rightward deflection of terminal 40 ms of QRS
- Prolonged QT_c and intraventricular conduction delays

Be aware of **CCCA** in tricyclic antidepressants:

- **C**oma
- **C**onvulsions
- **C**ardiac dysrhythmias
- **A**cidosis

Give activated charcoal only if the patient presents within an hour and is at low risk for aspiration (i.e., no seizures, normal mental status, or intubated). Clinical benefit of charcoal is minimal. Protect the airway with intubation if needed. Check the ECG: QRS duration > 100 msec indicates potential cardiac toxicity, as does an increased R wave in aVR. If the patient has QRS prolongation or an arrhythmia, give sodium bicarbonate to alkalinize the serum pH to 7.50–7.55. Monitor for decreasing QRS intervals to assess adequacy of treatment. Give IV fluids and vasopressors to treat hypotension. Treat seizures with benzodiazepines; avoid phenytoin, which can precipitate dysrhythmias. Also avoid physostigmine and flumazenil, because they may provoke seizures.

SEROTONIN SYNDROME AND NEUROLEPTIC MALIGNANT SYNDROME

Serotonin syndrome is most often seen in patients who commingle medications and chemicals from among a wide variety of classes of psychoactive substances, including the selective serotonin reuptake inhibitors (SSRIs), monoamine oxidase inhibitors (MAOIs), and 3,4-methylenedioxymethylamphetamine (MDMA; a.k.a. Ecstasy). Linezolid (an antibiotic) and the opioid pain medications meperidine, fentanyl, and tramadol are also known to cause serotonin syndrome.

Diagnosis is clinical. Symptoms include tachycardia and hypertension, hyperthermia, confusion and/or hallucinations and agitation, sweating, diarrhea, lower extremity rigidity, hyperreflexia, and myoclonus. Of these, **myoclonus** is the most specific finding. It helps distinguish the serotonin syndrome from its mimics, including neuroleptic malignant syndrome. If the patient has bruxism or hyponatremia, Ecstasy is likely to be one of the culprits. Treatment is predominantly supportive. If asked to choose a pharmacologic therapy, benzodiazepines and cyproheptadine are reasonable choices.

Neuroleptic malignant syndrome (NMS) is an idiosyncratic drug reaction to antipsychotics and related medications (e.g., metoclopramide). NMS is characterized by hyperthermia, muscle rigidity, confusion, and autonomic instability (difficult- or impossible-to-control heart rate and blood pressure), all in the context of exposure to antipsychotic agents. Usually, the medication taken by the patient or the underlying disorder (schizophrenia vs. depression) can help you differentiate NMS from serotonin syndrome. Treatment is supportive; benzodiazepines, dantrolene, bromocriptine, and amantadine are commonly used but controversial, as data is scant and conflicting.

Note: Antipsychotics (especially phenothiazines, such as chlorpromazine) can cause a dystonic reaction that potentially could be confused with the muscle rigidity of NMS. Remember that phenothiazines (e.g., promethazine) are often used in the treatment of nausea/vomiting, even in the absence of psychosis, and can cause similar side effects when used for this indication. The muscle rigidity of NMS is generalized and often severe. It causes a stable resistance to all passive joint movement, which leads to the term "lead pipe rigidity." On the other hand, acute dystonia is a contraction of a major muscle group, often in the head and neck area. Typical examples are torticollis, buccolingual reaction (protruding of the tongue), or oculogyric crisis. Effective treatment for acute dystonic reaction is an anticholinergic agent, such as diphenhydramine or benztropine.

ORAL HYPOGLYCEMIC AGENTS

The insulin secretagogues (e.g., glipizide, glyburide) are very dangerous, "one pill can kill" drugs. They can cause profound persistent hypoglycemia, leading to seizures, coma, and death.

Scenario: You are presented with a child who got into his diabetic grandma's medicine cabinet and then suddenly became ill and confused. Your best initial diagnostic test? A bedside fingerstick for glucose level. The best initial treatment is to administer glucose. Octreotide is also used in patients requiring frequent glucose replacement.

Always admit a child who has ingested even a single pill of an insulin secretagogue for close monitoring and glucose replacement.

Metformin does not typically cause hypoglycemia. Metformin is particularly famous for causing gastrointestinal upset and lactic acidosis.

METHEMOGLOBINEMIA

Methemoglobinemia occurs when the iron in hemoglobin is converted to the ferric form, resulting in normal oxygen uptake in the lungs but decreased oxygen release to tissues. It can be congenital or acquired; common sources include nitrites and nitrates (e.g., cardiac medications, fertilizer, foods, amyl nitrites [a.k.a. "poppers"]), aniline dyes, and local anesthetics (e.g., topical lidocaine or benzocaine preparations for teething).

Incidence of methemoglobinemia is increasing in adolescents and young adults who use amyl nitrites for sexual enhancement.

Findings are dependent on the methemoglobin level and range from otherwise asymptomatic to skin discoloration, headache, dyspnea, syncope, confusion, chest pain, seizures, dysrhythmia, coma, acidosis, and death.

Classic lab features include chocolate brown blood and a "saturation gap" between pulse oximetry and the arterial blood gas. For instance, a patient might have a pulse oximeter reading of 85%, unchanged with administration of oxygen, with a normal P_aO_2. Actually, both P_aO_2 and pulse oximetry results are incorrect! P_aO_2 measures oxygen tension in the plasma, which normally correlates with the oxygen saturation of normal hemoglobin (oxyhemoglobin saturation). When the hemoglobin is compromised, as with methemoglobinemia (and with CO poisoning), this correlation is lost and the P_aO_2 always reads normal to high. Pulse oximetry uses a single wavelength of light to measure light absorption through a pulsing capillary to determine oxyhemoglobin saturation; readings are incorrect in methemoglobinemia (and CO poisoning).

As with CO poisoning (see Carbon Monoxide (CO)), oxyhemoglobin saturation is accurately determined only by CO-oximetry. This previously required an arterial blood sample, but now there are CO-oximeters that work similarly to pulse oximeters. These pulse CO-oximeters measure several wavelengths of light to determine oxyhemoglobin and methemoglobin percentage and actual oxyhemoglobin saturation. Therefore, methemoglobinemia should be on the differential for a patient with a low oxygen saturation (usually mid-80s) and a normal-to-high P_aO_2.

Treat methemoglobinemia by removing the offending agent, providing oxygen, and administering methylene blue (note: contraindicated with glucose-6-phosphate dehydrogenase [G6PD] deficiency). Remember: Treat your blue patients with the blue medication!

ENVIRONMENTAL INGESTIONS AND EXPOSURES

PREVIEW | REVIEW

- What finding on peripheral smear is seen in lead poisoning?
- What lab test is useful in diagnosing carbon monoxide (CO) poisoning?
- True or false? A pulse oximetry reading of 98% rules out CO poisoning.
- True or false? Acid ingestions can cause severe gastritis, perforation, or late stricture even without oral/esophageal burns.
- Is ipecac routinely recommended for use?
- Know the similarities and differences among ethanol, methanol, and ethylene glycol poisonings.
- Can isopropyl alcohol poisoning cause an anion gap acidosis?
- What is the antidote for both methanol and ethylene glycol poisoning? How does it work?
- What are the symptoms of organophosphate poisoning? Treatment?
- What type of drug effect can occur after eating foxglove?
- Know which foreign body ingestions pose a higher risk for complications.

LEAD

Lead can be ingested orally or in an aerosolized form. Children in older homes may ingest paint chips, so ask about a history of pica. Most patients with lead poisoning are asymptomatic and are discovered to have elevated blood lead levels during routine screening. A venous blood level of > 5 μg/dL confirms the diagnosis. If symptoms are present, there is a wide spectrum. These range from vague abdominal pain, vomiting, fatigue, and malaise to significant behavioral changes (including ADHD), poor academic performance, and encephalopathy. Chronic lead poisoning can produce a blue line along the gums with bluish-black edging to the teeth (called **Burton line**) and metaphyseal densities on the radiographs of long bones (called **lead lines**, although long bone radiographs are not routinely recommended in the evaluation).

Lead poisoning may or may not be associated with anemia. Lead inhibits several enzymes involved with the production of hemoglobin, thus impairing the ability of iron to incorporate into heme. Classic laboratory findings include a hypochromic microcytic anemia and elevated levels of free erythrocyte protoporphyrin (FEP), due to failure of the heme biosynthetic pathway that incorporates iron into heme. Although FEP is often elevated in both lead poisoning and iron deficiency, extremely high levels are more often seen with lead intoxication.

Review of the peripheral smear often reveals **basophilic stippling,** which is characterized by the presence of bluish granules of various sizes scattered throughout the cytoplasm of RBCs. Although not diagnostic of lead poisoning, it is a common finding in this disorder. Basophilic stippling is also seen in patients with thalassemias, chronic alcohol use, heavy metal poisoning, sickle cell anemia, megaloblastic anemia, and sideroblastic anemia.

Treatment depends on the lead level and presence of symptoms. Patients with lead levels < 45 μg/dL do not require chelation, but must be monitored with the help of a toxicologist. The treatment for lead poisoning must also include lab confirmation, abdominal radiography (looking for intestinal sources of lead), and an environmental inspection of the child's home and surrounding area to identify and remove potential sources of lead exposure. For patients with moderate lead intoxication (venous blood lead level of 45–69 μg/dL), chelation with meso-2,3-dimercaptosuccinic acid (DMSA; a water-soluble analog of dimercaprol) is required. Severe intoxication is defined as venous blood lead levels ≥ 70 μg/dL or symptoms of encephalopathy. This is a medical emergency, and initial treatment must include management of seizures, if present, and maintaining adequate urine output without fluid overloading the patient. Immediately after this, chelation with dimercaprol and calcium disodium edetate is required.

CARBON MONOXIDE (CO)

CO binds to hemoglobin ~ 100× stronger than oxygen. It also impairs the ability of the 3 other oxygen-binding sites of the hemoglobin to release oxygen to tissues (shifts the curve to the left) and thus impedes oxygen utilization; the hemoglobin can bind the oxygen but cannot deliver it to the tissues. CO is colorless and odorless; poisoning occurs in settings of smoke inhalation or improperly vented stoves, automobile exhaust, or portable generators. CO poisoning is more common during winter months in cold climates.

Patients with mild poisoning present with nonspecific symptoms such as headache, malaise, and nausea— i.e., flulike symptoms. Distinguishing these symptoms from typical winter viral illnesses can be difficult, but the simultaneous presence of symptoms in multiple household members, including pets, is suspicious for CO toxicity. Infants and young children are more susceptible to CO poisoning due to their higher minute ventilation and oxygen utilization, but they can present with even more subtle, less-specific symptoms such as fussiness or

lethargy. Also know that frequent or continuous exposure to low levels of CO has a cumulative effect, because it binds so strongly to hemoglobin. On the exam (and in clinical practice!), look out for the whole family with similar flulike symptoms (commonly without fever). "Cherry-red" skin is classically described but seldom seen, except postmortem.

Diagnose CO poisoning by measuring carboxyhemoglobin (COHb) percentage by CO-oximetry. Most patients with COHb levels > 15–20% have symptoms.

Usually, the P_aO_2 and pulse oximetry reflect normal to high oxyhemoglobin levels. Both are wrong. Read the discussion under Methemoglobinemia regarding P_aO_2, pulse oximetry, and pulse CO-oximetry.

A measurable COHb level can be normal (≤ 1% for most patients, 5% for urban dwellers, and 10% for heavy smokers). COHb levels do not correlate precisely with toxicity. In general, however, higher levels result in more symptoms:

- Moderate exposure (20–40%): severe headache, dizziness, visual changes, syncope, vomiting, and ataxia
- Severe exposure (> 50%): coma, seizures, myocardial injury, and death

Treat with high-flow oxygen via a well-fitting nonrebreather mask with a reservoir. The CO half-life is ~ 4–6 hours in room air but ~ 60–90 minutes on 100% oxygen via nonrebreather and ~ 20 minutes with hyperbaric oxygen. Correct any metabolic acidosis and underlying anemia. Patients with altered mental status, neurologic symptoms, or cardiovascular dysfunction warrant admission. Severely affected patients may benefit from hyperbaric oxygen. Consider coexisting cyanide poisoning in patients from a fire, especially those with persistent metabolic acidosis and hemodynamic instability.

CYANIDE

Cyanide is an extremely deadly and infamous poison. Do not confuse cyanide with CO. Both are seen in patients who are exposed to smoke inhalation; however, they are very different. CO impairs oxygen delivery. Cyanide, on the other hand, is a cellular poison: It interferes with oxygen utilization by mitochondria. Clinically, patients present with a history of smoke inhalation (or intentional cyanide exposure), shock, and profound lactic acidosis. Cyanide is extremely toxic, so mild cases are relatively rare. Another common cause of cyanide poisoning is a nitroprusside infusion (because nitroprusside is metabolized to cyanide). A venous blood gas is bright red and shows high oxygen content, which reflects the fact that oxygen is not being extracted at the capillary level. Treat in an ICU-type setting with oxygen and hydroxycobalamin (precursor of vitamin B_{12}) or sodium thiosulfate with or without the addition of amyl nitrite.

CAUSTIC SUBSTANCE INGESTION

Generally, ingestion of caustic substances involves either alkaline or acidic agents.

Alkaline agents and characteristics:

- Industrial bleach, ammonia, oven and drain cleaners, automatic dishwasher detergent, hair relaxers, lye, and laundry detergents, including gel packets, tablets, and "pods" (Note: Everyday household bleach [5%] is only an irritant.)
- Tasteless in liquid form
- Cause severe, deep, liquefaction necrosis
- Can lead to scar tissue with strictures

Acidic agents and characteristics:

- Toilet bowl cleaner, grout cleaner, rust remover, automotive battery liquids, muriatic or sulfuric acid for swimming pools, and metal cleaners (e.g., gun bluing)
- Bitter taste
- Coagulation necrosis, which is more superficial and less severe than liquefaction necrosis
- Can lead to thick eschar formation, severe gastritis, metabolic acidosis, or acute kidney injury

Caustic ingestions cause major problems with esophageal and gastric inflammation and can potentially cause perforation.

Symptoms with both alkaline and acidic ingestions include:

- Oropharyngeal: mouth/throat pain, drooling, and refusal to drink
- Gastric/Esophageal: vomiting, hematemesis, chest or abdominal pain, and dysphagia
- Respiratory: wheezing, stridor, hoarseness, and respiratory distress (can cause epiglottitis)

The absence of any symptoms commonly implies little or no injury; however, the absence of oral lesions does not preclude severe esophageal or stomach injury. Remember that 20–40% of patients have no burns in the mouth! Note that acids in particular can cause severe gastritis, perforation, or late stricture even without apparent mouth/esophageal burns. Stricture formation occurs in up to 20% of caustic ingestions.

Do not induce vomiting or attempt to chemically neutralize the substance (by giving milk), as this can lead to more severe injury. Charcoal is ineffective and can interfere with endoscopy. Remove contaminated clothing and rinse the affected skin. Intubation is often required for airway obstruction. Check chest and abdominal films for pneumomediastinum and aspiration pneumonitis. Give IV fluids and analgesia, and keep NPO in symptomatic patients. Upper endoscopy should be done 12–24 hours from time of ingestion in all symptomatic children. (See the Gastroenterology section.) Teens with a suicidal overdose should be admitted and watched closely even if asymptomatic. Strictures often require treatment with dilatation; eventually they may even require surgical resection and reconstruction.

There is controversy regarding other medications, due to minimal literature. Gastric acid suppression with H_2 blockers or proton pump inhibitors may prevent stress ulcers and promotes faster mucosal healing. Literature supports steroids and antibiotics for deep focal or circumferential lesions. Sucralfate has been associated with improved healing and decreased frequency of stricture formation.

HYDROCARBON POISONING

Hydrocarbons are classified chemically (e.g., aromatic, aliphatic) or by risk of toxicity. Examples of various hydrocarbons and their potential toxicity include:

- **Low toxicity** (unless gross aspiration)—mineral, motor, baby, or suntan oils (high viscosity)
- **Aspiration risk**—mineral spirits, lamp oil, gasoline, kerosene, furniture polish, lighter fluid, and turpentine
- **Systemic effects** (including cardiac and CNS)—halogenated/aromatic hydrocarbons, including benzene, toluene (in glues and paints), methylene chloride, and pesticide-containing hydrocarbons

Highly toxic hydrocarbons can be remembered by the mnemonic **CHAMP** (**c**amphor, **h**alogenated, **a**romatic, **m**etal [e.g., arsenic, mercury], and **p**esticide). The most frequent toxicity from ingestion in children is **aspiration pneumonitis**, which can be severe. The aspiration hazard of a particular agent depends on its volatility, surface tension, and viscosity. Highly volatile compounds with low surface tension pose greater aspiration hazards.

Clinical findings typical of hydrocarbon aspiration include coughing, choking, gagging, wheezing, and respiratory distress, as well as mild CNS depression and fever, sometimes with an elevated WBC count. Chest x-ray (CXR) findings generally manifest at 2–6 hours after aspiration and consist initially of multiple, patchy, ill-defined densities that coalesce. Resolution of x-ray abnormalities often lags behind clinical improvement.

Teens who inhale ("huff," "sniff," or "bag") hydrocarbons can present with asphyxia or dysrhythmias. Hydrocarbon inhalation sensitizes the myocardium to the child's own catecholamines, and children/teenagers who inhale halogenated hydrocarbons can die from ventricular arrhythmias (sudden sniffing death). Get an ECG and cardiac monitor on these patients and consider this possibility if a preteen or teen presents with a ventricular arrhythmia. Chronic hydrocarbon inhalation can cause encephalopathy and organ-specific damage with certain hydrocarbons (e.g., toluene causes renal tubular acidosis).

Systemic toxicity is uncommon with most common hydrocarbon ingestions, but CNS depression or seizure can occur with certain hydrocarbons. Halogenated hydrocarbons can also cause hepatic or renal failure, and benzene is associated with aplastic anemia.

Do not forget external decontamination! Generally, asymptomatic children who have swallowed a hydrocarbon can be observed for 6 hours. They can be discharged if they remain asymptomatic, the CXR is normal, and they have normal oxygen saturation. In the presence of concerning symptoms or CXR findings, consider supportive care with oxygen, inhaled β-agonists, and (rarely) airway protection. Any CXR infiltrate noted within the first 24 hours is more likely to represent a pneumonitis than an infection. Acute respiratory distress syndrome (ARDS) occurs in severe cases, sometimes requiring extracorporeal membrane oxygenation (ECMO) or high-frequency ventilation. Use β-blockers if needed for patients with cardiac symptoms from sniffing.

Do not give ipecac. It is an unacceptable course of therapy because inducing emesis only increases the risk of aspiration. In addition, do not give activated charcoal (ineffective), steroids (no benefit), prophylactic antibiotics (alter lung flora and no benefit), or epinephrine (can induce ventricular fibrillation). Do not do gastric lavage (except in special circumstances, such as very toxic coingestant; e.g., insecticide).

ETHANOL INGESTION

Ethanol is found in many household substances besides spirits and liquor, including mouthwash and perfume. Signs and symptoms of ethanol intoxication include:

- CNS depression (slurred speech, ataxia, and stupor to coma)
- Respiratory depression
- Nausea, vomiting
- Hypothermia
- Hypoglycemia (inhibits hepatic gluconeogenesis, leading to hypoglycemia, particularly in children < 5 years of age)

A high osmolal gap is suspicious for ingestion of an alcohol (ethanol, methanol, ethylene glycol, or isopropyl alcohol). Diagnosis is confirmed by ethanol level. While the ethanol level does not necessarily correlate with severity of symptoms, especially in habitual drinkers, any measurable ethanol level would be of concern in a small child. Ethanol, methanol, and ethylene glycol ingestions can cause a high anion gap metabolic acidosis as well. Isopropyl alcohol does not cause anion gap acidosis.

Treatment includes the usual ABCs and intravenous fluids. Treat hypoglycemia and electrolyte abnormalities as needed. Activated charcoal is not recommended for ethanol ingestion alone but is considered if a coingestion is suspected. Hemodialysis can be done but is rarely needed. Some patients are sufficiently intoxicated that airway protection is indicated. Consider screening for other toxins in the face of presumed isolated ethanol ingestion.

METHANOL INGESTION

Methanol is found in windshield washer fluid and deicer and is used as a fuel additive. Methanol can cause **blindness** and death. Once ingested, it is metabolized by alcohol dehydrogenase and, ultimately, to formic acid.

This toxic metabolite is responsible for the symptoms. Onset of toxicity can be delayed if coingested with ethanol due to the competition of both substances for alcohol dehydrogenase.

Symptoms:

- Initially nonspecific: malaise, headache, abdominal discomfort, nausea, and vomiting; can appear "drunk"
- As methanol is metabolized, the child develops:
  - Visual disturbances with photophobia and blurry vision (described as a "snowstorm")
  - Optic nerve damage leading to blindness
  - CNS depression

Look for a triad of:

- Visual complaints
- Abdominal pain
- Metabolic acidosis with high anion gap but without lactic acidosis or ketonuria

The metabolic acidosis is often profound (HCO_3^- < 8 mEq/L); marked anion gap metabolic acidosis without high lactate or ketones suggests poisoning with methanol or ethylene glycol. An elevated osmolal gap is typically seen. Methanol itself is responsible for the osmolal gap and formic acid for the acidosis. As methanol gets metabolized, the high osmolal gap gives way to anion gap acidosis. Therefore, patients can demonstrate primarily an osmolal gap, primarily an anion gap acidosis, or components of both.

Because of rapid absorption, gastric decontamination and activated charcoal generally do not work. Obtain an ethanol level to rule out coingestion (and to account for ethanol in the calculated osmoles) and, if available, a methanol level (ideally obtained with a toxic alcohol screen that includes ethylene glycol and isopropyl alcohol). Monitor blood gases, electrolytes, and osmolality. Treat metabolic acidosis with sodium bicarbonate. The preferred antidote is IV 4-methylpyrazole (fomepizole), which competitively inhibits alcohol dehydrogenase. It is critical to treat early, before significant metabolism to formic acid has occurred. Ethanol was used to treat methanol poisoning in the past, but fomepizole has largely replaced it due to superior safety and easier dosing. Give folinic acid to enhance the metabolism of formic acid to less toxic metabolites. Hemodialysis should be considered in severe poisoning (e.g., visual symptoms, significant acidosis). Consult a poison control center or a toxicologist.

ETHYLENE GLYCOL INGESTION

Ethylene glycol is sweet tasting and found in antifreeze (a.k.a. radiator fluid) and other coolants. Once ingested, it is metabolized via alcohol dehydrogenase to glycolate, glyoxylate, and oxalic acid. As in the case of methanol, the metabolites are toxic and cause the most tissue injury. The kidney is most affected by ethylene glycol ingestion.

There are 3 stages of ethylene glycol intoxication:

- **Stage 1**—CNS; appears drunk with vomiting, drowsiness, slurred speech, and lethargy
- **Stage 2**—as ethylene glycol is metabolized, toxicity develops, including acute kidney injury, coma, and cardiorespiratory findings such as tachypnea from metabolic acidosis.
- **Stage 3** (after 24–72 hours)—renal failure

Flank pain and hematuria indicate renal involvement. Like methanol, ethylene glycol causes a high anion gap metabolic acidosis (without lactic acidosis/ketonuria) and often a high osmolal gap.

Because of rapid absorption, gastric decontamination and activated charcoal are not effective. Obtain an ethanol level and, if available, an ethylene glycol level (along with methanol and isopropyl alcohol levels). Monitor blood gases, electrolytes, osmolality, calcium, and urinalysis. Oxalic acid chelates calcium; calcium oxalate crystals are seen in the urine, but this is a late, nonspecific finding. Urine can fluoresce with a Wood lamp if antifreeze was the source, but this finding is not sensitive.

Treatment is similar to methanol poisoning, including sodium bicarbonate for metabolic acidosis and inhibition of alcohol dehydrogenase with IV fomepizole. Additionally, give thiamin and pyridoxine, which are cofactors in the metabolism of ethylene glycol. These help shunt metabolism to less toxic metabolites. Hypocalcemia is common and requires therapy if symptomatic. Order hemodialysis for patients with significant ethylene glycol poisoning, although some patients with high levels have been successfully treated without dialysis when fomepizole was started early (before the development of acidosis). As usual, involve a toxicologist in management.

ORGANOPHOSPHATE POISONING

Organophosphates are found in some pesticides (e.g., parathion, fenthion, diazinon, malathion) and nerve agents (e.g., sarin). Exposure can occur from inhalation, skin absorption, or oral ingestion. Many have a characteristic petroleum or garlic odor. Organophosphates bind to and inhibit the enzyme cholinesterase enzymes, causing **cholinergic** toxicity. Once bonds become permanent (1–3 days), it can take weeks to months for enzyme regeneration. Carbamates (e.g., methomyl, aldicarb) cause similar symptoms but bond reversibly with cholinesterase. Management is similar, although pralidoxime (which prevents irreversible binding) is not needed for carbamates.

Inhibition of cholinesterase leads to the cholinergic toxidrome **DUMBELS: d**efecation, **u**rination, **m**iosis, **b**ronchorrhea/**b**ronchospasm/**b**radycardia, **e**mesis, **l**acrimation, and **s**alivation.

Other symptoms seen with organophosphate poisoning include **nicotinic** muscular effects such as twitching, weakness, and paralysis. CNS effects, such as confusion, coma, convulsions, and slurred speech, can occur as well.

Some patients develop delayed neurotoxicity, typically 1–3 weeks after ingestion.

Diagnosis is confirmed by decreased RBC cholinesterase activity, but many hospitals cannot perform this test (so do not wait on it to treat).

Involved health care workers must wear proper protective gear to avoid self-contamination; surgical masks and latex gloves alone are not effective. For skin exposures, vigorously irrigate and wash with soap and water after removal of contaminated clothing.

If needed, cardiopulmonary resuscitation and intubation (avoid succinylcholine) are priorities. For treatment of the exposure, give 2 antidotes:

1) Atropine: temporarily blocks muscarinic effects of acetylcholine. Large, repeated doses are often needed. Treat until secretions dry up and bronchospasm resolves.
2) Pralidoxime: hydrolyzes the bonds between the organophosphorus compound and cholinesterase if given before they become irreversible (a process called "**aging**"). Pralidoxime does not cross the blood-brain barrier, so always use pralidoxime with atropine unless you are certain the exposure was a carbamate. Although it remains standard to give pralidoxime (or medications in this class) in this setting, their efficacy has recently been questioned and is under further study.

Use diazepam and other benzodiazepines for seizures and CNS symptoms.

PLANT EXPOSURES

For exams, you need to know about a few toxic plants:

- Digitalis effects (e.g., confusion, arrhythmia, nausea, vomiting)—foxglove, lily of the valley, and oleander
- Atropine effects—jimson weed, deadly nightshade
- Cyanide-like effects—pear and apple seeds, peach pits, bitter almonds
- Liver toxicity—Amatoxin-containing mushrooms provoke symptoms > 6 hours after ingestion. (Benign mushrooms quickly cause vomiting after exposure.)
- Oral pain—dieffenbachia and philodendron
- Mild GI symptoms—poinsettia, mistletoe, and holly

ESOPHAGEAL FOREIGN BODIES

The peak age for retained esophageal foreign body ingestion is 6 months to 3 years. Esophageal foreign bodies, of which coins are the most common, usually lodge at these 3 locations:

1) Upper esophageal sphincter (i.e., thoracic inlet and cricopharyngeus muscle): This is the most common area.
2) Aortic arch
3) Lower esophageal sphincter

Up to 35% of foreign bodies are asymptomatic. If present, the signs and symptoms are drooling, dysphagia, choking, gagging, pain in the neck or chest, and vomiting. In contrast, airway foreign bodies present with cough, stridor, and wheezing.

The diagnostic test of choice is a 2-view x-ray of the chest and abdomen. Flat, round objects, such as coins, appear circular on anteroposterior (AP) films if they are in the esophagus (Figure 7-2). If in the trachea, it is often oriented on-end and appears linear on AP film. However, it is important to recognize that foreign bodies can be radiolucent, and a normal radiograph does not exclude the possibility in a symptomatic patient or one with a concerning history. The lateral films allow for identification of multiple stacked coins or can show the silhouette of a button battery. If there are any signs of airway compromise, keep the child calm and prepare for removal by a skilled practitioner.

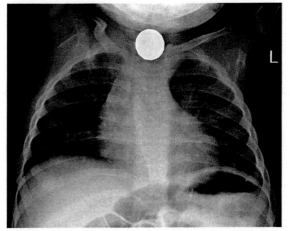

Figure 7-2: Coin in esophagus appearing circular on AP chest radiograph

Esophageal foreign bodies associated with symptoms, such as pain, vomiting, or dysphagia, should be removed endoscopically. If an object is lodged in the esophagus and the child is asymptomatic, consider observation for 12–24 hours to see if it will pass into the stomach with plan for removal if it does not pass. For the child with a coin in the stomach who is asymptomatic, advise the parents to watch for pain, vomiting, and/or a coin in the stools; follow up with repeat imaging and endoscopic removal if it has not passed within 4 weeks. Children with long, sharp objects or multiple batteries in the stomach or intestine require close observation and often urgent foreign body removal.

Esophageal button battery ingestions are a special case because they can cause esophageal liquefaction necrosis within 2–3 hours due to caustic leakage and electrical current generation. A double ring or poker chip sign is often seen on the AP radiograph (Figure 7-3) and a sharp step-off on the lateral view. Button batteries in the esophagus must be removed immediately, regardless of symptoms. Newer studies (from 2017 and 2018) recommend administration of honey and/or sucralfate. If mucosal injury is found following removal, a number of delayed complications can occur, including tracheoesophageal fistula,

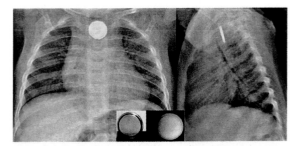

Figure 7-3: Button battery lodged in esophagus. Insert: photograph and x-ray

perforation, mediastinitis, pneumonia, and pneumothorax. While some practitioners will remove other foreign bodies with a balloon catheter, patients with button batteries are at increased risk of perforation and endoscopy is preferable. **Symptomatic** patients with button batteries in the stomach or intestines always require prompt removal, as they can lead to perforation or aortoenteric fistula. Urgent removal of button batteries in the stomach or intestines of **asymptomatic** patients is rarely indicated unless a larger button battery is in the stomach of a small child. Button batteries in other locations, such as the ear canal or nose, require immediate removal.

Magnet ingestions are concerning because multiple magnets can attract across layers of bowel leading to necrosis: 1 magnet is usually fine; 2 (or a magnet and a battery) can be trouble. These also require early consultation.

ENVENOMATION AND TRAUMA

BITES

PREVIEW | REVIEW

- Name the most common organism found in cat bite wound infections.
- What kind of human bites require thorough exploration?
- What kind of spider bite is initially painless?

DOG / CAT BITES

More than 4.5 million people in the U.S. are bitten by dogs each year; only about 50% of these bites are reported. Rottweilers, German shepherds, and pit bulls account for the majority of dog bite–related deaths in children. More than half of all attacks are unprovoked. In children, dog bites are most frequently (75%) on the head, neck, or upper extremities. Risk factors for infection from animal bites include the location (hand), type (puncture), interval to care (> 12 hours), and possibly type of animal (cat).

The most common organism in cat bite wound infections is *Pasteurella multocida*, an organism that is found in 60–75% of "normal" cats' mouths, followed by *Staphylococcus aureus*. Dog bites carry the same organisms plus *Capnocytophaga canimorsus*.

Clean all bites thoroughly with soap, water, and copious saline irrigation. Debride devitalized tissue. Tetanus immunization should be considered as well; bites are considered tetanus-prone wounds. (See more on bites and more about tetanus in the Infectious Disease section.) In the U.S., rabies prophylaxis is not indicated for bites from a nonrabid dog or cat. Patients bitten by bats or wild terrestrial carnivores (e.g., raccoons, skunks, foxes) should receive rabies prophylaxis unless the animal can be euthanized and tested.

In simple mammalian bites, there is clear evidence that prophylactic antibiotics decrease infection rates only for bites to the hand. Their use, however, may be justified in higher-risk body areas (e.g., foot, genitals), cosmetic areas (e.g., face), susceptible patients (e.g., immunocompromised, poor general health), or infection-prone wound types (e.g., deep puncture, massive crush injury, presentation > 12 hours from injury, wounds sutured closed). If antibiotic prophylaxis is given, use amoxicillin/clavulanate or, if the child is penicillin allergic, use clindamycin plus trimethoprim/sulfamethoxazole for 5 days. Close follow-up is needed.

If a wound already looks infected, then use the same antibiotics mentioned above for 7–10 days. Systemically ill patients or those who have failed outpatient antibiotics should receive ampicillin-sulbactam or a carbapenem (i.e., imipenem, meropenem, or ertapenem) intravenously.

Newer evidence suggests that most low-risk mammalian bites can be closed primarily without a significant increase in risk of infection. Significant crush injury, puncture wounds, wounds to hands or feet, wounds > 12 hours old, immunocompromised hosts, and cat/human bites are higher risk and should not be routinely closed.

Puncture wounds can be deceptive in appearance and are often more extensive than recognized on initial examination. Radiographs and local exploration are necessary when deep puncture wounds are close to bone or joints. Consultation is appropriate for bites with large areas of tissue loss or those with damage to complex structures such as joint, tendon, bone, or joint capsule.

HUMAN BITES

Clenched fist injuries (the "fight bite") are more serious than most other human bites. These occur when a fist "interfaces," so to speak, with another person's mouth. This injury is more of a laceration from the teeth than a true bite. The clinical history is often misleading because some patients, fearing ramification, are hesitant to admit involvement in a fight. Instead, patients might say that they "punched a wall" or another inanimate object in frustration.

These lacerations, which tend to occur over the knuckles (metacarpophalangeal or proximal interphalangeal joints), should be irrigated, x-rayed, and inspected very carefully for signs of tendon damage and infection. Maintain a low threshold for consultation.

Antibiotic prophylaxis has been shown to modify outcomes in many patients with a human bite, especially those over the hands or feet, those overlying a joint, and those that penetrate below the epidermis. The 2014 Infectious Diseases Society of America (IDSA) guideline states the following indications for antibiotic prophylaxis: lacerations undergoing closure or debridement; wounds over hands, face, or genitals; wounds close to bone or joint; wounds in areas of poor circulation; wounds in patients who are immunocompromised; and crush injuries. Empiric oral antibiotic therapy with amoxicillin/clavulanate is recommended for prophylaxis because it covers all potential flora found in human bite wounds, including aerobic bacteria (e.g., streptococci and *Staphylococcus aureus*) and anaerobic bacteria (e.g., *Eikenella corrodens*, *Fusobacterium*, *Peptostreptococcus*). Alternative treatment regimens include trimethoprim/sulfamethoxazole plus clindamycin. Copiously irrigate these bites. Closure depends on physician judgment when weighing the risk of infection with cosmesis and exposure of vital structures.

As with animal bites, the patient's tetanus immunization status must be determined and the patient treated when applicable. (See Lacerations and Punctures on page 7-16.) Patients unvaccinated against hepatitis B virus (HBV) who are bitten by an individual with HBV need hepatitis B immunoglobulin (HBIG) and the vaccine series. If the status of the source is unknown, the vaccine series is initiated. Although HIV and hepatitis C virus (HCV) are not typically transmitted through saliva, consider both if blood is in the saliva.

SNAKE BITES

More than 95% of venomous snake bites in the U.S. are from pit vipers (e.g., rattlesnakes, water moccasins, copperheads). They have a triangular head, elliptical pupils, and an obvious pit between each eye and nostril (Figure 7-4). These pits are openings of a very complex and exquisitely sensitive detection mechanism. Venom from these snakes can cause local tissue effects as well as systemic toxicity, including swelling and ecchymosis, necrosis, compartment syndrome (rare), vascular leak, coagulopathy, and (rarely) neurotoxicity. Most bites are sustained by young adult males while handling a snake. Rattlesnake bites tend to be more severe than water moccasin bites; copperhead bites usually cause only local tissue swelling and pain without severe systemic symptoms. Mojave rattlesnake bites can cause muscular weakness and respiratory failure; onset of neurologic symptoms may be delayed.

Figure 7-4: Pit viper

An envenomated patient develops signs of toxicity within 2–6 hours. However, many children presenting with snake bite have been bitten by a nonvenomous snake or have sustained a "dry bite" by a venomous snake. Dry bites have little or no local swelling and no systemic symptoms. Watch asymptomatic patients with no laboratory abnormalities for 6 hours (24 hours for lower extremity bites). Observe patients with local symptoms for 24 hours for development of progressive local swelling, systemic toxicity, or other concerning signs or laboratory abnormalities.

While identification of the snake is helpful, treatment is based on clinical signs and symptoms. First aid involves immobilizing the body part and removing any sources of possible constriction (e.g., watches, rings). Do not apply pressure, ice, or a tourniquet or use excision and suction. Remember: For pit vipers, including rattlesnakes, most of the effect is local tissue damage, so trapping the venom in the extremity is not advantageous.

Provide IV fluids and analgesia to patients with symptomatic envenomation. Check coagulation studies (including tests for disseminated intravascular coagulation [DIC]), CBC, electrolytes, creatine kinase (CK), and urinalysis (to check for rhabdomyolysis). Update tetanus immunization, if indicated. Infection after a snake bite is rare, so only give antibiotics for documented infection or massively contaminated bites.

The Crotalidae antivenins most widely used in the U.S. for North American pit viper envenomation are CroFab (crotalidae–polyvalent immune fab [ovine]; approved for rattlesnake, copperhead, and cottonmouth) and ANAVIP (crotalidae immune F(ab′)$_2$ [equine]; approved for rattlesnake). These are given as soon as possible after any signs of envenomation occur (local, systemic, or hematologic). Antivenin treats both local and systemic effects, including coagulopathy. Indications for treatment include coagulopathy, thrombocytopenia, systemic toxicity, significant edema, or edema crossing a joint. Multiple adult-size doses may be needed; dosage correlates with the amount of venom injected, not the size of the patient. Be ready to treat anaphylaxis! After discharge, children should be watched for signs of serum sickness.

The remainder of venomous snake bites in North America are those attributed to the Elapidae family. This includes the coral snakes, which have inspired the popular mnemonic "red on yellow, kill a fellow; red on black, venom lack." Elapidae bites produce minimal local reactions with prominent neurotoxicity. Treatment is symptomatic with species-specific antivenin.

SPIDER BITES

Brown recluse spiders (Figure 7-5), which are responsible for most toxic U.S. spider bites, are generally found in the Southeast, Southwest, and Midwestern regions of the U.S. (Figure 7-6). They tend to hide in dry and generally undisturbed areas such as woodpiles, attics, closets, and seldom-worn clothing. Adults have a leg span of ~ 25 mm, with a dark **violin** pattern on the dorsal front portion of the

body (cephalothorax); thus, they are called "fiddleback" or "violin" spiders. Their venom contains sphingomyelinase and other substances powerful enough to lyse cell membranes, which activates complement and causes local necrosis.

Figure 7-5: Brown recluse "fiddleback" spider

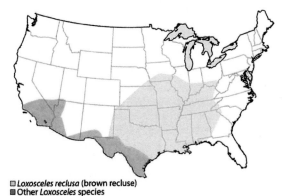

☐ *Loxosceles reclusa* (brown recluse)
■ Other *Loxosceles* species

Figure 7-6: Geographic distribution of Loxosceles spiders

Initially, the bite of a brown recluse spider is painless; pain develops at the site 2–8 hours later. Over the next day or two, a hemorrhagic blister develops that eventually progresses to a necrotic ulceration. **Cutaneous loxoscelism** is the term given for the ulcerative effect of the brown recluse bite (genus *Loxosceles*). Patients rarely have systemic symptoms such as fever, chills, nausea, vomiting, myalgias, rash; children can occasionally develop hemolysis (**systemic loxoscelism**). For systemic disease, steroids are recommended as treatment.

Treatment is supportive with local wound care. Despite their impressive appearance, these bites are seldom infected. (If there is obvious infection, think methicillin-resistant *Staphylococcus aureus* [MRSA].) The lesions sometimes continue to expand for as long as 10 days and last for weeks to months, but most eventually heal spontaneously without surgical or other intervention. Other treatments (e.g., dapsone) are not recommended because data on effectiveness is lacking.

Widow spiders are found throughout the U.S. (except Alaska); the southern black widow and western black widow spiders are most commonly responsible for serious symptoms. Widow spiders hide in dimly lit, warm, dry places such as outhouses and sheds. They are large, with a leg span of 40 mm. Patients usually have a recent history of outdoor activity, such as cleaning out a garage. Female spiders cause human envenomation. A mature black widow female has a **red/orange hourglass** marking on the ventral surface (Figure 7-7).

Figure 7-7: Black widow spider

The black widow spider's venom is a neurotoxin. Initial signs and symptoms begin within 30–60 minutes of the bite and include pain at the site, diaphoresis, muscle cramping, chest tightness, vomiting, malaise, sweating, abdominal pain (can mimic an acute abdomen/appendicitis), agitation, and hypertension. There may be a transient bull's-eye lesion at the bite site. Rhabdomyolysis with elevated creatine kinase can occur, along with nonspecific inflammatory labs (e.g., elevated white blood cell count, hyperglycemia).

Treatment includes local wound care, analgesia, and tetanus prophylaxis. Analgesia can consist of oral or parenteral opioids or benzodiazepines for muscle spasm. A black widow antivenin exists but, due to mortality associated with the antivenom, is no longer widely available. Typically, all symptoms resolve within 24–48 hours.

LACERATIONS AND PUNCTURES

PREVIEW | REVIEW

- What are some potential complications of lacerations?
- What organism can commonly cause infection with a puncture wound through the sole of a shoe?

Irrigation is the best way to clean a laceration; saline or tap water can be used. "Dilution is the solution to pollution." Irrigate with at least 100 mL/cm of laceration. Update tetanus immunization if needed. Do not use topical skin adhesives on the scalp or hair-bearing areas and take care to avoid getting them in the eyes. **LET** (**l**idocaine, **e**pinephrine, **t**etracaine) gel can be used for topical anesthesia in lieu of injected anesthetic. Do not shave eyebrows because this can cause difficulty in correct alignment with wound closure. Eyelid lacerations require an ophthalmologist if there is involvement of the globe, lid margin, lacrimal duct canaliculus, or tarsal plate. Lining up the vermillion border of the lip requires experience; this margin must be accurately approximated to avoid

a noticeable scar. A clenched-fist hand laceration (see Human Bites on page 7-14), especially if incurred from punching another individual in the mouth, is at high risk of infection or tendon damage and should be referred to a hand surgeon.

Potential complications of lacerations include:

- Tendon laceration with loss of function
- Arterial or vascular compromise
- Infection
- Scarring that limits function
- Cosmetic considerations; e.g., keloids, scarring

Puncture wounds are common and can lead to various problems, such as infection and retained foreign bodies (FB). Most occur on the feet when the child steps on an object, such as a nail. Wounds to the metatarsophalangeal joints are concerning because these weight-bearing areas have a high risk of complications, such as joint penetration and development of osteomyelitis. Punctures that penetrate through the sole of a shoe (especially sneakers) can result in *Pseudomonas aeruginosa* as well as *Staphylococcus* and *Streptococcus* infection.

X-rays are often indicated, particularly to evaluate for FBs or penetration into bone. Glass and metal are radiopaque; wood usually is not. Ultrasound or other modalities, such as MRI, are helpful if a retained foreign body is suspected but not seen on standard radiographs.

Puncture wounds should receive standard local wound care and tetanus prophylaxis. Aggressive wound "coring" is not recommended. Prescribe antibiotics if wound infection develops. Cover for *Staphylococcus* and *Streptococcus*, but, if the injury occurred through a shoe, also cover for *Pseudomonas*. Advise patients to return for persistent pain or signs of infection. Be sure to consider a retained FB if the child has lingering pain or infection. Consider cephalexin prophylaxis for puncture wounds that are higher risk (i.e., contaminated, through a shoe, or with retained foreign body).

BURNS

PREVIEW | REVIEW

- Explain the differences among superficial, partial-thickness, and full-thickness burns.
- How do you determine burn surface area in an adolescent vs. a young child?
- After being in a house fire, a child presents with singed facial/nasal hairs, stridor, hoarseness, and carbonaceous sputum. What should you do?

OVERVIEW

Burns are a leading cause of unintentional pediatric death. Additionally, 18% of burns are due to abuse. Burn first aid includes **ABCs** (**a**irway, **b**reathing, **c**irculation), removing clothing, washing off chemicals, and covering the burn with a clean dry sheet. For small burns, cold/wet compresses can be applied; for large burns, do not use cold/wet compresses because this can lead to hypothermia.

Prevention is key and includes:

- Keep matches out of reach.
- Use electrical outlet covers.
- Set water heater temperature to 120.0–125.0°F (48.9–51.7°C).
- Practice fireworks safety.

Burns suspicious for child abuse:

- Shaped like an object that could be used to burn (e.g., iron pattern)
- Circular
- "Stocking and glove" distribution
- Areas usually protected from burns (e.g., buttocks, perineum)
- Clear edges of burned area when splash marks would be expected

Burn depth classification:

- **Superficial** (previously **1st degree**): limited to epidermis; red, blanches with pressure, dry, minor swelling, and pain. Commonly resolves in 5–7 days.
- **Partial-thickness** (previously **2nd degree**) is divided into superficial and deep:
  ○ Superficial partial-thickness: papillary dermis; blistering, pink, moist, painful. Typically heals in 2–3 weeks without scarring.
  ○ Deep partial-thickness: reticular dermis; blistering, red and/or white with poor blanching and capillary refill, moist or dry, typically painful with variable sensation to light touch. Can take 3–9 weeks to heal, often with scarring.
- **Full-thickness** (previously **3rd degree**): entire epidermis and dermis; dry, leathery, waxy, and painless. Requires skin grafting unless small. When fully circumferential, a full-thickness burn can form a strangulating eschar that causes ischemia distally.
- **4th degree** involves skin, subcutaneous tissue, and underlying structures (i.e., fascia, muscle, bone).

Measurement of burn surface area (BSA) follows the **rule of 9s** in adults and adolescents > 14 years of age:

- Head and neck: 9%
- Each upper limb: 9%
- Thorax and abdomen, front: 18%
- Thorax and abdomen, back: 18%
- Perineum: 1%
- Each lower limb: 18%

Due to anatomic differences, such as larger head size, the rule of 9s is not accurate in children < 14 years of age. Use a pediatric Lund and Browder chart or estimate using the child's hand—the area of the child's palm is ~ 1% of the BSA. Include only partial-thickness and higher burns in estimating the total BSA burned (i.e., exclude superficial

burns). Burn size estimates are notoriously inaccurate and commonly overestimate the affected surface area. Also, be aware that the initial appearance of burn depth can be deceiving; some burns are deeper than they originally appear.

MINOR BURN CARE

Superficial partial-thickness burns require no therapy besides analgesia.

Small partial-thickness burn therapy:

- Leave intact blisters intact if they do not appear likely to rupture spontaneously.
- Debride skin from ruptured blisters.
- Apply temporary skin substitutes (if available) or other clean dressings.
- Apply antibiotic ointment (silver sulfadiazine or bacitracin).
- Give analgesics to control pain.
- Update tetanus if needed.
- Change standard dressings twice daily. (Some biologic/synthetic burn dressings are left on longer.)
- Reevaluate every 2–3 days, assessing for infection, poor healing, or progression.

MAJOR BURN CARE

Think ABCs: Singed facial hairs, carbonaceous sputum, and upper airway symptoms (e.g., stridor) indicate inhalation injury. Intubate early! Consider carbon monoxide and cyanide poisoning in house fires.

Check cardiovascular status. Anticipate excess fluid requirements for burns beyond superficial > 15% of BSA. The Parkland formula specified an additional 4 mL per kg body weight per percent body surface burned (excluding 1st degree or superficial). 2017 American Burn Association (ABA) criteria suggest slightly less fluid. For children < 14 years:

- 3 mL/kg for each percent of total BSA (partial- or full-thickness) is given in the first 24 hours, with 50% in the first 8 hours and the rest over the next 16 hours.
- Use Ringer's lactate for high-volume resuscitation.
- Administer Ringer's lactate with 5% dextrose at maintenance fluids, in addition to resuscitative fluids, to children < 30 kg to prevent hypoglycemia.
- Monitor blood sugar and electrolytes.
- Adjust fluid administration to clinical indicators, such as urine output, maintaining ~ 1 mL/kg/hour in children and 30–50 mL/hour in older children/adults. A Foley catheter is needed to monitor urine output in significant burns.

The 2017 ABA criteria for referral to a burn center include:

- Partial-thickness burns > 10% total BSA
- Burns involving face, hands, feet, perineum, or major joints
- 3rd degree burns

- Electrical, chemical, or inhalation burns
- Patients with preexisting medical disorders or concomitant trauma (if the burn poses the major risk)
- Special social, emotional, or rehabilitative needs (e.g., child abuse, substance use)
- The current hospital does not have qualified personnel or equipment to care for children

SUBMERSION INJURY

PREVIEW | REVIEW

- Is there a difference in management between freshwater and saltwater submersion/immersion injury?

Drowning is respiratory impairment that results from submersion/immersion in liquid and ranks 2nd to motor vehicles as a cause of accidental pediatric death. The peak risk groups for drowning include children < 5 years of age and males 15–25 years old. Young children can drown in swimming pools, bathtubs, toilets, and even small containers such as buckets. Drowning is sometimes due to child maltreatment. Submersion-related deaths in adolescents are often linked to risk-taking behaviors and alcohol consumption.

"Drowning" implies respiratory impairment either when the patient is submerged (the airway is below the surface of the liquid) or immersed (water splashes over the face). "Rescue" means that the process of drowning was interrupted, and thus the patient had a nonfatal drowning. Fatal drownings result in immediate or delayed death. The terms "near drowning," "dry drowning," and "wet drowning" are no longer used.

The sequence of events in the drowning patient lasts for no more than a few minutes and are as follows:

- Initially, water entering the mouth/nose is spat out.
- Conscious breath-holding (~ 60 seconds) occurs.
- The inspiratory drive becomes too hard to resist, and either water is aspirated into the airways or laryngospasm occurs, preventing this aspiration.
- Cerebral hypoxia terminates the laryngospasm response.
- Hypoxia and acidosis lead to bradycardia, pulseless electrical activity (PEA), and, ultimately, asystole, as well as hypoxic-ischemic neurologic injury.

In patients who survive the initial insult, ARDS or acute lung injury (ALI) can result from water in the alveoli washing out surfactant. Cerebral edema resulting from hypoxia is the most frequent cause of death, and many survivors have persistent neurologic deficits. Metabolic and respiratory acidosis are both seen. Electrolyte abnormalities, such as hyponatremia, are uncommon. Although one must consider cervical spine injuries in drowning victims, most of these are evident from the clinical scenario (e.g., diving into shallow water). Neurologic status is predictive of outcome. Children who are responsive at the scene and those who arrive to the emergency department awake and responsive generally do well; children with no spontaneous movements by 24 hours are likely to die or suffer severe neurologic impairment. Submersion of > 10 minutes is classically associated with a poor prognosis, though a large 2014 study suggested that outcomes worsen after 5 minutes. Delayed initiation of resuscitation (> 10 minutes), > 25 minutes of cardiopulmonary resuscitation in the emergency department, and asystole are associated with poor outcomes in patients with cardiopulmonary arrest.

Occasionally, hypothermic drowning victims have preserved neurologic function despite prolonged submersion. Hypothermia is thought to be protective only if the patient becomes hypothermic at the time of submersion and if rapid cooling occurs in water < 41.0°F (< 5.0°C); e.g., fell through ice into the water.

Freshwater and saltwater drownings are managed the same way. On the scene, ventilation is the most important intervention, followed by chest compressions if pulseless. Hospital measures include ABCs, with ventilatory support for significant respiratory distress/failure. Protect the spine as appropriate (e.g., abuse, diving injury). Vomiting is typical; place a nasogastric tube once the airway is protected. Administer supplemental oxygen as needed and order a CXR. Check blood glucose and electrolytes; metabolic and respiratory acidosis are common. After cold water submersion, warm the patient. Warm mildly hypothermic patients with external methods (e.g., removal of wet clothes, warm packs, blankets). Treat more severe hypothermia with internal techniques such as warmed IVFs, body cavity lavage (i.e., gastric, pleural, peritoneal, bladder), or ECMO if available. For drownings in freezing water, continue resuscitative efforts until the core temperature is 89.6–95.0°F (32.0–35.0°C). Remember: "not dead until warm and dead."

Observe asymptomatic children for ~ 6 hours; if the CXR is normal and no symptoms develop, discharge. Admit all patients who are symptomatic after drowning; some with mild symptoms will worsen over the first 24 hours.

HEAD INJURY

PREVIEW | REVIEW

- Describe physical findings compatible with a basilar skull fracture.
- In a child with a head injury, when should you definitely order a CT scan of the head?
- In a child with a head injury, when is it okay to send the patient home for observation?
- How should you determine when an athlete who has sustained an mTBI can return to play?

OVERVIEW

Head injuries are common. For all children, falls are the most typical cause of head injury, although motor vehicle trauma is the most common cause of serious head injury. Symptoms to watch for include loss of consciousness, amnesia, vomiting, lethargy, headache, irritability, seizures, and behavioral changes ("not acting right"). Significant brain injury is not ruled out in the absence of signs of external head trauma!

Some specific injury patterns to be aware of:

1) **Basilar skull fracture** (fracture at base of skull, involving temporal bone, occipital bone, and/or ethmoid):

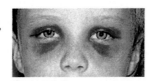

Figure 7-8: Raccoon eyes

- "Raccoon eyes" (Figure 7-8; presents 1–3 days after injury)
- Battle sign (Figure 7-9; presents 1–3 days after injury)
- Hemotympanum
- CSF leakage from ear or nose (puts patient at risk for meningitis)
- Cranial nerve palsy
- Hearing loss

2) **Abusive head injury**
- Retinal hemorrhages
- Subdural hematoma (particularly subacute or chronic)—see next category
- Other unexplained injuries

3) **Subdural hematoma**
- Hemorrhage in potential space between dura and arachnoid membrane
- Caused by nonaccidental trauma, fall from significant height, motor vehicle collision (MVC)
- Symptoms include headache, irritability, vomiting, lethargy, seizure, coma
- Crosses suture lines, not midline

4) **Epidural hematoma**
- Hemorrhage from middle meningeal artery into space between dura and calvaria
- Caused by fall from significant height, MVC, direct blow to temporal area
- Transient initial improvement in mental status ("lucid interval") followed by headache, vomiting, lethargy, seizure, and coma
- Can cross midline, not suture lines (where dura tightly adheres to the skull)
- Usually needs urgent surgical intervention
- Minimal underlying brain injury, with survivors having a better long-term neurologic outcome than with subdural hematomas

5) **Cushing triad**, representing increased intracranial pressure:
- Bradycardia
- Hypertension
- Hyperpnea and/or irregular respirations

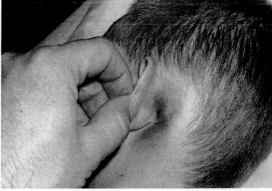

Figure 7-9: Battle sign

Signs of severe head injury include marked alteration in level of consciousness, focal neurologic signs, posturing, dilated or unequal pupils, abnormal vital signs (especially bradycardia and hypertension), and scoring < 8 on the Glasgow Coma Scale (GCS; Table 7-2) These children usually require intubation, as well as treatment directed at maintaining normal circulation/perfusion while lowering the increased intracranial pressure (ICP). Many have multisystem trauma, complicating their management. Be sure to protect the cervical spine until injury is excluded. Consult a pediatric neurosurgeon immediately or transfer to a pediatric trauma center with neurosurgical capabilities.

Table 7-2: Glasgow Coma Scale			
Activity	**Best Response (< 2 Years of Age)**	**Best Response (≥ 2 Years of Age)**	**Score***
Eye opening	Spontaneous	Spontaneous	4
	To verbal stimuli	To verbal stimuli	3
	To pain	To pain	2
	None	None	1
Verbal	Coos and babbles	Oriented	5
	Irritable/Cries	Confused	4
	Cries in response to pain	Inappropriate words	3
	Moans in response to pain	Nonspecific sounds	2
	None	None	1
Motor	Normal spontaneous	Normal spontaneous	6
	Withdraws to touch	Localizes pain	5
	Withdraws to pain	Withdraws to pain	4
	Abnormal flexion	Abnormal flexion	3
	Abnormal extension	Abnormal extension	2
	None	None	1

* Minimum score = 3; maximum score = 15.

In the prehospital setting, the patient should not be moved and the C-spine should be immobilized unless the patient is lucid enough to cooperate with C-spine evaluation. If necessary, the airway can be maintained with a jaw thrust maneuver. Remember that unless properly performed, removing helmets or other sporting equipment results in C-spine movement; therefore, clothing and protective equipment should not be removed if at all possible.

NEUROIMAGING

Most children with minor head trauma, GCS 15, and normal neurologic exams do not need imaging and should not be exposed to potentially harmful radiation.

When imaging is required for suspected intracranial injury, CT scanning is preferred because it detects virtually all injuries requiring acute neurosurgical intervention. Certain MRI sequences have excellent sensitivity and specificity for detecting traumatic injuries, but the utility of MRI in the acute setting is limited by availability, patient stability, need for sedation, and time required for scanning. Plain films detect skull fractures with suboptimal sensitivity. Additionally, only about 1/2 of the young children with an intracranial injury have an overlying skull fracture.

Unstable patients with persistently low GCS scores and those with focal neurologic findings, signs of elevated intracranial pressure (e.g., asymmetric or abnormal pupils, Cushing triad), or signs of basilar or depressed skull fractures need emergent CT scanning. Additionally, a low threshold should be maintained for imaging in suspected victims of child maltreatment and in patients on anticoagulant medications or with an underlying condition that predisposes them to intracranial hemorrhage.

For children with minor head injury and GCS 14 or 15, the largest study to date was published in 2009 by Pediatric Emergency Care Applied Research Network (PECARN). They developed low-risk criteria for children < 2 years of age and for those ≥ 2 years of age. Children meeting low-risk criteria have a negligible risk of a clinically important intracranial injury and can be observed at home. Those who do not meet low-risk criteria should be considered to be at measurable risk and can be evaluated by a period of observation or by imaging, at the discretion of the physician. Of note, minimally injured children can have a brief, immediate postimpact seizure (impact seizure), and an impact seizure in an otherwise low-risk child does not necessarily indicate the need for imaging.

PECARN criteria for children < 2 years of age:

- CT indicated for GCS < 15, altered mental status, or palpable skull fracture
- Observation or CT for nonfrontal scalp hematomas, loss of consciousness > 5 seconds, severe mechanism (see below), or not acting normally per parent
- Children without any of the above signs or symptoms are at low risk of clinically significant injury.

PECARN criteria for children ≥ 2 years of age:

- CT indicated for GCS < 15, altered mental status, or signs of basilar skull fracture
- Observation or CT for vomiting, loss of consciousness, severe headache, or severe mechanism (see below)
- Children without any of the above signs or symptoms are at low risk of clinically significant injury.

Mechanisms considered to be severe:

- MVC with ejection, rollover, or fatality
- Biker or pedestrian without a helmet vs. vehicle
- Struck by a high-impact object
- Fall > 3 feet in children < 2 years of age or > 5 feet in children ≥ 2 years of age

Children with abnormal imaging are admitted to the hospital with neurosurgical consultation. For asymptomatic children with simple linear skull fractures, most institutions discharge with close follow-up. In children < 3 years of age, be aware of the rare complication of a diastasis (widening) of the skull fracture and formation of a CSF-filled dural outpouching under the scalp (leptomeningeal cyst) in the weeks to months following a skull fracture.

MILD TRAUMATIC BRAIN INJURY (mTBI; CONCUSSION)

mTBI is a complex pathophysiological process affecting the brain, induced by traumatic biomechanical forces, with normal standard neuroimaging (if performed). Basically, it is a functional abnormality of the brain with no structural abnormality. 2018 CDC guidelines recommend replacement of the terms concussion and minor head injury with mild traumatic brain injury or mTBI. A blow to the head is the typical mechanism of injury, but transmitted or rotational forces can also cause mTBI.

mTBI questions on an exam are commonly sports-related. High-risk sports include football, soccer, rugby, ice hockey, basketball, and lacrosse. Children and adolescents often have more severe mTBI than adults; catastrophic head injuries due to football are 3× more likely in high school than in college.

Symptoms of mTBI include headache, amnesia, confusion, dizziness, nausea/vomiting, altered balance, and occasionally transient vision loss. Additional symptoms include difficulty concentrating, photophobia, emotional lability, and sleep disturbances. Most patients with mTBI do not have loss of consciousness.

While most symptoms resolve within days to weeks, a number of children suffer prolonged symptoms that affect their daily functioning, school performance, and ability to return to sports.

Since 2004, the International Consensus Conference on Concussion in Sport has recommended using a symptom-based approach rather than grading scales. CT scan is not required for diagnosis of mTBI. Use of a CT or MRI is reserved for ruling out other pathology in patients with more severe or worsening symptoms. Higher-level imaging (e.g., functional MRI) is considered a research tool, but not a clinical tool, at this point.

It is important to prevent a subsequent head injury from occurring before the original mTBI has healed. It appears that some children who sustain another head injury prior to complete recovery from the initial injury can have a devastating **second-impact syndrome**, which can be fatal. While there is some uncertainty as to the exact cause, this is thought to be due, at least in part, to loss of cerebral blood flow autoregulation with rapid development of cerebral edema. In addition, repeated mTBIs are more common in patients who return to play before complete recovery. The impact of repeated mTBI is not fully understood, but multiple episodes can eventually lead to chronic neuropsychological deficits.

Children with any signs of mTBI should not return to play the same day. Similarly, athletes sustaining any degree of mTBI should be removed from the game immediately and should not return to play the same day ("no same day return to play" and "when in doubt, sit them out"). Formal neuropsychological assessment (ideally compared with prior baseline testing) can be used in the office setting to diagnose mTBI or assess readiness to return to play.

Optimal timing for return to an aerobic program is not definitely established. Physical and cognitive rest (avoidance of intellectually demanding activity, including complex video games) are recommended in the first several days after mTBI. For most patients, complete cognitive and physical rest should be continued only for 24–48 hours, then the patient should gradually become more active but stay below their cognitive and physical thresholds. The best duration of rest, particularly cognitive rest, is not fully researched, but this recommendation was not altered in JAMA Pediatric's 2020 Consensus Statement on Sport-related Concussion. Longer periods of rest may be associated with an adverse effect of recovery. Upon resumption of physical activity, the athlete should follow the return-to-play protocol (Table 7-3), remaining at each stage for 24 hours if asymptomatic and progressing more slowly if symptomatic.

ELECTRICAL BURNS

PREVIEW | REVIEW

- What types of electrical burns typically cause more serious injury?

Current is defined in terms of type (direct current [DC] or alternating current [AC]) and voltage. AC burns are worse than DC burns. **DC** electricity, from an electric rail system, for example, tends to cause a single muscle contraction, throwing the patient away from the source. **AC** exposure is considered more dangerous at the same voltage because the alternating nature of the current causes tetany, preventing the victim from releasing the contracted muscles and, thus, prolonging the exposure. High voltage is considered > 500–1,000 V. The amount of resistance alters the effective current delivery to the person, and moisture on the person's skin can reduce resistance and significantly worsen an electrical burn.

Electrical burns due to contact with **low-voltage** household current (AC; 110–240 V) usually are minor, requiring no specific treatment beyond normal wound care. Children with a small burn from touching an electrical outlet while dry, for instance, do not require laboratory or ECG screening. Electrical burns that typically cause more serious injury include those that occur in water or wet areas, high-voltage contact, and those due to lightning (i.e., very high-voltage contact!).

Burns to the oral commissure from biting an electrical cord are concerning, as the labial artery can be injured and bleed profusely once the eschar begins to separate (~ 1–3 weeks after injury). Patients can also have significant scarring and should be followed by an appropriate surgical specialist. Advise families to seek immediate medical attention if the child begins to bleed.

High-voltage electrical burns can cause asystole, ventricular fibrillation, chest-wall tetany, central respiratory failure, surface thermal burns, and deep tissue injury, leading to compartment syndrome, myoglobin release, rhabdomyolysis, and renal failure. Give IV fluids (4 mL/kg for each percent of BSA burned over 24 hours) and check electrolytes, urinalysis/serum myoglobin, serum creatine

	Table 7-3: Mild Traumatic Brain Injury Rehabilitation — Graduated Return-to-Play Protocol	
	Rehabilitation Stage*	**Functional Exercise**
1	Symptom-limited activity	Gradual reintroduction of work/school activity
2	Light aerobic activity	Walking, swimming, stationary cycling at 70% maximal heart rate; no weight lifting
3	Sport-specific exercise	Specific sport-related drills with no head impact
4	Noncontact training drills	More complex drills; light resistance training
5	Full-contact practice (medical clearance first)	Normal training
6	Return to play	Normal game play

* Each stage should last at least 24 hours. If symptoms recur, the patient must stop the activity and wait until asymptomatic for at least 24 hours before resuming.

kinase, and ECG. Urine alkalization may be indicated if rhabdomyolysis is present and the urine pH is low. Patients who were thrown from the current require a workup for traumatic injuries as well. High-voltage exposures require cardiac monitoring for 24–48 hours. Establish a pediatric burn center referral for all high-voltage burn patients and for those with low-voltage AC current exposures with concurrent arrest or loss of consciousness.

OCULAR CHEMICAL BURNS

PREVIEW | REVIEW

- What is the difference between alkali burns and acid burns of the eye?

Chemical burns to the eye are ocular emergencies. Alkali burns often cause penetrating corneal injuries, whereas acid burns tend to cause more localized tissue damage. Severe alkali burns often cause corneal opacification. Emergency treatment involves immediate saline or water irrigation of the affected eye until neutralization of the ocular pH. This should be started prior to transporting the child to the emergency department, where irrigation should then resume. Ophthalmologic evaluation is required.

CHEST WALL TRAUMA

PREVIEW | REVIEW

- Which severe injuries are most common from chest wall blunt trauma?

Most (80%) chest wall trauma to children and adolescents is due to blunt injury—usually from motor vehicle collisions (MVCs) and falls from height. Injuries due to child maltreatment tend to occur in younger children. Falls from bicycles and skateboards occur more in school-age children. Sports injuries, MVCs, pedestrian injuries, and attempted suicide occur more in adolescents. Penetrating injuries, usually from gunshots, also occur more commonly in adolescents.

Most common severe injuries from chest wall blunt trauma are (in order):

1) Pulmonary contusion

2) Pneumothorax/Hemothorax

3) Rib fracture

The most common results of chest wall penetrating trauma are (in order):

1) Pneumothorax/Hemothorax

2) Pulmonary contusion

3) Lung laceration

4) Blood vessel injury

Pulmonary contusions can cause parts of the lung to consolidate with collapse of the alveoli and atelectasis (lung tissue collapse). Infection and ARDS may occur in up to 50%.

Pulmonary contusions are seen on x-ray as whitish areas but may take 6–48 hours to appear.

Children with chest wall trauma who have respiratory or cardiovascular compromise or collapse at presentation require stabilization before any imaging studies can be done. This can be due to severe pulmonary contusion, cardiac tamponade, pneumothorax, or disruption of the thoracic vessels and may require intubation, intravenous fluids, or emergent treatment for pneumothorax or tamponade.

Pneumothorax causing respiratory compromise requires an immediate needle thoracostomy.

Cardiac tamponade causing vascular compromise requires an immediate pericardiocentesis.

Cardiovascular compromise from blood loss requires rapid infusion of volume (blood or isotonic fluid).

BLUNT ABDOMINAL TRAUMA

PREVIEW | REVIEW

- Which organs are most commonly affected in blunt abdominal trauma?
- How do most patients with splenic injuries present?
- What is a common cutaneous finding that indicates possible abdominal injury?

The spleen and liver are the organs most commonly injured in blunt abdominal trauma. Pancreatic and intestinal injuries are less typical. Patients with splenic injuries often complain of left upper quadrant pain and/or left shoulder pain due to diaphragmatic irritation from subphrenic blood. Intestinal perforations can present with delayed symptoms (abdominal pain and vomiting) up to 24–48 hours after injury and can be missed on CT scan. Abdominal trauma may lead to development of a duodenal hematoma within 1–5 days. The intramural hematoma is caused by compression of the duodenal wall against the vertebral column. Clinical signs and symptoms may include gastric distention, abdominal pain, anorexia, bilious vomiting, and a palpable upper abdominal mass. Bruising of the abdominal wall may or may not be present. Plain radiographs often reveal an air-fluid level in a dilated duodenal loop proximal to a mass caused by the hematoma. A typical injury resulting in a duodenal hematoma is a bicycle accident with flexion over the handlebars. Duodenal hematomas may also be the result of child maltreatment.

Patients with a seat belt sign (abdominal ecchymosis) after a motor vehicle collision are at a significantly increased risk for abdominal injuries and Chance fractures (a type of lumbar spine fracture caused by extreme forward flexion, typically over a lap-only seat belt).

Severely injured patients may have associated hypovolemia and hemorrhagic shock, often heralded by tachycardia. These injuries also frequently present with diffuse distention, rigidity, tenderness, and ecchymosis on physical examination. Resuscitate with crystalloid and blood products. Hemodynamically unstable patients with a positive focused assessment with sonography in trauma (**FAST**), indicating hemoperitoneum, require surgical management.

A CXR should be ordered in trauma patients (unless undergoing immediate thoracic CT). While not definitive, it can show signs of most significant pneumo- or hemothoraces and pulmonary contusions. A widened mediastinum can indicate aortic injury. While the CXR is not sensitive for vessel injury, fortunately, this is rare in children. A FAST exam may be considered (controversial); a positive FAST in a stable patient, significant abdominal tenderness, and a seatbelt sign require a CT scan. PECARN developed a rule for abdominal trauma; abdominal pain, decreased breath sounds, thoracic wall trauma, vomiting, and GCS score < 14 should be considered as well in the assessment of abdominal trauma. Assess stable patients who have mild pain with laboratory studies (AST, ALT, amylase/lipase, CBC, and urinalysis) and serial exams.

Many children with splenic trauma can be managed nonoperatively to preserve splenic function and decrease the subsequent risk of bacterial sepsis, which occurs more frequently among asplenic individuals.

FRACTURES

PREVIEW | REVIEW

- Explain the Salter-Harris classification of fractures.
- What is the treatment for a greenstick fracture?
- In a 7-month-old infant with a spiral fracture of the left femur, what should you suspect?
- How do you treat a clavicle fracture?
- What is the major concern with distal humerus fractures?
- What are the symptoms of compartment syndrome?

OVERVIEW

Fractures are common in pediatrics. It is important to determine if serious conditions coexist with the fracture and if urgent reduction or orthopedic evaluation is required. For uncomplicated fractures, immobilization and pain management (i.e., ice, analgesics) are key.

Growth plate injuries (15% of all childhood fractures) are unique to childhood and involve the physis (growth plate) with variable involvement of the surrounding bone. The Salter-Harris classification is both a mnemonic and a clinical descriptor of the area involved. In Figure 7-10, the fracture line is depicted in red.

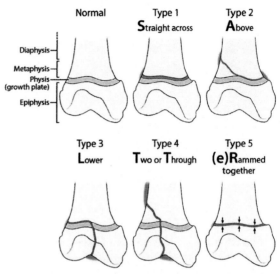

Figure 7-10: Salter-Harris classification of growth plate injuries

The **SALT(e)R** mnemonic can help you remember these fractures. As shown in Figure 7-10, picture the bone as epiphysis-down when using the mnemonic:

- Type 1—**S**traight across
- Type 2—**A**bove
- Type 3—**L**ower
- Type 4—**T**wo or **T**hrough
- Type 5—**R**ammed together

Type 1 (through the physis only, potentially separating the epiphysis from the metaphysis) and **Type 2** (fracture through the physis and metaphysis), which are common, have an excellent prognosis. Type 1 may be evident on radiographs or can be diagnosed based on tenderness over the growth plate despite a normal radiograph. Nondisplaced fractures simply require immobilization in a cast.

Type 3 (fracture through the epiphysis extending to the growth plate) and **Type 4** (fracture extending from the articular surface through the epiphysis, the physis, and metaphysis) are uncommon. An orthopedic consult and precise reduction are required. There is a greater risk of growth disturbance and functional impairment with these types of fractures, because the articular surface and germinal layer are affected. Manipulation usually requires an anesthetic.

Type 5 is a crush injury to the epiphysis and, fortunately, is rare. Because the epiphyseal blood supply is affected, the prognosis for the growth plate is poor. Unfortunately, this typically is diagnosed only after limb deformity becomes apparent, as the radiograph can initially be negative.

GREENSTICK FRACTURE

This incomplete fracture, in which the cortex is broken on one side and intact on the other (Figure 7-11), is somewhat unique to children. If there is no deformation, immobilization alone is effective therapy. Anatomic reduction may be required if there is an obvious bend to the affected limb.

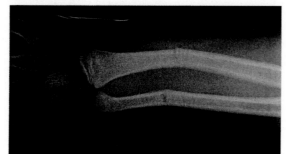

Figure 7-11: Greenstick fracture of the radius and ulna

TORUS (BUCKLE) FRACTURE

This is a typical fracture in children. Axial loading and compression of the bone (e.g., falling on an outstretched hand) produce a "buckle" of the metaphysis (Figure 7-12). It most frequently occurs in the distal radial metaphysis and usually heals with 3 weeks of immobilization.

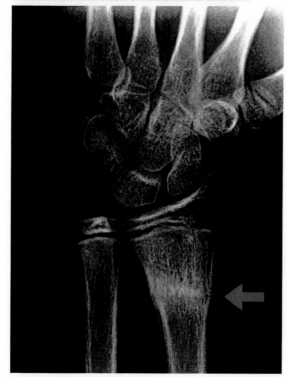

Figure 7-12: Torus (buckle) fracture

SPIRAL FRACTURE

This looks just like its name, with a fracture having a curvilinear course following a twisting mechanism of injury (Figure 7-13). Spiral fractures can be accidental. However, if you see a spiral fracture without an appropriate history, particularly in a nonambulatory child, consider child maltreatment. The exception to this is the "toddler's fracture," a spiral fracture of the tibia in a young child. The mechanism is frequently minor—a twist or a jump—and physical exam findings are often subtle, with minimal swelling and tenderness in a child who is not bearing weight. Toddler's fractures typically heal well with immobilization.

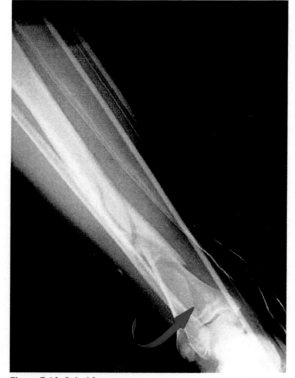

Figure 7-13: Spiral fracture

CLAVICLE FRACTURE

This is the most common fracture in children. Usually, the middle third of the clavicle is affected. Most cases occur as a result of falling on an outstretched arm or shoulder or from direct trauma. Neurovascular injury is uncommon. Diagnosis usually is made by physical exam and/or radiograph (Figure 7-14). While clavicle fractures can represent inflicted injury, particularly in nonambulatory children, neonates can sustain clavicle fractures during birth, and many go unrecognized until several weeks to months of age when the healing callus becomes prominent.

For most clavicle fractures, treatment is:

- In a young child—immobilization of the affected arm (e.g., sling and swathe)
- In an older child—a simple sling for 2–3 weeks

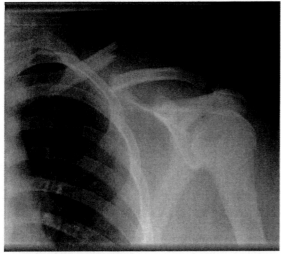

Figure 7-14: Clavicle fracture

Almost all medial third clavicle fractures heal well, but warn families about the prominent "lump" of callus that develops as the fracture heals and remodels. Orthopedic referral is needed for the following circumstances: open fractures, tenting of the skin (from fracture fragment), displaced medial or lateral clavicle fractures, comminuted fractures, and significant shortening. This includes medial third fractures with shortening of > 2 cm in adolescents > 12 years of age, especially high-level athletes, because surgical repair may be indicated.

DISTAL HUMERUS (ELBOW) FRACTURE

The most common pediatric elbow fracture is the **supracondylar fracture**, which usually occurs after a fall on an outstretched hand or elbow. Look for the posterior fat pad sign on x-ray, indicating joint effusion/hemarthrosis. Sometimes an elbow fracture is difficult to see, and presence of a posterior fat pad (which is normally absent) or displacement of the normally small anterior fat pad is the only clue (Figure 7-15). Displaced supracondylar fractures have a high risk of neurovascular complications, including compartment syndrome of the forearm. Untreated, this can lead to Volkmann contractures in the wrist and hand. Evaluate for damage to the brachial artery, median nerve, or radial nerve (e.g., absent or diminished pulse, abnormal motor or sensory function). Admit and monitor neurovascular status carefully with repeat exams.

Splint all suspected elbow fractures (i.e., localized pain, swelling, joint effusion) even if no definite fracture is seen, and always arrange orthopedic follow-up. Nondisplaced supracondylar fractures may be splinted or casted and require nonemergent orthopedic follow-up. Supracondylar fractures with any angulation or displacement require emergent orthopedic evaluation for precise reduction. Improper reduction can result in cubitus varus (a.k.a. gunstock deformity of the elbow). Document a

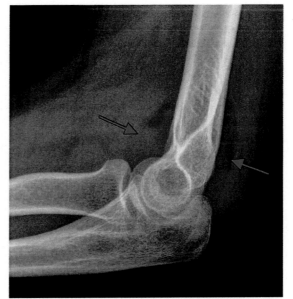

Figure 7-15: Fat pad sign of supracondylar (distal humerus) fracture

complete neurovascular examination in patients with supracondylar fractures—median and radial nerve and brachial artery injuries are potential complications.

FRACTURE COMPLICATIONS

Remember: Be on the lookout for neurovascular compromise with any fracture, especially supracondylar.

Compartment syndrome is most typical with tibial (anterior compartment) and supracondylar fractures. The fracture (or other injury such as crushing or circumferential burn) results in hemorrhage or swelling in an enclosed fascial compartment. Vascular compromise results, leading to ischemia and tissue damage. Classic signs include the "5 Ps": **p**ain, **p**allor, **p**aresthesias, **p**ulselessness, and **p**aralysis. However, these signs are unreliable, and pulses are sometimes still palpable in early compartment syndrome. The biggest clue is pain out of proportion to the fracture, especially pain that is remote from the fracture site. In contrast, remember that, once immobilized, most children with fractures have significantly reduced pain. Direct measurement of compartment pressure is often needed; get an emergent orthopedic consult!

Occult fractures are those not evident on x-rays. Possible clues:

- Clinical exam suggests fracture (i.e., swelling, localized tenderness)
- Persistent pain
- Gait disturbances, especially in younger children

Treat as if fractured (e.g., splint, elevation) and follow with x-rays in 7–10 days for the development of callus formation.

SUBLUXATION OF THE RADIAL HEAD

PREVIEW | REVIEW

- Know nursemaid elbow!

Know this topic. Subluxation of the radial head (a.k.a. "nursemaid elbow") is a very common injury in children < 5 years of age. The typical mechanism is axial traction on an extended and pronated arm, causing the annular ligament to slide over the radial head. See Figure 7-16. However, other mechanisms (including falls) can produce the same injury. Child maltreatment is highly unlikely. The child holds the arm limply to the side, but there is no localized swelling or bony tenderness. Pain mainly occurs with attempted pronation or supination of the forearm.

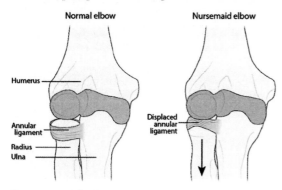

Figure 7-16: Subluxation of the radial head

X-rays are not necessary in typical cases and will be normal if obtained. Therefore, radiographs are reserved for patients with an unusual history (e.g., fall, unknown history) or physical exam finding (e.g., tenderness, swelling). To fix the problem, either hyperpronate the extended forearm or supinate the forearm and flex the elbow. Often a "click" or snapping sensation is palpable (and sometimes audible) over the radial head. There is evidence that the hyperpronation maneuver is more often successful. If the first maneuver fails, try the alternate method. After reduction, the child will begin using the arm within a short time.

SHOULDER INJURIES

PREVIEW | REVIEW

- What does the x-ray show in an acromioclavicular separation?
- How does a patient with an anterior shoulder dislocation present?

Acromioclavicular (AC) sprains and separations occur primarily in adolescents, usually from a direct blow to the shoulder. There is tenderness over the AC joint, and x-rays typically show widening or separation of the joint. A sling or shoulder immobilizer is effective for minor injuries; refer to orthopedics if the injury is more severe. AC separation is rare in prepubertal children—they commonly fracture the distal clavicle.

Anterior shoulder dislocation (Figure 7-17), also rare in children < 12 years of age, occurs usually in adolescents. The affected shoulder appears lower than the other, the normal deltoid contour is diminished, and the humeral head is palpated inferiorly and anteriorly to its normal position in most cases. Various methods, such as external rotation, scapular manipulation, and traction/counter-traction are used for reduction. Intraarticular anesthetic injection, narcotic pain medications, and/or sedation with muscle relaxation may be needed. Immobilize with a shoulder immobilizer for several weeks. Most patients should follow up with orthopedics, particularly those with recurrent dislocation.

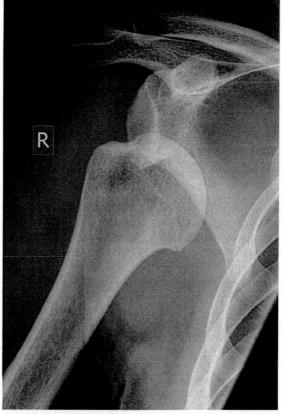

Figure 7-17: Anterior shoulder dislocation

SPRAINS

PREVIEW | REVIEW

- Which is more likely in a young child—ankle sprain or fracture? Why?
- Name the common physical findings in a sprain of the ankle.
- How do you treat an ankle sprain?

A sprain is an injury to the ligament around a joint when it is forced to move in an unnatural position. Many have always thought that sprains are rare in prepubescent children because the ligament is stronger than the growth plate. However, recently, sprains have been recognized as plausible injuries even in young children. The most common sprains are of the ankle and fingers. On physical examination, look for ligamentous tenderness, swelling, and bruising (Figure 7-18). Ankle sprains are graded from I to III (Table 7-4), with I representing a partial ligamentous tear, II an incomplete tear with moderate functional impairment, and III a complete tear.

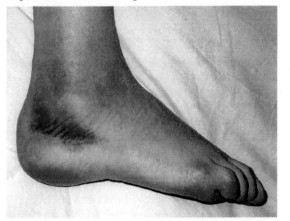

Figure 7-18: Bruising with ankle sprain

Table 7-4: Grades of Ankle Sprains			
	Grade I (Mild)	**Grade II (Moderate)**	**Grade III (Severe)**
Swelling	Mild	Moderate	Severe
Tenderness	Mild	Moderate	Severe
Loss of Function	Minimal	Difficult to ambulate	Unable to bear weight
Treatment	Rest 7–10 days	Rest 2–4 weeks	Rest 5–10 weeks

The **Ottawa ankle rules** have been found to be nearly 100% sensitive in detecting clinically significant fractures in both children ≥ 2 years of age and adults. Children with acute ankle injury who cannot bear weight for 4 steps or who have tenderness over the 6 cm of the distal posterior edge or tip of either malleolus should get x-rays of the ankle. Although the majority of children with ankle injuries get radiographs, those who can bear weight and who do not have bony tenderness are very unlikely to have a significant fracture. Be sure to examine the foot as well (especially over the navicular and base of the 5th metatarsal), and order foot views if either area is tender. Remember that Salter-Harris Type 1 fractures of the distal fibula are typical in children with open growth plates; the child has localized tenderness of the physis, but x-rays are often normal—this is a clinical diagnosis.

Ankle sprains are treated with **RICE** (**r**est, **i**ce, **c**ompression, and **e**levation), though little literature actually supports this practice. Significant sprains require a splint or removable air cast for protection and comfort. Occasionally, casting is needed for severe injuries. Rehabilitation, including early ambulation as tolerated with range-of-motion/stretching exercises, is an important component of ankle sprain treatment, because recurrences are common and often limit participation in sports and other activities.

OTHER EMERGENT EVENTS

BRIEF RESOLVED UNEXPLAINED EVENT (BRUE)

PREVIEW | REVIEW

- What are the low-risk criteria for a brief resolved unexplained event (BRUE)?

BRUE is the term used to describe a brief episode of cyanosis, irregular breathing, change in tone, or altered level of responsiveness in an infant. In 2016, the American Academy of Pediatrics recommended replacement of the term apparent life-threatening event (ALTE), which was considered imprecise and subjective. The term BRUE can be applied when no underlying diagnosis is evident as a cause of the event. Infants meeting all low-risk criteria are unlikely to have poor outcomes.

Low-risk criteria include:

- Age > 60 days
- Born at a gestational age of ≥ 32 weeks and current postconceptual age ≥ 45 weeks
- No CPR by a medical professional
- Event lasting < 1 minute
- Single event and no previous episodes
- No concerning findings on history or physical exam

Infants meeting all low-risk criteria may be discharged after a period of observation on continuous pulse oximetry and possibly a 12-lead electrocardiogram and/or pertussis testing. Manage with education, including training in cardiopulmonary resuscitation, and close follow-up. Routine testing and admission are not indicated.

Infants not meeting all of the aforementioned criteria are considered high risk and may require hospitalization for observation and potentially more extensive testing for underlying disorders. Specific causes of the symptoms are found in 50% of cases and can include gastroesophageal reflux, seizures, bronchiolitis, pertussis, child maltreatment, inborn errors of metabolism, and cardiac arrhythmias. Treatment is based on the final diagnosis.

SHOCK

PREVIEW | REVIEW
- What differentiates compensated shock from decompensated shock?

There are 4 categories of shock, based on mechanism:

1) **Hypovolemic shock**—most common; from hemorrhage or from extravascular fluid loss (e.g., osmotic diuresis, diarrhea). Patient may appear dehydrated and have concurrent tachycardia. Treatment is with fluid or blood repletion.

2) **Distributive shock**—decreased systemic vascular resistance (SVR); from sepsis, anaphylaxis, and transient neurogenic shock ("spinal shock"; from trauma to spinal cord). Hypotension with bradycardia in the setting of trauma is classic for a spinal injury. This is typically treated with fluids and vasopressors targeted at increasing systemic vascular resistance.

3) **Cardiogenic shock**—results from pump failure and is associated with decreased function and depressed cardiac output; from cardiomyopathies and arrhythmias (e.g., pulseless V-tach, V-fib, bradyarrhythmias). Common symptoms include difficulty breathing, fatigue or lethargy, and a recent viral prodrome (myocarditis). Clinical signs of cardiogenic shock may include tachycardia, hypotension, and tachypnea. This patient also has a gallop, which can indicate imminent heart failure, and has cardiomegaly on chest x-ray. Small fluid boluses of 5–10 mL/kg can be administered, with careful attention to fluid overload.

4) **Obstructive shock**—from massive pulmonary embolism, cardiac tamponade, tension pneumothorax, and congenital heart lesions. These conditions present differently and have different outcomes with fluid administration. Typical treatment is that of the underlying condition.

At first, the patient is typically in **compensated shock** where the body is able to maintain blood pressure primarily by peripheral vasoconstriction and tachycardia with decreased peripheral pulse pressure. **Decompensated shock** occurs when homeostatic mechanisms no longer compensate, resulting in decreased systolic blood pressure, altered mental status, lactic acidosis, and rapid deterioration.

Treatment is focused on stabilization and improvement of perfusion and organ function as soon as possible. Patients initially get supplemental oxygen and vascular access. Intubate the patient if there is respiratory compromise.

Lab work includes CBC, calcium, cultures, and electrolytes. Start antibiotics if the patient appears to be in septic shock.

The initial treatment is determined by how sick the patient is and their response to treatment in the 1st hour. The shock reversal goals are:

- Systolic BP > 5th percentile:
  - 60 mmHg for 1-month-old
  - 70 + (2× age in years) mmHg from 1 month to 10 years of age
  - 90 mmHg if > 10 years of age
- Good perfusion with warm skin and normal capillary refill (i.e., < 2 seconds)
- Pulses strong and equal
- Normal urine output (> 1 mL/kg/hour up to 30–50 mL/hour)
- Normal mental status

Aggressive fluid resuscitation: Any child with hypovolemic shock who is hypotensive requires fluid boluses of isotonic fluid (NS or RL) at 20 mL/kg. In 2020, PALS endorsed a recommendation for either 10-mL or 20-mL fluid boluses for septic shock. Multiple 20-mL/kg fluid boluses may be required. Fluid should be given rapidly and may require more than gravity to infuse quickly (e.g., 3-way stopcock on syringe, squeeze IV bag).

Slow the fluid resuscitation when shock reversal is achieved or if there are signs of fluid overload (e.g., pulmonary crackles) or in settings without capacity for respiratory support.

Do not give aggressive fluid resuscitation in the following circumstances:

- Cardiogenic shock: Extra isotonic fluid may help hypotensive cardiogenic shock, but being overly aggressive may result in poor outcomes.
- Obstructive shock: Fluids are usually not helpful and often deleterious in obstructive shock. For cardiac tamponade, a bolus sometimes temporizes the situation briefly while definitive care can be provided. As much as possible, the underlying cause of obstructive shock should be addressed.
- Several trials (mainly in resource poor settings) have demonstrated deleterious effects to large volume resuscitation. Based on these, be careful with fluids in patients with severe anemia or malnutrition.
- Note: If the patient has DKA, cerebral edema is a concern. Historically, recommendations were to limit bolus fluids to 10 mL/kg over the 1st hour. A 2018 study found that more rapid fluid administration with up to 20 mL/kg bolus fluids was not associated with adverse neurologic outcomes, and if the patient is in shock, fluids should be administered.

Cardiac arrhythmias should be addressed prior to fluid resuscitation.

Blood: Many experts recommend starting with blood rather than isotonic fluids if hemorrhage is the cause of shock, because isotonic fluids may result in increased blood loss and dilutional coagulopathy. If isotonic fluids are given, start transfusing blood if shock does not improve after 40 mL/kg of isotonic fluids.

Vasoactive drugs: If the patient has either distributive (i.e., septic) shock or cardiogenic shock and is still hypotensive after 40–60 mL/kg of fluid replacement or is showing signs of fluid overload before shock reversal, then epinephrine or norepinephrine is used. Dopamine is no longer recommended by PALS for septic shock.

Frequently reassess the patient throughout resuscitation. Once the shock reversal goals are reached, attention shifts to diagnosis of underlying etiology (if not evident) and transfer to an inpatient setting for continued monitoring and treatment. For septic shock not responsive to fluids and vasoactive drugs, consider stress-dose corticosteroid administration.

PEDIATRIC ADVANCED LIFE SUPPORT (PALS)

PREVIEW | REVIEW

- Explain how to do rescue breaths in an infant and a child. How are rescue breaths for an infant different from those for a child?

- Know Table 7-5 on page 7-30.

- What reversible causes should you think about for a child in cardiac arrest?

- How do you manage symptomatic bradycardia?

- How do you manage pulseless V-tach?

- True or false? After giving a shock to defibrillate, you should immediately pause CPR to check the pulse and rhythm.

- You are attending to a 5-year-old child who collapsed in a public place with an adult AED available. Is it safe to use adult pads on a pediatric patient?

OVERVIEW

In 2010, the guidelines for advanced cardiac life support (ACLS) changed from ABC to **CAB** (compressions-airway-breathing) with greater emphasis on minimizing the interruption of chest compressions. For many pediatric patients, though, airway and breathing are the key interventions needed since the most common cause of cardiac arrest in children is asphyxia.

We'll review **C** in great detail under Circulation on page 7-30.

For **A**, remember head tilt/chin lift or, if trauma is present, jaw thrust. Clear the airway of foreign bodies via back blows and chest thrusts for children < 1 year of age. For those 1–8 years of age, use the Heimlich maneuver.

For **B**, do not forget supplemental oxygen (if available). For infants, use mouth-to-mouth/nose breathing. For children, pinch the nose and use mouth-to-mouth

breathing. Breaths are delivered slowly over ~ 1 second. While "compression-only CPR" is recommended for adults, children should still get rescue breaths with compressions. For children requiring breaths without CPR or those with an advanced airway in place, the rate has been changed to 20–30 per minute. In the out-of-hospital setting, bag-valve-mask is a reasonable option when compared to advanced airway.

Postarrest care in patients who remain comatose involves continuous temperature monitoring and targeted temperature management of either 89.6–93.2°F (32.0–34.0°C) for 2 days followed by 96.8–99.5°F (36.0–37.5°C) for 3 days or just 96.8–99.5°F for a total of 5 days, maintenance of systolic blood pressure above the 5th percentile, and an oxygen saturation of 94–99%.

For newborns requiring resuscitation, remember the ABCs and temperature (warm and dry). Use the inverted pyramid (Figure 7-19), which outlines the most frequently needed resuscitative measures at the top (position, clear airway, stimulate by drying), less frequently needed procedures in the middle (establish ventilation with bag and mask or endotracheal intubation), and the least frequently required measures (chest compressions, oxygen, and medications) at the bottom. Resuscitation of newborns > 35 weeks gestational age requiring positive pressure ventilation begins with 21% F_iO_2 and resuscitation of newborns < 35 weeks gestational age begins with 21–30% F_iO_2.

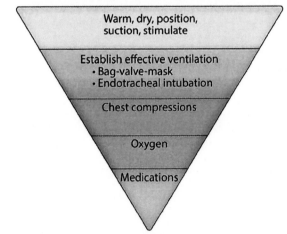

Figure 7-19: Resuscitative measures

Important changes in neonatal resuscitation (Neonatal Resuscitation Program 2020 Update):

1) Delay clamping the cord for 30–60 seconds.

2) Routine intubation for tracheal suctioning in infants born with meconium staining is not recommended. If nonvigorous with evidence of obstruction, intubation with tracheal suction and positive pressure ventilation can be beneficial.

3) Skin-to-skin contact in healthy newborns not requiring resuscitation can be beneficial.

4) Umbilical venous is preferred access (if required).

5) 20 minutes without heart rate despite accomplishing the steps of resuscitation is a reasonable time frame to reassess goals of care.

CIRCULATION

Where should you do a pulse check? In newborns, ECG monitoring is now recommended (although pulse can often be palpated in the umbilical cord). In infants, brachial or femoral pulses are used. In children, carotid or femoral pulses are used. Start compressions if the HR is < 60 bpm with poor perfusion.

The 2020 PALS resuscitation guidelines (Table 7-5) stress the need for high-quality, uninterrupted chest compressions to maximize coronary perfusion, and this was unchanged in the 2020 update. Remember "push hard and push fast." For infants and children, compress at least 1/3 of the anteroposterior diameter of the chest, up to adult recommendations of at least 2 inches (5 cm) but not greater than 2.4 inches (6 cm). Allow full recoil. Avoid excessive ventilation. Deliver breaths at a 15:2 (2 rescuers) or 30:2 (1 rescuer) ratio with compressions, using a goal of 100–120 compressions/minute, and PALS recommends 20–30 breaths/minute after establishment of an advanced airway in all patients requiring assisted ventilation.

For all critically ill children, including those in cardiac arrest, consider reversible causes, including the 5 Hs and 4 Ts:

- **5 Hs:** hypoxemia, hypothermia, hypovolemia, hypoglycemia, and hypo- or hyperkalemia
- **4 Ts:** tamponade, tension pneumothorax, thrombosis (pulmonary or coronary), and toxins

Tachycardia

According to the PALS algorithm for tachycardia with a pulse and poor perfusion, a wide complex tachycardia in a patient with pulses who is unstable (i.e., shock, low blood pressure, changes in mental status) should receive immediate synchronized cardioversion.

For a patient with tachycardia and shock who has pulses, initial steps are as follows:

1) Maintain a patent airway.

2) Provide oxygen.

3) Obtain IV or intraosseous (IO) access.

4) Obtain a 12-lead electrocardiogram.

For signs of cardiogenic shock and wide complex tachycardia, immediate synchronized cardioversion is indicated at a dose of 0.5–1 J/kg. If ineffective, give a second dose of 2 J/kg. The physician should consider providing sedation prior to cardioversion as it can be uncomfortable or painful, but this should not delay cardioversion in an unstable patient. In the stable patient, adenosine may be attempted if the QRS is monomorphic.

For more information on tachycardia, see the Cardiology section.

Bradycardia

Possible causes of bradycardia include the "Hs" and "Ts" (see Circulation), as well as head injury with increased ICP, heart block, ingestions, and cervical spine injury.

Support CABs, especially oxygen/ventilation, and reevaluate frequently. If there is no cardiovascular compromise (e.g., hypotension, poor perfusion, altered consciousness), continue supportive care and try to determine the cause. Consider consultation/transfer if bradycardia persists.

Table 7-5: Pediatric Advanced Life Support — CPR Guidelines		
Component	**Infant < 1 Year of Age**	**Child 1–8 Years of Age**
Recognition	Unresponsive, no breathing or only gasping No pulse palpated within 10 seconds (health care providers only)	
CPR sequence	Compressions-airway-breathing	
CPR technique	2 thumbs with encircling hands Allow complete recoil.	Heel of one hand; other hand can be on top. Allow complete recoil.
Compression depth	Push hard: at least 1/3 AP diameter, ~ 1½ inches	At least 1/3 AP diameter, ~ 2 inches
Compression rate	At least 100–120 compressions/minute; rotate compressor every 2 minutes.	
Airway	Head tilt/Chin lift (Use jaw thrust if there is trauma with a need for C-spine protection.)	
Obstructed airway	Back blows and chest thrusts	Abdominal thrusts
Rescue breaths	2–3 gentle breaths, about 2 seconds apart; verify chest rise. Check for signs of response; repeat if there are none.	
Ventilation	15:2 for 2 health care providers (30:2 for single rescuer in the field), asynchronous with chest compressions If advanced airway or ventilatory support without compressions, 20–30 breaths/minute	
Pulse check location	Brachial/Femoral artery	Carotid/Femoral artery

Adapted from the 2020 PALS guidelines.

For bradycardia (HR < 60 bpm) with cardiovascular compromise (e.g., low BP, altered level of consciousness):

- Assist breathing if needed with positive pressure ventilation.
- Place on monitors.
- Perform chest compressions if HR remains < 60 bpm with ventilatory support.
- Epinephrine (can repeat every 3–5 minutes):
  ◦ 0.01 mg/kg (1:10,000, 0.1 mL/kg) IV/IO (preferred) or
  ◦ 0.1 mg/kg (1:1,000, 0.1 mL/kg) endotracheal tube
- Continue CPR for 2 minutes after drug administration before checking pulse.
- Atropine for increased vagal tone or primary AV block: 0.02 mg/kg (minimum dose 0.1 mg, maximum dose 0.5 mg).
- Consider pacing.

Pulseless Algorithm

For a pulseless arrest, start CPR, open the airway, give rescue breaths, and obtain IV or IO access. Attach monitors, including pulse oximetry, cardiac, and exhaled CO_2 to monitor rhythm and effectiveness of resuscitation. These interventions typically are accomplished simultaneously in the health care setting. For most situations with a single rescuer, the 2020 American Heart Association guidelines recommend starting compressions first (CAB instead of ABC), noting a delay of < 6 seconds until first rescue breath with this model.

For a pulseless child with V-fib or V-tach:

- Start CPR; attach monitor or defibrillator.
- Shock: Attempt defibrillation with 2 J/kg.
- Resume CPR for 2 minutes before checking pulse/rhythm.
- Give epinephrine every 3–5 minutes. There is a new emphasis in 2020 to start epinephrine within 5 minutes of starting chest compressions:
  ◦ 0.01 mg/kg (1:10,000, 0.1 mL/kg) IV/IO or
  ◦ 0.1 mg/kg (1:1,000, 0.1 mL/kg) endotracheal
- Repeat shocks if ventricular arrhythmia persists:
  ◦ 2nd shock (4 J/kg)
  ◦ 3rd and subsequent shock (4 J/kg)
- Pattern is **CPR → shock → CPR → drug → shock (repeat)**.
- Consider other drugs: amiodarone, lidocaine (magnesium for torsades de pointes or hypomagnesemia).

Automatic external defibrillators (AEDs) can be used in children. If available, use child-size pads and a pediatric dose attenuator for children < 8 years of age. Manual defibrillators are preferred in infants. If child-size pads are not available, use the adult pads (place 1 on the front and 1 on the back if needed to avoid the pads touching each other) and settings.

For a pulseless child with a nonshockable rhythm (i.e., PEA, asystole):

- Start CPR.
- Give epinephrine every 3–5 minutes. There is a new emphasis in 2020 to start epinephrine within 5 minutes of starting chest compressions:
  ◦ 0.01 mg/kg (1:10,000, 0.1 mL/kg) IV/IO or
  ◦ 0.1 mg/kg (1:1,000, 0.1 mL/kg) endotracheal
- Continue CPR for 2 minutes after drug administration before checking pulse.
- Continue to search for etiology/reversible causes.

CHILD MALTREATMENT

CHILD MALTREATMENT SYNDROMES

PREVIEW | REVIEW

- Are boys or girls more commonly sexually abused?

- A 1-year-old presents with a left femur fracture. The mother says the child was with his father for most of the day and that the child was refusing to bear weight on the leg when she returned, but she doesn't know how the child was injured. Should you be suspicious of physical abuse?

- You note a small bruise on the cheek of a 2-month-old child presenting for a well-child check. The mother states the child got the bruise when she rolled over a toy in her crib. Should you be suspicious of physical abuse?

- A 1-year-old boy presenting for an otitis media follow-up visit has dark-purple bruises on his shins. The father says his son fell against the steps 2 days ago when attempting to walk. A few scrapes are also noted on the child's shins. Should you be suspicious of physical abuse?

- What is the most common cause of death due to child physical abuse?

- What eye finding is important to look for in a child you suspect was shaken violently?

- True or false? Rib fractures should make you suspect child abuse.

- What radiologic test should be done to screen for fractures in children < 2 years of age suspected of abuse?

- True or false? In a child with suspected sexual abuse, a normal genital and rectal examination rules out sexual abuse.

OVERVIEW

There are multiple types of child maltreatment. Neglect is reported much more commonly than physical and sexual abuse.

The highest rate of maltreatment is in the birth to 1-year-old age range. Caregivers who are related to the child inflict the majority of abuse. More physical abuse cases involve boys, whereas 75% of sexual abuse cases involve girls. In fact, it is estimated that 1 in 4 girls and 1 in 10 boys have been sexually abused. Rates are doubled in children with physical or intellectual impairments, and those already in foster care are not immune to further abuse.

Child maltreatment occurs in children of all races/ethnicities and socioeconomic groups; be careful to avoid bias in evaluating children who possibly have been abused. Abuse can lead to mood disorders, including post-traumatic stress disorder and poor school performance. Conditions such as ADHD and learning disorders are associated with child abuse but causality has not been established. Abusive caretakers may be abuse victims themselves, young parents, affected by domestic violence, or have a mental illness or substance use problem. Poverty and financial stress are significant risk factors, as is living in a home with unrelated adults. Frequently, caretakers have unrealistic expectations regarding the child's behavior (e.g., amount of crying, toileting accidents). Siblings, especially twins, of abuse victims are at increased risk of abuse as well. Overall, a slight majority of the perpetrators are female, and a significant majority are parents of the victim. Perpetrators of sexual abuse are almost always male and known to the abused child, and about 20% are < 18 years of age.

NEGLECT

Neglect, the most common form of child abuse, includes "acts of omission," such as failure to provide adequate food, shelter, clothing, or supervision. It also includes abandonment and failure to provide a child with adequate health care and/or education.

A typical manifestation of neglect is poor growth and developmental delay. Older neglected children can seem emotionally needy, or they can be very adult-like in their behaviors due to forced early independence and self-reliance.

PHYSICAL ABUSE

The classic definition of physical abuse is "an act against a child that results in harm or intended harm to the child." Many areas limit this to "deformation or leaving a lasting mark on the child's body." This definition tries to separate physical abuse from common practices, such as "spanking," but the difference between these definitions remains blurry. Common injuries due to abuse include bruising/soft tissue injuries, fractures, burns, and head trauma.

The following features on history should raise suspicion of physical abuse:

- Vague or unknown history of how the child sustained the injury
- Injury history that is not appropriate for the child's age and development (e.g., a 2-month-old can't roll off a bed), not compatible with the injury, or is inconsistent either over time or between witnesses
- Unexplained delay in seeking medical care for a significant injury
- History of recurrent injuries, especially those with inconsistent explanations
- History of abused sibling or unexplained death of a sibling

Always consider developmental ability with findings on physical exam—a 1-year-old just learning to walk frequently has bruises on the shins from falling, but it is unusual to see bruising on a child who is not yet cruising or crawling ("those who cannot cruise rarely bruise"). Intraoral injuries, such as bruising/lacerations to the lip or tongue frenula, may be due to attempts to force-feed the child, particularly in nonambulatory patients. A 2013 study found that over 25% of infants with severe physical abuse had previously been seen for more minor sentinel injuries (i.e., a previous injury reported in the medical history that was suspicious for abuse because the explanation was implausible). Common sentinel injuries include bruising and intraoral injuries. Failure to thrive can sometimes indicate abuse and neglect; thus, pay attention to growth percentiles for age.

Common Presentations

Soft tissue injuries, such as bruises, welts, and contusions, are suspicious if they occur in an area not usually harmed with normal falls (e.g., ears, neck, trunk, genital area, posterior body surfaces) or if not consistent with the story (e.g., buttocks bruising from falling forward). Patterned bruises, such as slap marks or imprints of objects (e.g., belts/belt buckles, looped cords), are not consistent with accidental bruising. Bite marks can be inflicted by adults as well as other children; typically, an interdental distance of > 2 cm can help determine that the biter was an adult.

The earliest sign of soft tissue injury is often redness and swelling; if the child is seen soon after injury, the full extent of bruising does not usually develop for several hours to days. It is not possible to accurately date bruises based on color. Various factors affect bruise appearance and color, such as depth of the injury and the patient's skin color. Bruises heal at different rates on different people and even on different areas on the same person. Document skin findings suspicious for abuse with detailed drawings or photographs.

Certain skin findings can be mistaken for soft tissue injuries resulting from abuse, including the slate-gray patches of Mongolian spots, phytophotodermatitis, and marks left by alternative medical and folk remedies, such as cupping and coining.

Burns account for 5% of physical abuse. Children with forced immersion burns commonly present with bilateral burns to the buttocks, genitalia, back, lower extremities, or hands and have a sharp area of demarcation between normal and burned skin, the "stocking and glove" distribution. Nonabusive burns usually are asymmetric; e.g., only 1 foot injured due to stepping on a hot surface. Accidental scald burns from hot liquids typically involve the upper body and have characteristic splash marks. Children occasionally get accidental burns from hot objects (e.g., grabbing a curling iron), but contact burns on > 1 surface (front and back) or that follow the curve of the body are concerning. Multiple cigarette burns are strong evidence for abuse; a single burn may be non-abusive (i.e., child ran into a lit cigarette) but is more concerning for abuse in areas such as the back, buttocks, or genital area. Skin is thickest on the palms and soles and children can often easily pull away from the heat source if not restrained; make certain the mechanism is explanatory in children with substantial burns in these areas. Nonabusive skin conditions, such as impetigo or severe diaper rash, are sometimes confused with inflicted burns. Lesions of impetigo generally vary in size, whereas cigarette burns are all the same size.

Serious head injury in infants < 1 year of age is most commonly due to physical abuse and is the leading cause of child maltreatment fatalities. Terms describing head injuries due to physical abuse include abusive head trauma (AHT; formerly shaken baby syndrome), inflicted head trauma, and nonaccidental head trauma. Infants with AHT frequently have subdural and/or subarachnoid hemorrhages, and most (62–100%) have bilateral retinal hemorrhages (Figure 7-20) as well. Retinal hemorrhages from birth can be seen in newborns without AHT, but these typically resolve by 2–6 weeks, depending on location. Subdural hemorrhages of various ages can be seen in children who have been repeatedly injured. These injuries are caused by repeated acceleration, deceleration, and rotation of the brain, producing shearing of the bridging vessels, intracranial bleeding, and often diffuse brain injury. Subsequent hypoxia and ischemia cause additional damage. Some babies with AHT also have injuries to the skull/scalp (e.g., skull fractures, hematomas) due to impact with the floor or crib, for example, but remember that a child with serious inflicted head injury may have no external signs of trauma. 54% have bruises, 25% also have a long-bone fracture, and 4% have an intraabdominal injury. Skull fractures due to abuse, if present, are often extensive, compared with simple linear fractures, which are more likely to be caused by a fall of a short

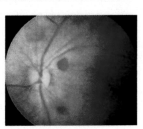

Figure 7-20: Retinal hemorrhages

distance. Presenting symptoms of AHT can be subtle (e.g., vomiting, fussiness, lethargy, seizures, "not acting right") or life-threatening, with coma, apnea, or cardiac arrest. Severe AHT can also cause spinal cord injuries.

Fractures are a typical sign of child abuse. The "corner" fracture or "bucket handle" fracture are classic metaphyseal bony fracture patterns, characteristic of injuries related to child abuse; they are caused when an extremity is yanked and the periosteum—most tightly adherent to metaphysis—causes a small bone fragment to avulse. Consider abuse with fractures of the ribs (especially posteromedial rib fractures) and complex skull fractures or in infants and toddlers, midshaft femur and humerus fractures. Rib fractures in children are seldom due to CPR and, although not pathognomonic, require consideration of abuse. Fractures should raise suspicion if they are of the types usually seen only with major trauma (e.g., vertebral spinous process, sternum, pelvis, scapulae), if they indicate a twisting mechanism (e.g., spiral fracture of humerus), or if the patient's developmental stage makes the fracture otherwise unlikely. Abused children can have multiple, bilateral fractures in various stages of healing.

It can be difficult to distinguish accidental from nonaccidental fractures. For example, it is common for 2- to 3-year-olds to have a supracondylar humerus fracture from a fall or a spiral tibial fracture ("toddler's fracture") from a minor injury. Clavicle fractures and subluxed radial heads ("nursemaid elbow") usually are accidental, unless the history or age of the child makes the injury implausible. Spiral fractures by themselves are not diagnostic of abuse because they can occur with various injuries involving a twisting mechanism, but spiral fractures other than the classic toddler's fracture of the tibia should raise concern for abuse if the history does not seem consistent with the injury. Accidental fractures are less common under 2 years of age and are exceedingly uncommon outside of the setting of major trauma in nonambulatory infants.

Rare conditions, such as osteogenesis imperfecta (OI) and metabolic bone diseases, can present with multiple, poorly explained fractures that mimic abuse. The physical finding of blue sclera can be a tip-off that a child has OI.

Other injuries that raise suspicion of abuse are unexplained intraabdominal injuries, such as lacerations to the liver or spleen, bowel injuries, or pancreaticoduodenal trauma. Abdominal trauma is the leading cause of abuse-related fatality in toddlers. These injuries can be hard to detect on physical exam and have a high morbidity and mortality.

Multiple sudden infant death syndrome (SIDS) deaths in a family have been linked to infanticide by suffocation. Other features that make an infant death more suspicious for inflicted injury include > 6 months of age at the time of death and multiple brief resolved unexplained events (BRUEs) while in the care of the same person. When > 1 infant in a family dies of SIDS, investigate for both child abuse and other genetic causes, such as metabolic diseases.

Children can also be intentionally poisoned.

Factitious disorder imposed on another (formerly Munchausen syndrome by proxy) is a form of maltreatment in which the caregiver (more frequently the mother) exaggerates, fabricates, or creates illness symptoms in the child, resulting in the child undergoing multiple tests, procedures, and hospitalizations. Presentation varies and can include factitious hematuria, diarrhea due to laxatives, or repeated BRUEs. Children typically undergo extensive workups in which no plausible medical explanation for their symptoms is discovered. Affected children frequently experience significant long-term psychological sequelae. Additionally, 30% of children who suffer medical abuse also have a true underlying medical condition.

Management of medical child abuse requires a multidisciplinary approach, including interventions such as therapy, monitoring ongoing usage of medical services, potential hospital admission, involvement of child protective services, and ultimately removal of the child from the home if warranted. Involvement of a pediatrician with child abuse expertise is highly advisable. See the Behavioral Medicine & Substance Use Disorders section for more information.

Evaluation

For children with head injuries, immediately order a CT scan of the brain and an ophthalmology consult within 72 hours to look for retinal hemorrhages. MRI can add information regarding timing of injury and identify additional subtle findings. Also obtain a screening head CT in children < 1 year of age who present with suspicious injuries (e.g., fracture) that do not involve the head.

Obtain lab tests as needed to treat the child and to exclude other disorders. Transaminases (AST and ALT) are advisable in children with serious injuries, and elevations > 80 U/L are a good marker of occult liver injury. Amylase/lipase, CBC, and urinalysis are also recommended. Order an abdominal CT scan if there are symptoms of abdominal injury or concerning abnormalities in the lab tests. Consultation with a child abuse specialist and/or hematologist is very helpful in directing further workup and for children suspected to have other disorders.

In children with bruising or bleeding potentially attributable to abuse, consider a bleeding disorder. If careful history and physical exam uncovers this potential, order appropriate laboratory tests (prothrombin time/partial thromboplastin time, CBC, Factor 8 and 9 levels, and von Willebrand panel).

Children < 2 years of age and nonverbal children with suspected physical abuse of any kind should have skeletal survey radiographs performed because many nonaccidental fractures are not apparent on physical exam. Also, consider ordering a skeletal survey in children with developmental impairments who cannot provide a history and in whom abuse is suspected. Radiographic images should include detailed views of the skull, chest/ribs, spine, pelvis, and extremities. In addition, consider performing selected radiographs of areas clinically concerning

for fractures. Radionuclide bone scanning has been used to screen for fractures in the past, but it often requires sedation and is less commonly used. Dating of fractures can be difficult; in general, remember that a callus starts to form at 7–14 days (7–10 days in infants), followed by eventual remodeling.

Some injuries are not apparent on initial skeletal survey; if there is high clinical suspicion, do a follow-up survey in 2 weeks when healing fractures typically are more visible. Siblings and household contacts of abused children should undergo complete history and physical examination (including skeletal surveys for those < 2 years of age).

SEXUAL ABUSE

Sexual abuse is involvement of a child or adolescent in sexual activities they do not comprehend, to which they are unable to consent, or that violate societal norms. These sexual activities can involve fondling or other sexual physical contact but also can include noncontact forms, such as using the child to produce pornography. Sexual abuse often occurs in families with related problems, such as physical abuse, domestic violence, and drug use. The child usually knows the perpetrator (often a relative).

Clinical manifestations: These can be behavioral—either specific (e.g., excessive masturbation, developmentally inappropriate explicit sexual behaviors) or nonspecific (e.g., poor school performance, anxiety, suicidal gestures). Consider and thoroughly investigate sexual abuse when an older child includes genitals in a drawing. Similarly, physical findings can be specific (e.g., genital or rectal laceration, pregnancy) or nonspecific (e.g., vaginal discharge, abdominal pain, dysuria). Vaginal discharge alone is unlikely to indicate sexual abuse, but it still requires consideration.

A child's disclosure of sexual contact must be taken seriously; history is often much more important than the physical exam in determining whether abuse likely occurred. Question children in a developmentally appropriate, nonleading manner. Detailed questioning of the child is a specialized skill best deferred to forensic interviewers, typically social services or law enforcement (see evaluation protocols below). The medical history should focus on relevant aspects such as the type of alleged contact, current symptoms, and menstrual history to help determine what tests and treatment are indicated.

Physical exam: Few sexually abused children have abnormal genital or anal findings; even if injuries occurred, they often heal rapidly and completely. Although parents and other authorities often expect the physician to be able to determine on examination whether the child was molested, the majority of children evaluated for sexual abuse have normal examinations. Proper evaluation for sexual abuse in children takes skill and experience. The examiner must be familiar with normal developmental changes in genital appearance, as well as numerous normal variants such as hymenal bumps, tags, and septae. Magnification using colposcopy or other techniques is helpful in detecting subtle injuries. Gentle labial traction (pulling toward the examiner, not laterally) allows enhanced visualization of the hymen and vagina. Examining the child in the prone, knee-chest position can sometimes be helpful in clarifying findings. In the pre-pubescent child, a speculum exam requires procedural sedation; any internal exam in this age group should be performed under anesthesia. When findings are present, abrasions, lacerations, or hematomas are seen acutely, whereas past abuse can manifest as hymenal clefts or a decreased rim of tissue posteriorly. Measurement of hymenal diameter is not useful. For children reporting anal penetration, physical findings of sexual abuse are rare, but look for acute anal fissures and thickened rugae.

Accidental injuries and skin conditions can be mistaken for sexual abuse. Girls frequently injure the genital area by falling; e.g., while riding a bike ("straddle injury"). Findings in accidental straddle injuries typically include hematomas and shallow lacerations to the perineum and anterior genitalia (i.e., clitoral area and adjacent labia). Penetrating trauma to the hymen or vagina is not likely in accidental injury, unless the child falls on a protruding object. Other conditions sometimes mistaken for abuse include vulvovaginitis, labial adhesions, urethral prolapse, lichen sclerosis, and even diaper rash.

Lab: Sexually transmitted infections (STIs) are found in 8% of girls experiencing sexual abuse (less in boys). Recall, however, that HPV, HSV, HIV, syphilis, gonorrhea, and chlamydia can be acquired perinatally; therefore, additional history and testing is needed to determine the source of infection, including history of maternal infections and symptoms.

Indications for specific STI testing depend on patient history, symptoms, physical exam, and other risk factors, such as characteristics of the perpetrator. Testing includes cultures, nucleic acid amplification tests (NAATs), and serology for *Neisseria gonorrhoeae*, *Chlamydia*, *Treponema pallidum* (syphilis), *Trichomonas*, HIV, hepatitis B, hepatitis C, and HSV. In young girls, use swabs of the fourchette or shallow portions of the vaginal vault in lieu of cervical swabs. Urine NAAT is another option for initial diagnosis. Cultures are still considered the legal gold standard. Depending on the age of the child, the child's vaccine status, the details of the abuse, and the health status of the perpetrator, prophylaxis against STIs, HIV, hepatitis, and pregnancy should be considered.

Evaluation protocols: Most cities and hospitals have protocols for the evaluation of sexual abuse/assault. These include contacting appropriate law enforcement and child protection authorities, gathering appropriate forensic evidence, obtaining indicated laboratory tests, and prophylaxis against STIs and pregnancy. All children in whom sexual abuse is confirmed or suspected, regardless of time from event, should be screened for suicidality and referred to a mental health professional for evaluation and counseling. Asymptomatic children without recent (within 24 hours, depending on state) or ongoing contact with the alleged perpetrator can be referred for nonemergent

evaluation by specialized child abuse medical professionals or clinics if available; such facilities offer additional expertise and resources beneficial for the child and family undergoing this stressful evaluation. It is very important to avoid repeated questioning of the child; ideally, a single forensic interview is arranged with a trained professional. However, if the child spontaneously discloses abuse to the pediatrician ("daddy put his pee-pee on my privates"), document this verbatim in the medical record because such statements are admissible in court.

PSYCHOLOGICAL MALTREATMENT

Psychological maltreatment is probably one of the most common forms of abuse, but it is difficult to define or identify. It includes repeated verbal denigration, belittling, "making fun," and scapegoating of the child. These attacks result in a child with low self-esteem and feelings of worthlessness.

Long-Term Psychological Effects of Maltreatment

Every healthcare provider must know how to recognize child maltreatment. This is necessary to protect the child and to support the caregiver to avoid or minimize long-term consequences.

Behavioral consequences: Unfortunately, many victims of child abuse exhibit risky behavior as they grow older. This includes unhealthy sexual practices, substance use, and criminal activity.

Cognitive and intellectual consequences: These children often have language and cognitive deficits as reflected in poor school performance and underperformance in extra-curricular activities such as sports and arts. Maltreated children commonly misinterpret social cues and have difficulty handling personal problems.

Psychosocial consequences: Abused children often have a difficult time trusting others and suffer from low self-esteem. These consequences are more apparent in children who were abused from an early age. These children may have difficulty expressing their emotions in the same way as their peers, and they often become involved in bullying, either as a victim or as a perpetrator.

As pediatricians, there are 2 components to the care of abused children: supporting the child and supporting the family and caregivers:

- Supporting the child involves addressing physical, emotional, and psychological needs. This often involves an interdisciplinary approach with specialists (e.g., child life specialists, psychologists, counselors).
- Supporting the family and caregivers involves addressing their ongoing practical and psychological needs. This includes providing accurate information and referring to support groups and counseling.

MANAGEMENT OF MALTREATMENT

PREVIEW | REVIEW

- As a pediatrician, what should you do if you suspect child maltreatment but do not have confirmation of abuse?

For all types of maltreatment, good communication between the parents and the clinician is essential. Child maltreatment investigation is stressful for families, even when maltreatment is not substantiated. However, the 1st priority is the safety and well-being of the child. As a pediatrician, you are mandated to report suspected child maltreatment; you must report your suspicions to the appropriate local child protective agency and often the police. You need to provide relevant medical information to designated authorities, as well as your assessment of the child's safety and whether it is appropriate for the child to return to the home environment. Although the ultimate decision to keep the child in the home (perhaps with additional services/supervision) or to remove the child and find alternate placement (such as foster care) is typically determined by the child protection agency, you must advocate for the best interest of the child. Children with serious injuries or an unsafe home situation require hospitalization. A team approach to child maltreatment is valuable and involves social workers, child abuse experts, and trained interviewers. Children who suffer maltreatment are at risk for lifelong adverse health effects.

THE MEDSTUDY HUB: YOUR GUIDELINES AND REVIEW ARTICLES RESOURCE

For both review articles and current pediatrics practice guidelines, visit the MedStudy Hub at

medstudy.com/hub

The Hub contains the only online consolidated list of all current guidelines focused on pediatrics. Guidelines on the Hub are easy to find, continually updated, and linked to the published source. MedStudy maintains the Hub as a service to the medical community and makes it available to anyone and everyone at no cost to users.

FIGURE SOURCES

Figure 7-2: Samir, CC BY 3.0

Figure 7-3: Anand Swaminathan

Figure 7-5: Matt B

Figure 7-8: Thomas Krzmarzick, MD

Figure 7-9: Thomas Krzmarzick, MD

Figure 7-12: Hellerhoff, CC BY-SA 3.0

Figure 7-13: Thomas Krzmarzick, MD

Figure 7-14: Majorkev, CC BY 3.0

Figure 7-15: Hellerhoff, CC BY-SA 3.0

Figure 7-18: Boldie

Figure 7-20: Choi YJ, Jung MS, Kim SY - Korean Journal of Ophthalmology : KJO (2011)

The remaining figures are from the MedStudy archives.

Pharmacology and Pain Management

SECTION EDITOR

Sara Marie Reed, MD, PhD
Pediatric Hospitalist
Cherokee Nation W.W. Hastings Hospital
Tahlequah, OK

MEDICAL EDITOR

Lynn Bullock, MD
Colorado Springs, CO

Table of Contents

PHARMACOLOGY.....................................8-1
  OVERVIEW 8-1
  PHARMACOKINETICS...............................8-1
    Absorption..8-1
    Distribution.......................................8-1
    Metabolism.......................................8-2
    Excretion..8-3
  PHARMACODYNAMICS 8-3
    Adverse Drug Reactions 8-3
    Drug Interactions...............................8-3
  BIOEQUIVALENCE...................................8-3

SEDATION 8-4
  OVERVIEW 8-4
  PATIENT CHARACTERISTICS 8-4
  DEGREES OF SEDATION 8-4
  RISK FACTORS FOR SEDATION-RELATED
    ADVERSE EVENTS (SRAEs) 8-5
  SRAEs...8-5
    Airway Obstruction.............................8-5
    Hypoventilation and Apnea 8-5
    Aspiration...8-6
    Cardiac Depression 8-6
  REDUCTION OF SRAEs.............................8-6
  SEDATION AGENT PROFILES 8-6
    Propofol...8-6
    Dexmedetomidine 8-7
    Midazolam 8-7
    Pentobarbital....................................8-7
    Methohexital.....................................8-7
    Ketamine..8-7
    Nitrous Oxide (N_2O) 8-8
    Fluranes 8-8

ANALGESIA 8-8
  OVERVIEW 8-8
  LOCAL AND TOPICAL AGENT PROFILES 8-9
    LET (Lidocaine, Epinephrine, and Tetracaine)....8-9
    Eutectic Mixture of Local Anesthetics (EMLA)..8-9
    Lidocaine..8-9
    Magic Mouthwash 8-9
  SYSTEMIC TREATMENT PROFILES 8-10
    Acetaminophen.................................8-10
    Nonsteroidal Antiinflammatory
      Drugs (NSAIDs) 8-10
    Opioids..8-10

**THE MEDSTUDY HUB: YOUR GUIDELINES
AND REVIEW ARTICLES RESOURCE**...............8-10

FIGURE SOURCES 8-12

PHARMACOLOGY

PREVIEW | REVIEW

- High first-pass effect causes what difference in dosage between oral and parenteral forms of the same drug?
- What is first-order kinetics?
- Approximately how many half-lives does it take for a first-order drug to reach steady state if no loading dose is given?
- What is zero-order kinetics?
- What is an adverse drug reaction?
- Drug-drug interactions are caused by what mechanisms?

OVERVIEW

Pharmacokinetics refers to "how the body affects the drug" (i.e., drug absorption, distribution, metabolism, elimination). **Pharmacodynamics** refers to "how the drug affects the body" (i.e., the relationship between the concentration of the drug and the biochemical and physiologic effects). Pharmacokinetics, in concert with pharmacodynamics, determines dose and dosing schedule of a particular drug.

PHARMACOKINETICS

There are 4 main components of pharmacokinetics:

1) Absorption—the process by which the drug gains access to the bloodstream from the site of drug administration (bioavailability)
2) Distribution—the process by which the drug, after absorption, moves around the body and distributes throughout the body tissues
3) Metabolism—the process by which the drug's chemical structure changes in order to increase the ease of its excretion
4) Excretion—the process by which the drug is removed from the body

Absorption

Absorption can be enteral (i.e., given and absorbed into the gastrointestinal [GI] tract) or parenteral (i.e., any route that avoids absorption via the GI tract—such as intramuscular [IM], intravenous [IV]).

First-pass effect: Oral drugs are absorbed from the GI tract, pass through the portal vein, and then enter the liver. Some drugs are rapidly metabolized by the liver and undergo "first-pass" metabolism, which means the concentration of the drug is greatly reduced before it reaches the systemic circulation. These drugs require a much higher oral dose to reach similar serum concentrations as a parenteral dose of the same medicine.

Common drugs that are subject to the first-pass effect include:

- Opioids—meperidine, morphine, and naloxone
- Calcium channel antagonists—nifedipine, verapamil, and diltiazem
- Some β-blockers—labetalol, metoprolol, and propranolol
- Tricyclic antidepressants
- Some benzodiazepines (e.g., midazolam)
- Others—e.g., lidocaine, terbutaline

Some drugs require an acidic environment for absorption—especially the azole antifungals (except fluconazole and voriconazole), iron, and thyroid hormone. Patients taking H_2 blockers or proton pump inhibitors (PPIs) may require a dose adjustment; giving the medication with acidic foods and vitamins (e.g., vitamin C, orange juice) can help. PPIs can also decrease calcium absorption.

Important! The ingestion of cations (e.g., calcium and iron supplements, antacids containing magnesium and aluminum) can interfere with the absorption of thyroid hormone or quinolones.

The absorption of most drugs is better on an empty stomach, because food delays gastric emptying (hence delaying absorption) and some drugs may interact with food and form complexes that are poorly absorbed. Drugs like levothyroxine, amoxicillin, PPIs, and alendronate are preferably taken on an empty stomach. However, some drugs are better tolerated when taken with food (e.g., aspirin, other antiinflammatory drugs). Also, absorption of griseofulvin is enhanced when taken with fatty foods.

Distribution

Volume of distribution (V_D) describes the relationship between the total amount of a drug in the body and the concentration of the drug in the plasma. Know: V_D is already known for most drugs; it is used to determine the total amount of drug in the body at a certain plasma level and to determine the loading dose.

The total amount of drug in the body (D_T) is equal to the volume of distribution (V_D) × plasma concentration (C_P):

$$D_T = V_D \times C_P$$

The volume of distribution is the total amount of drug in the body (D_T) divided by the plasma concentration (C_P):

$$V_D = D_T/C_P$$

If the drug is primarily found in the tissues, then the volume of distribution will be higher.

Factors that affect the V_D include:

- Drugs tightly bound to plasma proteins have a low V_D (~ 8 L). Side note: A protein-bound drug is inactive; only unbound drug has a biological effect.
- Hydrophilic drugs also have a low V_D (~ 8 L).
- Drugs that disperse into both plasma and tissue fluids have a V_D of ~ 30–40 L.

- Lipid solubility increases V_D. (For example, chloroquine sequesters in the fat and has a V_D of 15,000 L!)
- Blood flow
- Size of drug

Note that the loading dose does not depend on excretion capability! The loading dose in a patient with renal failure is the same as that in a healthy patient, but if the drug is cleared by the kidney, the subsequent maintenance dose is very different.

Metabolism

Drug metabolism refers to the series of enzyme reactions that transform a drug into various products, ultimately to facilitate its elimination from the body. The main site for metabolism is the liver. Normally, a constant proportion of a drug is eliminated per unit of time, so the higher the drug concentration, the quicker the elimination rate. But when the enzyme-based elimination system becomes saturated, only a constant amount can be eliminated per unit of time, no matter how much higher the drug level (i.e., enzyme system is working at max). The pharmacokinetics of these are called first-order (constant proportion; set half-life) and zero-order (constant amount) reactions.

The Michaelis-Menten saturation curve plots elimination rate vs. plasma concentration and demonstrates both zero-order and first-order kinetics. As a drug's plasma concentration increases, the rate of drug elimination is roughly linear (first-order) and then plateaus (zero-order) when all enzyme systems are saturated. See Figure 8-1. Now we'll go a bit more into these kinetics.

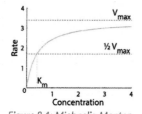

Figure 8-1: Michaelis-Menten saturation curve of an enzyme reaction

First-Order Kinetics

First-order elimination kinetics describe the rate at which a drug is cleared when it is dependent on (and proportional to) the drug concentration. The rate of drug elimination increases as the plasma concentration of the drug increases (in a linear progression when you plot elimination rate vs. concentration). After a dose of the drug is given and maximum concentration achieved, then, in 1 half-life, the drug concentration in the serum is half of the initial concentration. After 2 half-lives, the drug concentration is half again (1/4 the initial level). It is possible to determine the half-life of a drug by checking 2 separate blood levels between doses.

Assuming first-order elimination kinetics, which virtually all drugs follow, the half-life defines the time it takes for the drug to reach steady state. 5 half-lives after a patient is started on a first-order drug without a loading dose, the drug concentration is 97% of steady state (Table 8-1). So, when starting patients on a medication with no loading dose, wait 5 half-lives before checking blood concentration (or for expected effect) before considering an adjustment in dosage.

| Table 8-1: First-Order Drug Half-Lives ||
Number of Half-Lives	Percentage of Steady State
1	50
2	75
3	88
4	94
5	97

Zero-Order (Saturable) Kinetics

Zero-order elimination rate has a flat, rather than a linear, relationship with the drug concentration (i.e., this is called nonlinear in this context). A constant amount of drug is eliminated per unit time regardless of the concentration of the drug. Zero-order clearance happens only when the metabolizing enzyme sites are saturated, which is not the case with most drugs. However, if a patient overdoses on a medication, the kinetics can shift from first-order to zero-order due to saturation of metabolic enzymes. Also, certain drugs, like warfarin and phenytoin, can change from first-order to zero-order kinetics at higher therapeutic doses. In these examples, the plasma concentration of the drug increases disproportionately with increase in dose.

Therapeutic Range and Drug Monitoring

The difference between the lowest drug concentration that produces a minimal therapeutic effect and the concentration that causes maximal acceptable adverse effects is called the "therapeutic range." Defining a therapeutic range is often difficult given variability in response of individual patients; hence, monitoring drug levels is not a routine practice in most cases. Therapeutic drug monitoring may be useful for drugs with a low safety margin (e.g., digoxin, lithium), to measure compliance to medications (e.g., antiseizure medications), and in patients with suspected drug toxicity. Drug levels should be measured after steady state is reached (at 5 half-lives), except in cases of drug toxicity. Drug levels are typically drawn prior to the next anticipated dose (trough levels). For some drugs (e.g., aminoglycosides), both trough and peak levels are important.

Cytochrome P450 (CYP) Isoenzymes

CYP represents the major system for oxidative metabolism of drugs. CYP enzyme activity can be affected by genetic and environmental factors (e.g., drugs). In case of polypharmacy, pay attention if ≥ 1 drug is metabolized by the same CYP enzyme. Induction or inhibition of a specific CYP enzyme by one drug can respectively increase or decrease another drug's metabolism. Some important drugs that can induce CYP system include phenytoin, phenobarbital, carbamazepine, griseofulvin, and rifampin. Important inhibitors include erythromycin, clarithromycin, azole antifungals, and protease inhibitors.

Excretion

The primary routes by which drugs are removed from the body are the kidneys (e.g., aminoglycosides, levetiracetam) and the liver (e.g., acetaminophen). The kidneys are responsible for the majority of excretion using 3 main mechanisms: glomerular filtration, tubular secretion, and tubular reabsorption. Liver excretion involves metabolizing and converting the drug, usually into inactive or less active products after the first-pass effect, and then excreting into the bile.

Remember that in a person with cirrhosis, the decreased first-pass increases the bioavailability of the drugs that are metabolized in the liver. Clearance is also decreased, so the effective dose of a drug can be very small. Example: Meperidine is metabolized by the liver to normeperidine, which is an active metabolite that causes central nervous system (CNS) stimulation (including seizures); therefore, in liver disease, there is less of a first-pass effect. Normeperidine is cleared by the kidney; so, watch carefully when using meperidine in a patient with hepatic or renal dysfunction!

PHARMACODYNAMICS

Pharmacodynamics refers to the body's response to the drug at specific drug concentrations. The response can be either desirable (therapeutic effect) or undesirable (adverse effect).

Adverse Drug Reactions

Adverse drug reaction refers to any unwanted or dangerous effect caused by a drug. These can be predictable or unpredictable reactions, as follows.

Predictable reactions: These are based on pharmacological properties of the drug and include dose-related exaggerations of the therapeutic effect of the drug, effects of drug toxicity, as well as withdrawal. These can also be secondary to decreased drug clearance in a patient with hepatic or renal dysfunction.

Unpredictable reactions: These include drug allergies and idiosyncratic adverse drug reactions. These reactions are rare and refer to effects that are not dose dependent or related to the known pharmacologic actions of the drug, such as primaquine causing nonimmune hemolytic anemia in patients with glucose-6-phosphate dehydrogenase deficiency. Idiosyncratic drug reactions are hard to predict, can result from genetic alterations in the patient, and have variable presentations. Adverse drug reaction reporting is voluntary in the U.S. and can be submitted either to the Food & Drug Administration (FDA) or to the manufacturer of the product.

Drug Interactions

Drug interactions occur when a drug's effect is altered because of another drug, food, or supplement. Certain foods or supplements can alter the absorption of medications. One such example is grapefruit juice, which increases the absorption of certain statin drugs (e.g., simvastatin), resulting in an increased likelihood of side effects. Drug-drug interactions take place when > 1 drug is taken concurrently. These interactions can be caused by various mechanisms including:

- Absorption—PPIs can impair the absorption of iron supplements.
- Distribution and protein binding—administration of diclofenac in a patient on warfarin can increase free warfarin levels and hemorrhagic complications.
- Metabolism—use of enzyme-inducing agents (e.g., phenytoin, phenobarbital) can decrease efficacy of birth control pills.
- Excretion—use of NSAIDs can potentiate complications of methotrexate and lithium by blocking their renal clearance.
- Competition for same receptor—use of aminoglycosides enhances the effects of neuromuscular blocking agents.
- Same clinical effect—the combination of aminoglycosides and loop diuretics can cause ototoxicity. Aminoglycosides given in combination with cephalosporins increase nephrotoxicity. Angiotensin-converting enzyme inhibitors, angiotensin receptor blockers, spironolactone and other potassium-sparing diuretics, and heparin can cause severe hyperkalemia. Combining antiseizure medications and psychiatric medications increases the risk of sedation.

A clinician must take a careful drug history, including over-the-counter medications and supplements. When prescribing medications, carefully consider drug interactions and remember that the fewest drugs for the shortest amount of time is best.

Patients do not always include complementary medications when they provide drug lists, so always inquire about them when taking a thorough history. For example, coadministration of indinavir and St. John's wort must be avoided because both induce the same hepatic CYP enzyme, resulting in the decreased bioavailability and effectiveness of indinavir. Always caution patients about complementary therapies that could interfere with their medications.

BIOEQUIVALENCE

Bioequivalence is commonly discussed in the context of generic drugs. The FDA Orange Book definition of bioequivalence requires the products to be pharmaceutical equivalents or pharmaceutical alternatives when studied under similar conditions. **Pharmaceutical equivalents** have exact amounts of the active drug ingredient in the same dosage form and route of administration and meet applicable standards of purity, quality, strength, and identity.

Pharmaceutical alternatives have the same therapeutic moiety, though not necessarily the same inactive ingredients, strength, or dosage form (e.g., they may contain different salts or esters). Pharmaceutical equivalents and pharmaceutical alternatives must have no significant difference in the rate and extent of absorption compared to the original drug in order to be considered bioequivalent.

SEDATION

PREVIEW | REVIEW

- What are the different degrees of sedation?
- What are some health conditions that increase the risk for sedation-related adverse events?

OVERVIEW

When considering sedation for a child, it is important to keep in mind the following:

- Patient characteristics
- Purpose of sedation, clinical setting, and degree of sedation desired
- Risk factors for sedation-related adverse events (SRAEs)
- Sedation agent profiles, including common adverse events (AEs)

PATIENT CHARACTERISTICS

As always, obtain a good history and physical. Some of the important things to know about the child include:

- Age
- Developmental stage
- Airway type (Figure 8-2; the Mallampati classification measures the degree of intubation difficulty.)
- Anxiety level
- Ability and willingness to cooperate
- Drug allergies
- Comorbidities
- Fasting status

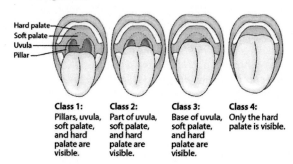

Figure 8-2: Mallampati airway classification

In many situations, nonpharmaceutical methods—such as distracting the patient (e.g., child life assistance, vibration stimulus, cold stimulus), swaddling the baby, or coaching the patient in using self-coping and relaxation—prevent the need for sedation.

DEGREES OF SEDATION

Over the years, sedation definitions have evolved. For example, "conscious sedation" has fallen out of favor. More standardized definitions, attesting to the varying degrees of sedation, are now used.

Sedation is a continuum ranging from minimal sedation to general anesthesia (Table 8-2).

Table 8-2: Degrees of Sedation and Anesthesia				
	Minimal Sedation	**Moderate Sedation**	**Deep Sedation**	**General Anesthesia**
Responsiveness	Normal response to verbal commands	Purposeful response to light tactile stimulation and verbal commands	Purposeful response to painful stimulation	No response to painful stimulation
Airway	Maintained	Maintained	Partial or complete loss of protective reflexes	Requires assistance to maintain
Ventilation	Intact	Intact	May require respiratory support	Requires respiratory support
Cardiovascular Function	Maintained	Maintained	Usually maintained	Possible cardiac assistance required
Monitoring	Observation via intermittent assessment	Continuous pulse ox and HR; intermittent RR and BP	Continuous pulse ox, RR, and cardiac monitoring; BP every 3 minutes	Leave this to the pros— the anesthesiologists!

BP = blood pressure   ox = oximetry
HR = heart rate   RR = respiratory rate

RISK FACTORS FOR SEDATION-RELATED ADVERSE EVENTS (SRAEs)

Risk assessment is crucial to successful sedation, recovery, and the avoidance of SRAEs. Risk assessment also addresses potential complicating compromises in cardiopulmonary function and the risk of aspiration events. The possible risk factors for SRAEs are:

- Airway obstruction history
- Obstructive sleep apnea
- Inability to properly handle airway secretions
- Craniofacial anomalies
- Chronic lung disease
- Myocardial dysfunction
- Mental status changes
- Poorly controlled seizures
- Hydrocephalus (and other causes of increased intracranial pressure [ICP])
- Acute illness (e.g., upper respiratory infection [URI], cough, GI symptoms)
- Gastroesophageal reflux disease (GERD)
- Bowel obstruction
- Obesity

Another tool to assess sedation suitability is provided by the American Society of Anesthesiologists (ASA):

- **Class 1**—normal healthy patient
  - Unremarkable medical history
  - Excellent sedation suitability
- **Class 2**—mild systemic disease without functional limitation
  - Examples include mild asthma, controlled seizure disorder, anemia, and controlled diabetes mellitus.
  - Good sedation suitability
- **Class 3**—severe systemic disease with definite functional limitation
  - Examples include moderate-to-severe asthma, poorly controlled seizure disorder, pneumonia, poorly controlled diabetes mellitus, and moderate obesity.
  - Intermediate-to-poor sedation suitability
- **Class 4**—severe systemic disease with a constant threat to life
  - Examples include severe bronchopulmonary dysplasia, sepsis, advanced pulmonary, cardiac, hepatic, or endocrine insufficiency, and chronic kidney disease.
  - Poor sedation suitability (The benefits rarely outweigh the risks.)
- **Class 5**—a very ill patient not expected to survive without operative intervention
- **Class 6**—a declared brain-dead patient whose organs are being removed for donor purposes

A thorough evaluation of comorbidities and the ASA class gives you a practical way to gauge risk prior to any sedation. For example, a patient with an ASA Class 3 with comorbidities of seizure disorder and cleft lip and palate should give you plenty of pause. Vigilance is the motto

of the ASA; when performing sedation, this becomes the clinician's motto and duty. When in doubt, consult with the experts (e.g., anesthesiologist, intensivist).

SRAEs

Intuitively, as the degree of sedation increases, the risk of AEs also increases. Overdose is an ever-present concern. Risk of drug-drug interaction and oversedation increases with multiple drugs (especially > 3). As a rule of thumb, combining a sedative with another sedative or analgesic agent amplifies the risk of AEs, such as respiratory issues and cardiac depression. The key events to watch for are airway obstruction, hypoventilation and apnea, aspiration, and cardiac depression.

Airway Obstruction

Pharyngeal obstruction is a common AE during sedation due to the inhibition of upper airway neuromuscular control. The upper airway can be divided into 3 sections: the nasal segment, the pharyngeal segment, and the tracheal segment. The pharyngeal segment is innervated by cranial nerves 9 and 10. It is this portion of the upper airway that is most susceptible to collapse, resulting in airway obstruction. Address pharyngeal obstruction by proper airway positioning, chin lift/jaw thrust, bag and mask ventilation, and nasal/oral airway devices.

Laryngospasm results in partial or complete airway obstruction. The risk factors for laryngospasm include:

- Upper airway secretions
- Airway manipulation
- Recent URI
- GERD
- Passive smoking
- Airway devices
- Young age
- Higher ASA classifications

Treat laryngospasm with positive pressure ventilation (PPV) with 100% oxygen, deepening the depth of sedation, or neuromuscular blockade for nonresponsive cases.

Hypoventilation and Apnea

With increased sedation, ventilation decreases and likelihood of apnea (cessation of breathing) increases. Note that apnea is generally due to either a decrease in respiratory drive (central apnea) or obstruction of the airway (obstructive apnea). Central apnea is most commonly due to drugs that cause sedation. If a sedated patient develops apnea, discontinue the sedation agent and give its antidote (e.g., naloxone, flumazenil). If no antidote is available, you will need to provide ventilatory support until help arrives or the sedation wears off sufficiently.

In a heavily sedated patient, apnea is identified clinically by assessing airway patency, observing chest wall rise, and monitoring S_pO_2 and carbon dioxide. End-tidal CO_2 is the best indicator of proper ventilation. S_pO_2 is a good indicator only in patients who are not on supplemental oxygen. So never rely solely on pulse oximetry with a sedated patient on supplemental oxygen.

Aspiration

Remember that there is often a loss of the protective airway reflexes during sedation. Vomiting and copious oral secretions are concerns and can lead to aspiration events as well as obstruction of the airway. The suctioning apparatus and other interventions, such as bag and mask ventilation system, should be set up and readily at hand during sedation.

Cardiac Depression

Hypotension, hypertension, bradycardia, and inadequate perfusion can result via various mechanisms. Whereas propofol and morphine cause vasodilation, barbiturates can directly depress cardiac function. Most of these AEs are directly related to the dosing and the degree of sedation. Patients with preexisting cardiovascular compromise often decompensate much sooner.

REDUCTION OF SRAEs

The literature reports many reasons for SRAEs. Some of the main reasons are:

- Lack of knowledge of specific drugs (e.g., death after discharge in patients given drugs with a long duration of effect)
- Lack of adequate patient information (e.g., limited evaluation due to emergent need for sedation)
- Rule violations (e.g., inadequate protocols for pre-assessment, sedation delivery, recovery)
- Lack of an independent observer

The successful administration of sedation involves training and experience in multiple areas:

- Proper patient evaluation prior to sedation, including good history and physical with current and chronic medical conditions, sedation/anesthesia history, airway history, allergies, and fasting status. The minimum duration of fasting depends on the type of food ingested. See Table 8-3.
- Active vigilance of the medical team prior to, during, and after the sedation-related event
- Strict monitoring of oxygenation, ventilation, and other respiratory parameters
- Proper sedation protocols prior to, during, and after the sedation-related event
- Rescue management for the overly sedated and decompensating patient
- Access to medications, antidotes, and medication delivery systems
- Resuscitation equipment and practices (i.e., basic life support, pediatric advanced life support, neonatal resuscitation program)

- Airway management (i.e., suction, oxygen delivery, crash carts with airway tools)
- Clinicians with experience and knowledge in addressing cardiovascular compromise

Table 8-3: Suggested Duration of Fasting Prior to Elective Sedation	
Type of Food	**Hours of Fasting Recommended**
Clear liquids	2
Breast milk	4
Infant formula or light meal (no fat)	6
Full meal	8

SEDATION AGENT PROFILES

When choosing an agent, consider:

- Onset of action
- Desired clinical effects
- Sedation duration
- Common AEs of the agent

Many of these agents have a fine balance between the therapeutic window and overdose. Too much of a drug results in AEs, and too little results in inadequate sedation. As previously stated, the combination of multiple drugs increases the risk of AEs, especially respiratory and cardiac depression.

The onset of action and duration of drug effects vary due to the route of drug administration, the drug's bioavailability, and the drug's water solubility. For example, midazolam can be administered via oral (PO), rectal (PR), intranasal (IN), intramuscular (IM), and intravenous (IV) routes; onset and duration for each of these delivery mechanisms vary due to midazolam's water solubility.

The sedative-hypnotic agents discussed provide sedation, motion control, anxiolysis, and variable amnestic properties. In addition, ketamine, dexmedetomidine, and nitrous oxide (N_2O) provide analgesia.

Propofol

Propofol (Diprivan) initially gained use as an induction agent to general anesthesia. Not all clinical settings allow for the use of this agent. There are careful protocols in place using capnography and pulse oximetry to monitor for respiratory depression, apnea, bradycardia, and hypotension. Propofol can be administered as a continuous infusion or as a bolus, depending on the desired duration of sedation. While even IV dosing alone carries the risk of overshooting the desired sedation, bolus dosing increases this risk. Thus, a thorough understanding of the patient's hemodynamic status and cardiac comorbidities is of the utmost importance. Propofol is painful during injection, but this is mitigated by using an analgesic agent such as lidocaine, ketamine, or an opioid. This agent reduces ICP and becomes useful in hemodynamically stable patients with head trauma, but it can cause hypotension. Propofol does not provide analgesia.

Consider:

- Onset: < 1 minute
- Duration: 5–15 minutes after a single bolus; longer with repeated boluses and prolonged infusions
- Uses: diagnostic imaging (e.g., computed tomography [CT], magnetic resonance imaging [MRI]) and anesthesia
- Absolute contraindications: porphyria (Although egg and soy allergies are listed as contraindications in product information, most egg- and soy-allergic patients tolerate propofol.)

Dexmedetomidine

Dexmedetomidine (Precedex) doubles as a sedative with some analgesic properties. The greatest benefits of this agent are minimal respiratory depression and minimal recovery agitation. These traits become especially advantageous in the treatment of children with intellectual disabilities and those undergoing weaning from mechanical ventilation. There is dose-related hypotension. Initial-dose hypotension is addressed with saline bolus. Use this agent with caution in those with arrhythmias and cardiac conduction abnormalities. Dexmedetomidine can cause profound bradycardia, especially in those receiving medications that slow atrioventricular (AV) node conduction, such as digoxin. In patients receiving nifedipine (vasodilator), it can cause profound hypotension due to additive effects.

Consider:

- Onset: 5–10 minutes
- Duration: 1–2 hours
- Uses: diagnostic imaging (e.g., CT, MRI), procedural sedation, intensive care unit (ICU) sedation, and adjunct to anesthesia
- Absolute contraindications: digoxin or other medications slowing conduction to the AV node, cardiac conduction abnormalities, and other cardiac dysfunction

Midazolam

Midazolam, a short-acting BDZ, has good effects on anxiety, amnesia, and muscle relaxation. Being water soluble, it has multiple routes of administration via IV, IM, PR, IN, sublingual (SL), and, of course, PO. This carries the prized advantage of not requiring IV access. The route of administration affects the onset and duration of action. Of note: Midazolam has poor oral bioavailability. Flumazenil is used for the reversal of respiratory depression or apnea. Other AEs include inconsolable crying, hyperactivity, and aggressive behavior. These events are reversed by flumazenil as well. Midazolam does not provide analgesia.

Consider:

- Onset: 1–3 minutes (IV), 20–30 minutes (other routes)
- Duration: 15–60 minutes (IV, dose dependent), 30–60 minutes (other routes, route dependent)
- Uses: procedures not requiring full immobility (e.g., laceration repairs, orthopedic reduction) and nonpainful procedures (e.g., sexual assault exam, routine exam in children with intellectual disability, echocardiogram, electroencephalogram [EEG])
- Relative contraindication: myocardial depression

Pentobarbital

Of the 2 short-acting barbiturates in use, pentobarbital (Nembutal) is the most efficacious and has the lowest incidence of respiratory depression and apnea. It can be given either IV or IM. Prolonged sleepiness is a common side effect of pentobarbital. Hypotension and increased HR are other side effects. Pentobarbital and other barbiturates are used for sedation and do not provide analgesia.

Consider:

- Onset: 1–5 minutes (IV), 10–20 minutes (IM)
- Duration: 15–90 minutes (IV, dose dependent), 1–2 hours (IM)
- Uses: procedural sedation and diagnostic imaging for those without IV access
- Relative contraindications: cardiac insufficiency, hepatic insufficiency, or pregnancy (fetal anomalies in 1st trimester; neonatal withdrawal if used in 3rd trimester)
- Absolute contraindication: porphyria and acute severe asthma (a.k.a. status asthmaticus)

Methohexital

The other short-acting barbiturate in use is methohexital (Brevital). It is delivered via IV. Methohexital has more AEs than pentobarbital, which include respiratory depression, hypotension, and myocardial depression.

Consider:

- Onset: 0.5–1 minute (IV)
- Duration: 5–10 minutes (IV)
- Uses: noninvasive diagnostic procedures
- Relative contraindications: respiratory disease (e.g., asthma, chronic obstructive pulmonary disease [COPD]), cardiovascular disease, renal dysfunction, and focal seizure disorder (a.k.a. partial seizure disorder)
- Absolute contraindication: porphyria

Ketamine

This dissociative sedative is a phencyclidine (PCP) derivative that oddly has a dichotomous "all-or-nothing" sedation. At anesthetic doses, ketamine (Ketalar) produces a trance-like state accompanied by sedation, analgesia, amnesia, and immobilization. All the while, upper airway muscle tone, airway protective reflexes, and spontaneous breathing remain intact. Its rapid onset and short

PHARMACOLOGY/PAIN

duration, along with analgesic properties, make it an ideal agent for painful procedures. Vomiting (pretreated with ondansetron), laryngospasm (remember PPV with bag mask), and longer recovery times are more frequent with IM dosing. Emergence phenomenon—characterized by agitation, impaired awareness, and hallucinations as a patient wakes from anesthesia—is another AE of ketamine; incidence of emergence phenomenon increases with age.

Consider:

- Onset: 1–2 minutes (IV)
- Duration: 15–30 minutes (IV)
- Uses: moderately to severely painful procedures (e.g., orthopedic reduction, laceration repair, bone marrow aspiration, central line placement, lumbar puncture [LP])
- Relative contraindications: uncontrolled hypertension, active pulmonary infection, cardiac disease, increased ICP, glaucoma, acute eye injury, porphyria, or thyroid disease
- Absolute contraindications: < 3 months of age or those with psychosis

Nitrous Oxide (N$_2$O)

N$_2$O ("laughing gas") is the dentist's favorite sedative. This anesthetic gas provides mild analgesia, sedation, amnesia, and anxiolysis. Protective airway reflexes, spontaneous breathing, and hemodynamic stability are all preserved. It is always delivered via inhalation with oxygen. Due to its low solubility in blood and adipose tissue, N$_2$O has a fast onset with an equally quick recovery after discontinuation and washout of the drug. Its safety profile in children is excellent, and no major cardiopulmonary events were reported in several large observational studies.

The AEs reported are vomiting (most common), nausea, and dysphoria. Studies show N$_2$O causes a dose-dependent blunting of the ventilatory response to hypoxemia. It has also, to a lesser degree, demonstrated the blunting of the ventilatory response to hypercapnia. These respiratory effects become more of a concern with the combination of different agents and in patients with COPD.

Consider:

- Onset: dependent on patient, concentration, and gas delivery (most within a few minutes)
- Duration: immediate recovery after termination of gas delivery
- Uses: nonpainful procedures (e.g., sexual assault exam, routine exam in children with intellectual disability, echocardiogram, EEG) and certain painful procedures (e.g., LP, dental work)
- Absolute contraindications: inability to use a nasal mask, patients on psychotropic agents, conditions in which gas can get trapped (i.e., bowel obstruction, pneumothorax, middle ear and eustachian tube pathologies, sinusitis, retinal surgery) due to the increased capability of N$_2$O to enter air-filled cavities, pregnancy (increased risk of spontaneous abortion), and COPD (rely on hypoxemic drive)

Fluranes

Fluranes (halothane, desflurane, isoflurane, sevoflurane, and enflurane) are fluorinated hydrocarbons that are used as inhaled anesthetics. Due to potential severe AEs (i.e., halothane hepatitis, cardiac arrhythmias), halothane and enflurane are rarely used in pediatric patients now that there are faster-acting inhalants with less severe AEs. Isoflurane and desflurane have a pungent odor that can lead to coughing and laryngospasm, so they are mostly utilized for anesthesia maintenance, not induction. Sevoflurane has a shorter induction time and a less pungent odor, so it can be used for induction. These agents can be used in combination with other sedation agents.

Fluranes can cause nausea, vomiting, depressed ventilation, hypercarbia, hepatic injury, prolonged QT, and decreased blood pressure. These inhaled anesthetics can also cause muscle relaxation and potentiate the effects of muscle relaxers. Infants (6–12 months of age) require a higher concentration of inhaled anesthetic to obtain the desired effect than older children and teens. These agents are utilized in the operating room or ICU setting and are best given by highly trained anesthesiologists and intensivists.

Consider:

- Onset: dependent on age of patient, concentration, and fat- and water-solubility (most within minutes)
- Duration: rapid recovery after termination of gas delivery (usually within minutes)
- Uses: induction of anesthesia (only sevoflurane), maintenance of anesthesia (desflurane, sevoflurane, isoflurane), severe bronchospasm, refractile status epilepticus
- Relative contraindications: hypovolemia, severe intracranial hypertension, prolonged QT (especially sevoflurane), liver dysfunction
- Absolute contraindications: malignant hyperthermia

ANALGESIA

PREVIEW | REVIEW

- How is pain assessed in young children who cannot self-report?
- What is the 1st line treatment for mild pain? Moderate-to-severe pain?

OVERVIEW

The measurement of pain in children is more challenging than its treatment. While self-reporting is the gold standard of pain assessment, it is only available to older children with normal cognitive and communication abilities. To assess the level of distress in younger children and infants, rely on vital signs (e.g., elevated BP, tachycardia) and behaviors (e.g., not using a particular limb, inconsolable crying, posturing). The other tools for the assessment of pain in children include the face, legs, activity, cry, and consolability (**FLACC**) tool and the Wong-Baker FACES Pain Rating Scale.

Pain management is not limited to pharmacologic remedies. Quite frequently, the treatment of a child's stress and anxiety by physical, behavioral, and cognitive measures leads to a significant amount of relief. The most important thing is to minimize separation from parents. Physical stimulation by cold, heat, massage, and vibration is often used with success in minimally painful procedures, such as IV placement and blood sampling. Child life specialists are available in many institutions and aid in the process with the use of play therapy, relaxation, and distraction during painful and anxiety-provoking procedures.

The following describes a few of the most common pain control medications used in the clinic, urgent care, and emergency department settings. The 2012 World Health Organization (WHO) Guidelines on the Pharmacological Treatment of Persisting Pain in Children with Medical Illnesses (analgesic ladder) recommends a simple stepwise strategy for the treatment of pain. First, treat mild pain with either ibuprofen or acetaminophen. For moderate-to-severe pain, add a weak opioid. This, of course, can be followed by a stronger opioid agent until analgesia is achieved. In Local and Topical Agent Profiles and Systemic Treatment Profiles on page 8-10, we describe common local and topical agents, followed by the commonly used systemic agents.

LOCAL AND TOPICAL AGENT PROFILES

LET (Lidocaine, Epinephrine, and Tetracaine)

LET is frequently used topically (placed under occlusive dressing) for the purposes of IV placement and laceration repair. LET is a combination of 4% lidocaine, 1:2,000 epinephrine, and 0.5% tetracaine. The safety profile of this drug is excellent.

Consider:

- Onset: 20–30 minutes
- Duration: not established
- Use: uncomplicated small facial or scalp laceration
- Contraindication: Do not use over mucous membranes and in regions with an end arterial supply (i.e., penis, nose, tips of the digits).

Eutectic Mixture of Local Anesthetics (EMLA)

EMLA is also used topically (placed under occlusive dressing) on intact skin for procedures such as IV placement and lumbar puncture. EMLA cream contains 2.5% lidocaine and 2.5% prilocaine.

Consider:

- Onset: 1 hour
- Duration: maximum dermal anesthesia at 2–3 hours; lasts up to 1–2 hours after removal
- Relative contraindications: Class 3 antiarrhythmic therapy (e.g., amiodarone, sotalol, dofetilide)
- Absolute contraindications: open wounds, allergy to amide anesthetics (i.e., lidocaine, prilocaine, bupivacaine, mepivacaine, ropivacaine), or methemoglobinemia (congenital or idiopathic)

Lidocaine

Lidocaine is one of the most commonly used local anesthetics in the emergency department and urgent care setting. It belongs to the family of amide anesthetics (others include prilocaine, bupivacaine, mepivacaine, and ropivacaine). Solutions of 1–2% are injected locally or for purposes of nerve block. It is often mixed with a small amount of epinephrine to prolong the anesthetic duration and aid in hemostasis via vasoconstriction. This feature becomes useful when repairing highly vascular areas like the scalp. Decreasing the pain of injection (commonly a burning sensation) is accomplished by buffering the pH of lidocaine, warming it, and slowly injecting it. Lidocaine is available in many forms. Of note, lidocaine spray is used prior to intubation, and the 2% jelly formulation is useful for mucous membranes (e.g., urethral catheterization, intraoral lesions, intubation). Although AEs are rare with local use, the rapid absorption of large amounts can lead to CNS and cardiovascular toxicity.

Consider:

- Onset: < 2 minutes
- Duration: 90–120 minutes; 2–6 hours (with epinephrine)
- Relative contraindications: treatment of arrhythmia or heart failure
- Absolute contraindications: heart block without pacemaker and allergy to amide anesthetics (very rare—usually a reaction to a preservative, such as methylparaben). Do not use lidocaine with epinephrine in the penis, digits, nose, ears, and other spaces with limited blood flow.

Magic Mouthwash

This solution is a 1:1:1 mixture of 2% viscous lidocaine, aluminum and magnesium hydroxides (liquid antacid), and diphenhydramine suspension. This combination deserves special mention because of its very specific but important role in the treatment of oral pain related to the conditions of coxsackievirus infection, herpetic gingivostomatitis, and other oral mucositis due to chemotherapy and/or radiation therapy. Such painful lesions often lead to poor intake and subsequent hospitalization for dehydration.

SYSTEMIC TREATMENT PROFILES

Acetaminophen

Acetaminophen remains a key medication in the treatment of mild pain and headache. This drug is also an antipyretic and is administered PO, PR, and IV. This remains a very safe drug when kept at or below total daily dosing recommendations. Overdose carries the risk of acute liver injury and failure. *N*-acetylcysteine is a well-known antidote.

Consider:

- Onset: 30–60 minutes
- Duration: peak effect at 1–3 hours
- Relative contraindications: chronic liver disease, alcoholism, chronic malnutrition, severe hypovolemia, or severe renal disease
- Absolute contraindications: acute liver disease or failure

Nonsteroidal Antiinflammatory Drugs (NSAIDs)

Ibuprofen also remains a commonly used option for mild pain and headache. It does triple duty, having antiinflammatory, antipyretic, and analgesic effects. Among the nonselective NSAIDs, ketorolac is the only IV form available in the U.S. Ketorolac is useful as a nonopioid option in treating moderate pain in migraine, sickle cell crisis, and minor urologic procedures involving the bladder. Other commonly used NSAID options include naproxen, ketoprofen, and aspirin. Aspirin is used only in certain circumstances in children due to its association with Reye syndrome. Aspirin's main pediatric indication is the treatment of Kawasaki disease. The main AEs of NSAIDs as a group are the inhibition of platelet function and gastric mucosal injury.

Consider:

- Contraindications and cautions: acute bleeding; peptic ulcers; upper GI bleeding; renal, hepatic, or cardiac dysfunction

Opioids

Opioids (a.k.a. narcotics) have a broad range in their route of administration, duration of effect, and analgesic strength. The WHO guidelines from 2012 recommend morphine as the 1st line treatment for moderate-to-severe pain, and this agent becomes the prototype agent by which all the other opioids are compared. The other commonly used opioids include hydromorphone, oxymorphone, fentanyl, oxycodone, hydrocodone, and codeine. The common AEs of opioids are nausea, vomiting, constipation, pruritus, dysphoria, and mydriasis.

Respiratory depression remains the biggest concern in treatment with opioids, especially in patients who are opioid-naïve or using combined therapy with benzodiazepines or other sedatives. Slow titration of opioids and careful monitoring of the respiratory function, availability of bag and mask ventilation, and access to naloxone plays a key role in preventing and reversing this serious AE. Naloxone is a very well-known reversal agent for opioid overdose and reverses not only respiratory depression but also the aforementioned AEs. Nausea and vomiting can accompany naloxone administration, so access to good suctioning for airway clearance is crucial.

Infants carry an increased risk for apnea and hypoventilation due to a decreased response to hypoxia and hypercapnia. Immature kidney and liver function, an immature blood-brain barrier, and decreased plasma protein binding results in increased free fractions of opioids in the blood and impaired clearance of the same.

Contraindications: hypersensitivity to opioids, acute respiratory depression, substance use disorder, acute asthma, paralytic ileus, use of monoamine oxidase (MAO) inhibitors, increased ICP or head trauma, uncontrolled ventilation, coma, or use within 24 hours before or after surgery.

After several reports of death due to codeine use in children with obstructive sleep apnea who underwent adenoidectomy and/or tonsillectomy, the FDA has issued a black box warning for codeine use in this group of children. The mortality is ascribed to ultrarapid metabolism of codeine in the liver leading to dangerously elevated levels of its metabolite, morphine.

Precautions: cardiovascular (e.g., bradycardia, hypotension, shock), pulmonary (e.g., asthma, impaired respiratory function), GI (e.g., obstructive or inflammatory bowel disease, biliary disease, acute pancreatitis, hepatic impairment), endocrine (e.g., hypothyroidism, adrenocortical insufficiency, diabetes mellitus), CNS and psychiatric (e.g., seizure disorder, altered mental status, toxic psychosis), renal impairment, and myasthenia gravis.

Opioid profiles are presented in Table 8-4, and specific dosages are included to demonstrate comparative strengths, termed opioid equianalgesic dose (i.e., estimated opioid dose equivalents). For example, the bioequivalent dose for 10 mg of IV morphine is 30 mg of PO morphine and 1.5 mg of IV hydromorphone.

Table 8-4: Characteristics of Common Opioids			
	Routes	**Duration of Action**	**Equianalgesic Dose**
Morphine	IV, SQ, IM, PO	3–6 hours	10 mg (IV, SQ, IM) 30 mg (PO)
Hydromorphone	IV, SQ, IM, PO	3–6 hours	1.5 mg (IV, SQ, IM) 7.5 mg (PO)
Oxymorphone	IV, SQ, IM, PO	3–6 hours	1 mg (IV, SQ, IM) 10 mg (PO)
Fentanyl	IV, TD*	0.5–2 hours	0.1 mg (100 mcg)
Oxycodone	PO	3–6 hours (short-acting) 12 hours (long-acting)	15–20 mg (short-acting) 20 mg (long-acting)
Hydrocodone	PO	3–6 hours	30–45 mg
Codeine	PO	4–6 hours	180–200 mg

* Transdermal dosing not discussed

IM = intramuscular
IV = intravenous
PO = per os, by mouth

SQ = subcutaneous
TD = transdermal

PHARMACOLOGY/PAIN

FIGURE SOURCES

Figure 8-1: MedStudy illustration
Figure 8-2: MedStudy illustration

Musculoskeletal & Sports Medicine

SECTION EDITOR

Kate E. Berz, DO
Assistant Professor of Pediatrics, Division of Sports Medicine and
Emergency Medicine
Cincinnati Children's Hospital Medical Center
University of Cincinnati College of Medicine
Cincinnati, OH

MEDICAL EDITOR
Lynn Bullock, MD
Colorado Springs, CO

Table of Contents

CONGENITAL DISORDERS 9-1
  TORTICOLLIS 9-1
  CLUBFOOT 9-1
  INTOEING 9-1
    Metatarsus Adductus..............................9-1
    Internal Tibial Torsion 9-1
    Internal Femoral Torsion 9-1
  POLYDACTYLY 9-1
  SPRENGEL DEFORMITY...............................9-2
  KLIPPEL-FEIL SYNDROME 9-2
  OSTEOGENESIS IMPERFECTA 9-2
  ACHONDROPLASIA......................................9-2

CHEST WALL MALFORMATIONS.......................9-2
  SCOLIOSIS...9-2
  KYPHOSIS 9-3
    Scheuermann Kyphosis 9-3
  PECTUS EXCAVATUM 9-4
  PECTUS CARINATUM....................................9-4

DISORDERS OF THE LOWER EXTREMITY 9-4
  DEVELOPMENTAL DYSPLASIA OF THE
    HIP (DDH)..9-4
  BLOUNT DISEASE 9-5

LIMB PAIN 9-6
  OVERVIEW 9-6
  EVALUATION OF THE LIMPING CHILD..............9-6
  GROWING PAINS 9-6
  BONE NEOPLASMS 9-7
  OSTEOID OSTEOMA....................................9-7
  OSGOOD-SCHLATTER DISEASE AND LIMB
    PAIN..9-7
  TRANSIENT SYNOVITIS 9-7
  LEGG-CALVÉ-PERTHES DISEASE 9-7
  SLIPPED CAPITAL FEMORAL EPIPHYSIS (SCFE)..9-8

HEEL AND FOOT PAIN 9-8

BONE INJURIES AND BENIGN LESIONS..............9-9
  COMPARTMENT SYNDROME.......................9-9
  GROWTH PLATE INJURIES..........................9-9
  BONE LESIONS..9-9
  OSTEOCHONDROMA 9-9
  TRAUMATIC MYOSITIS OSSIFICANS...............9-9
  FRACTURES..9-9

PREPARTICIPATION PHYSICAL
  EVALUATION (PPE)....................................9-10

SPORTS INJURY PREVENTION AND
  TREATMENT 9-10
  OVERVIEW 9-11
  HEAT ILLNESS 9-11
  CONCUSSION 9-11
  OVERUSE INJURIES 9-11
    Sever Disease 9-12
    Osgood-Schlatter Disease 9-12
    Patellofemoral Syndrome (PFS)...................9-12
    Iliotibial Band Syndrome 9-12
    Medial Elbow Apophysitis (Little
      League Elbow) 9-12
    Lateral Epicondylitis (Tennis Elbow) 9-13
    Osteochondritis Dissecans (OCD) 9-13
    Stress Fractures 9-13
    Spondylolysis / Spondylolisthesis..................9-14
  SPRAINS AND STRAINS...............................9-15
  SHOULDER DISLOCATION / SUBLUXATION 9-15

KNEE INJURIES...9-15
  Patellar Dislocation / Subluxation 9-15
  Anterior Cruciate Ligament (ACL) Injury..........9-15
  Medial Collateral Ligament (MCL) Injury..........9-15
  Prepatellar Bursitis..................................9-15
  Meniscal Tears 9-16
  ANKLE SPRAIN 9-16

NUTRITIONAL REQUIREMENTS.......................9-16

FEMALE ATHLETE TRIAD...............................9-16

PERFORMANCE-ENHANCING
  SUBSTANCES (PESs)...................................9-16

THE MEDSTUDY HUB: YOUR GUIDELINES
  AND REVIEW ARTICLES RESOURCE.................9-17

FIGURE SOURCES 9-18

CONGENITAL DISORDERS

PREVIEW | REVIEW

- What is the most common cause of torticollis?
- What are the most common causes of intoeing?
- What are some of the conditions that can be associated with Sprengel deformity?
- What is the classic triad of symptoms for Klippel-Feil syndrome?

TORTICOLLIS

Torticollis refers to an abnormality in the neck muscles causing the head to tilt and rotate. It can be congenital or acquired. Acquired torticollis is most commonly caused by injury or inflammation of the sternocleidomastoid or trapezius muscle and sometimes by atlantoaxial rotary displacement.

Congenital causes include:

- Tightening of one sternocleidomastoid muscle with the other one absent or atretic
- Traumatic delivery resulting in a hematoma within the sternocleidomastoid muscle
- Fixed positioning in utero resulting in fibrosis
- Cervical spine lesions

In children, another common etiology is acute infection resulting in referred pain or muscle spasm. Fever, upper respiratory, and other symptoms are usually present in this case. Serious causes of torticollis include retropharyngeal abscess, suppurative jugular thrombophlebitis (Lemierre syndrome), cervical spine injury, or central nervous system tumor.

The correct etiologic diagnosis is imperative because treatment is dependent on the underlying cause. Good history and physical exams (H&Ps) are important and, in most situations, are all that is needed. When there is trauma or prolonged/severe pain, plain radiographs may be required. Most cases of torticollis can be treated with nonsteroidal antiinflammatory drugs (NSAIDs); however, if there is no improvement, refer to physical therapy. Treat acute infection with antibiotics. If one of the more serious causes is suspected, refer immediately to a specialist for management.

CLUBFOOT

Clubfoot (a.k.a. equinus varus) is a congenital defect in which the foot appears plantarflexed and medially rotated (i.e., inverted). It is usually idiopathic and results from shortened ligaments. Refer early to an orthopedic surgeon for treatment; the goal is to correct the problem before the infant begins to walk. The 1st step is stretching and casting (the Ponseti method, or manipulation and casting in an orderly sequence). This consists of repositioning and recasting once a week for 6–8 weeks. If stretching and casting are unsuccessful, surgery may be needed to lengthen tendons.

INTOEING

Intoeing refers to the feet turning inward while walking instead of pointing forward. Causes include metatarsus adductus, internal tibial torsion, and internal femoral torsion.

Metatarsus Adductus

Metatarsus adductus occurs from intrauterine crowding and typically resolves spontaneously within the 1st year. In metatarsus adductus, the forefoot is adducted; the adduction can be flexible or rigid. This disorder can be identified by following a line that bisects the base of the hindfoot forward to the toes. In the normal foot, this line should pass between the 2nd and 3rd toes. If it passes lateral to this, metatarsus adductus is present. A flexible foot that can be passively abducted past midline will resolve by 1 year of age. A semiflexible foot that can only be abducted to midline needs follow up at 6 months and orthopedic referral if not becoming more flexible. A rigid foot cannot be abducted to midline and requires orthopedic referral for possible serial casting.

Internal Tibial Torsion

Internal tibial torsion is the most common cause of intoeing and presents in the 2nd year when the child starts walking. It results from medial rotation of the tibia. On physical exam (PE), the medial malleolus is even with or posterior to the lateral malleolus and, although the toes are rotated medially, the patella faces forward when walking. Most cases spontaneously resolve by school age; reserve surgery for severe cases causing functional or cosmetic deformity that persist past 8 years of age.

Internal Femoral Torsion

Internal femoral torsion (a.k.a. femoral anteversion) is due to medial rotation of the femur caused by intrauterine molding and genetic inheritance. It presents in children 3–5 years of age. These children find the "W" sitting position comfortable. Exam reveals inward rotation of the toes and patella when walking, and increased internal rotation with decreased external rotation of both hips while the patient is lying prone with knees bent. Most cases spontaneously resolve by 7–11 years of age. Orthopedic referral is recommended if rotation is present past 11 years of age with cosmetic concerns, if it interferes with ambulation, or if unilateral.

POLYDACTYLY

Polydactyly is the condition of having > 5 digits per hand or foot. Isolated polydactyly (which is much more common) is typically inherited as an autosomal dominant trait, whereas syndromic polydactyly is more often inherited as an autosomal recessive trait. Any newborn with extra digits should be examined closely, looking for other anomalies.

Polydactyly occurs during the 6th or 7th week of embryonic development as the hand (in the shape of a paddle) splits into separate fingers.

The extra digit may consist of just skin and soft tissue, but may also include bone. The most important factor that dictates intervention is the presence of a bony articulation of the extra digit with the remaining hand structure. An x-ray of the involved hand or foot is obtained to determine if bone is involved. If so, refer to an orthopedic surgeon for surgical intervention. If bone is not involved and the extra digit is attached by a thin stalk of tissue, then a vascular clip can be used to remove the extra digit.

SPRENGEL DEFORMITY

In Sprengel deformity, there is a congenital malposition and dysplasia of the scapula. The adjacent muscles are also hypoplastic. Usually this condition is sporadic but, in some cases, it can be inherited in an AD fashion. Associated malformations include Klippel-Feil syndrome (see Klippel-Feil Syndrome), **VATER** (vertebral defects, anal atresia, tracheoesophageal, radius, and renal anomalies), absent or fused ribs, cervical ribs, and congenital scoliosis.

These patients have shoulder asymmetry with the affected scapula elevated, adducted, and medially rotated inferiorly. There is restricted shoulder movement of the affected side. The anomalies are best visualized with plain film. In most patients, nonsurgical treatment is sufficient; this consists of physical therapy to improve range of motion and strengthen surrounding muscles. Severe cases require surgery.

KLIPPEL-FEIL SYNDROME

In Klippel-Feil syndrome, there is abnormal vertebral segmentation resulting in congenitally fused cervical vertebrae. The classic triad consists of:

1) Short neck
2) Limited neck motion
3) Low occipital hairline

Associated anomalies include Sprengel deformity (small, high riding scapula), scoliosis, renal anomalies, synkinesia (involuntary movement of one body part when moving another), congenital heart disease, and deafness. Evaluate with a careful PE, x-ray of the entire spine, and renal ultrasound.

Advise the family of the risks of contact sports due to cervical spine instability. Treat unstable spine segments and neurologic abnormalities with vertebral fusion. The risk of serious neurologic sequelae is highest with abnormalities at the occipito-C1 junction.

OSTEOGENESIS IMPERFECTA

See the Genetics section.

ACHONDROPLASIA

See the Genetics section.

CHEST WALL MALFORMATIONS

PREVIEW | REVIEW

- What degree of thoracic curvature in scoliosis can result in respiratory symptoms?
- What is pectus excavatum?
- What is pectus carinatum?

SCOLIOSIS

Scoliosis refers to an abnormal lateral curvature of the spine. Idiopathic scoliosis is most common but is a diagnosis of exclusion after careful evaluation for other causes of scoliosis—including congenital, neuromuscular, and compensatory (e.g., leg length discrepancy, tumor). If significant pain is associated, look for underlying causes (e.g., spondylolysis, spondylolisthesis, herniated disc). The most common causes of congenital scoliosis are inherited neuromuscular diseases and rib/vertebral anomalies. Scoliosis results in spinal rotation and abnormal positioning of the ribs, which cause an abnormal configuration of the chest cavity.

Scoliosis is most often diagnosed by a simple back examination with forward flexion and plain radiographs to assess the degree of curvature using the Cobb angle (> 10° = scoliosis). Risser grading (Table 9-1) plus sexual maturity rating (SMR) help to predict which curves will progress. Risser grading is the measurement of ossification of the iliac crest; low SMR + low Risser grade = increased risk for curve progression.

Table 9-1: Risser Grading — Measurement of Ossification of the Iliac Crest	
Risser Grade	Percentage Ossification of Iliac Epiphysis (on X-Ray)
0	0
1	< 25
2	25–50
3	50–75
4	> 75

Idiopathic scoliosis comprises 80–85% of all scoliosis and is divided into **infantile** (0–3 years of age), **juvenile** (4–9 years of age), and **adolescent** (> 10 years of age), depending on the age of onset. ~ 3% of the general school population has a scoliotic curve of ≥ 10°, and 0.5% have a curve of ≥ 20°. Curves < 30° are less likely to progress after physical maturity. Severe scoliosis (thoracic curve > 90° to 100°) increases mortality, sometimes occurring in the 4th or 5th decade, due to cardiopulmonary insufficiency. The American Academy of Pediatrics (AAP) recommends screening asymptomatic adolescents for idiopathic scoliosis as follows:

• Girls: Screen at 10 and 12 years of age.
• Boys: Screen once at either 13 or 14 years of age.

Mild scoliosis is asymptomatic, but when the thoracic curve is > 50°, you may find pulmonary function abnormalities. Alveolar hypoventilation is common. Respiratory symptoms sometimes occur with lesser curves when there is weakness, poor secretion control, or dysphagia from coexisting neuromuscular disease.

Severe scoliosis causes respiratory abnormalities, including restrictive lung disease and/or distortion of the airways or large pulmonary vessels. Cardiopulmonary compromise, including cor pulmonale and right heart failure, generally occurs if the Cobb angle (of the scoliosis curvature) exceeds 90°.

In milder cases of curvature (< 20°), particularly with limited symptoms, encourage activity without restrictions. For skeletally immature curves between 25° and 45°, use bracing to prevent or minimize curve progression. Curves > 45° to 50° frequently require spinal fusion or the placement of a Harrington rod.

Ideally, congenital forms of scoliosis are diagnosed early in childhood. If diagnosed early enough, bracing usually corrects or limits progression of the curve. Surgical intervention is often required when scoliosis is congenital or is caused by neuromuscular weakness.

KYPHOSIS

Kyphosis is an anteroposterior (AP) curvature of the spine (Figure 9-1). The normal spine has curves ranging from 20° to 40° in the cervical, thoracic, and lumbar regions. Kyphosis is diagnosed when these curves are greater than normal, causing an abnormally convex spine. It typically involves the upper thoracic spine and does not cause respiratory compromise. Kyphosis can be congenital or caused by trauma, infection, tumor, neuromuscular disease, Scheuermann disease (see Scheuermann Kyphosis), or other underlying conditions. Symptoms include a hump in the back, abnormal shoulder position, and back pain.

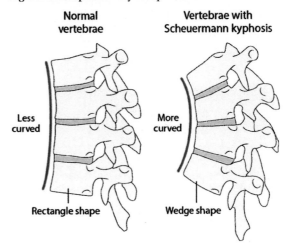

Figure 9-1: Kyphosis

Diagnose by x-ray. Treatment can include bracing, physical therapy, and NSAIDs. For more severe cases (i.e., progressive kyphosis > 70° to 80°, severe pain), surgery is often indicated.

Scheuermann Kyphosis

In Scheuermann kyphosis (a.k.a. Scheuermann disease), there is ≥ 5° anterior wedging of at least 3 adjacent thoracic vertebrae (Figure 9-2). The cause is unknown, but it appears that damage to the vertebral growth plate is followed by abnormal vertebral growth. In genetically susceptible individuals, mechanical forces associated with repetitive flexion (e.g., weight lifting) likely result in microtrauma, producing endplate injury to thoracic or thoracolumbar vertebrae. Similar radiographic changes have also been identified in some individuals after an extended period of bed rest, suggesting that wedging is the result of compression fractures due to transient osteopenia/osteoporosis. It is more common in males and typically begins during the prepubertal growth spurt (10–15 years of age). Most patients with the deformity are asymptomatic; if present, pain and stiffness are the most common associated symptoms. It is rare to have neurologic or cardiopulmonary compromise.

Figure 9-2: Scheuermann kyphosis

Diagnose with plain radiographs. In addition to the anterior wedging, additional radiographic manifestations include abnormalities of the vertebral endplates and, in some cases, Schmorl nodes (nodules)—which represent herniation of the nucleus pulposus through the vertebral body endplate into the adjacent vertebrae.

Initial management is conservative, consisting of avoiding pain triggers, treatment with NSAIDs, and exercises to increase strength and flexibility. Curves > 60° in the skeletally immature may be improved with bracing. Curves > 70° to 80° that are uncontrolled by bracing sometimes require surgery.

PECTUS EXCAVATUM

Pectus excavatum (hollowed chest; a.k.a. funnel chest) is a depression of the midsternum (Figure 9-3). It is sometimes seen with connective tissue disorders and other genetic conditions (e.g., Marfan syndrome, Ehlers-Danlos syndrome). It can occur in response to underlying pulmonary conditions. By itself, pectus excavatum rarely causes respiratory or cardiac problems—though some affected individuals complain of exercise intolerance. More severe pectus excavatum can shift the heart leftward. Spirometry is usually normal but can show mild restriction in severe cases. Normal spirometry does not exclude the possibility of cardiopulmonary limitation with exercise. A chest CT can help define the severity, and exercise testing can help identify impairment in those with severe pectus excavatum.

Consider surgical referral in those who also have an associated thoracic scoliosis or who have significant cardiopulmonary limitation. Many affected individuals choose elective surgery to improve the aesthetic appearance of the chest.

PECTUS CARINATUM

Pectus carinatum (keeled chest; a.k.a. pigeon breast) is the anterior protrusion of the sternum with lateral depression of the costal cartilages. Pectus carinatum is rarely symptomatic (Figure 9-4). Bracing and surgery are recommended only to improve appearance.

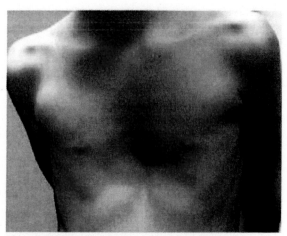

Figure 9-3: Pectus excavatum

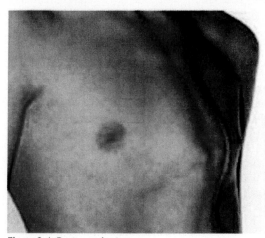

Figure 9-4: Pectus carinatum

DISORDERS OF THE LOWER EXTREMITY

PREVIEW | REVIEW

- What are some risk factors for developmental dysplasia of the hip (DDH)?
- How is DDH diagnosed in an infant < 4–6 months of age?
- What is Blount disease?
- What are the 2 forms of Blount disease, and how do they differ?

DEVELOPMENTAL DYSPLASIA OF THE HIP (DDH)

DDH affects the proximal femur and acetabulum (pelvic portion of hip joint) and is a spectrum from mild instability of the hip joint to frank dislocation. Disruption of the normal contact between the acetabulum and the femoral head prevents the hip joint from developing normally. DDH is more common among females, firstborn children, infants swaddled incorrectly, and infants with a history of intrauterine crowding and breech presentation. Newborns at high risk routinely undergo hip ultrasound by 4–6 weeks of age. Early diagnosis and treatment are critical because failure to diagnose can lead to significant morbidity. Screen for DDH on PE from the time of birth until the child is walking well.

DDH can involve several age-specific clinical findings:

- Both the Barlow and Ortolani maneuvers (Figure 9-5) are positive only in the newborn period as affected hips are no longer reducible by 8–10 weeks of age. Any positive testing in an infant > 4 weeks of age should be referred to an orthopedist:
  - A positive **Barlow test** is defined by movement ("clunk") of a dislocated femoral head from the acetabulum as the examiner adducts the flexed hip while pushing the thigh posteriorly. If this test is positive in an infant < 2 weeks of age, the test should be repeated. The Barlow test is a less significant test than the Ortolani test.
  - A positive **Ortolani test** is defined by movement ("clunk") of the dislocated femoral head back into the acetabulum as the examiner holds the thigh between the thumb and index finger and lifts the greater trochanter while abducting the hip. This is the most important clinical test and is negative after 3 months of age.

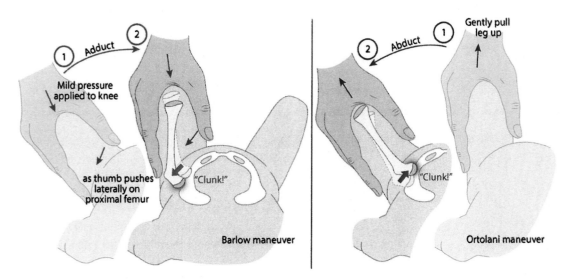

Figure 9-5: Barlow maneuver (left) and Ortolani maneuver (right)

- The **Galeazzi** sign initially presents at 8–10 weeks of age and is defined by asymmetry in the height of the knees due to shortening of the thigh on the affected side (Figure 9-6). It is best observed with both hips placed in 90° flexion.
- In addition to the Galeazzi sign, clinical findings in infants > 8–10 weeks of age include:
  - Limb-length difference
  - Limited or asymmetric hip abduction
  - Asymmetry of the gluteal and thigh folds
  - **Telescoping** (a.k.a. pistoning sign) is a sign of hip instability elicited with the hip flexed to 90°. One hand stabilizes the pelvis at the anterior iliac spine while the other hand grasps the femur and applies gentle anterior-to-posterior force, causing the femur to slip out of the acetabulum in the unstable hip.

Figure 9-6: Galeazzi sign

In infants < 4–6 months of age, evaluate with hip ultrasound. The femoral head has not yet ossified; the cartilage and soft tissues are better delineated by this imaging modality.

When to image an infant > 6 months of age:

- Suspicious or inconclusive exam
- History of improper swaddling
- History of breech presentation
- Family history of developmental dysplasia
- History of clinical instability
- Parental concern

In older infants and children, plain radiographs are appropriate because the femoral heads are ossified and no longer cartilaginous.

The goal of DDH treatment is early recognition and treatment to restore contact between the femoral head and acetabulum (i.e., reduce the joint). Maintain reduction while the acetabulum develops. Refer to a pediatric orthopedist if the patient has risk factors or questionable exam findings, or if pediatrician or parent is concerned. In infants ≤ 6 months of age, use a Pavlik harness or similar device to hold the hip flexed so the femoral head stays in the socket and allows for proper hip joint development. From 6 months to 2 years of age, use a spica splint to attempt closed reduction. If these procedures are unsuccessful, surgery is indicated.

BLOUNT DISEASE

Blount disease is a pathologic varus malformation caused by abnormally slow growth of the medial portion of the proximal tibial physis (Figure 9-7 on page 9-6). The exact cause is unknown but appears to be multifactorial, consisting of both hereditary factors and mechanical overload. Risk factors include African American ethnicity, early walking, obesity, and female gender.

MSK / SPORTS MED

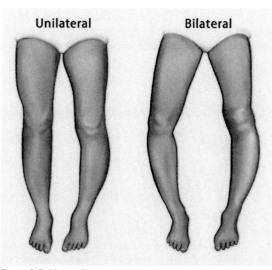

Figure 9-7: Blount disease

There are 2 forms of Blount's. The **infantile form** is diagnosed at < 4 years of age, is usually bilateral, and is seen in children of normal weight. The **adolescent form** is diagnosed at ≥ 4 years of age, is often unilateral, and is more commonly seen with obesity. The adolescent form also can have pain and leg length discrepancy. Both forms present with genu varum deformity.

Infantile Blount disease must be distinguished from physiologic varus. The normal physiologic progression in children is genu varum up to 2 years of age followed by genu valgum at ~ 3 years of age. By 7 years of age, most children return to the normal physiologic valgus, which has a tibial metaphyseal-diaphyseal angle (MDA) ≤ 11°. A patient with a greater angle should be referred to a pediatric orthopedist.

If PE demonstrates significant or asymmetric genu varus with a lateral thrust while walking, radiographic examination must be performed. In Blount disease, plain radiographs show **metaphyseal beaking** (more common in the infantile form) and MDA is > 16°.

Treatment depends on the age of the patient. Treat infantile Blount disease with bracing for ~ 2 years. If bracing is unsuccessful or the MDA is > 20°, surgery is indicated. Surgical intervention is usually needed for the adolescent form.

LIMB PAIN

PREVIEW | REVIEW

- What is the initial workup, after history and physical, for a limping child?
- What are the characteristics of growing pains?
- Osteoid osteoma does not respond to which common analgesic?
- How does Legg-Calvé-Perthes disease typically present?
- What are some risk factors for slipped capital femoral epiphysis?

OVERVIEW

Limb pain is very common in children and adolescents. Musculoskeletal pain can be difficult for children to characterize and can cause them great anxiety.

Diagnostic evaluation is guided by the H&P and may include complete blood count (CBC), acute phase reactants, and plain radiographs of the limb and/or hip. See Growing Pains for differential diagnosis of leg pain. Differential diagnosis of hip pain includes infection, tumor, transient synovitis, Legg-Calvé-Perthes disease, and slipped capital femoral epiphysis (SCFE).

EVALUATION OF THE LIMPING CHILD

In children, causes of limping range from the benign (77%) to the life threatening. Overuse, sprains, minor problems such as splinters or bruises, and transient synovitis are the most common diagnoses.

The H&P can rapidly narrow the differential diagnosis. Gather information regarding the location, duration, and characteristics of the pain, history of any injury or repetitive activity, and systemic symptoms.

Acute and recent symptom onset suggests infection or trauma. Consider infection, inflammation, or malignancy when there are constitutional symptoms (e.g., fever, night sweats, poor appetite, weight loss).

During the PE, localize the affected area by noting swelling, tenderness, and decreased range of motion with joint movement. Additionally, look for systemic signs such as ill appearance, fever, and diffuse rashes. Fever with limp is seen with septic arthritis and osteomyelitis but rarely with rheumatic arthritis.

Initial workup should include blood culture, CBC, CRP, ESR, and muscle enzymes. Get an AP and lateral x-ray of a suspect joint. Do entire lower extremity x-rays if there are no focal findings on PE.

If septic arthritis is suspected, CBC, C-reactive protein (CRP), and erythrocyte sedimentation rate (ESR) are helpful in evaluation. CRP > 2 mg/dL has high specificity for septic arthritis. CRP < 1 mg/dL has an 87% negative predictive value. The WBC and ESR are sensitive but lack specificity. Confirm septic arthritis by aspiration of the joint.

Check muscle enzymes. Recent infection with influenza A or B and increased muscle enzymes suggests a transient myositis.

GROWING PAINS

Growing pains are recurrent, self-limited, benign limb pains of unknown etiology that are not due to growing; i.e., there is no evidence that growth "hurts."

Typically bilateral, they are often described as deep, sharp, aching pain in the muscles of the legs. Pain usually occurs late in the day or during the night and resolves by morning. There is no joint involvement, and inflammation is absent. Growing pains occur in up to 40% of children 3–5 years of age and in 10–20% of school-age children.

Exclude possible organic etiologies before making the diagnosis of benign leg pain.

Specific etiologies to exclude or consider:

- Neoplasms (e.g., leukemia, osteosarcoma, Ewing sarcoma, metastatic disease)
- Infections (e.g., osteomyelitis, septic arthritis, viral myositis)
- Trauma (e.g., fracture, myositis ossificans)
- Bone disorders (e.g., chondromalacia, Osgood-Schlatter disease)
- Collagen vascular disease
- Juvenile idiopathic arthritis
- Transient synovitis
- Metabolic disorders (e.g., osteomalacia, rickets)
- Hypervitaminosis A
- Patellofemoral pain syndrome

Psychosomatic pain (somatization) is sometimes mistaken for growing pains but is associated with, for example, school phobia, bullying, or conversion reactions.

BONE NEOPLASMS

The most common types of malignant bone neoplasms in children and adolescents are osteosarcoma and Ewing sarcoma. See the Oncology section for more information.

OSTEOID OSTEOMA

Osteoid osteoma is a benign lesion that produces prostaglandins; it is most commonly found in the proximal femur, followed by the tibia. Although it is often seen on plain radiographs, CT scan is sometimes necessary for further evaluation. The CT scan reveals a sharp, round or oval lesion < 2 cm in diameter with a 1- to 2-mm peripheral radiolucent zone surrounding a homogeneous dense center (Figure 9-8). Osteoid osteoma often presents with severe nighttime pain and responds to salicylates and NSAIDs. Osteoid osteoma does not respond to acetaminophen. Treatment depends on the symptoms. For those with mild or tolerable pain, treat

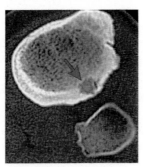

Figure 9-8: CT of osteoid osteoma

with NSAIDs and observe with serial exams and x-rays every 4–6 months. Most spontaneously resolve within several years. In patients with severe pain or limp, surgical resection or radiofrequency ablation of the lesion is sometimes needed.

OSGOOD-SCHLATTER DISEASE AND LIMB PAIN

Osgood-Schlatter disease is a repetitive stress injury to the patellar tendon insertion at the tibial tuberosity. See more on Osgood-Schlatter Disease on page 9-12.

TRANSIENT SYNOVITIS

Transient synovitis (previously known as toxic synovitis) is thought to be a postinfectious arthritis and is characterized by hip pain, limp, or refusal to walk. It typically presents between 3 and 10 years of age; the median age at presentation is 6 years. It is more common in males than in females. The etiology is unclear but most often follows a viral infection (e.g., recent upper respiratory infection). Children with transient synovitis appear well. Imaging is not necessary, but ultrasound shows effusion. Hip infection must be excluded in any patient with clinical or laboratory findings of concern; e.g., high fever, toxic appearance, severe pain, and elevated CBC and/or acute phase reactants. After ruling out a disorder requiring specific treatment and intervention, treat with ibuprofen.

LEGG-CALVÉ-PERTHES DISEASE

Legg-Calvé-Perthes disease is characterized by a partial or complete idiopathic avascular necrosis (osteonecrosis) of the femoral head, most often in boys between 3 and 12 years of age, with a peak incidence between 5 and 7 years of age. Patients present with hip or knee pain and a limp. The pain is insidious and worsens with activity. PE reveals reduced hip movement and pain with passive range of motion. Counsel patients to not bear weight on the affected limb, and refer them to an orthopedist. Treat by maintaining the femur in an internally rotated and abducted position so that the femoral head is held within the acetabulum; this can be accomplished through activity modification, abduction exercises, or bracing. The disorder typically resolves with time; however, pelvic osteotomy may hasten femoral remodeling or the return of normal blood flow to the femoral head. Avascular necrosis secondary to an underlying disease—such as renal failure, collagen vascular disease, or sickle cell disease—or secondary to glucocorticoid use can present in a similar manner.

See Figure 9-9; note the misshapen and "ratty" appearance of the left femoral head.

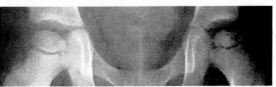

Figure 9-9: Legg-Calvé-Perthes disease with avascular necrosis of left femoral head

MSK / SPORTS MED

SLIPPED CAPITAL FEMORAL EPIPHYSIS (SCFE)

SCFE ("skiffy") is one of the most common hip disorders of adolescence and can be unilateral or bilateral. It is characterized by posterior and inferior slippage of the epiphysis off the metaphysis, causing hip, groin, or knee pain and a limp. Mean age of onset is 12 years in girls and 13.5 years in boys, near the time of peak linear growth. The incidence is higher among boys, obese children, and those with endocrine dysfunction (especially hypothyroidism and growth hormone deficiency).

On PE, there is altered gait, pain with movement of the hip, and impaired internal rotation and flexion of the hip. The diagnosis is usually made with plain radiographs. A common radiographic finding in SCFE is lack of extension of the epiphysis past the Klein line (a line along the superior edge of the femoral neck; Figure 9-10).

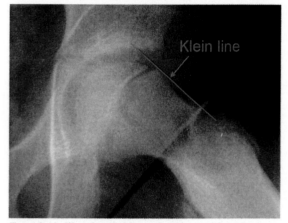

Figure 9-10: Slipped capital femoral epiphysis with minimal displacement

Treatment involves immediate nonweightbearing status, emergent orthopedic referral, and surgical repair.

Remember: Hip pathology often presents with a limp associated with anterior thigh, groin, and/or knee pain.

HEEL AND FOOT PAIN

PREVIEW | REVIEW

- Which drug increases the risk for Achilles tendon rupture?

Heel pain can originate from any of the structures on or overlying the heel. A careful H&P can generally localize the pain and clarify the etiology.

Typical causes of heel pain are cuts, plantar puncture wounds, blisters, heel contusions, and overuse injuries. Sever disease is also common in the skeletally immature and is discussed separately under Sever Disease on page 9-12.

If there is any suspicion of a **retained foreign body**, plantar puncture wounds must be imaged. X-rays identify radiopaque objects, whereas ultrasounds show radiolucent objects. If a retained foreign body is strongly suspected despite negative initial imaging, follow with CT or MRI.

Calcaneal osteomyelitis can result from a retained foreign body—typically after a plantar puncture wound or from hematogenous spread. Exam reveals difficulty weightbearing, calcaneal swelling, erythema, and tenderness. Patients may have constitutional symptoms and elevated white blood cell (WBC) count, ESR, and CRP. Check x-rays for characteristic findings: periosteal elevation, periosteal new bone formation, and sclerotic or lytic bony lesions.

Achilles tendonitis is an overuse injury from prolonged or intense running or hiking. On PE, there is tenderness and swelling over the Achilles tendon at the back of the ankle.

The same activities that cause Achilles tendonitis can also cause inflammation of the bursa near the distal insertion of the Achilles tendon.

Achilles tendon rupture can occur from overuse or trauma. Both Achilles tendon rupture and bursitis are rare in children. Fluoroquinolone antibiotic use carries a slightly increased risk for Achilles tendon rupture.

Plantar fasciitis can occur in adolescents who participate in sports or jobs with repetitive standing, running, or walking. In plantar fasciitis, the pain and tenderness generally occurs along the plantar surface of the foot and commonly over the calcaneal tubercle or origin of the plantar fascia at the anterior portion of the calcaneus.

Heel contusions are sometimes confused with plantar fasciitis; however, these usually localize to midheel, and the tenderness does not vary.

Enthesitis of juvenile idiopathic arthritis can cause heel, foot, and knee pain.

Calcaneal fracture is unusual and typically results from high-energy trauma to the heel after a high fall or jump. On PE, the heel area is very swollen and tender, and weightbearing is intolerable. Get x-rays with lateral and axial views. CT is sometimes required to fully assess the bone and any surrounding bony injuries (which are common).

There are many causes of pain occurring in other areas of the foot, including:

- Tarsal coalitions
- Pes planus (flat feet)
- Accessory navicular
- Sesamoiditis and bipartite sesamoid (1st metatarsophalangeal [MTP] joint)
- Metatarsal stress fractures
- Trauma

OSTEOCHONDROMA

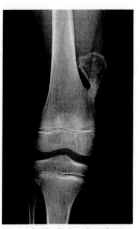

Osteochondroma occurs spontaneously and is a bone spur with a cartilaginous cap on the bone surface (Figure 9-12). These benign lesions occur around growth plates and are common in the humerus, proximal tibia, and distal femur. Osteochondroma is often discovered as a painless mass on exam or as an incidental finding on x-ray. If the osteochondroma is painful or keeps the patient from activity, refer to a pediatric orthopedist for resection.

Figure 9-12: Osteochondroma

TRAUMATIC MYOSITIS OSSIFICANS

Traumatic myositis ossificans (a.k.a. traumatic heterotopic ossification) is characterized by extraskeletal (heterotopic) ossification following blunt soft tissue trauma. The etiology is uncertain, but it is thought that the underlying process is an inflammatory response to tissue injury. This disorder typically occurs in active adolescents after trauma and presents as a painless, enlarging mass most often located in the quadriceps, brachialis, or deltoid muscles. The mass is usually located away from a joint, is rounded, and is characterized on x-ray by mature peripheral ossification with a distinct margin surrounding a radiolucent center of immature osteoid and primitive mesenchymal tissue. This peripheral maturation is the reverse of that seen with a neoplasm. Also in contrast to a neoplasm, the bony mass is always slightly separated from the long shaft of the bone.

Treatment of myositis ossificans consists of rest, muscle stretching, and antiinflammatory agents (e.g., indomethacin). Surgical excision is rarely warranted, and only after a period of 6–12 months and with a negative bone scan. Earlier removal will likely result in return of new bone formation within the muscle; therefore, myositis ossificans is surgically excised only if it interferes with joint mobility or is irritating a nerve.

FRACTURES

See the Emergency Medicine & Maltreatment Syndromes section.

BONE INJURIES AND BENIGN LESIONS

PREVIEW | REVIEW

- What is the treatment for unicameral bone cysts?
- What are the characteristics of traumatic myositis ossificans seen on x-ray?

COMPARTMENT SYNDROME

See the Emergency Medicine & Maltreatment Syndromes section.

GROWTH PLATE INJURIES

See the Emergency Medicine & Maltreatment Syndromes section.

BONE LESIONS

Nonossifying fibromas (NOF; a.k.a. fibrous cortical defects) are common benign lesions made up of fibrous tissue (Figure 9-11). Bone cysts are either fluid-filled lesions (unicameral) or blood-filled lesions (aneurysmal) within a bone.

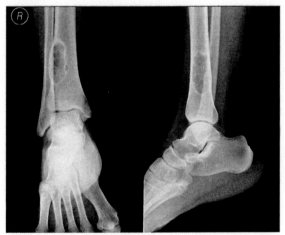

Figure 9-11: Nonossifying fibromas

Cysts and fibromas are noncancerous, typically solitary, and occur in children and young adults. Symptoms can include pain, limp, and fracture (because of weakened bone), but most are asymptomatic. Many are found incidentally on imaging studies for other reasons.

No treatment is necessary for NOF. Treatment for unicameral bone cysts includes observation with serial plain films and, for large lesions (> 50% of the bone), activity restriction to prevent fracture. Unicameral bone cysts often resolve spontaneously with physeal closure. Aneurysmal bone cysts, on the other hand, are aggressive and require surgical treatment.

PREPARTICIPATION PHYSICAL EVALUATION (PPE)

PREVIEW | REVIEW

- What are some conditions that restrict participation in sports?

- What special consideration is there for persons with Down syndrome before their participation in sports?

- What types of sports are inadvisable for patients with Marfan syndrome?

The main purpose of the PPE (i.e., sports physical) is to identify conditions that would carry life-threatening risks during participation in a sport, would require a treatment plan for participation, or would require rehabilitation prior to participation. The athlete's history is the major component of evaluation and must include general health, injury history, and past medical history, including family history of cardiovascular conditions. It is important to ascertain if the athlete has ever had chest pain, shortness of breath, syncope, palpitations, dizziness with exercise, seizures, or any previous cardiac testing. An affirmative answer requires further cardiac workup, including electrocardiogram (ECG) and echocardiogram. A thorough PE can identify additional abnormalities that may need to be addressed. No routine lab testing is recommended. As of 2019, ECG screening remains controversial and is not currently recommended by the American Heart Association.

Conditions having life-threatening complications, and therefore restricting sports participation, include:

- Hypertrophic cardiomyopathy
- Prolonged QT interval
- Aortic stenosis
- Coronary artery anomalies
- Myocarditis
- Uncontrolled Stage 2 hypertension
- Fever (increases risk of heat illness)
- Concussion (if still symptomatic)

Conditions that require a treatment plan for participation in sports include:

- Asthma
- Hypertension
- Diabetes mellitus
- Eating disorders
- Musculoskeletal disorders/injuries
- Concussion

Certain conditions require specific considerations.

Individuals with **Down syndrome** have a predisposition to atlantoaxial (C1–C2) instability and must be examined for this. If the exam is abnormal and/or patients are symptomatic, order cervical imaging and a pediatric neurosurgeon or orthopedist consult. Athletes with **seizure disorder** should not participate in free climbing, hang-gliding, or scuba diving. Water sports are fine if the seizure disorder is well controlled and there is adequate supervision. Certain sports—such as horseback riding, harnessed rock climbing, and gymnastics—are permissible if precautions are taken. Individuals with **Type 1 diabetes** can participate in sport activities but must closely monitor their blood glucose levels before, during, and after exercise (for up to 12 hours). Coaches must be trained to recognize and treat hypoglycemia. They can even participate in scuba diving as long as specific guidelines and restrictions are followed. Persons with **Marfan syndrome** can typically participate in low-to-moderate intensity exercise (e.g., bowling, walking). Contact sports and scuba diving are not advisable, due to risk of cardiovascular bleed/lens dislocation and precipitating a pneumothorax, respectively.

Along with reviewing history and completing a symptoms checklist, a computerized neurocognitive function assessment is sometimes used to establish a baseline score before participation in contact sports. This baseline score is used for postconcussion evaluation of changes in cognitive function. It provides an objective comparison to facilitate return-to-play decisions.

The National Collegiate Athletic Association (NCAA) requires all participants to have confirmation of sickle cell trait status through newborn screening or recent blood test.

SPORTS INJURY PREVENTION AND TREATMENT

PREVIEW | REVIEW

- What steps can an athlete take to prevent heat illness?

- Why are children at increased risk for overuse injuries?

- What is Sever disease?

- What is the most common cause of anterior knee pain?

- What is the difference between spondylolysis and spondylolisthesis?

- Are anterior cruciate ligament tears more common in males or females?

- What is the typical mechanism of injury for meniscal tears?

OVERVIEW

Risk for injury includes trauma or overuse. Most common injuries are caused by abnormal stress to bone or soft tissue resulting in a sprain, strain, or fracture. The AAP released its recommendations to reduce the risk of injury in its 2017 Sports Injury Prevention Tip Sheet:

1) Take time off. Plan to have at least 1 day off per week from a particular sport to allow the body to recover. Take 1 month off per year from a specific sport. This time off does not have to be consecutive.

2) Wear the right gear. Players should wear appropriate and properly fitting protective equipment: pads (e.g., neck, shoulder, elbow, chest, knee, shin pads), helmets, mouthpieces, face guards, protective cups, and/or eyewear. Young athletes should not assume that protective gear will protect them completely when engaging in more dangerous or risky activities.

3) Strengthen muscles. Conditioning exercises during practice strengthen muscles used in play.

4) Increase flexibility. Stretching exercises before and after games or practice can increase flexibility and should also be incorporated into a daily fitness plan.

5) Use the proper technique. This should be reinforced during the playing season.

6) Take breaks. Rest periods during practice and games can reduce injuries and prevent heat illness.

7) Play safe. Strict rules against headfirst sliding (baseball and softball), spearing (football), and checking (ice hockey) should be enforced.

8) Stop the activity if there is pain.

9) Avoid heat injury by drinking plenty of fluids before, during, and after exercise or play; decrease or stop practices or competitions during high heat/humidity periods; wear light clothing.

10) Children jumping on a trampoline should be supervised by a responsible adult; only 1 child should be on the trampoline at a time.

11) The main goals of sports participation should be having fun and building lifelong physical activity skills. Emotional stress caused by the pressure to win can be avoided by emphasizing effort, sportsmanship, and hard work.

HEAT ILLNESS

Heat illness occurs when the body cannot cool itself with the typical sweating mechanism. It usually occurs in hot, humid weather with strenuous activity. Risk factors include young age, old age, illness, being overweight, alcohol consumption prior to activity, and certain medications (e.g., stimulants). Prevention includes heat acclimatization, staying well hydrated, replenishing salt with sports drinks, and limiting the amount of outdoor activity.

Heat cramps are muscle cramps occurring during exercise and are the mildest form of heat illness. Treat with rest, hydration, salt replenishment, and stretching of the affected muscle.

Heat exhaustion refers to the inability of the body to maintain a normal temperature during exercise and presents with tachycardia, profuse sweating, and weakness. The body temperature is between 102.0°F and 104.0°F (38.9°C and 40.0°C), and there are no significant CNS symptoms. Treatment consists of stopping the activity, moving to a cool place, removing any unnecessary clothing or equipment, drinking fluids, and taking an ice-water bath or using ice packs. Monitor temperature during the cooling process; discontinue monitoring when the temperature falls to < 102.0°F (38.9°C) or shivering occurs.

Heat stroke is the most severe form of heat illness and refers to hyperthermia (≥ 104.0°F [≥ 40.0°C]) and CNS dysfunction. Other symptoms include altered mental status, nausea/vomiting, headache, tachycardia and tachypnea, and flushed skin. This is a medical emergency, and the longer that treatment is delayed, the higher the risk of serious complications or death. Rectal temperature is the only reliable method of obtaining an accurate core temperature measurement. Rapid cooling is the most effective treatment to prevent organ damage and must be initiated immediately (prior to transportation). Total body immersion in ice water is the most effective cooling technique; others include massage with ice-water towels, evaporative cooling (cool water misted on skin with fans on the body), or cooling blankets/ice. Complications of heat illness can include seizures, rhabdomyolysis, respiratory failure, acute kidney injury, myocardial injury, and death.

CONCUSSION

See the Emergency Medicine & Maltreatment Syndromes section.

OVERUSE INJURIES

Overuse injuries can affect bones, growth plates, and soft tissues. Because these structures grow at an uneven rate, children are at increased risk for these types of injuries. Overuse injuries are increasing in frequency due to the competitive nature of youth sports and the year-round playing of a single sport. This puts repetitive stress on specific areas of the body without allowing for adequate rest. The main symptom is pain that is not due to an acute injury and that increases with activity. Other signs and symptoms can include joint or tendon swelling and change in playing technique due to the injury. Prevention consists of limiting the number of teams on which an athlete participates in one season and not allowing an athlete to play one sport year-round without taking breaks or playing other sports. General management includes resting athletes until they are pain free. Do not use medication to mask symptoms in order to participate.

MSK / SPORTS MED

Sever Disease

Sever disease is a common cause of heel pain and refers to inflammation of the calcaneal growth plate (apophysis) where the Achilles tendon inserts. It usually occurs with running and jumping activities (e.g., soccer, basketball) in the setting of a child's growth spurt. Make a clinical diagnosis when palpation of the calcaneal apophysis causes pain. Treatment consists of decreased participation in the activity until the patient feels symptom relief, ice, stretching, heel cups, and NSAIDs.

Osgood-Schlatter Disease

Osgood-Schlatter disease is a traction apophysitis of the proximal tibial tubercle at the point of patellar tendon insertion (Figure 9-13). It typically occurs during the adolescent growth spurt, is more common among males, and usually presents bilaterally—although it can be unilateral. Osgood-Schlatter disease is most common in sports that require running and jumping, such as basketball, volleyball, and gymnastics. Pain worsens during exercise and is relieved by rest and NSAIDs. The patient presents with anterior knee

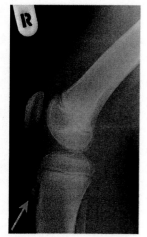

Figure 9-13: Osgood-Schlatter disease

pain that is made worse with activity and improves with rest. Clinically, patients complain of worsening knee pain and point tenderness over the area of the patellar tendon insertion on the tibial tubercle, where a painful "bump" may be palpated. Pain with resisted knee extension or pain with full knee flexion may be present. While unnecessary, radiographic findings may be limited to soft tissue swelling or, in more severe cases, may include evidence of fragmentation of the tibial tubercle.

Osgood-Schlatter disease is usually self-limited and often resolves once the growth plate ossifies. Treat with NSAIDs, ice, and physical therapy (quadriceps, hamstring, and calf stretching). Continuation of play is permissible if the pain is tolerable and there is no limp.

Patellofemoral Syndrome (PFS)

PFS is the most common cause of anterior knee pain in young athletes, particularly females. Symptoms include vague anterior knee pain, especially with prolonged sitting, and patellar pain with squatting, climbing stairs, or physical activities that require bending the knees. The pathophysiology seems to be related to overuse and muscle weakness. In patellofemoral syndrome, the patella does not track straight down the middle but instead rubs against the lateral trochlea, resulting in the patellofemoral

joint becoming inflamed and painful. If the condition progresses, the articular cartilage on the underside of the patella or trochlea softens, causing decay. This syndrome is referred to as **chondromalacia patella**. Diagnosis of PFS or chondromalacia patella is made mostly by history, but certain PE findings can help clarify the diagnosis:

1) Positive patellofemoral compression test (with the leg extended, pain with compression of the patella)
2) Patella facet tenderness (while leg is extended, pain with manipulation of the patella and palpation of the facets)

Imaging studies are not typically necessary. Treat with activity modification, ice, and NSAIDs. Physical therapy for hip and core strengthening, knee sleeves, and orthotics can also be helpful.

Iliotibial Band Syndrome

The iliotibial band passes over the lateral femoral condyle and inserts over the lateral aspect of the proximal tibia just distal to the knee. It can become inflamed as it passes over the lateral femoral condyle secondary to overuse injury. Repeated friction between the iliotibial band and lateral epicondyle causes chronic inflammation and is referred to as iliotibial band syndrome or iliotibial band friction syndrome (ITBFS).

Iliotibial band syndrome is common among long-distance runners, cyclists, and soccer players. Pain, sometimes described as "stinging," is generally reported only during activity and is localized over the lateral femoral epicondyle, just proximal to the lateral knee joint. Pain is often worsened by running on a banked surface (such as an indoor track) as well as excessive uphill and downhill running. With the patient lying on the unaffected side, beginning with the knee flexed at 90° and the hip flexed at 45°, passive extension of the knee to 30° leads to reproducible pain when palpating over the lateral femoral epicondyle. Diagnosis is based on H&P findings. Imaging is usually not necessary.

Symptomatic treatment with rest, NSAIDs, knee sleeve, and icing resolves the pain in most cases. Sometimes there are associated findings that can suggest the need for physical therapy and/or orthotics; these include hamstring and/or iliotibial band tightness, hyperpronated feet, and hip abductor weakness. Injection with corticosteroids can be helpful in refractory cases.

Medial Elbow Apophysitis (Little League Elbow)

Medial elbow apophysitis is inflammation of the growth plate of the medial epicondyle. It occurs in athletes who are skeletally immature (typically 9–14 years of age) and results from the valgus stress placed on the elbow during overhead throwing. Most patients present with medial epicondyle pain with overhead throwing.

On PE, pain can be elicited by palpation of the medial epicondyle and with valgus maneuvers of the elbow. X-rays are often normal but can show widening/fragmentation of the apophysis. Treatment consists of rest from throwing, ice, NSAIDs, and physical therapy for scapular stabilization stretching of wrist flexors and forearm pronators (and reviewing proper throwing mechanics). 2–3 months of rest should be consecutive.

Lateral Epicondylitis (Tennis Elbow)

Lateral epicondylitis is an overuse injury causing inflammation and pain around the lateral epicondyle of the humerus at the origin of the wrist extensors and supinators. It is caused by repetitive motions in which the wrist deviates from a neutral position (e.g., backhand motions). In addition to racket-sport players, this condition can also be found in carpenters, plumbers, painters, and butchers. Pain results from inflammation and microtears of the common extensor origin, in particular the extensor carpi radialis brevis tendon (extensor of the wrist and middle finger).

Examination reveals pain on palpation of the lateral epicondyle. There can also be pain during resisted wrist/finger extension and supination. There is usually no warmth or surrounding erythema on PE. Treat symptomatically with rest, NSAIDs, counterforce strap, and icing. Coaches should also evaluate athletes to correct any stroke technique errors and to check for correct racket grip size.

Osteochondritis Dissecans (OCD)

OCD is a condition in which necrosis of subchondral bone causes a piece of bone to break off into the joint, with resultant pain and mechanical symptoms. It occurs either after a single injury or after repetitive trauma from overuse. OCD most often affects older boys and adolescent males between 8 and 18 years of age. Usual locations are the knee, elbow, and ankle, with the most common site being the nonarticular surface of the lateral aspect of the medial femoral condyle (Figure 9-14). Symptoms include pain that worsens with activity, decreased range of motion of the joint, and joint popping/locking.

On PE, there is pain and swelling over the affected joint; crepitus and decreased joint mobility may also be present. On plain radiographs, the lesion is well demarcated and radiolucent. The subchondral fragment may be intact or there may be evidence of separation. In some patients, the subchondral fragment can become an intraarticular loose body; in these cases, a radiograph may reveal loss of continuity of the articular cartilage. Plain radiographs can be used to make the diagnosis, but MRI is better for staging the lesion as stable or unstable.

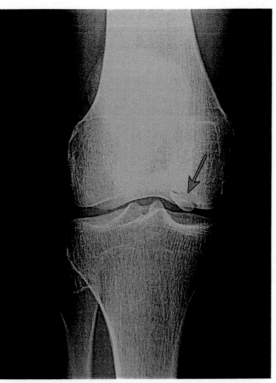

Figure 9-14: Osteochondritis dissecans

If the physis is still open, treatment of OCD is usually conservative and consists of rest, ice, NSAIDs, bracing, and physical therapy until the patient is pain free and there is evidence of healing on repeat radiographs. If there are loose bodies, closed physes, or lack of improvement with conservative therapy after 4–6 months, surgery is often warranted.

Stress Fractures

A stress fracture is a tiny crack in the bone that typically results from overuse in weight-bearing bones of the lower leg and foot. The cause is usually due to an increase in the amount or intensity of activities that require running and jumping. Certain conditions increase the risk for developing stress fractures, including the female athlete triad (see Female Athlete Triad on page 9-16). The presenting symptom is pain with activity that is relieved with rest. Exam reveals bony point tenderness and pain with hop or fulcrum testing. For symptoms lasting > 3–4 weeks, the diagnosis can be made by plain radiographs (Figure 9-15 on page 9-14); early stress fractures are often not visible on x-rays. MRI is sometimes necessary if plain films are negative but symptoms persist.

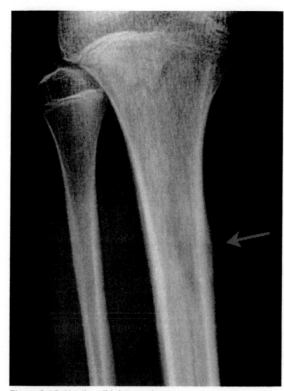

Figure 9-15: Healing tibial stress fracture

For **low-risk stress fractures** (metatarsal, femoral shaft, and most tibial/fibular fractures), treat with rest from the offending activity for 6–8 weeks. Sometimes crutches or a boot might be necessary. For **high-risk stress fractures** (femoral neck, anterior tibia, tarsal navicular, and Jones fractures of the 5th metatarsal), treatment includes strict nonweightbearing. Nonunion requires open reduction internal fixation surgery.

Spondylolysis / Spondylolisthesis

Spondylolysis is a unilateral or bilateral vertebral injury involving a stress fracture of the pars interarticularis. It usually involves the 5th lumbar vertebra but can involve the others. Any activity that causes hyperextension of the spine—such as gymnastics, football, wrestling, and ballet—can put patients at increased risk of spondylolysis.

A related condition is spondylolisthesis, a spontaneous translation subluxation (usually forward) of one vertebra over another, most commonly L5 on S1. Occasionally, spondylolisthesis results in sciatica, but generally it does not affect the nerves of the cauda equina. Do not confuse either of these terms with spondylosis, which refers to osteoarthritis of the spine.

Although many patients are asymptomatic, activity-related lower back pain usually occurs with both conditions. Clinical findings include localized lower back pain, which characteristically increases with lumbar extension, during sporting activities, and with heavy lifting.

Spondylolysis is sometimes evident on plain film, where the fracture in the pars interarticularis is especially visible on the oblique view of a lumbar x-ray; this break appears as a "collar on the neck of a Scottie dog" (Figure 9-16). However, spondylolysis is more accurately identified with single-photon emission computed tomography (SPECT) imaging or MRI with short tau inversion recovery (STIR; a.k.a. short T1 inversion recovery) sequences.

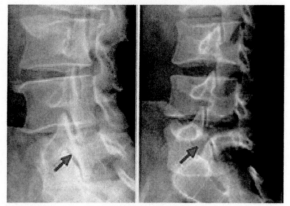

Figure 9-16: Left, normal; right, spondylolysis

Significant slippage with spondylolisthesis is associated with noticeable lordosis on exam and can be seen on lateral radiographs (Figure 9-17).

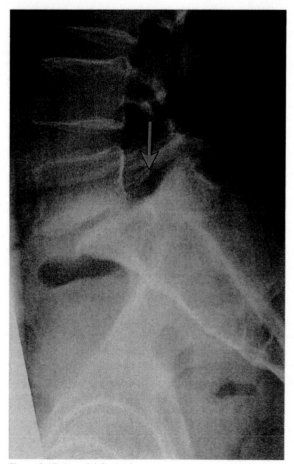

Figure 9-17: Spondylolisthesis

Initial treatment is conservative for both spondylolysis and spondylolisthesis and consists of rest from the offending activity (until the patient is pain free), ice, heat, and NSAIDs. Physical therapy can improve hamstring flexibility and core strength. Occasionally, a back brace is needed if pain persists. Once the patient is free of pain, allow gradual return to activity. If pain does not improve or the patient has worsening slippage, refer for a surgical consultation.

SPRAINS AND STRAINS

Soft tissues can be injured from direct trauma or twisting mechanisms. A sprain is stretching or tearing of a ligament, and a strain is tearing of muscle fibers or tendon. In either situation, the patient presents with pain of the affected area, and diagnosis is typically made clinically by history, exam, and negative x-rays. In the acute phase, treatment consists of rest, ice, compression, NSAIDs, bracing, and elevation. Subsequently, strengthening exercises and a gradual return to activities are important to prevent reinjury. Sometimes physical therapy is needed. In rare cases, surgery is required when sprains are severe or instability is recurrent.

SHOULDER DISLOCATION / SUBLUXATION

The shoulder is the most mobile joint in the body, making it susceptible to dislocation. Because the shoulder moves in many directions, it can dislocate anteriorly, posteriorly, or inferiorly, with anterior dislocation being the most common. Extreme external rotation or a forceful blow that occurs during sports or from a fall are typical causes. Symptoms include severe pain, inability to move the joint, and a visible shoulder deformity. Treat initially with closed reduction, after plain radiograph if possible. Postreduction radiographs confirm successful reduction and rule out fractures. After reduction, a short period in a sling is usually needed with referral to an orthopedist within 1 week. Ice, NSAIDs, rest, and physical therapy are the conservative treatments. Recurrent dislocation occurs in 50–90% of teenagers. Refer for a surgery consult if the condition is recurrent.

KNEE INJURIES

Patellar Dislocation / Subluxation

Patellar dislocation can result from a contact or noncontact injury. Risk factors include quadriceps or hip weakness, a shallow femoral groove, and ligament laxity. Symptoms include pain, swelling, shifting of the patella, and a deformed appearance of the knee. Physical examination shows an effusion and a positive apprehension test (fear with lateral displacement of the patella).

Initial treatment of a patellar dislocation is closed reduction. Postreduction radiographs (i.e., AP, lateral, sunrise views) can show fractures. Further treatment includes ice, NSAIDs, brief immobilization, a patellar stability brace, and physical therapy. Sometimes surgery is required if the knee remains unstable after rehabilitation.

Anterior Cruciate Ligament (ACL) Injury

ACL tears are more common in female athletes than in male athletes and usually occur in sports that require jumping, sudden stops, or quick changes in direction (e.g., basketball, volleyball, soccer, football). A "pop" is often heard or felt, followed by pain, loss of motion, swelling, and inability to bear weight.

The most sensitive and specific test for an ACL tear is the Lachman test, which evaluates the anterior translation of the tibia on the femur. Perform the test with the knee in 30° flexion by stabilizing the femur with one hand placed on the thigh and the other hand placed behind the tibia and pulling the tibia forward. Anterior translation of the tibia, associated with a soft endpoint (i.e., the endpoint of its forward motion feels soft or "mushy"), is indicative of a positive test. A difference of > 2 mm of anterior translation, when compared to the uninvolved knee, is diagnostic of an ACL tear, as is ≥ 10 mm of total anterior translation. Diagnosis is usually made clinically. MRI is useful to show any associated meniscus injury, collateral ligament injuries, and bone bruises.

Surgical reconstruction is required, in most cases, to allow return to cutting-and-jumping sports.

Medial Collateral Ligament (MCL) Injury

MCL tears are common injuries among athletes. Such a tear occurs in contact sports when the lateral knee sustains a blow causing valgus stress or in activities that require significant torque of the leg (e.g., basketball, football, tennis). Symptoms include pain, swelling, and instability over the medial knee.

Most MCL injuries can be diagnosed clinically, with tenderness to palpation over the MCL and valgus laxity with high-grade injuries.

Treatment is usually nonsurgical and includes rest, ice, NSAIDs, bracing, and physical therapy.

Prepatellar Bursitis

Prepatellar bursitis is an inflammation of the bursa that is anterior to the kneecap. It is caused by a fall or direct blow to the anterior knee that can occur in sports such as wrestling and basketball. Symptoms include pain with activity, swelling, and tenderness. Bursal wall thickening can be demonstrated by palpation of a fluid-filled mass anterior to the patella or the patellar tendon.

Diagnosis is usually made clinically. Treatment consists of rest, ice, elevation, and NSAIDs. If there is no improvement with time and treatment, needle aspiration of the bursa is sometimes needed.

MSK / SPORTS MED

Meniscal Tears

Meniscal injuries are common, and tears usually occur due to twisting injuries while the foot is planted. The medial meniscus is injured more frequently than the lateral unless it is a discoid variant. Often symptoms are vague and nonspecific. Isolated meniscal tears usually cause localized pain and moderate effusion, whereas more diffuse pain and significant effusion occur if there is an associated injury to a cruciate ligament or a fracture.

During the duck walk test, the patient is asked to squat down and walk like a duck. A positive test is one that causes reproducible pain in the joint line with this maneuver. Palpation also causes pain in the joint line of the injured meniscus. The McMurray test is repeated passive knee flexion and extension with tibial internal and external rotation. A positive result produces pain and sometimes "clicking." Plain radiographs of the knee are normal, but these injuries are clearly visible on MRI.

Isolated tears without associated ligamentous injury—or a mechanical block to full extension of the knee—often require only symptomatic treatment with ice, compression, NSAIDs, and rest, followed by strengthening exercises and gradual return to activity as tolerated. Surgery is needed in patients who have large tears, persistent effusions, or continuing symptoms that interfere with activity.

ANKLE SPRAIN

Ankle sprain is a common sports-related injury and occurs when the ankle is pushed past its normal range of motion, causing stretching or tearing of the involved ligaments. Lateral ankle sprains, caused by inversion of the foot, occur more frequently than medial sprains. Symptoms include pain, swelling, decreased range of motion, and inability to bear weight.

The diagnosis is typically made by PE with added x-rays in the skeletally immature athlete to rule out fracture. The growth plate of the fibula is the weak link, and a child more often injures the growth plate than the ligaments.

Treat with rest, ice, compression, bracing, NSAIDs, and elevation. Emphasize the importance of strengthening, balancing, and stretching exercises. Formal physical therapy and a lace-up ankle brace can help prevent recurrence.

NUTRITIONAL REQUIREMENTS

PREVIEW | REVIEW
- When is the best time to start hydration for exercise?

Hydration, including water and electrolyte replacement, is very important for the athlete. Hydration helps regulate body temperature and replaces losses that occur during exercise. For physical exertion < 1 hour, recommend 16 ounces of water or sports drink 1 hour prior to exertion and 4–8 ounces every 15–20 minutes during exercise. For physical exertion > 1 hour, use a sports drink to replace electrolytes; begin hydrating 3–4 hours prior to activity and continue throughout and after exercise. Higher environmental temperatures and humidity necessitate more fluids. After exercise, recovery foods that contain both carbohydrates and protein need to be consumed to help replenish muscle glycogen and protein.

FEMALE ATHLETE TRIAD

PREVIEW | REVIEW
- What is the female athlete triad?
- What is the most sensitive piece of history that can be used to detect female athlete triad?

The female athlete triad is a combination of:

- Energy deficiency (typically from disordered eating)
- Menstrual dysfunction
- Low bone mineral density

At-risk patients may have only 1 component of the triad. It is especially common in sports where a low body weight is favorable (e.g., ballet, gymnastics, running, figure skating). A history of **menstrual dysfunction** is the earliest symptom of female athlete triad and should prompt obtaining a detailed history of diet, supplements, exercise, and fractures.

A careful PE (and often labs) is necessary to look for causes of amenorrhea and hypothalamic-pituitary dysfunction (e.g. pregnancy test, thyroid studies). Evaluate bone mineral density with a dual-energy x-ray absorptiometry (DXA) in patients with < 6 menses in 12 months and history of ≥ 2 stress fractures. Initial treatment is nonpharmacologic and aims to increase energy availability by increasing calories and decreasing activity.

Treatment requires a multidisciplinary, team-based approach that includes the pediatrician, coach, athletic trainer, eating disorder specialist, nutritionist, and psychologist.

PERFORMANCE-ENHANCING SUBSTANCES (PESs)

PREVIEW | REVIEW
- Which athletes are most prone to misuse of androgenic steroids?

The highly competitive nature of sports today results in many athletes looking for an advantage over their opponents. Unfortunately, some athletes turn to PESs, known as "doping," and do not take into consideration the risks of using these substances. These supplements include, but are not limited to, anabolic steroids, human growth hormone, erythropoietin, diuretics, creatine, and stimulants.

Androgenic steroids (a.k.a. anabolic-androgenic steroids), especially when taken in conjunction with weight training, increase muscle mass and strength. Athletes requiring short bursts of excessive power (e.g., weight lifters, football linemen) are most apt to misuse these preparations. Side effects include acne, gynecomastia, hirsutism, testicular atrophy, azoospermia, hypertension, aggressive behaviors, depression, and inhibited skeletal growth (from premature closure of growth plates). Cardiac, liver, and kidney toxicities can also occur with the use of anabolic steroids and are associated with cardiac arrhythmias, cardiomyopathy, hepatic adenomas and carcinomas, and even sudden death. Withdrawal symptoms can include insomnia, mood disorders with suicidal ideation and suicide, anorexia, and muscle and joint pain.

Growth hormone is used by athletes to increase muscle mass and decrease body fat, despite lacking evidence of performance benefit. Side effects can result in insulin resistance, cardiomegaly, hypertension, joint pain, muscle weakness, and peripheral edema (especially swelling of the hands).

Erythropoietin is used by athletes to increase the body's number of red blood cells (and thereby oxygen-carrying capacity) in an attempt to enhance performance. It leads to an increased risk of stroke, heart attack, and pulmonary embolism.

Diuretics are used in sports for 2 reasons:

1) To lose water weight quickly in order to compete in a lower weight division (such as in boxing or wrestling)

2) To dilute the urine and make it more difficult to detect other drugs (e.g., steroids) in the urine, thereby masking the use of other banned substances

Adverse effects of diuretics can include dehydration, potassium deficiency, hypotension, and death.

Athletes who take **creatine** do so with the intent of increasing their strength and improving performance during times that require brief bursts of intense performance, such as wrestling, weight lifting, and football. Effects have not been evaluated in children. Intramuscular stores of creatine may be increased by the ingestion of supplemental creatine—often in conjunction with high-glycemic carbohydrates—in an attempt to improve skeletal muscle performance. Creatine can cause muscle cramps and weight gain. The long-term risks are uncertain but can potentially damage the kidneys or liver.

Stimulants suppress the appetite, increase alertness and aggressiveness, and improve endurance. Side effects include insomnia, irritability, dehydration, gastrointestinal upset, cardiac arrhythmias, and heat stroke.

The primary care physician must be prepared to identify risk factors, signs, and symptoms of PES use and to ask appropriate screening questions. It is important to discuss the risks of PES use with young athletes and their parents, as well as present healthy alternatives for achieving their goals. Emphasize that the effects of PESs on the growing adolescent body are not well studied. Involvement of the coach, athletic trainer, and nutritionist is often needed.

THE MEDSTUDY HUB: YOUR GUIDELINES AND REVIEW ARTICLES RESOURCE

For both review articles and current pediatrics practice guidelines, visit the MedStudy Hub at

medstudy.com/hub

The Hub contains the only online consolidated list of all current guidelines focused on pediatrics. Guidelines on the Hub are easy to find, continually updated, and linked to the published source. MedStudy maintains the Hub as a service to the medical community and makes it available to anyone and everyone at no cost to users.

MSK / SPORTS MED

FIGURE SOURCES

Figure 9-1: BruceBlaus, CC0 1.0
Figure 9-2: MedStudy illustration
Figure 9-5: MedStudy illustration
Figure 9-6: MedStudy illustration
Figure 9-7: MedStudy illustration
Figure 9-8: Hellerhoff, CC BY-SA 3.0
Figure 9-9: Keith Boyd, MD
Figure 9-10: Keith Boyd, MD
Figure 9-11: Nevit Dilmen, CC BY-SA 3.0
Figure 9-13: Lucien Monfils, CC BY-SA 3.0
Figure 9-14: Nevit Dilmen, CC BY-SA 3.0
Figure 9-17: Lucien Monfils, CC BY-SA 3.0
The remaining figures are from the MedStudy archive.

Gastroenterology

SECTION EDITOR

William E. Bennett, MD
Associate Professor of Pediatrics
Adjunct Associate Professor of Urology
Indiana University School of Medicine
Pediatric Gastroenterology, Hepatology and Nutrition
Pediatric and Adolescent Comparative Effectiveness Research
Indianapolis, IN

MEDICAL EDITOR
Lynn Bullock, MD
Colorado Springs, CO

Table of Contents

VOMITING..10-1
  OVERVIEW 10-1
  INFANT REGURGITATION..............................10-1
  CYCLIC VOMITING SYNDROME (CVS) 10-2
  RUMINATION SYNDROME.............................10-2
  GASTROPARESIS...10-2

ABDOMINAL PAIN 10-3
  OVERVIEW 10-3
  HISTORY / WORKUP.......................................10-3
  FUNCTIONAL ABDOMINAL PAIN 10-4

ACUTE DIARRHEA..10-5
  HISTORY / WORKUP.......................................10-5
  ORAL REHYDRATION THERAPY.....................10-5
  FEEDING DURING ACUTE DIARRHEA..............10-6
  USE OF ANTIDIARRHEAL AGENTS.................10-6

CHRONIC DIARRHEA..10-6

CONSTIPATION 10-7
  OVERVIEW 10-7
  "THEY STRAIN WHEN THEY POOP"
  SYNDROME...10-7
  FUNCTIONAL CONSTIPATION 10-7
    Etiology and Diagnosis 10-7
    Treatment...10-8

ESOPHAGUS DISORDERS 10-8
  TRACHEOESOPHAGEAL FISTULAS (TEFs)
  AND ESOPHAGEAL ATRESIAS (EAs) 10-8
  ACHALASIA 10-9
  GASTROESOPHAGEAL REFLUX (GER).............10-10
    Reflux in Infants 10-10
    Reflux in Older Children 10-10
    Diagnosis..10-10
    Treatment...10-10
  EOSINOPHILIC ESOPHAGITIS (EoE)..............10-11
  INFECTIONS OF THE ESOPHAGUS 10-11
  CAUSTIC INGESTIONS 10-12
  PILL-INDUCED ESOPHAGITIS.......................10-12
  INGESTION OF FOREIGN BODIES..................10-12
  ESOPHAGEAL PERFORATION.......................10-13
  ESOPHAGEAL VARICES 10-14

STOMACH DISORDERS 10-14
  PYLORIC STENOSIS 10-14
  EROSIVE AND HEMORRHAGIC
  GASTROPATHY...10-14
    Stress Gastropathy....................................10-14
    Prolapse Gastropathy 10-15
    Drug-Induced Gastropathy.......................10-15
  NONEROSIVE GASTROPATHY 10-15
    Occurrence...10-15
    Nonspecific Gastritis 10-15
    Helicobacter pylori Gastritis......................10-15
  PEPTIC ULCER DISEASE (PUD) 10-15
    Diagnosis..10-15
    Treatment...10-16
    Follow-Up..10-16
    PUD Due to Acid Hypersecretory Diseases 10-16

INTESTINAL DISORDERS...................................10-17
  MALROTATION OF THE INTESTINE................10-17
  INTUSSUSCEPTION 10-18
  MECKEL DIVERTICULUM 10-18

CONGENITAL INTESTINAL ATRESIAS 10-19
  Occurrence...10-19
  Duodenal Atresia..10-19
  Jejunoileal Atresia..10-19
  Colonic Atresia...10-19
GASTROINTESTINAL (GI) DUPLICATIONS.........10-19
MECONIUM ILEUS...10-20
CARBOHYDRATE MALABSORPTION 10-20
  Lactose Intolerance 10-20
  Fructose and Sorbitol Malabsorption 10-20
  Sucrase-Isomaltase Deficiency 10-21
  Secondary Carbohydrate Malabsorption........10-21
CONGENITAL TRANSPORT DEFECTS 10-21
  Disorders of Fat Transport 10-21
  Amino Acid Transport Defects 10-21
  Zinc Deficiency 10-21
SHORT BOWEL SYNDROME...........................10-22
SUPERIOR MESENTERIC ARTERY (SMA)
  SYNDROME..10-22
GLUTEN-SENSITIVE ENTEROPATHY
  (CELIAC DISEASE)..10-23
TROPICAL SPRUE...10-24
WHIPPLE DISEASE 10-24
APPENDICITIS...10-24
  Treatment...10-25
NEUTROPENIC ENTEROCOLITIS 10-25

INFLAMMATORY BOWEL DISEASE (IBD) 10-25
  OVERVIEW 10-25
  ULCERATIVE COLITIS (UC)............................10-26
    Presentation..10-27
    Diagnosis..10-27
    Colon Cancer...10-27
  CROHN DISEASE..10-27
    Presentation..10-27
    Diagnosis..10-28
    Colon Cancer...10-28
  TREATMENT OF IBD.......................................10-28

COLONIC POLYPS AND TUMORS.....................10-29
  OVERVIEW 10-29
  JUVENILE POLYPS AND JUVENILE POLYPOSIS..10-29
  PEUTZ-JEGHERS SYNDROME 10-29
  SYNDROMES LINKED TO PTEN GENE
  MUTATIONS 10-30
    PTEN Hamartoma Tumor Syndrome (PHTS) 10-30
    Bannayan-Riley-Ruvalcaba Syndrome 10-30
    Cowden Syndrome.....................................10-30
  PROTEUS SYNDROME 10-30
  FAMILIAL ADENOMATOUS POLYPOSIS 10-30
    Incidence..10-30
    Gardner Syndrome....................................10-30

CONGENITAL VENTRAL ABDOMINAL WALL
DEFECTS 10-31
  OCCURRENCE...10-31
  OMPHALOCELE..10-31
  GASTROSCHISIS 10-31

ANORECTAL DISORDERS 10-32
  OCCURRENCE...10-32
  MALE ANORECTAL DISORDERS 10-32
    Perineal Fistula...10-32
    Rectourethral Fistula 10-32
    Rectovesical Fistula....................................10-32

FEMALE ANORECTAL DISORDERS..................10-32
    Perineal Fistula.......................................10-32
    Vestibular Fistula 10-32
    Persistent Cloaca 10-32
ANORECTAL DISORDERS PRESENTING
    SIMILARLY IN BOTH SEXES 10-32
    Imperforate Anus (Anal Atresia) without
        Fistula 10-32
    Rectal Atresia 10-33
    Rectal Prolapse 10-33
    Hemorrhoids 10-33
    Anal Fissures 10-33
    Perianal Itching 10-33

HIRSCHSPRUNG DISEASE...........................10-34
    OCCURRENCE..10-34
    PATHOGENESIS 10-34
    PRESENTATION 10-34
    DIAGNOSIS..10-35
    TREATMENT 10-35

DISORDERS OF THE EXOCRINE PANCREAS 10-35
    NOTE 10-35
    CYSTIC FIBROSIS (CF)...............................10-35
    SHWACHMAN-DIAMOND SYNDROME 10-35
    ACUTE PANCREATITIS................................10-36
    Causes...10-36
    Clinical Manifestations............................10-36
    Diagnosis...10-36
    Treatment 10-36
    CHRONIC PANCREATITIS............................10-37

DISEASES OF THE LIVER AND BILIARY TREE 10-37
    JAUNDICE BEYOND NEONATAL PERIOD 10-37
    CONGENITAL DISORDERS OF LIVER
        STRUCTURE..10-37
    Liver Location Abnormalities 10-37
    Congenital Anomalies of the Portal Vein 10-38
    CONGENITAL ANOMALIES OF THE
        BILIARY TREE 10-38
    Extrahepatic Biliary Atresia 10-38
    Choledochal Cysts 10-38
    Structural Anomalies of the Gallbladder.........10-38
    Congenital Hepatic Fibrosis........................10-38
    Caroli Disease..10-38
    Alagille Syndrome 10-39
    LIVER TRAUMA..10-39
    VIRAL HEPATITIS......................................10-39
    Hepatitis A..10-40
    Hepatitis B..10-40
    Hepatitis C..10-42
    Hepatitis D..10-43
    Hepatitis E..10-43
    Hepatitis G..10-43
    Differential Diagnosis 10-44
    METABOLIC LIVER DISEASES.......................10-44
    Glucuronosyltransferase Defects.................10-44
    Dubin-Johnson Syndrome 10-45
    α_1-Antitrypsin Deficiency....................10-45
    Wilson Disease 10-45
    Hemochromatosis...................................10-46
    Progressive Familial Intrahepatic
        Cholestasis (PFIC)..................................10-46
    Reye Syndrome 10-47
    DRUG-INDUCED LIVER INJURY (DILI) 10-47

AUTOIMMUNE HEPATOBILIARY DISEASE 10-47
    Autoimmune Hepatitis (AIH)........................10-47
    Primary Sclerosing Cholangitis 10-48
BILIARY ATRESIA..10-48
CHOLELITHIASIS...10-49
ACUTE CHOLECYSTITIS................................10-49
HYDROPS OF THE GALLBLADDER..................10-50
TUMORS OF THE LIVER AND BILIARY TREE......10-50

THE MEDSTUDY HUB: YOUR GUIDELINES
    AND REVIEW ARTICLES RESOURCE.................10-50

FIGURE SOURCES 10-51

VOMITING

PREVIEW | REVIEW

- What disorders are characterized by vomiting of undigested food?
- What does bilious vomiting suggest?
- What is the initial treatment for gastroesophageal reflux in infants?
- What is cyclic vomiting syndrome?

OVERVIEW

Vomiting is a coordinated motor response of the gastrointestinal (GI) tract, abdominal muscles, and thoracic muscles, resulting in the forceful expulsion of stomach contents. Nausea often precedes retching, which typically precedes emesis.

Vomiting is controlled by 2 separate centers in the brain:

1) The vomiting center (neural)

2) The chemoreceptor trigger zone (chemical)

The vomiting center is located in the nucleus solitarius and a series of nuclei in the medulla of the brainstem. Stimuli to these areas can come from cortical afferents (e.g., migraine, increased intracranial pressure), vestibular afferents (e.g., dizziness), and vagal afferents such as in the posterior pharynx (i.e., gagging) and the GI tract (i.e., distention). Also, the chemoreceptor trigger zone, located in the floor of the 4th ventricle, receives stimuli from drugs, toxins, and metabolic products (e.g., acidemia, ketonemia, hyperammonemia).

Vomiting, like most GI problems, can be divided into **organic** diagnoses and **functional** diagnoses. We use an international standard to diagnose functional GI problems, called the Rome criteria, which was last updated in 2016 (Rome IV). If a patient meets criteria for these diagnoses, you usually do not need to pursue further workup. Functional GI diagnoses represent > 50% of all outpatient visits in pediatric gastroenterology. Examples of functional disorders that cause vomiting include infant regurgitation, cyclic vomiting syndrome, rumination syndrome, and gastroparesis.

Some associations can be helpful in suggesting the possible etiology:

- Red blood or "coffee grounds" in vomitus: upper GI bleed
- Undigested food in vomitus: achalasia, delayed gastric emptying, rumination
- Projectile emesis: pyloric stenosis, antral web
- Bilious vomiting: GI obstruction beyond the duodenum (e.g., malrotation)
- Fever: gastroenteritis or systemic infection
- Tense fontanelle in infants or headache/neurologic symptoms in an older child: increased intracranial pressure due to hydrocephalus, meningitis, or tumor
- Adolescent: pregnancy, migraine, bulimia, drugs (especially chronic heavy marijuana use)
- Vomiting seconds to minutes after eating: rumination syndrome

In cases of chronic vomiting, proceed with a careful history and physical and then a stepwise evaluation that can include abdominal ultrasound, upper GI contrast x-rays, or endoscopy. In one study of vomiting patterns, children with vomiting for over a month were evaluated, and a histologic diagnosis was made in ~ 60% of the cases. The main causes were esophagitis and gastritis (including *Helicobacter*-induced vomiting). Less commonly found (< 5%) were duodenitis and giardiasis. Endoscopy is the best test for diagnosis of chronic vomiting. Remember to think about GI disorders like Crohn disease, which can be present in multiple areas of the GI tract.

However, most patients have a functional cause for vomiting, which is more common in adolescents, children with significant social stressors, and those with psychiatric diagnoses (e.g., anxiety, depression).

INFANT REGURGITATION

Infant regurgitation (a.k.a. gastroesophageal reflux [GER]) is a common problem and a frequent topic for the general pediatrician. Half of infants 0–3 months of age vomit at least once daily, and 2/3 of infants 4–6 months of age do. This decreases rapidly after 8 months of age. Most infants with daily vomiting outgrow this problem by 2 years of age and do not require special treatment.

The 2016 Rome IV criteria define infant regurgitation as follows:

1) In a child 3 weeks to 12 months of age, who regurgitates ≥ 2 times per day for ≥ 3 weeks, and

2) None of the following:
- Retching—think upper airway obstruction or immature swallowing.
- Hematemesis—think malrotation with volvulus.
- Aspiration or apnea—think immature swallowing or neurologic problems preventing airway defense.
- Failure to thrive—think inadequate caloric intake or underlying metabolic/genetic disorder.
- Swallowing dysfunction—think developmental or genetic disorders.
- Abnormal posturing—think neurologic disorders.

Diagnosis is typically made by history and physical exam. In uncomplicated GER, with no signs suggesting underlying pathology, no further work up is needed.

Because most infantile GER is normal, guide initial therapy toward parental reassurance. Management includes providing small meals and keeping the infant upright for 20–30 minutes following a meal. Do not give medications to infants with uncomplicated GER. For those parents who are upset or having difficulty dealing with the vomiting child, suggest thickening formula with rice cereal, using 1–2 tablespoons per ounce of formula. This often requires

GASTROENTEROLOGY

cutting the bottle nipple, which can worsen the infant's cough or feeding problems. The 2018 North American Society for Pediatric Gastroenterology, Hepatology and Nutrition (NASPGHAN) guidelines also suggest avoiding positional treatment in infants (prone or side sleeping or elevating the head). Always ask about the infant's sleep position and discourage prone sleeping because of the definite increased risk of SIDS in babies who sleep in the prone position.

For information about pathologic disease, see Gastroesophageal Reflux (GER) on page 10-10.

CYCLIC VOMITING SYNDROME (CVS)

CVS occurs with paroxysms of vomiting followed by symptom-free periods. These children develop intense vomiting episodes that last from hours to days, with vomiting often occurring many times per hour. The "well spells" last from several weeks to many months between episodes. Median age of onset is ~ 5 years of age. There is a strong association with a family history of migraine headaches and many patients progress from CVS to migraine headaches by adolescence. The underlying mechanism is unknown, but thought to be due to dysfunction of the vasovagal axis, so similar disorders (such as migraines and vasovagal syncope) can occur at the same time and are often treated in similar ways.

The 2016 Rome IV criteria define CVS as follows:

1) ≥ 2 periods of unremitting paroxysmal vomiting with or without retching, lasting hours to days, within a 6-month period
2) Episodes are stereotypical in each patient
3) Episodes are separated by weeks to months with return to baseline health between episodes of vomiting

Think about the diagnosis when the history is characteristic and the physical examination is normal.

The 2008 NASPGHAN pediatric guidelines for CVS suggest ordering a CMP and UGI series on all patients with episodic vomiting. However, if they have characteristic symptoms of CVS, and do not have associated symptoms (see below), then no further workup is necessary.

The diagnosis of CVS is made using the 2016 Rome IV criteria. However, if other symptoms are present, further testing is needed to exclude other diagnoses:

- Laboratory testing including a CBC, CMP, inflammatory markers, and a tissue transglutaminase (tTG) IgA antibody to test for celiac disease if weight loss or abdominal pain also occur
- Metabolic workup specific for underlying inborn errors of metabolism (even if history is unremarkable, because mild cases can present late or atypically): ammonia, lactate +/– blood and urine ketones, plasma amino acids, plasma acylcarnitine, urine organic acid profiles
- Upper GI contrast study with small bowel series (to rule out gut malrotation)

- Electroencephalogram (to rule out seizures)
- Consider brain imaging if there is an abnormal neurologic examination, severe altered mental status, or elevated intracranial pressure.
- Consider esophagogastroduodenoscopy/ultrasound/ serum amylase and lipase if hematemesis or severe abdominal pain is present.

Treatment for cyclic vomiting can be difficult and includes avoidance of triggers plus lifestyle changes. Ondansetron is often used to abort the acute episode, as is rapid rehydration with either oral rehydration or IV fluids (this "turns off" the vasovagal signal that causes the episodes). For prophylaxis, most practitioners prescribe cyproheptadine, propranolol, or amitriptyline. Cyproheptadine is the 1st choice for children ≤ 5 years of age. Most patients have spontaneous resolution of cyclic vomiting with age.

RUMINATION SYNDROME

Many patients have episodes of vomiting that occur immediately after eating. This is often semipurposeful and small in volume, often within seconds or minutes of initiating a meal. Consider rumination for an adolescent patient who leaves the table multiple times during dinner to "throw up" mouthfuls of food in the bathroom. Many patients have comorbid anxiety or depression. It also occurs in patients with intellectual disabilities. Treatment is supportive, relying on psychotherapy and cognitive behavioral therapy.

The 2016 Rome IV criteria define rumination syndrome as follows:

1) Repeated regurgitation and rechewing or expulsion of food that occurs soon after a meal
2) Not preceded by retching
3) After appropriate medical evaluation, another disorder cannot explain the symptoms. Specifically, an eating disorder must be ruled out.

GASTROPARESIS

Gastroparesis is defined as delayed gastric emptying in the absence of mechanical obstruction. The most common cause of gastroparesis in children is **postinfectious gastroparesis**, which usually occurs after an episode of viral gastroenteritis. The infectious agent causes a neuropathy of the autonomic ganglia either directly or indirectly via the inflammatory response. Other causes of gastroparesis in children include gastric hypomotility (in children with static encephalopathy, for instance) and Type I diabetes.

Symptoms include nausea, vomiting, abdominal pain, early satiety, abdominal distention, and (if caloric intake is decreased because of these symptoms) weight loss. The classic presentation that you will see in a board question is vomiting undigested food in the middle of the night, many hours after the meal. It is helpful to rule out mechanical obstruction using an upper GI series. Gastric acid scintigraphy (a gastric emptying study) is the gold standard for diagnosing gastroparesis and consists of measuring the rate of gastric emptying of a radiolabeled meal over a defined period of time. Postinfectious gastroparesis is self-limited and usually resolves within 1–3 months, although sometimes it takes up to 24 months. In postinfectious gastroparesis that does not resolve quickly, or in children with diabetic gastroparesis, erythromycin ethylsuccinate is the 1st line therapy. Other options include metoclopramide, although its use should be limited due to the potential for serious neurologic side effects (e.g., dystonia).

ABDOMINAL PAIN

PREVIEW | REVIEW

- The finding of "currant jelly" stool suggests what possible diagnosis?
- What clues suggest an organic cause for abdominal pain that would require a targeted workup?
- True or false? Abdominal pain that is nonorganic in nature presents with growth and development problems in the child.
- What is the most common cause of abdominal pain in children?
- What clues are useful in diagnosing functional abdominal pain?

OVERVIEW

Acute abdominal pain is a common complaint in children. However, < 5% who present to emergency departments require admission for observation or surgery. It can be very difficult to differentiate the emergent cases from the nonemergent. Careful history and serial physical examinations are usually the most important strategy for delineating the etiology. Supplement your investigation with laboratory and diagnostic studies, as appropriate, to confirm normalcy.

HISTORY / WORKUP

Some clues in the history and presentation can be helpful in diagnosing acute abdominal pain:

- Functional abdominal pain—coinciding with psychosocial stress
- Presenting with the acute onset of pain as the 1st symptom—intussusception, midgut volvulus, ovarian or testicular torsion
- Trauma—perforated viscus, hemorrhage, musculoskeletal injury, pancreatitis
- Bilious vomiting—intussusception, malrotation with volvulus, incarcerated hernia, adhesions
- Peritoneal signs—appendicitis, cholecystitis, pelvic inflammatory disease (PID)
- Adolescent female—PID, pregnancy, ectopic pregnancy, ovulatory pain (mittelschmerz)
- "Currant jelly" stool—intussusception

- Melena (dark, tarry, pungent stools)—upper GI bleed
- Nonbilious vomiting and diarrhea—gastroenteritis
- RUQ pain after meals, with or without vomiting (biliary colic)—cholecystitis, biliary obstruction, sphincter Oddi dysfunction

A nonspecific history can occur with many of the above conditions (e.g., appendicitis, cholecystitis) if the patient presents at an early stage. Also with a nonspecific history, consider gastroenteritis, toxins (e.g., food poisoning), urinary tract infection (UTI), and even pneumonia (although cough is usually in the history).

Initial laboratory studies for a child with acute abdominal pain include a CBC, U/A, and, for the adolescent female, pregnancy test. These are relatively nonspecific (well, except for the pregnancy test!). Perform ultrasound and/or CT scan in patients who do not improve over several hours and who do not have defining peritoneal signs. Avoid indiscriminate and routine use of imaging.

If the pain is postprandial, check for biliary-pancreatic disease (i.e., bilirubin, γ-glutamyl transferase [GGT], amylase, lipase; fasting abdominal ultrasound). If the history and physical examination are classic for appendicitis, refer immediately to surgery. You can rule out pneumonia or pneumothorax with chest x-ray.

You do not need to order a wide spectrum of tests to confirm your clinical suspicions. What are the clues for an organic cause of acute abdominal pain that indicate the need for a targeted workup? Target the workup as follows if a patient has abdominal pain and:

- **Vomiting**—suspect upper GI problems like gastritis, duodenitis, or esophagitis, as well as anatomic disorders such as malrotation. If brief (a few days), viral gastroenteritis is a very common cause. An upper GI series can confirm normal anatomy. An upper endoscopy is the only way to reliably diagnose any upper GI "-itis." If pain occurs with eating, suspect pancreatitis (order an amylase and lipase) or biliary disease, such as cholecystitis (order an ultrasound).
- **Weight loss**—think chronic inflammatory conditions such as celiac disease (order a tTG IgA antibody) and Crohn disease (look for anemia, hypoalbuminemia, and guaiac-positive stools).
- **Hematochezia**—think of chronic inflammation such as IBD (look for anemia and check a stool guaiac). If brief, have a high suspicion for bacterial colitis (order a stool enteric culture and *Clostridioides difficile* [formerly *Clostridium difficile*] toxin assay).
- **Diarrhea**—the most common cause is still IBS, but suspect IBD. Celiac disease (order an anti-tTG IgA and a total IgA) and giardiasis (order a stool *Giardia* antigen) are also common causes of pain with diarrhea.
- **Nighttime awakening from pain**—classic test question! Suspect *Helicobacter pylori* infection.
- **Fever, rash, oral ulcers, or joint pain**—suspect IBD or celiac disease.
- **Melena**—suspect an upper GI bleed, such as bleeding peptic ulcer or gastritis. Most patients need upper endoscopy.

FUNCTIONAL ABDOMINAL PAIN

Children often complain of abdominal pain, with a peak incidence at ~ 7–10 years of age. Up to 35% of children, at some point in time, report abdominal pain lasting ≥ 2 weeks. It is more common in girls than boys.

Recurrent abdominal pain is defined by ≥ 3 episodes of pain during the course of at least 3 months that interferes with activities of daily living. Pain may be described as dull, crampy, or sharp in character. Pain can occur in any location of the abdomen, but most commonly involves the periumbilical area. It is not associated with eating or defecation. Although the pain often affects daily living, growth and development are normal. The frequency and duration of functional abdominal pain are increased by environmental stressors (e.g., school, sports, social interactions, family), temperament of the child (e.g., anxious, a perfectionist, lack of coping skills, disordered peer relationships), and secondary gain (e.g., extra attention, getting out of school early).

Approximately 5% of children with recurrent abdominal pain have an organic etiology such as cholelithiasis, inflammatory bowel disease (IBD), peptic ulcer disease (PUD), PID, celiac disease, pregnancy, UTI, intestinal parasite (giardiasis), or lactase deficiency. Signs and symptoms of concern that suggest an organic etiology include:

- Pain that awakens the child at night
- Unexplained intermittent fever
- Weight loss or lack of weight gain
- Deceleration of linear growth
- Heme-positive and/or chronically loose stools
- Bilious emesis or protracted vomiting
- Localized right upper or lower quadrant tenderness
- Hepatosplenomegaly
- Costovertebral angle tenderness
- Oral ulcers
- Perianal abnormalities

A complete physical examination with emphasis on the oral, abdominal, rectal, pelvic, and genitourinary regions is an essential part of the evaluation. Obtain laboratory and radiographic studies only to confirm or exclude possible organic conditions suggested by history and findings on physical examination.

Functional abdominal pain, also called pain-predominant functional gastrointestinal disorder (FGID), is the most common cause of abdominal pain in children and one of the most common presenting complaints seen by pediatricians. School absenteeism is a major problem in nearly 1/3 of children with functional abdominal pain. Recognizing the difference between an organic disorder requiring intervention and a functional disorder requiring reassurance can be challenging, but it is an essential skill for any practitioner.

Note: There are typically some exam questions that require recognizing that a child has a benign disorder, so do not be afraid to put "reassurance" for answers when it seems appropriate.

Let us start by defining the common functional causes of pediatric abdominal pain, because these are by far the most common causes of both acute and chronic abdominal pain in children.

The 2016 Rome IV criteria specify 4 disorders with abdominal pain as the primary symptom:

1) **Functional abdominal pain syndrome** is most often seen in school-aged children. Pain is typically periumbilical. Growth is normal and appetite is usually not affected. Symptoms tend to get better on the weekends and during vacations and worse in the morning before school or in the evening before bed. Ask about social stressors (e.g., recent divorce, trouble at school). Treat with reassurance. Workup is usually unnecessary, and medications are not effective. This disorder was previously referred to as "chronic recurrent abdominal pain syndrome." (What a great acronym!)

2) **Functional dyspepsia** is the medical term for "indigestion." Pain is typically in the midepigastric area and strongly correlates with meals. Most patients are school age or adolescents. Some children describe a burning sensation. There should not be associated symptoms such as vomiting. (If there is vomiting, consider an organic disorder such as peptic ulcer, gastritis, or esophagitis.) As many as 50% of patients respond to acid suppression, although there is no acid-related damage. Again, growth is normal in these patients.

3) **Irritable bowel syndrome** (IBS) is more common in adolescents. Pain is typically in the lower abdomen or can be multifocal. The hallmarks of IBS are pain that improves with defecation and frequent changes in stool caliber or frequency. If a patient has constipation one day, normal stools another day, and loose stools another, then it is IBS. IBS has 4 subtypes, which categorize patients as having diarrhea, constipation, diarrhea and constipation, or having only pain. Other symptoms include bloating, urinary urgency, and incomplete bowel evacuation. Growth and appetite are normal. Anxiety, depression, and social stressors can greatly influence symptoms. (Studying for exams is a likely stressor!) Treatments and treatment responses vary widely. Treatments include antispasmodic medications, such as hyoscyamine and dicyclomine; SSRIs; a high-fiber diet; probiotics or elimination of certain foods (e.g., spicy foods, FODMAPs [fermentable oligo-, di-, and monosaccharides and polyols]); acupuncture; and caffeine avoidance, to name a few. Nonpharmacologic interventions, such as exercise and psychotherapy, have been shown to be some of the most effective treatments. Do not confuse IBS with IBD! Irritable bowel syndrome (IBS) is a chronic, benign, functional disorder that causes no long-term damage and can be managed supportively. Inflammatory bowel disease (IBD) is much more severe and is characterized by chronic inflammatory changes that can cause anemia, weight loss, and malnutrition! See more on IBD under Inflammatory Bowel Disease (IBD) on page 10-25.

4) **Abdominal migraine** is a form of migraine seen mainly in children from 2 to 10 years of age in which the abdominal pain, ranging from dull to severe, is poorly localized. The pain is accompanied by ≥ 2 of the following: loss of appetite, nausea, vomiting, and pallor. Etiology is uncertain, but the majority of these kids have a family history for migraines. The child is normal in between attacks. Diagnosis is clinical. Treatment consists of hydration, good sleep habits, NSAIDs, antinausea medication, and the triptans. For frequent attacks, consider preventive therapies used for other forms of migraines. Abdominal attacks in most of these patients resolve by early adolescence; however, most go on to develop migraine headaches later in life.

ACUTE DIARRHEA

PREVIEW | REVIEW

- What is the most common cause of diarrhea in children?
- What are the indications for intravenous therapy in a child with diarrhea?
- Do children with resolving diarrhea require special diets?

HISTORY / WORKUP

Acute diarrhea is defined as loose or watery stools lasting < 14 days. Almost all diarrhea in children is due to an infectious agent, most commonly viruses such as norovirus, astrovirus, and rotavirus. Rotavirus was previously the most common cause, but with the current widespread use of the vaccine, it is far less common in developed countries. For most cases of acute diarrhea, aim therapy at rehydration and providing nutritional needs.

In most instances of diarrhea, you do not need to search for an etiologic agent because most are self-limited. Certain findings, though, prompt further evaluation:

- Infants < 2 months of age (but remember that many infants have watery/loose stools, which is normal)
- Gross blood in the stool
- Toxic-appearing child
- Immunocompromised child
- Diarrhea developing during hospitalization or following a course of antibiotics

Stool cultures were the mainstay of diagnosis for many years, but since these fail to find an etiology in the majority of cases (even if the bacteria is present), the 2016 AGA guidelines on infectious diarrhea suggest using culture-independent methods (enzyme-linked immunosorbent assay [ELISA], PCR) if available. The newer PCR-based methods can assess for many bacterial infections at once (the "GI pathogen panel" or "multipathogen molecular panel") and were previously reserved for immunocompromised or medically fragile patients to find a diagnosis quickly but are now more widely available. If you do get a positive result on a multipathogen panel, you should do a confirmatory culture for that antigen.

If these molecular panels are not available or don't cover your suspicions, then stool studies can include:

- Rotavirus ELISA
- If WBCs are in the stool, stool cultures for bacteria including
  ◦ *Salmonella*
  ◦ *Shigella*
  ◦ *Campylobacter*
  ◦ *Yersinia*
  ◦ *Escherichia coli* (including O157:H7)
  ◦ Aeromonas
- *Clostridioides difficile* (formerly *Clostridium difficile*) toxin
- *Giardia* ELISA
- *Cryptosporidium* ELISA

A complete ova and parasite microscopic exam is usually not done for acute diarrhea. It is reserved for diarrhea lasting > 7 days when all other antigen tests are negative.

Note: *C. difficile* toxin assays in children < 1 year of age are not reliable because enterocytes in infants have not yet developed the receptor for the toxin.

Some associations that can give clues to the infectious etiologic agent are:

- Recent travel—toxigenic *E. coli* (traveler's diarrhea) or *Giardia*
- Exposure to pet reptiles—*Salmonella*
- Fever and high WBC count—*Shigella*
- Hemolytic uremic syndrome—*E. coli* O157:H7, also known as enterohemorrhagic *E. coli*
- Swimming in lakes or drinking well water—*Giardia*
- Consumption of pork intestine (chitterlings)—*Yersinia*
- Recent antibiotic use—*C. difficile*

See the Infectious Disease section for more information.

ORAL REHYDRATION THERAPY

Treat acute diarrhea with oral rehydration therapy (e.g., Pedialyte). There are many brands and they are formulated to be iso- or hypotonic with appropriate amounts of electrolytes. Infants < 2 months of age require special care because of the risk of rapid development of dehydration, as well as the many noninfectious etiologies that appear in this age group. All oral rehydration solutions contain both glucose and sodium. The glucose is present to facilitate sodium-glucose co-transport via SGLT-1.

Note: Do not recommend using clear liquids since most "clear" liquids (juices, soft drinks, and most sports drinks) are hypertonic and have excess glucose or fructose. These often result in ongoing diarrhea-like stools even after the illness has resolved, and do not provide sufficient acute rehydration.

GASTROENTEROLOGY

In patients with evidence of hypovolemic shock, altered mental status, or intestinal obstruction such as ileus, IV rehydration is likely needed.

Note: Vomiting is not a contraindication to using oral rehydration therapy and does not reduce its success rate. The recommended course with these patients is a clinical trial of oral rehydration. The goal of rehydration is not the relief of symptoms, but support of intravascular volume.

FEEDING DURING ACUTE DIARRHEA

After achieving rehydration (usually 12–24 hours or less), resume the child's age-appropriate regular diet. Breastfed infants can resume breastfeeding, and infants on solid foods and children can resume their normal diets. Recommend feeding small amounts of the child's regular diet at frequent intervals. Avoid high-sugar foods, such as juices, which can result in osmotic diarrhea. The traditional bland **BRAT** (bananas, rice, applesauce, toast) diet results in a longer recovery time and has never been validated in a clinical trial. It contains a large amount of sugar and other carbohydrates and is specifically discouraged by 2004 American Academy of Pediatrics (AAP) guidelines for managing acute gastroenteritis.

Children who are on cow's milk or commercial milk formulas can resume their diets, although a small number develop acidosis or recurrent diarrhea. If diarrhea persists 2 weeks, withhold milk/formula for 1–2 days, temporarily using a lactose-free formula instead. There is a higher incidence of transient lactose intolerance in very young infants.

USE OF ANTIDIARRHEAL AGENTS

Antidiarrheal agents are widely available over the counter (OTC) and by prescription. The most commonly used agents are known as **adsorbents** and include magnesium aluminum silicates, bulk-forming agents, and bile acid–binding resin. Magnesium aluminum silicates are found in OTC brands (e.g., Donnagel, Kaopectate) as well as generic products. They mainly alter stool consistency and do not affect absolute fecal water loss, but they do give the illusion that the diarrhea is better. Bulk-forming agents (e.g., methylcellulose, psyllium seed, soy fiber) also improve stool consistency. Although the stools appear more normal, use of these adsorbents does not shorten the length of the infection.

Antimotility drugs are not recommended in children. Generally, these are opiates, such as codeine, diphenoxylate, or loperamide. They do not shorten the course of illness and can be quite dangerous in children; thus, do not use routinely. Opiates can induce ileus and worsen underlying bacterial infections.

Another available antidiarrheal is **probiotic** treatment. These are microorganisms that can be taken to modulate diarrhea due to bacterial or viral etiologies. *Saccharomyces boulardii* is a nonpathogenic yeast that is helpful in reducing the recurrence rate of *Clostridioides difficile* diarrhea.

(For more on diagnosing and treating *C. difficile*, see the Infectious Disease section.) Studies have shown that *Lactobacillus rhamnosus GG* lessens the severity of rotavirus infection.

Antisecretory agents, including somatostatin and octreotide, act by stimulating sodium and chloride absorption and inhibiting chloride secretion.

Additionally, a special type of agent is **bismuth subsalicylate**. Bismuth has both antimicrobial and antisecretory properties; it also contains magnesium aluminum silicate, which is an adsorbent. Warn parents that this agent results in black stools. Also, the bismuth can be radiopaque, so if you see flecks of white on a patient's abdominal x-ray, ask about recent OTC medications. Children and adolescents who are recovering from a flulike illness or varicella should not use bismuth subsalicylate due to the association with Reye syndrome (all salicylates in children can do this!).

Finally, the 2016 ACG guidelines do not recommend empiric use of antibiotics for suspected bacterial GI infections, because the likelihood of side effects outweighs the small benefit in reduction of disease duration. In patients who have a known bacterial cause, or in patients who are immunocompromised or have a chronic GI infection (IBD, CF, liver disease), many experts recommend antibiotic therapy.

CHRONIC DIARRHEA

PREVIEW | REVIEW

- When is diarrhea considered chronic?
- What is the most common cause of chronic diarrhea in older children and adolescents?
- By what age does a patient with functional diarrhea (toddler's diarrhea) typically obtain a normal stool pattern?

Diarrhea is considered chronic when loose or watery stools occur ≥ 3×/day for > 14 days. In developing countries, the main causes are infections and malnutrition (often both). Because there are many etiologies for chronic diarrhea, the discussion here is limited to some common causes in developed countries.

Irritable bowel syndrome (IBS) is the most common cause of diarrhea in older children and adolescents. Patients tend to have a variable number of loose bowel movements, especially after eating. This disorder is heavily influenced by stress and diet (recommend the low FODMAP [short-chain carbohydrate] diet).

Functional diarrhea (a.k.a. toddler's diarrhea) occurs in otherwise healthy infants or toddlers who have ≥ 3 loose stools per day without a specific cause. There is no pain with the passage of stool. In some patients who have a carbohydrate intake with high osmotic load (e.g., prune juice, apple juice), improvement occurs with reduction of these carbohydrates. Most children obtain a normal stool pattern by 4 years of age.

Postenteritis syndrome occurs in a small number of cases of otherwise healthy children following an infectious gastroenteritis. The offending agent causes mucosal damage to the small intestines, resulting in chronic diarrhea. Probiotic treatment can be helpful for recovery of the mucosa. In infants, this can be particularly severe.

Carbohydrate malabsorption syndromes can be the cause of chronic diarrhea. (See Carbohydrate Malabsorption on page 10-20.)

Celiac disease often presents with chronic diarrhea due to small bowel inflammation and malabsorption from villous blunting. (See Gluten-Sensitive Enteropathy (Celiac Disease) on page 10-23.)

Inflammatory bowel disease presents with a gradual onset of chronic diarrhea, especially if the colon is involved. (See Ulcerative Colitis (UC) on page 10-26 and Crohn Disease on page 10-27.)

Cystic fibrosis causes pancreatic exocrine insufficiency resulting in fat malabsorption and chronic fatty diarrhea. (See the Pulmonary Medicine section.)

Giardia is the most common parasite to cause chronic diarrhea in the U.S. Other parasitic causes are *Cryptosporidium, Cyclospora, Entamoeba histolytica,* and microsporidia. A complete ova and parasite microscopic exam is usually ordered if the multipathogen panel and other antigens tests are negative. (See the Infectious Disease section.)

CONSTIPATION

PREVIEW | REVIEW

- Is it rare for a breastfed infant to pass a stool less often than once every 5 days?
- What is the treatment for infant dyschezia?
- What is the most common cause of constipation in children?

OVERVIEW

Constipation is a symptom and not a disease. Only a very small minority of children who present with constipation have an organic or anatomic cause. The majority of constipation cases are due to a functional or behavioral problem.

Constipation has no standardized definition and varies from person to person. Some breastfed infants pass a stool only once every 5–10 days; in the absence of other signs or symptoms, they do not need treatment. Some older children pass a stool only every 3–4 days; they do not have any other symptoms, and this pattern often continues into adulthood.

Constipation due to organic causes makes up ~ 5% of cases in childhood. Consider Hirschsprung disease in all neonates with constipation, especially when the 1st passage of meconium occurs > 48 hours after birth (see Hirschsprung Disease on page 10-34). Constipation is a common presenting symptom in hypothyroidism (see the Endocrinology section) and a frequent complaint in cystic fibrosis (see the Pulmonary Medicine section).

"THEY STRAIN WHEN THEY POOP" SYNDROME

A common complaint parents have during the first 9 months of their infant's life is: "My child strains all the time and cries before every bowel movement." The clinical term is **infant dyschezia**, which is defined by the Rome IV criteria as ≥ 10 minutes of straining or crying before successful or unsuccessful passage of soft stools. This is perfectly normal due to the fact that some infants have difficulty coordinating an increase in intraabdominal pressure and relaxation of the pelvic floor at the same time. These cries, grunts, and facial expressions are typical and are part of getting these mechanisms coordinated. Do not use or recommend constipation treatment for these infants! They don't have hard stools—they just don't know how to poop yet! Provide parental reassurance and discuss that this is a normal phase of development.

FUNCTIONAL CONSTIPATION

Etiology and Diagnosis

Functional constipation is the most common cause of constipation. It is also responsible for most cases of encopresis in children. (Encopresis is the soiling of underwear in children past the age of toilet training.) The fecal retention is due to voluntary withholding of stool secondary to the fear of defecation. The disorder occurs at 2 peaks: toilet-training time and the start of school. It also can develop before toilet training has even been attempted. In most cases, there is no clear social or behavioral cause. Some children also have had past experiences with painful defecation, anal fissures, or perianal infections, all of which can cause discomfort to the point that they learn to equate defecation with pain.

The whole cycle begins with the child voluntarily "holding in" a bowel movement. Stool accumulates in the rectum, and the child must increasingly contract the pelvic floor muscles and buttocks to prevent stool from passing. As the stool continues to amass, the child's mood and appetite are adversely affected, and the child can experience abdominal pain. Soiling frequently occurs when the child has flatus because the child cannot keep all the rectal contents contained. The withholding cycle is reinforced when the parent becomes angry at the child for soiling and the child is already trying to prevent any stool passage. Eventually, many affected children develop a negative self-image.

It is important to differentiate functional constipation from other etiologies. Physical examination can show anal fissures, perianal fecal staining, and/or a firm mass (i.e., stool) in the suprapubic area.

Other causes of constipation, such as Hirschsprung disease (see Hirschsprung Disease on page 10-34), do not typically present with fecal soiling, and the rectal vault is empty instead of full of stool. The finding of a deep sacral pit or a vascular or pigmented hairy patch on the sacrum suggests spinal dysraphism (see the Neurology section). Consider lumbosacral ultrasound or MRI in these cases. IBS can present with constipation; see Functional Abdominal Pain on page 10-4.

Treatment

Treatment of functional constipation requires a mixed behavioral and medical approach, including positive reinforcement schedules and the use of stool softeners (e.g., docusate) or osmotic laxatives (e.g., polyethylene glycol). Usually, some sort of clean-out of the fecal impaction is required, generally using a large amount of an oral osmotic laxative or enemas. Occasionally, prokinetic agents are needed and, in very rare instances, disimpaction under anesthesia. Give osmotic laxatives or stool softeners to make stool passage painless, and advise parents to make sure the child has unhurried time on the toilet 2–3×/day after meals. Instruct parents to have the child sit on the toilet with feet pressed firmly against the floor (or a footstool, if necessary) to help with defecation. Once the fecal mass is cleared, maintenance therapy is necessary to stop the cycle of withholding. The most commonly used agents include polyethylene glycol, mineral oil, and lactulose. Titrate doses up or down to reach the desired results. After ≥ 6 months of pain-free and accident-free success, discontinue the agents. Failure rates approach 20% regardless of the treatment used. Relapses are also common in children who were treated for this previously. Avoid excessive oral phosphates and hypertonic enemas, as they can be absorbed by the rectal mucosa.

ESOPHAGUS DISORDERS

PREVIEW | REVIEW

- How do 90% of tracheoesophageal abnormalities present?
- At the bedside, how do you diagnose esophageal atresia with distal tracheoesophageal fistula?
- What does VACTERL stand for?
- What is achalasia?
- True or false? Achalasia in infancy can be due to a congenital disorder.
- Is gastroesophageal reflux a normal process for many infants?
- What is the definition of eosinophilic esophagitis (EoE)?

- What are the 2 types of EoE, and how are they treated?
- Which children are at risk for having infection of the esophagus?
- How long after ingestion of a caustic substance should upper endoscopy be performed?
- What are the most common pills that cause pill-induced esophagitis?
- What is the best way to determine if an ingested coin is in the esophagus?
- Spontaneous esophageal perforation is rare but has increased frequency in patients with which 2 disorders?

TRACHEOESOPHAGEAL FISTULAS (TEFs) AND ESOPHAGEAL ATRESIAS (EAs)

TEFs and EAs occur in ~ 1/4,000 live births (Figure 10-1). A clue for most esophageal abnormalities can occur prenatally; ~ 50% of these mothers have **polyhydramnios** (excessive buildup of amniotic fluid).

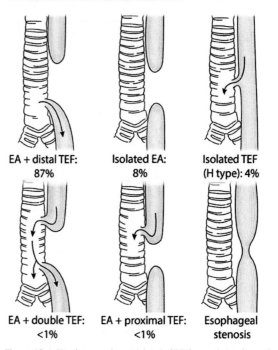

EA + distal TEF: 87%   Isolated EA: 8%   Isolated TEF (H type): 4%

EA + double TEF: <1%   EA + proximal TEF: <1%   Esophageal stenosis

Figure 10-1: Tracheoesophageal fistula (TEF), esophageal atresia (EA), and esophageal stenosis

Nearly 90% of tracheoesophageal abnormalities present as a blind, upper EA with a fistula between a lower esophageal segment and the lower portion of the trachea, near the carina, known as **EA with distal TEF**. Look for this in the delivery room or early in the nursery. The infant presents with excessive oral secretions and appears to be choking frequently, especially with attempted feeding. Diagnose by trying to place a nasogastric (NG) tube into the stomach; the blind pouch of the esophagus prevents its passage. A simple x-ray of the chest shows the abnormality fairly well, often with the NG tube coiled in the upper chest. For example, in Figure 10-2, the catheter tip stops in the blind pouch of the esophagus. Also, look for a dilated proximal esophagus with air distention of the entire GI tract. Initially in these infants, discontinue all oral feedings, place an orogastric catheter into the blind pouch and tape it into position, and then connect it so there is continuous drainage of the saliva from the pouch to prevent aspiration. Also, it is important to keep the head elevated at ~ 30°, which prevents stomach contents from being refluxed back into the trachea. After a cardiac evaluation rules out potential cardiac abnormalities, perform surgery as soon as possible.

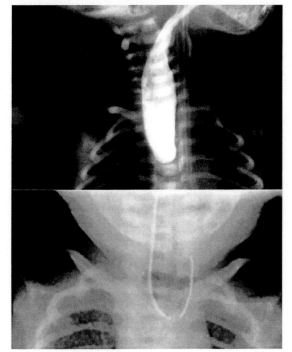

Figure 10-2: Esophageal atresia

The next most common abnormality is **isolated EA** with 2 blind pouches (the esophagus is closed distally, and the stomach is closed proximally, without a connection between the 2—classified as a TEF). Neonates with isolated EA have excessive oral secretions with choking and a flat, gasless abdomen on x-ray, which is not seen in those with a TEF. Treat with esophageal lengthening, followed by surgical repair.

An **"H-type" TEF**, which has a connection between a normal esophagus and a normal trachea, often presents in early infancy with choking during feeding. Others present later with cough, pneumonia, or reactive airway disease. This variant is not associated with maternal polyhydramnios because the esophagus is normal and without GI obstruction. Diagnosis can be tricky; barium swallows frequently miss the H-type fistula, requiring an esophagoscopy and/or bronchoscopy to confirm the diagnosis. Surgery to tie off the fistula is curative.

Esophageal stenosis alone can also occur and is not classified as a TEF.

Know that nearly 1/3 of these infants also have other congenital anomalies. The most common association is known by an acronym, **VACTERL: v**ertebral, **a**nal atresia, **c**ardiac (e.g., patent ductus arteriosus [PDA], atrial septal defect [ASD], ventricular septal defect [VSD]), **t**racheo**e**sophageal fistula, **r**enal (e.g., urethral atresia with hydronephrosis), and **l**imb anomalies (e.g., humeral hypoplasia, radial aplasia, hexadactyly, proximally placed thumb).

In all children with any form of EA, long-term outcomes are generally good. However, many present later with anastomotic strictures, dysphagia, or esophagitis because they lose lower esophageal sphincter (LES) tone or have abnormal esophageal motility.

ACHALASIA

Achalasia is a disorder of the esophagus characterized by incomplete relaxation of the LES and a lack of normal esophageal peristalsis. Thus, it is a motor problem, not an anatomic problem. Achalasia appears to be due to an autoimmune-mediated loss of ganglion cells in the esophagus and/or to dorsal motor nuclei reduction of vagus nerve signals. Only ~ 5% of all achalasia cases occur in children; the mean age for presentation in children is 9 years.

Patients present with dysphagia, often with regurgitation/vomiting of undigested food. Weight loss and chest discomfort are often present as well. Recurrent aspiration pneumonia may accompany the presentation of achalasia.

Figure 10-3: Achalasia

Barium swallow typically reveals a dilated esophagus that terminates in a beaklike manner due to persistent contraction of the LES (Figure 10-3). Manometric examination is needed to confirm the diagnosis and demonstrates elevated resting LES pressure, incomplete relaxation of the sphincter, and loss of peristalsis of the smooth muscle portion of the body of the esophagus. Endoscopy findings include a dilated and sometimes inflamed or ulcerated esophagus, often containing residual food particles.

If achalasia presents in infancy or early childhood, it may be due to a congenital disorder. A genetic syndrome in which achalasia is associated with adrenal insufficiency and alacrima is known as triple A syndrome (a.k.a. Allgrove syndrome).

GASTROENTEROLOGY

The preferred treatment for achalasia is a myotomy, which separates the muscle fibers in the LES so they can relax. This can be done laparoscopically or endoscopically.

GASTROESOPHAGEAL REFLUX (GER)

GER is defined as return of gastric contents into the esophagus. This is actually a normal process and is referred to as spitting up or vomiting if the refluxed material passes out of the mouth. The age of the patient has an important impact on the need for diagnostic testing and treatment.

Although pathologic reflux is rare in normal children, it is commonly seen in children with disabilities—especially those with neurologic dysfunction, in obese patients, or in patients with reactive airway disease. In infants and children without adequate airway protective measures, reflux is more likely to cause airway complications such as aspiration pneumonia or reactive airway disease exacerbations.

Reflux in Infants

Infant regurgitation (or GER) is very common, especially in the first 6 months of life. This is a normal physiologic process and most children outgrow this by 18 months of age. For more information, see Infant Regurgitation on page 10-1.

In a small percentage of infants, GER becomes a more pathologic process, at which point it is called **gastroesophageal reflux disease** (GERD). This can manifest as poor weight gain or failure to thrive (FTT) due to the inability to consume and maintain enough calories in the digestive tract. The 2018 NASPGHAN guidelines for GERD recommend attention to the following "red flags" as the distinction between GER and GERD:

- Systemic—FTT, feeding refusal, dystonic neck posturing, dental erosions, anemia
- Respiratory—wheezing, stridor, cough, hoarseness, recurrent aspiration pneumonia
- GI—esophagitis, esophageal stricture, hematemesis, dysphagia

Many of these symptoms can be caused by other non-GI disorders, which caregivers sometimes misinterpret as being caused by reflux, such as airway symptoms with hoarseness, laryngitis, cough, pneumonia, and apnea. Intermittent irritability is often blamed on GER, although this is present in many normal infants and is a nonspecific sign.

Reflux in Older Children

Older children often have symptoms similar to adults: heartburn, acid brash (a nasty taste in their mouth—some parents report very bad breath), frequent sore throat, or intermittent vomiting. Abdominal pain, especially epigastric pain, is often blamed on reflux, but it rarely proves to be the actual etiology (think functional abdominal pain syndrome or functional dyspepsia instead). A hiatal hernia—when a portion of the stomach herniates through the diaphragmatic esophageal hiatus—can present with symptoms of GERD and requires surgery if symptomatic.

Diagnosis

Diagnosis of a pathologic reflux disorder in children is difficult, and there is no absolute test that defines it. It is typically diagnosed by history, although that can be inaccurate as well. In most infants without concerning symptoms of GER, no workup is needed.

An **upper GI series** can show anatomic abnormalities in the vomiting child (e.g., malrotation, pyloric stenosis, esophageal stricture, antral webs). It can also show evidence of esophageal motility problems like achalasia. So, the upper GI is good for showing anatomic or motility problems only, but not diagnosing GER.

Upper endoscopy with biopsy of the esophagus is the only way to definitively diagnose esophagitis. Also use this procedure to diagnose other diseases, such as eosinophilic esophagitis or infectious causes of esophagitis. So, the upper endoscopy is good for diagnosing the mucosal complications of GER but not for diagnosing it.

A **pH probe**, usually inserted by gastroenterologists, records the duration and number of acid reflux episodes that occur in an infant or child. This is performed by inserting an intranasal catheter or a wireless device that is attached to the lower esophagus during endoscopy. The test is helpful for determining the risk of esophagitis. A normal pH probe study does not exclude GER. A positive test also does not always mean that recurrent wheezing or pneumonia is due to the GER detected; it just increases the likelihood that GER is a contributing factor. The pH probe is most useful when attempting to correlate troublesome symptoms (dysphagia, cough, heartburn) with GER or to determine if treatment has been effective.

Treatment

Treatment of GER in infants is initially aimed at **dietary measures** and **reassurance**. See Infant Regurgitation on page 10-1 for more information.

Treat infants with GERD and FTT. The 2018 NASPGHAN guidelines on GERD recommend a 2-week trial of a low-allergy formula due to the common occurrence of reflux in children with milk-protein allergy. These new guidelines also specifically recommend against positional treatment (head elevation, side sleeping, or prone sleeping) in infants, which has been common practice in pediatrics for decades.

Rule out other causes in infants with GERD who have poor weight gain, but know that inadequate caloric intake is the most common cause for FTT in infants. If no other causes are found, therapy is indicated. You can suggest food thickening and/or increasing the caloric content of food. On rare occasions, the vomiting is so severe that the infant requires NG feedings or postpyloric feedings. Do not recommend surgery (such as a fundoplication) for infants when GERD is the etiology for their poor weight gain. If there is delayed stomach emptying, promotility therapy can be helpful.

Therapy is indicated for patients with advanced GERD symptoms. Treat esophagitis with an **antisecretory agent**, such as a proton pump inhibitor (PPI; e.g., omeprazole). Unlike in infants, positional changes like head elevation or left lateral positioning are recommended in older children. The 2018 NASPGHAN guidelines and a 2013 AAP review of GERD suggest that PPIs are superior to H_2-receptor blockers in healing esophagitis and improving symptoms. If esophagitis is severe and prolonged for many years without therapy, the esophagus can develop strictures or **Barrett esophagus** can occur. Barrett esophagus presents with intestinal metaplasia in the distal esophagus. It is a premalignant condition requiring surveillance endoscopies and biopsy every 3–5 years. Barrett esophagus is rare in children and is normally seen in the context of an underlying neurologic disorder or esophageal anomaly.

Although the use of PPIs and H_2-receptor blockers has become common in children with asthma, recurrent respiratory symptoms, or recurrent sore throat/hoarseness, there is little evidence to support this practice.

Long-term acid blockade was previously thought to have few negative consequences, but recent evidence suggests otherwise. Infants taking acid-suppressing drugs have increased rates of pneumonia and viral gastroenteritis. Older children and adults appear to have increased risk for other GI infections, such as *Clostridioides difficile*.

Do not use antacids, especially the aluminum-containing compounds, because they can cause toxicity. Bethanechol and metoclopramide are both prokinetic drugs, but neither has demonstrated effectiveness in the treatment of GERD.

Surgical therapy is the final option, especially for those children with severe respiratory or neurologic disease. The most commonly used procedure is the **Nissen fundoplication**. In this operation, the fundus of the stomach is pulled up and wrapped around the lower esophagus, forming a "valve." The operative mortality from Nissen fundoplication is ~ 1%, and there are many long-term consequences of the altered anatomy, including "gas-bloat syndrome" and dysphagia from a tight fundoplication. Studies in adults have shown that prolonged medical therapy is more cost effective and has lower morbidity.

EOSINOPHILIC ESOPHAGITIS (EoE)

EoE is a chronic inflammatory condition of the esophagus that has become much more prevalent over the past 2 decades.

EoE is the most common cause of dysphagia or food impaction in children (60–80% of cases) and is an increasingly common cause for feeding difficulties in infants and toddlers. Suspect this disorder in any child with a history of a food bolus becoming stuck or who describes frequent odynophagia (pain with swallowing) or dysphagia.

Chest pain that does not occur with swallowing is also a common presenting complaint.

Many patients with EoE also have some other form of atopy (e.g., asthma, eczema, allergic rhinitis, food allergies), so this is a strong clue to the answer if an exam question mentions esophageal symptoms and atopic symptoms in the same patient.

The only way to establish a diagnosis is via upper endoscopy. The surface can appear inflamed or ulcerated, but in many cases, it looks normal. The key is the biopsy—a large number of eosinophils (usually > 15/high power field) indicates the patient has EoE.

Treatment is often difficult, although most experts recommend high-dose acid suppression with a PPI, specific food elimination, or swallowed steroids (fluticasone or budesonide is administered via metered dose inhalers but the medicine is swallowed rather than inhaled). Endoscopy is repeated after several months of treatment to determine if inflammation has decreased.

The 2013 ACG and 2017 ESPGHAN guidelines for EoE suggest dividing patients into 2 categories: (1) **PPI-responsive EoE**, and (2) **PPI-nonresponsive EoE**. The usual strategy is to perform a trial of high-dose PPI as monotherapy first, and then repeat endoscopy weeks or months later to determine if the eosinophilia is resolved. If it has, the patient can stay on PPI monotherapy. If it has not, they will likely need swallowed steroids or an elimination diet. The updated guidelines from 2017 suggest that these 2 categories may in fact lie along a continuum with many similar features, but most clinicians continue to find this division useful when making management decisions. GERD and EoE are separate entities, but they often coexist and can worsen each another.

As many as 60% of children with EoE improve symptomatically with the elimination of dietary cow's milk. Some patients, if they fail medical management, require a more complex "6-food elimination diet," which restricts cow's milk, soy, shellfish, wheat, eggs, and legumes (e.g., peanuts). Unfortunately, a specific food can be identified as the cause in only about 1/3 of these patients in this way. Allergy testing (either by serum IgE or by skin-prick test) rarely correlates either positively or negatively with empiric food challenges. The last resort for some patients is nutritional maintenance on an elemental formula. In very rare or severe cases, other immunosuppressants (e.g., immunomodulators, biologics) may be helpful.

INFECTIONS OF THE ESOPHAGUS

Infections of the esophagus are rare in children, except for those who are immunocompromised. Generally, children at risk are those with HIV, diabetes mellitus (DM), cancer, and long-term, high-dose steroid usage.

Candida, cytomegalovirus (CMV), and herpes simplex virus (HSV) are the most common organisms to cause infection in the esophagus. Dysphagia is the most common symptom with which children present. Odynophagia and retrosternal burning are also seen.

GASTROENTEROLOGY

Diagnose by upper endoscopy and obtain biopsies and a KOH prep to look for fungal hyphae. *Candida* esophagitis has white plaque-like lesions, and CMV and HSV have discrete "volcano-like" ulcers with normal intervening mucosa. Treat *Candida* with fluconazole, CMV with ganciclovir and/or foscarnet, and HSV with acyclovir.

CAUSTIC INGESTIONS

Ingestion of various products around the house can induce severe esophagitis. The most common products ingested include bleach, laundry detergents, bathroom cleansers, drain cleaners, oven cleaners, and swimming pool products.

Acidic agents taste bad, cause immediate pain, and are rapidly spit or vomited out; because of this, significant ingestions are unusual. They generally cause more injury to the stomach than to the esophagus but can nevertheless cause esophageal damage, although this is rare. Alkaline agents are tasteless and swallowed without initial consequences. The alkalis produce a liquefactive necrosis with intense inflammation of the surrounding tissue. Granular alkalis, like drain cleaners, cause more injury to the mouth, pharynx, and proximal esophagus, whereas liquid drain openers cause severe injury to the entire esophagus but rarely to the stomach.

Children and infants present with drooling, dysphagia, or abdominal discomfort. Some present with airway symptoms only, including stridor, retractions, and nasal flaring. The symptoms can be immediate or delayed for hours, and the lack of symptoms or the lack of significant oral findings do not necessarily correlate with the amount of esophageal or stomach damage. Severe damage can occur without outward signs or symptoms. Observe the child who has no symptoms and no physical findings—and a questionable history of ingestion—for several hours and give clear liquids to see if the child can tolerate them. Have those with a definite history of ingestion undergo additional tests (see below) no matter what their current symptoms or signs are, and they should remain NPO until after endoscopy.

Initial management of a caustic product ingestion is observation. Do not induce emesis because it leads to further esophageal exposure to the agent. Use of neutralizing agents, milk, and large amounts of water are no longer recommended because of the risk of inducing vomiting. NG tubes are also not recommended because they can perforate damaged areas. If the child has developed upper airway disease, steroids and/or intubation are likely needed.

Labs (like a CBC) are not helpful to determine degree of GI injury. Order plain films initially if perforation is suspected. CT is helpful to detect perforation, especially in more severe injuries, but it should not replace endoscopy. Neither PPIs nor steroids have been proven to decrease the risk of perforation or subsequent stricture. Use antibiotics in the setting of a patient with perforation. Follow patients closely to monitor for stricture formation.

Upper endoscopy is recommended 12–24 hours after the ingestion, but no later than 48 hours afterward due to increased risk of wall perforation. Doing the endoscopy before 12 hours may not show the full extent of injury.

Burn injuries are divided into 4 grades:

- **Grade 1 burns** are only superficial and consist of mucosal edema or redness. These lesions heal without scars and are well tolerated.
- **Grade 2 burns** extend into the submucosa and muscle layers. These lesions cause scarring and can result in strictures of the esophagus.
- **Grade 3 burns** extend through the esophagus and/or stomach and are associated with complete thickness burns and extensive necrosis. For most patients with more severe injury (Grade 2 or 3), repeat endoscopy or fluoroscopic imaging within a few months to assess for the presence of a stricture.
- If you suspect perforation, a **Grade 4 burn**, consult a pediatric surgeon immediately.

PILL-INDUCED ESOPHAGITIS

Pill-induced esophagitis is fairly common in children old enough to take pills, especially adolescents who swallow their pills dry. The most common location for the pill to become stuck is in the midesophagus. Tetracycline, doxycycline, aspirin, NSAIDs, and slow-release potassium are the pills most often implicated. The pills adhere to the side of the esophagus, dissolve, and cause local irritation. Symptoms usually begin soon after ingestion, and patients have retrosternal pain and dysphagia. Look for the adolescent who comes in with chest pain and a history of doxycycline for acne. If the diagnosis is not clear cut, an endoscopy is helpful.

Symptoms generally resolve in 1–3 weeks. Agents to stop acid production can be helpful for severe cases, but, generally, no specific therapy is necessary other than advising the patient to swallow pills with water.

INGESTION OF FOREIGN BODIES

In children, the most commonly ingested foreign bodies by far are coins. Sharp pointed objects carry an increased risk of perforation, with the most common of these being needles, straight pins, straightened paper clips, and fish bones. For the most part, foreign bodies pass without incident. Only about 10–20% require endoscopic removal, and < 1% require surgical intervention. Once in the stomach, nearly 95% of foreign bodies pass without problem.

Symptoms, if they occur, are likely due to the foreign body getting stuck just below the cricopharyngeal muscle. Children can present with drooling, choking, or poor feeding. Older children can usually describe retrosternal pain and/or dysphagia. Respiratory symptoms alone can also occur and are typically due to the foreign body pushing against the posterior tracheal wall.

You can diagnose ingestion of most objects with standard chest x-ray, because nearly 90% of them are radiopaque. On a posteroanterior projection, coins in the esophagus tend to lie in the coronal plane ("face forward"; Figure 10-4) and in the sagittal plane ("on edge") in the trachea (Figure 10-5). A lateral chest or neck x-ray can be helpful to delineate the exact location of a foreign body. Sometimes contrast material or fluoroscopy is needed to show nonopaque items, such as plastic toys or pieces of toys; however, with a good history of ingestion and physical symptoms, you can usually bypass this option.

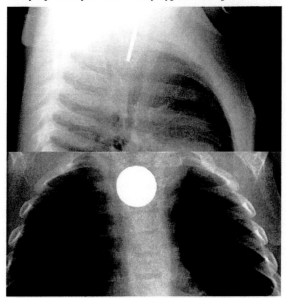

Figure 10-4: Coin in esophagus

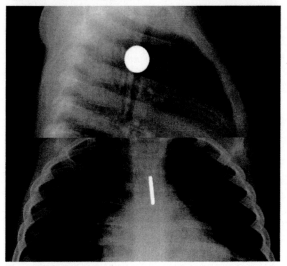

Figure 10-5: Coin in trachea

The 2015 European Society for Paediatric Gastroenterology, Hepatology and Nutrition (ESPGHAN) and NASPGHAN guidelines are more conservative and recommend removal of most foreign bodies. Endoscopy is the method of choice to grab and remove objects under direct visualization. "Blind" removal with a Foley catheter or other method is not recommended. The child or infant who presents with inability to swallow secretions or who is in respiratory distress requires immediate evaluation and intervention, regardless of the type of foreign body.

Remove button batteries emergently from the esophagus, as they can cause immediate liquefactive necrosis. They should be removed urgently from the stomach or small bowel in asymptomatic children < 5 years of age and battery width ≥ 20 mm but otherwise can be observed for passage.

Magnets should be removed, especially if multiple magnets are present, because they can attract to each other once they reach the small bowel and cause a perforation and fistula.

Urgently remove sharp or long objects if in the esophagus or stomach.

Coins in the esophagus can be observed for up to 24 hours after ingestion if the child is asymptomatic. In 20–30% of these cases, the coin will pass into the stomach during the observation period. If the patient is symptomatic or if the coin remains in the esophagus after 24 hours, removal with fiberoptic endoscopy is required. Coins can be observed if in the stomach or beyond, as the vast majority will pass without any problem.

By definition, "emergent" removal means < 2 hours from presentation, regardless if NPO or not, whereas "urgent" removal means < 24 hours from presentation if patient is NPO.

Food impaction is a special case and usually occurs in older children and adolescents; it requires intervention if the patient is in respiratory distress or cannot swallow secretions. Do not use meat tenderizer! It can cause hypernatremia and esophageal perforation.

Foreign bodies or food impaction in adolescents and older children often indicate an underlying etiology—most commonly EoE.

ESOPHAGEAL PERFORATION

Esophageal perforation is rare in children. However, there are a few things you must remember. Spontaneous perforation can occur with increased frequency in patients with **Ehlers-Danlos** and **Marfan** syndromes. Chest and upper back pain, as well as subcutaneous emphysema, occur. Fever and hypotension are common. Do not perform endoscopy in these patients! The safest thing to do is to get plain film x-rays, followed by instillation of a small amount of water-soluble contrast material. If the water-soluble contrast material does not show the perforation, proceed with a barium examination to better outline the abnormality.

Treat surgically, and then begin IV antibiotics and parenteral feeds. You can do enteral feeds by positioning the tube past the healing perforation.

ESOPHAGEAL VARICES

Esophageal varices are dilated esophageal veins caused by increased pressure in the portal circulation. Most cases are caused by cirrhosis, which leads to scarring and decreased portal blood flow through the liver (causing portal hypertension). In children, the most common causes are from congenital biliary obstruction, such as **biliary atresia** or **Alagille syndrome**. Patients with portal venous thrombosis can also develop portal hypertension, leading to esophageal varices. Increased portal hypertension also leads to increased pressure in other venous plexi, like the umbilical veins (causes caput medusa) and rectal veins (causes hemorrhoids, which are rectal varices).

Patients often present with severe, life-threatening hematemesis. Typically, the patient will have the sudden onset of vomiting frank blood with or without melena, a rapidly falling hemoglobin, tachycardia, and hypotension. Treatment is urgent support of intravascular volume, blood transfusion, and urgent endoscopy with esophageal band ligation within 12 hours of presentation. Band ligation involves using a rubber-band gun to squeeze esophageal varices flat against the esophageal wall and decompress the large volume of blood pooled there.

STOMACH DISORDERS

PREVIEW | REVIEW

- How does pyloric stenosis typically present?
- What type of acid-base disorder is seen with pyloric stenosis?
- What causes stress gastropathy?
- What is the most common identifiable cause of chronic gastritis in children?
- Which organism is responsible for most peptic ulcer disease (PUD) in children?
- When and how do you diagnose *Helicobacter pylori* infection?
- Are antibody tests useful in diagnosing active PUD?
- What is the treatment for *H. pylori* infection?
- What is Zollinger-Ellison syndrome?

PYLORIC STENOSIS

Pyloric stenosis is fairly common, occurring in 1/200 to 1/750 live births. It is more common in males than females (4:1 to 6:1), but do not dismiss a female infant with compatible symptoms. White infants are 2–3× more likely to be affected. It is more closely associated with smaller family size and higher socioeconomic status rather than with birth order. Prematurity and a positive parental history of pyloric stenosis are risk factors. Early (< 2 weeks of age) exposure to erythromycin is also a risk factor for pyloric stenosis that is frequently tested on exams.

Studies show that the pyloric muscle is normal at birth but hypertrophies soon after and causes obstruction of the pyloric outlet. The etiology is unknown but is probably multifactorial, involving both genetic and environmental factors.

Know! Pyloric stenosis usually presents between 3 weeks and 2 months of age, with progressively worsening, nonbilious vomiting. The infant is hungry and eager to feed. If vomiting is prolonged, **hypochloremic hypokalemic metabolic alkalosis** can develop, along with dehydration. Hypokalemia occurs due to exchange of hydrogen ion and potassium in the kidney.

Physical examination will sometimes reveal visible peristalsis and rarely a mobile pyloric mass known as an "olive." Finding the "olive" means you have made the diagnosis because it is pathognomonic for pyloric stenosis. The diagnostic test of choice is a pyloric ultrasound, which shows a thickened and lengthened pyloric muscle. The 2012 American College of Radiology guidelines define pyloric stenosis as a pyloric length > 18 mm and a pyloric wall thickness > 4 mm on pyloric ultrasound. An upper GI series is sometimes ordered for pyloric stenosis, which shows elongation and thickening of the pylorus, as well as obstruction of the pyloric outlet by thickened mucosa (Figure 10-6).

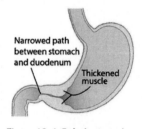

Narrowed path between stomach and duodenum

Thickened muscle

Figure 10-6: Pyloric stenosis

Aim initial treatment at correcting dehydration and electrolyte abnormalities, particularly hypokalemia and alkalosis, before surgery. The surgical procedure of choice, pyloromyotomy (which can be done laparoscopically), is curative and has a very low mortality rate (< 0.5%). Full oral feeds can commence quickly after surgery. Recurrence rate is < 1%.

EROSIVE AND HEMORRHAGIC GASTROPATHY

Stress Gastropathy

Stress gastropathy is due to severe physiologic stress, such as occurs with shock, metabolic acidosis, sepsis, burns, and head injury. (Think sick ICU patient with an upper GI bleed!) Initially, the mucosal ischemia occurs in the fundus and proximal body, and later it spreads to the antrum, resulting in a diffuse erosive and hemorrhagic appearance. Prompt control of the underlying disorder improves the gastropathy more than any acid-neutralizing therapy. Because control of the underlying disorder is often impossible, acid suppression is standard clinical practice. Gastropathy in a burn patient is called a **Curling ulcer** (think of a burning object "curling") and in a patient with head injury or brain surgery is called a **Cushing ulcer** (remember Dr. Cushing was a neurosurgeon).

Prolapse Gastropathy

Prolapse gastropathy is usually due to forceful retching or vomiting (termed "emetogenic gastritis/gastropathy") that causes subepithelial hemorrhages in the fundus and proximal body as the proximal stomach is pulled up into the distal esophagus. The hemorrhages tend to resolve quickly, but large amounts of bleeding can occur in a short time period.

Mallory-Weiss tears occur in the distal esophagus at the gastroesophageal junction and can extend into the gastric cardia from profound/extended retching, but note that Mallory-Weiss tears are rare in children. NG tubes and foreign bodies can also cause hemorrhages and erosions.

Drug-Induced Gastropathy

Nonsteroidal antiinflammatory drugs (NSAIDs) are common causes of minor erosions and hemorrhages in the body and antrum of the stomach. On occasion, NSAIDs can cause more extensive erosions and hemorrhages, resulting in perforation and excessive bleeding. The injuries result from local, as well as systemic, effects. Alcohol is a well-known cause of gastropathy. Corticosteroids are frequently implicated in upper GI bleeding, but this observation often coincides with stress gastropathy, and studies have not shown a clear drug-induced effect.

NONEROSIVE GASTROPATHY

Occurrence

Nonerosive gastropathy is the most common gastritis in children and adults. It usually occurs in the antrum and is a histologic diagnosis because endoscopy may not show anything visually. Etiologies are varied.

Nonspecific Gastritis

Nonspecific gastritis is fairly common in children, with no identifiable etiology. On biopsy, the inflammation is chronic and superficial, as well as being focal instead of diffuse. The antrum is commonly involved.

Helicobacter pylori Gastritis

H. pylori is the most common identifiable cause of chronic gastritis in children. An acute infection of *H. pylori* can result in nausea, vomiting, decreased appetite, and epigastric abdominal pain, with a short period of increased acid secretion followed by a marked decrease in acid production. The acute symptoms only last about 1 week. Then, over the next 3–6 months, gastritis resolves and acid secretion returns to normal. Most patients then have a chronic infection with the organism; however, in a large majority of individuals, this causes no symptoms. The incidence of *H. pylori* is decreasing in the U.S., but it remains endemic in many parts of the world, including Africa, the Middle East, India, Southeast Asia, and South America. Note that *H. pylori* is also the primary cause of PUD.

The most sensitive way *H. pylori* is diagnosed is with endoscopic visualization and biopsies with a rapid urea test on the tissue. Positive gastric biopsies show the gram-negative spiral rods on the surface of the glandular epithelium under the mucous layer when using special stains (Figure 10-7). *H. pylori* gastritis often results in the gastric mucosa appearing nodular. Remember that the endoscopic appearance can be normal with nonerosive gastritis, so you must biopsy with endoscopy. However, endoscopy with biopsies is an invasive test. A less invasive manner, but still sensitive, is to do a urea breath test and fecal antigen test to confirm the diagnosis of *H. pylori*. These tests are also used to confirm eradication.

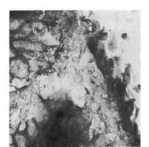

Figure 10-7: H. pylori seen with Giemsa stain

Treatment and follow-up is essentially the same as for PUD caused by *H. pylori* (see Treatment on page 10-16).

Chronic gastritis due to *H. pylori* can cause atrophic gastritis and intestinal metaplasia in adults. *H. pylori* is the primary identified cause of **gastric adenocarcinoma**; however, there appears to be no association between early childhood acquisition of *H. pylori* and the development of gastric cancer in adults. *H. pylori* is also the cause of a rare, slow-growing gastric lymphoma called mucosa-associated lymphoid tissue (**MALT**). MALT lymphomas respond well to antibiotic therapy that eradicates *H. pylori*.

PEPTIC ULCER DISEASE (PUD)

PUD is rare in children, and most cases are caused by *H. pylori* (especially duodenal ulcers) or NSAIDs (especially gastric ulcers). The cause is unknown in 20% of affected children. Important: *H. pylori* infection in children is common and ~ 80% of those infected are asymptomatic. If symptomatic, patients usually present with epigastric pain or discomfort. The rate of *H. pylori* infection has fallen dramatically in developed countries over the past 10 years, but rates remain high in the developing world and in recent immigrants.

Diagnosis

If you suspect PUD, perform an upper endoscopy. Remember, endoscopy is the best test for children with:

- upper GI bleeding,
- recurrent vomiting, or
- persistent, unexplained abdominal pain.

An upper GI series is unacceptable in children for diagnosis of PUD because there is both low sensitivity and specificity: Many ulcers are missed and many normal gastric or duodenal folds are misinterpreted as ulcers.

When the pathology is determined with endoscopic visualization and biopsy, immunologic staining of the tissue, a urea breath test, or a rapid urea test on the tissue is done to confirm *H. pylori* is present.

Remember that serum antibody tests confirm only past exposure, not necessarily active, ongoing infection, so do not use them for diagnosis of active *H. pylori* infection.

The stool antigen test can be helpful to determine if a known infection is eradicated, but the 2011 ESPGHAN and NASPGHAN pediatric guidelines discourage its use for initial diagnosis. Newer guidelines for adults from the AGA issued in 2017 suggest that stool antigen is a reasonable test for most patients with no previous history of *H. pylori*.

Only ~ 20% of *H. pylori* infections cause chronic gastritis or PUD. This is why it is important to first diagnose the pathology and only then look for *H. pylori*. Do not test for *H. pylori* initially as an aid for diagnosis of abdominal pain because the presence of *H. pylori* alone is not helpful as a diagnostic indicator.

Treatment

The most important treatment for PUD (of all causes) is acid suppression, ideally with a PPI. This promotes immediate healing of gastric or intestinal tissue by removing ongoing tissue damage caused by acid exposure. According to the 2011 ACG guidelines for management of peptic ulcers, if an ulcer is actively bleeding, it must be treated endoscopically with injection of epinephrine, cauterizing the ulcer bed, or applying clips to the bleeding artery. Patients with hemodynamically significant bleeding should receive packed red blood cells to maintain hemoglobin > 7 mg/dL. Somatostatin infusion may be necessary to slow bleeding, usually in the pediatric intensive care unit.

Treatment of *H. pylori*–induced PUD requires both antibiotics and acid suppression. Treat *H. pylori* infection with 2 weeks of a PPI plus clarithromycin, plus either amoxicillin or metronidazole. Give all 3 drugs in divided doses, twice a day. The 2017 AGA *H. pylori* guidelines suggest that sequential therapy, which uses antibiotics in a series rather than in parallel, increases the chance of cure with 1 course, and are also acceptable as a 1st line therapy. In areas where clarithromycin resistance is high, quadruple therapy is used: bismuth salicylates are used along with PPIs, tetracycline, and either amoxicillin or metronidazole (but resistant *H. pylori* remains very rare in North America).

The key in treatment of *H. pylori*–induced PUD is to eradicate the infection. However, in the presence of a positive *H. pylori* test, give anti-*H. pylori* therapy only when PUD is proven or in MALT lymphoma. In children, do not treat *H. pylori* colonization indiscriminately. Asymptomatic individuals should not be screened for *H. pylori* infection.

Surgery is rarely indicated for PUD except for the following circumstances: perforation of the stomach or duodenum, active bleeding that cannot be controlled, gastric outlet or duodenal obstruction, or failed medical therapy, as in hypersecretory syndromes (see PUD Due to Acid Hypersecretory Diseases).

Follow-Up

Ulcers with complications (bleeding, perforation, or penetration) commonly relapse, so confirm healing (and eradication of *H. pylori* if present) with follow-up endoscopy.

For uncomplicated ulcers, confirm healing and/or *H. pylori* eradication with symptom resolution and a follow-up urea breath test or stool antigen test. Hold off on the follow-up urea breath test or stool antigen test until at least 4–6 weeks after acid suppression therapy has ended. Do not recommend dietary modification.

To recap, *H. pylori* is the primary identified cause of chronic gastritis, PUD, gastric adenocarcinoma, and MALT lymphoma. Again, invasive tests (endoscopic visualization and biopsy) are done only for initial diagnosis, and noninvasive tests are typically done for follow-up.

PUD Due to Acid Hypersecretory Diseases

There are only a few acid hypersecretory diseases. Note that, for the ones discussed next, about 10% present with diarrhea and no ulcers. Mucosal resistance (likely due to genetic factors) prevents ulcer formation in these individuals.

Zollinger-Ellison Syndrome

Zollinger-Ellison syndrome is rare in children. It produces markedly excessive stomach acid due to a gastrin-secreting tumor (**gastrinoma**), typically located in the pancreas or duodenal wall. Multiple ulcers are common in the stomach and duodenum and frequently involve unusual sites for ulcers, such as the esophagus or jejunum. The majority of gastrinomas are malignant but slow-growing tumors.

Gastrinomas are strongly associated with multiple endocrine neoplasia Type 1 (MEN1). Approximately 25% of people with gastrinoma have MEN1 (so evaluate them for hyperparathyroidism and pituitary disease as well), and 25–30% of those with MEN1 have gastrinoma.

Perform surgical resection of the tumor if possible, but metastasis to the lymph nodes and liver indicates poor prognosis.

Systemic Mastocytosis

Systemic mastocytosis is also characterized by acid hypersecretion. It is a disease wherein mast cells accumulate in the skin, marrow, liver, spleen, and GI tract. Hyperparathyroidism is also noted with this disorder. See the Allergy & Immunology section for more information on mastocytosis.

INTESTINAL DISORDERS

PREVIEW | REVIEW

- At what age do infants with malrotation classically present?

- What does an upper gastrointestinal (GI) series show in an infant with malrotation?

- At what age does intussusception usually occur?

- Describe the presenting symptoms of a child with intussusception.

- What is the diagnostic procedure of choice in patients with suspected intussusception?

- What test is preferred to diagnose Meckel diverticulum?

- Which is associated with other congenital anomalies—jejunoileal or duodenal atresia?

- What do abdominal plain x-rays show in neonates with duodenal atresia?

- What is the common carbohydrate metabolism deficiency that starts after 2 years of age?

- What is the most reliable noninvasive test to diagnose lactase deficiency?

- What does the absence of apolipoprotein B result in?

- What is Hartnup disease?

- How do children with abnormal zinc absorption present?

- Which dietary protein induces celiac disease?

- How does the classic gastrointestinal form of celiac disease present in children < 2 years of age?

- Children with Type 1 diabetes mellitus or selective immunoglobulin A deficiency should be screened for what disease(s)?

- What organism causes Whipple disease?

- What is the most common surgical emergency in children?

- If the pain of appendicitis suddenly resolves, what has likely happened?

- What is neutropenic enterocolitis?

MALROTATION OF THE INTESTINE

Malrotation of the intestine can present anytime in infancy or childhood and is due to nonrotation, incomplete rotation, paraduodenal hernia, or reverse rotation. Malrotation occurs in ~ 1/6,000 births. Omphalocele and gastroschisis always have malrotation as well.

Nonrotation is the most common malrotation abnormality and presents with the cecum on the left and the small intestine to the right of the superior mesenteric artery.

This results in a short mesentery and relatively little fixation of the bowel. The duodenum is small and fuses with the colon, using a common mesentery around the superior mesenteric artery.

Infants with malrotation classically present with the acute development of bilious emesis in the 1st month of life (90% present within the 1st year). These infants present with abdominal distention, diffuse tenderness, and irritability. If a volvulus develops, septic shock is likely. As the bowel necrosis worsens, the infant develops hematemesis, melena, or both.

In an infant who has bilious vomiting, always perform an upper GI series for diagnosis. More recently, ultrasound has been used to diagnose volvulus, and in experienced hands, can be superior to the upper GI series. The upper GI series can demonstrate the classic "bird's beak" of the 2nd or 3rd portion of the duodenum, where the gut is twisted (Figure 10-8). A corkscrew pattern is visible if the duodenum is partially obstructed. For the older child with intermittent symptoms, the upper GI series can identify an abnormal location of the duodenojejunal junction (the ligament of Treitz). Normally, the ligament of Treitz is to the left of the spine at the level of the gastric antrum and is fixed to the posterior body wall. In malrotation, the ligament of Treitz is on the right side of the spine and is inferior to the duodenal bulb. Thus, in malrotation, contrast from the upper GI series fills the jejunal loops on the right side of the abdomen.

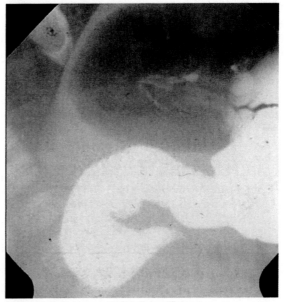

Figure 10-8: Volvulus with "bird's beak" sign

After initial management of shock and cardiovascular compromise, emergent surgery (the Ladd procedure) must be performed. The Ladd procedure consists of opening the abdominal wall and taking out the intestines to inspect the mesenteric root. If the surgeon finds volvulus, it is untwisted and the bowel is inspected for viability.

During surgery, they resect nonviable or necrotic areas and perform enterostomies. If questionable areas of bowel are found, they are generally left in place; after 12–36 hours, a "2nd look" surgery is performed to assess viability.

If a child is diagnosed with a malrotation but is asymptomatic, most will recommend an elective Ladd procedure.

INTUSSUSCEPTION

Intussusception occurs when 1 part of the intestine invaginates ("telescopes") into the lumen of the adjoining bowel. With this telescoping, mesentery is dragged in the process, which can cause venous obstruction, swelling, and/or edema of the bowel wall. Eventually, the edema can cause arterial obstruction, ischemia, and perforation. Intussusception usually occurs between 6 and 36 months of age, with the majority occurring < 2 years of age. Almost all in this age group are idiopathic; that is, no pathologic lead point is discovered. Most originate near the ileocecal junction, and many believe these are due to a virus-induced swelling of Peyer patches. The original rotavirus vaccine was removed from the market due to concerns of an increased rate of intussusception (never proven).

In older children and adolescents, intussusception is much less common, and the cause is often much more apparent. The development of intussusception in this age group is often generated by an intraluminal lesion that serves as a "leading edge;" the most common cause is a Meckel diverticulum (see Meckel Diverticulum). Polyps, duplication cysts, and immunoglobulin A vasculitis (IgAV; formerly Henoch-Schönlein purpura [HSP]) are also culprits.

Patients with intussusception present with repeated episodes of severe abdominal pain interspersed with asymptomatic intervals. Vomiting (if obstruction occurs) and hematochezia (if bowel ischemia occurs) are symptoms as well.

An infant with intussusception awakens with crying and has flexion of the knees and hips. Frequently, the pain subsides, and the child appears comfortable. A normal bowel movement is common with the pain, but subsequent bowel movements can have blood admixed with mucus ("currant jelly" stool) and can occur hours or days after the abdominal pain. Eventually, the pain episodes increase in severity and frequency. Lethargy is a late, ominous sign and likely results from worsening metabolic acidosis. Examination between episodes shows a soft abdomen, and, during an episode, you may be able to palpate a mass in the right side of the abdomen.

Ultrasound is the best initial imaging study. Look for a "target sign" of telescoped bowel (Figure 10-9). Plain abdominal x-rays sometimes show a soft tissue mass displacing loops of bowel and a gasless right abdomen.

An air contrast enema is the diagnostic and therapeutic procedure of choice. Nearly 90% can be reduced with this procedure. For an air-contrast enema, peritonitis is

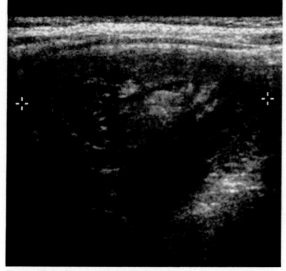

Figure 10-9: Ultrasound showing intussusception with target sign. Note the concentric layering of tissue between the 2 markers.

an absolute contraindication—and bowel obstruction is a relative contraindication. Recurrence rates are 3–10%, and most recommend admission for 24-hour observation. Consult a pediatric surgeon early in the process, because it is helpful to have a surgeon immediately present to perform surgery if air-contrast enema reduction fails.

MECKEL DIVERTICULUM

A Meckel diverticulum is an embryologic leftover and occurs when the vitelline (omphalomesenteric) duct fails to obliterate. It is a true diverticulum of the small intestines containing all 3 tissue layers. Ectopic tissue is often present (~ 20% of the time) and is typically gastric in origin. Meckel diverticula are present in ~ 1% of the population.

In most instances, a Meckel diverticulum is clinically asymptomatic; a large series from Mayo Clinic showed that 16% of diverticula are symptomatic. When found, it is typically an incidental finding discovered during surgery done for a different purpose. The lifetime risk of complication from a Meckel diverticulum is 4%. Symptoms occur more commonly in patients who are < 2 years of age. The main symptoms are due to painless GI bleeding from ectopic gastric mucosa or small bowel obstruction. Large diverticula (> 2 cm in length) and those with ectopic tissue are more likely to be symptomatic.

A Meckel diverticulum is usually an isolated finding, but is sometimes associated with other congenital anomalies, including esophageal atresia (6× risk), imperforate anus (5× risk), neurologic anomalies (3× risk), and cardiovascular anomalies (2× risk).

Painless rectal bleeding is the most common presenting symptom in adults, but in children, small bowel obstruction is most common (sometimes as a lead point for intussusception). Occasionally, colicky abdominal pain accompanies the bleeding. The color of the blood can be bright red or maroon and can resemble intussusception with "currant jelly" character. Transfusions are often required because of the large amount of bleeding that occurs. Bleeding tends to stop and start spontaneously.

Diagnosis is difficult. Most prefer a technetium-99m pertechnetate scan (a.k.a. Meckel scan). This scan works because a majority of bleeding Meckel diverticula contain ectopic gastric mucosa. The technetium-99m pertechnetate concentrates in the parietal cells of gastric mucosa and the bladder. So, if isotope uptake appears outside of the stomach and bladder, the scan is positive. Histamine H_2 blockers can enhance the accuracy of the scan. The Meckel scan is a great example of a test with a high positive predictive value (if a test is positive, a Meckel diverticulum is likely to be present), but a low negative predictive value (a negative scan does not rule out the disease very well).

A Meckel diverticulum requires surgical intervention. IV fluids and blood are usually required before surgery if the antecedent lower GI bleed is hemodynamically significant. If a Meckel diverticulum is found incidentally during an abdominal surgery in a young child, most pediatric surgeons resect it.

CONGENITAL INTESTINAL ATRESIAS

Occurrence

Atresias of the gut happen in ~ 1/5,000 births, with most occurring in the duodenum or other areas of the small intestines.

Duodenal Atresia

Duodenal atresia accounts for more than 50% of the intestinal atresias. Duodenal atresia is associated with multiple anomalies, including cardiac, genitourinary (GU), anorectal, and esophageal. About 50% of patients are born prematurely; 40% of patients with duodenal atresia have **trisomy 21** (Down syndrome). Polyhydramnios and a dilated stomach are often visualized on prenatal ultrasound. A majority have their obstruction distal to the ampulla of Vater; therefore, they also have bilious vomiting on the 1st day of life. Abdominal plain x-rays show the classic "**double bubble**" formed by air in the stomach and proximal duodenum (Figure 10-10). This is diagnostic when the rest of the bowel is airless. If there is distal gas, confirm with an upper GI study. Surgery is necessary, and most of the complications occur due to the associated cardiac abnormalities.

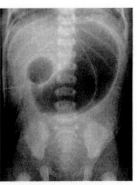

Figure 10-10: Duodenal atresia. Note the "double bubble sign" and lack of gas in the bowel distal to the obstruction.

Jejunoileal Atresia

Jejunoileal atresia is different from duodenal atresia in that jejunoileal atresia is not usually associated with other congenital anomalies. Risk factors include situations that may limit mesenteric blood flow in the developing fetus, such as low birth weight from placental insufficiency, multiple births, and maternal tobacco/cocaine use. Prenatal diagnosis is possible with maternal ultrasound. Postnatally, patients present with abdominal distention and bilious emesis, and they may or may not have meconium stools. Abdominal x-rays show multiple, dilated loops of bowel with air-fluid levels. Diagnosis is best made with an upper GI or lower GI contrast study. The differential diagnosis includes meconium ileus, which is seen with cystic fibrosis. Surgery is necessary for jejunoileal atresia, with the goal of salvaging as much small bowel as possible.

Colonic Atresia

Colonic atresia is the rarest of the intestinal atresias. If the colon is the only segment involved, patients present with distal bowel obstruction, abdominal distention, bilious emesis, and failure to pass meconium. Confirm diagnosis with a contrast enema, which shows a distal microcolon and the point of obstruction. Surgical reanastomosis is the treatment of choice.

GASTROINTESTINAL (GI) DUPLICATIONS

Intestinal duplications are rare and can occur anywhere from the mouth to the anus, but the most common location is in the ileum.

By definition, 3 characteristics are required:

- contiguous and strongly adherent to some part of the GI tract,
- 2-layered muscular coat, and
- epithelial lining similar to that of the stomach, small intestine, or colon.

Intestinal duplications are located on the mesenteric instead of the antimesenteric side of the bowel and share a common blood supply with the adjacent bowel. This differs from a Meckel diverticulum, which occurs on the antimesenteric side of the bowel. About 1/4 have ectopic mucosa, which is often gastric but occasionally pancreatic in character. Remember that having ectopic gastric mucosa predisposes to bleeding (just like in Meckel's) and peptic ulceration.

Complications from intestinal duplications can include obstruction, intussusception, bleeding, pain, and perforation. It is common for patients to present with abdominal pain and frequent vomiting. You can confirm diagnosis with exploratory laparotomy.

Gastric duplications are much rarer than the ileal location and make up only ~ 5% of GI duplications. Gastric duplications are usually cystic and are located on the greater curvature of the stomach. They do not typically

GASTROENTEROLOGY

communicate with the stomach lumen. Major complications include bleeding and ulcerations because these duplications contain gastric mucosa and secrete acid. Treat by resecting the duplication.

Colonic and rectal duplications are very rare and are associated with GU malformations. Rectal duplications can be confused with rectal prolapse, hemorrhoids, or fistulas.

MECONIUM ILEUS

See the Neonatology section for the discussion of meconium ileus and meconium plugs.

CARBOHYDRATE MALABSORPTION

If a patient is unable to digest carbohydrates in the gut, bacteria will do it. Bacterial fermentation produces gas (H_2), which can cause bloating and pain. The undigested carbohydrates cause a high solute concentration in the intestinal lumen, which leads to osmotic diarrhea.

Lactose Intolerance

Lactose intolerance is a common disorder in patients who are > 2 years of age, with prevalence varying substantially by race. Lactase is an enzyme normally found on the brush border near the tips of the intestinal villi, and it breaks down lactose into glucose and galactose. Lactose intolerance is an impaired ability to break down lactose due to a deficiency in lactase. The deficiency can be either partial or complete, resulting in varying degrees of symptoms.

Primary lactose intolerance (adult type) is the most common cause of carbohydrate malabsorption in the world. It is due to a postweaning decline in intestinal lactase-specific activity. Infants are universally able to ingest lactose-containing breast milk and other milk products. Milk intolerance in infants can be due to other causes such as milk-protein intolerance. In individuals with this genetic programming, the lactose gene (located on chromosome 2q21) downregulates and produces a much lower lactase level. This can occur as early as the 2nd year of life and can persist into adulthood. Most of the world's population is genetically prone to become lactase deficient by early adulthood, except for Caucasian populations of northern and central European descent. As much as 90% of those of Asian descent and 75% of those of African descent are affected. Symptoms of diarrhea and recurrent abdominal pain can occur in those with low levels of lactase who consume a large amount of lactose-containing foods.

Secondary lactase deficiency, sometimes seen in infancy, is usually transient and due to a secondary cause (e.g., infectious diarrhea). In addition, premature infants can have a transient developmental lactase deficiency that resolves as they reach term.

Finally, there is also a very rare **congenital** lactase deficiency that presents at birth. It is autosomal recessive (AR) and is due to a complete absence of lactase. Symptoms (most notably severe diarrhea) resolve with complete removal of lactose from the diet or addition of lactase to the diet when consuming lactose-containing foods.

The diagnosis of lactase deficiency is usually made solely on clinical grounds. However, be familiar with the following tests:

- Endoscopic biopsy with measurement of mucosal enzyme activity is the gold standard study for disaccharide activity but is relatively expensive and invasive.
- The breath hydrogen test is the most reliable noninvasive diagnostic test. When carbohydrate is malabsorbed, bacteria in the colon produce hydrogen gas, which is then absorbed across the colon mucosa into the bloodstream, transported to the lungs, and expired. In the breath hydrogen test, breath is sampled sequentially after the patient is given a test carbohydrate substance. A rise of > 10–20 ppm in expired hydrogen indicates that the carbohydrate is not being digested and, therefore, is not absorbed properly. If the rise is too early, this typically indicates small bowel bacterial overgrowth. A child on antibiotics sometimes produces a false-negative test because the bacteria needed for hydrogen production are missing due to the presence of the antibiotics.

Advise older children and adults with lactase intolerance to avoid large quantities of lactose-containing foods (e.g., milk, ice cream, soft cheeses) and to limit their intake of lactose to foods like hard cheeses and yogurt that contain relatively small amounts of lactose (due to the fermentation process used to make them). As an alternative, a microbial-derived lactase enzyme (e.g., Lactaid) supplement can be used with meals.

In the past, many practitioners recommended lactose avoidance for infants during acute infectious diarrhea (which often causes a secondary lactase deficiency). However, 2012 AAP guidelines on acute gastroenteritis advise continuation of a regular diet throughout the diarrheal illness because early refeeding of milk does not prolong diarrhea.

Fructose and Sorbitol Malabsorption

Fructose and sorbitol are used extensively in commercial food products. Fructose is used as a sweetener, especially as high-fructose corn syrup in soft drinks. Sorbitol is a poorly absorbed sugar best known for its use in "diet" foods.

Both fructose and sorbitol can cause malabsorption symptoms if consumed in quantities that exceed the ability of the intestine to break down and absorb these sugars. The transport carrier protein can be overwhelmed by excessive quantities of these sugars. Fructose malabsorption presents with diarrhea, abdominal pain, and distention. Fruit juices with high fructose-to-glucose ratios and those with sorbitol (e.g., apple, pear) can cause nonspecific diarrhea and recurrent abdominal pain. High fructose diets are associated with a nonspecific childhood diarrhea called **toddler's diarrhea.**

Sucrase-Isomaltase Deficiency

Sucrase-isomaltase deficiency is an AR disorder that affects the ability to break down and absorb sucrose and maltose. It first appears when sucrose-containing formula or fruits are introduced to the older infant. (Remember that breast milk contains lactose, and most formulas contain maltodextrin, a polymer of glucose). In those of European descent, the incidence of this condition is approximately 5/1,000; however, in some indigenous populations in Alaska, Greenland, and Northern Canada, it has been reported to occur as commonly as 1/10. These children have low levels of sucrase and maltase and cannot digest starches easily. They can present with mild-to-severe diarrhea and abdominal pain. Sacrosidase, an enzyme derived from *Saccharomyces cerevisiae*, is a potent sucrase and can be taken with meals to overcome sucrase deficiency.

Secondary Carbohydrate Malabsorption

Secondary carbohydrate malabsorption is very common in diseases that cause intestinal mucosal damage or atrophy. Viral gastroenteritis is the most common etiology. *Giardia* infection and HIV can also cause carbohydrate malabsorption. Conditions of bacterial overgrowth can lead to impaired monosaccharide transport. Secondary carbohydrate malabsorption can also affect infants with short bowel syndrome who do not have enough surface area to complete carbohydrate digestion. Finally, children with CF or other causes of pancreatic insufficiency have low levels of amylase, so they cannot break down starches into simple sugars.

CONGENITAL TRANSPORT DEFECTS

Congenital transport defects are rare. For exam questions, you generally just have to know the syndrome and the defect, but a few require further discussion (Table 10-1.)

Table 10-1: Congenital Transport Defects

Name	Defect	Symptoms
Hypo- and abetalipoproteinemia	ApoB deficiency	Steatorrhea Failure to thrive
Chylomicron retention	Chylomicron exocytosis	Steatorrhea Failure to thrive
Hartnup disease	Free neutral amino acid transport	Pellagra-like
Blue diaper syndrome	Tryptophan transport	Bluish urine-stained diapers
Lowe syndrome	Lysine and arginine transport	Intellectual disability Cataracts Hypotonia Rickets
Acrodermatitis enteropathica	Zinc transport	Rash Diarrhea Failure to thrive Alopecia Blepharitis Conjunctivitis

Disorders of Fat Transport

Abetalipoproteinemia is an AR disorder due to congenital absence of apolipoprotein B (apoB), which results in an inability to synthesize chylomicrons and very-low-density lipoprotein. Patients present with malodorous steatorrhea and FTT. Fat-soluble vitamins (i.e., A, D, E, K) cannot be absorbed, eventually leading to development of problems such as night blindness, sensory ataxia, and nystagmus. Retinitis pigmentosa is present. Acanthocytosis is visible on peripheral blood smear because the red blood cells have abnormal membrane lipids. Serum cholesterol is extremely low, and triglyceride levels are just barely detectable. Confirm by observing an absence of plasma β-lipoprotein. Treat by limiting dietary intake of long-chain fatty acids and giving medium-chain triglycerides. Supplement with vitamins A, D, E, and K. Prognosis is poor.

Hypobetalipoproteinemia is an autosomal dominant (AD) disorder and presents in a manner that is similar to abetalipoproteinemia. A family history with an AD pattern (1 or more 1st degree relatives with the disease) is a distinguishing feature.

Chylomicron retention disease (Anderson disease) is an AR disorder that occurs due to defective exocytosis of chylomicrons. It presents mainly with diarrhea, steatorrhea, and low serum cholesterol without the severe acanthocytosis, retinitis pigmentosa, and neurologic abnormalities typical of the abeta- and hypobetalipoproteinemias.

Amino Acid Transport Defects

Amino acid transport defects are rare and can involve the small intestine enterocyte as well as the proximal renal tubule. Clinically, these can be asymptomatic to severe.

Hartnup disease is due to a defect in transport of free neutral amino acids. It results in a deficiency of nicotinamide synthesized from tryptophan and leads to pellagra-type findings.

Blue diaper syndrome is due to isolated malabsorption of tryptophan. In addition to bluish urine–stained diapers, symptoms can include digestive disturbances, irritability, and visual difficulties.

Lowe syndrome is due to malabsorption of lysine and arginine and presents with intellectual disability, cataracts, hypotonia, and vitamin D–resistant rickets, all of which can be detected with analysis of urine amino acids.

Zinc Deficiency

Acquired zinc deficiency is common, especially in infants and older adults (as high as 30–40% in some populations). It is often seen in inflammatory conditions such as Crohn disease or other disorders causing malabsorption. In Crohn disease and ulcerative colitis, low zinc is linked to worse disease outcomes, so most gastroenterologists recommend checking zinc levels and supplementing if low.

GASTROENTEROLOGY

Acrodermatitis enteropathica (AE) is an extremely rare AR disease with an abnormal chromosome 8q24.3. In patients with AE, zinc is not adequately absorbed. Consequently, these patients develop bullous and pustular dermatitis. Additionally, alopecia, blepharitis, conjunctivitis, diarrhea, and FTT are common. Breast milk contains the missing zinc-binding factor, so symptoms will not appear in a breastfed infant until 2–3 weeks after weaning has occurred. Deficiency develops 1–2 months after birth in a nonbreastfed infant.

You can confirm diagnosis by the above classic clinical findings and by demonstrating a zinc concentration < 50 µg/dL. Treat with oral elemental zinc 35–100 mg daily for life. Expect prompt improvement (1–2 days) after initiation of therapy. (See the Dermatology section for more information.)

SHORT BOWEL SYNDROME

Short bowel syndrome is a malabsorption disorder caused by shortened intestinal length, due to congenital anomalies of the gut or to resection of the small intestine. Common causes include necrotizing enterocolitis, volvulus (e.g. from malrotation), intestinal atresia, and gastroschisis. Malabsorption occurs because of a lack of sufficient mucosal absorptive surface. Other contributing factors can include bile acid deficiency and bacterial overgrowth syndromes.

Just how much bowel is required for normal health is not clear. Normally, infants have 200–300 cm of small intestine. This lengthens to 600–800 cm by adulthood. We do know that most infants with at least 38 cm of small intestine survive, and those with < 15 cm die or require small bowel transplantation. There have been reports of survival with shorter bowel lengths, so it appears that a more important factor is the functional capacity of the remaining bowel.

The length and functional capacity of the small bowel are the most important factors, but board exams like to test the specific nutrient defects seen with loss of specific sections:

- If the defect is in the **duodenum**, expect decreased iron, folate, and calcium absorption, which results in anemia and osteopenia.
- If the defect is in the **jejunum**, there is impaired nutrient absorption, which results in osmotic diarrhea and inadequate enteral caloric intake, especially of protein.
- If the defect is in the **ileum**, expect fluid and sodium losses, as well as specific vitamin deficiencies. Remember that the ileum is responsible for absorption of vitamin B_{12} and bile salts; therefore, a shortened ileum results in vitamin B_{12} deficiency and hypovitaminosis A, D, E, and K. (A diminished level of bile salts results in fat malabsorption, which in turn results in reduced absorption of the fat-soluble vitamins.)

If the short gut is due to surgery, adaptive measures in the remaining small intestine usually kick in and eventually result in improved absorption. Again, this depends largely on how much and what part of the small intestine remains, as well as how much functionality of the mucosal area is left. If the small intestine's capacity to absorb nutrients does not improve, then total parenteral nutrition (TPN) is required for survival. If chronic TPN use results in either chronic liver damage, or frequent central line infections, an intestinal transplant is often performed. Unfortunately, intestinal transplant is not curative, and outcomes and survival remain poor even after successful transplant.

SUPERIOR MESENTERIC ARTERY (SMA) SYNDROME

SMA syndrome occurs when the bifurcation of the superior mesenteric artery from the abdominal aorta compresses the third portion of the duodenum (see Figure 10-11). This results in a proximal small bowel obstruction causing bilious vomiting, weight loss, gastric distension, and abdominal pain. Normally, a pad of adipose tissue cushions the space between the SMA and the aorta, allowing the duodenum to pass through. In states of malnutrition this fat pad decreases in volume, decreasing the angle of the bifurcation and squeezing the duodenum, causing obstruction. This most commonly occurs in situations involving rapid weight loss, such as anorexia nervosa (see the Behavioral Medicine & Substance Use Disorders section), or after major surgery (such as spinal fusion), but it can occur in any condition that causes weight loss. Children with scoliosis who have repositioning of the spine with spinal fusion are at particularly increased risk, because the operation causes repositioning of abdominal contents.

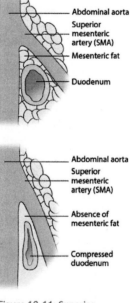

Figure 10-11: Superior mesenteric artery syndrome

Diagnosis is with a contrast study of the upper GI tract (e.g., upper GI series, abdominal CT with oral contrast). These will show narrowing of the duodenum as it crosses the midline, which often changes with repositioning of the patient. Treatment is challenging, but usually involves passing a naso- or gastrojejunal tube past the obstruction and then feeding the patient with an elemental formula for weeks until they gain enough weight for the fat pad to increase in size and relieve the obstruction.

GLUTEN-SENSITIVE ENTEROPATHY (CELIAC DISEASE)

Celiac disease (a.k.a. celiac sprue or gluten-sensitive enteropathy) occurs in genetically predisposed children and adults after exposure to specific gluten proteins and resultant intestinal inflammation and damage due to immunologic cross-reaction. In susceptible individuals, gluten from wheat products (and similar proteins found in rye, barley, and malt) can induce the immune reaction to human transglutaminase and the resulting mucosal damage.

Celiac disease is a common disorder, and many studies using serology-based screening have determined the incidence to be 0.5–2% (between 1/50 and 1/200) in the general population of the developed world, with considerable racial differences. Non-Hispanic Whites have ~ 4–8× the risk of celiac disease than do other populations. There is also evidence that the overall incidence has been increasing over the past 20 years. Remember, celiac disease is not the same as a wheat allergy, which is a Type I hypersensitivity to wheat proteins causing mast cell degranulation. Nor is celiac disease the same as **nonceliac gluten sensitivity** (a.k.a. "gluten intolerance"), which is a nonallergic clinical response to dietary gluten similar to IBS.

Human leukocyte antigen (HLA) typing shows only 2 HLA types are associated with celiac disease: DQ2 and DQ8. Penetrance is variable, and people with known genetic markers for celiac disease do not necessarily develop HLA. Initially, the immune response occurs in the duodenum, but it eventually spreads to the jejunum and ileum. The mucosal lesions are characterized by increased numbers of lymphocytes, plasma cells, and macrophages in the lamina propria and by increased numbers of intraepithelial lymphocytes. Patients with DQ2 or DQ8 are also at increased risk for autoimmune thyroiditis and Type I diabetes, so many clinicians screen for celiac disease regularly in these populations.

Clinically, patients can present with a variety of symptoms. The classic GI form of the disease presents in the child < 2 years of age, with symptoms that include malabsorptive diarrhea, poor weight gain, abdominal distention, and proximal muscle wasting. If the malabsorption is significant, look for resulting vitamin D deficiency and hypocalcemia in the patient who presents with seizures and hypocalcemic tetany. Iron deficiency anemia is common at diagnosis, and unexplained iron deficiency should prompt you to look for celiac disease. Some patients present without any of the classic GI complaints and only have growth failure, delayed puberty, rash, or oral ulcers. You should have a low threshold to check celiac serology in these situations. Other vitamin and mineral deficiencies, including iron (and less often, folate and vitamin B_{12}), are common in untreated celiac disease because the ileum is relatively spared compared with the proximal small intestine.

Patients with celiac disease may have an associated affective disorder—typically anxiety or depression. Common symptoms include anger, moodiness, and impatience. Important: Sometimes celiac disease is misdiagnosed or significantly contributes to disruptive behavior disorders, including attention deficit hyperactivity disorder, oppositional defiant disorder, and conduct disorder.

Dermatitis herpetiformis is an itchy, vesicular rash that erupts symmetrically on the extensor surfaces of the arms and legs and on the buttocks. It can occur with or without GI symptoms. The lesion is pathognomonic for celiac disease (Figure 10-12).

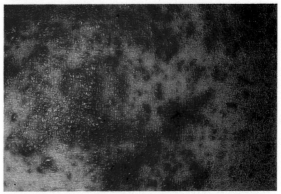

Figure 10-12: Dermatitis herpetiformis (DH). DH is a chronic vesicular eruption that is extremely pruritic and symmetric in distribution.

Comorbid autoimmune disorders are common with celiac disease and can include Type 1 DM, autoimmune thyroid disease, Sjögren syndrome, collagen vascular disease, liver disease, and IgA glomerulonephritis. Celiac disease is so common in children with Type 1 DM and selective IgA deficiency that many physicians recommend universal screening for both diseases in these patients.

Additionally, there is a 5–16× increased risk of celiac disease in children with trisomy 21 (a.k.a. Down syndrome). There is also an increased risk in patients with Turner syndrome or Williams syndrome.

Dental enamel defects are more common in patients with celiac disease. The defect occurs symmetrically and in the secondary teeth, especially the incisors. The abnormalities include brown or yellow opacities, pits, or grooves.

Both 2013 adult and 2016 pediatric guidelines for celiac disease recommend testing for celiac disease using anti-tTG IgA level and total IgA level for all children ≥ 2 years old. For children < 2 years of age, a combination of tTG IgA and deaminated gliadin IgG is recommended. Other serologic tests, or combinations of tests, are not recommended for initial screening as they are less cost effective or have lower sensitivity/specificity. Total IgA levels are measured so that patients with selective IgA deficiency can be identified, as their anti-tTG IgA levels would be falsely low, even in the presence of celiac disease.

IgA tends to be a better immunoglobulin to test than IgG because tTG-IgA is involved in the disease—it is secreted into the gut lumen.

If the serologic testing is positive (or if clinical suspicion is high in the face of negative serologic testing), confirm the diagnosis with a biopsy of the small intestine. Important: Do not place the patient on a gluten-free diet prior to endoscopy because this can cause a false-negative result.

There are 2 mandatory requirements for diagnosis:

1) Characteristic histology on small intestine biopsy: villous blunting and subepithelial lymphocytes
2) Complete clinical remission with a gluten-free diet

Treat with dietary exclusion of gluten (wheat, barley, and rye). Preventing exposure to these products is the only way to make symptoms go away, including the dermatitis herpetiformis. An increasing number of commercial products are becoming available to these patients. You can monitor for low or zero anti-tTG levels to determine if gluten and other products are being effectively excluded from the diet.

TROPICAL SPRUE

Tropical sprue is mainly seen in long-term visitors (at least 3 months) or inhabitants of endemic regions of the tropics, which include India, parts of Asia, the Philippines, areas of South America, Central America, parts of the Caribbean, and areas of central and southern Africa. Sprue can occur in children but is more common in adults. It is probably infectious, but so far, no pathogen has been found. Most patients have a combination of malnutrition and chronic GI infections. It is difficult to distinguish between tropical sprue and celiac sprue (celiac disease) clinically or histologically, so if asked, order celiac serologic testing!

Malabsorption of sugars, fats, folate, and vitamins A and B_{12} occurs. Early in the disease, fatigue, diarrhea, and anorexia are common. The diarrhea is accompanied by abdominal cramps and flatulence. Nutritional deficiencies eventually occur and present as night blindness, cheilosis, glossitis, stomatitis, and hyperkeratosis. Edema and muscle wasting occur in the final stages of the disease. It can take 6 months to several years for the final stages to occur.

Treat with oral broad-spectrum antibiotics and nutritional supplements, including folate and vitamins A and B_{12}.

WHIPPLE DISEASE

Whipple disease is very rare in children and presents as a multisystem disorder resulting in severe malabsorption. Arthritis, polyserositis, and central nervous system symptoms frequently occur. Fever is also prominent. The etiology is a gram-positive actinomycete called *Tropheryma whipplei*. The hallmark is finding periodic acid-Schiff (PAS)-positive granules in the lamina propria, but this has low sensitivity and specificity, so molecular techniques like ELISA and PCR are now used on small bowel biopsies. You need a biopsy for diagnosis, so an upper endoscopy is necessary in most patients. You must treat with antibiotics for ≥ 6 months to cure.

APPENDICITIS

Appendicitis is the most common surgical emergency in children. The peak age of onset is 12 years, and it is unusual before 2 years of age. This disease progresses much more rapidly in children; in ~ 1/3 of cases, the appendix ruptures before surgery.

Fatigue and anorexia are frequently the common symptoms at initial presentation. This can accompany indigestion, which is followed by periumbilical discomfort. Soon after, fever between 100.0°F and 102.0°F (37.8°C and 38.9°C), with nausea and vomiting, often occurs. Over several hours, the inflammation involves the parietal peritoneum and localizes to the right lower quadrant (RLQ) of the abdomen. But remember, younger children are notoriously poor at localizing pain, and many children with appendicitis do not point to their RLQ. Depending on the location of the appendix, the pain can be in different locations: pelvic appendix—hypogastric pain; retrocecal appendix—psoas and obturator muscle pain (pain with hip flexion or rotation, respectively); and retrocolic appendix—right flank pain.

Pain that suddenly resolves can indicate rupture, which has relieved the appendix's pressure, but remember that most other causes of abdominal pain in children also can stop suddenly. Soon, however, high fever, persistent vomiting, thirst, and signs of peritonitis develop. Signs of systemic infection can occur; alternatively, the infection is "walled off" and a local abscess forms.

Early on, the patient may not have a lot of pain and can be in minimal distress; however, pain starting in the midabdomen and migrating to the RLQ, RLQ rebound tenderness, and guarding eventually become prominent. Rebound RLQ tenderness is a key indicator that results with pain being caused with abrupt release of pressure after slow, deep palpation of the RLQ. You see psoas irritation with extension of the thigh and obturator irritation with passive internal rotation of the thigh. **Rovsing sign** occurs when abdominal palpation remote to McBurney's point (i.e., LLQ) results in RLQ pain. Figure 10-13 shows typical locations of appendicitis pain.

In children, inflamed appendices perforate within 24–48 hours after onset. CBC is not helpful (WBC is often normal in children), but microscopic pyuria and hematuria can occur with appendicitis. Abdominal x-ray is rarely helpful.

Admit for observation if the diagnosis is unclear, and preferably have the same physician conduct serial examinations. Ultrasound can sometimes be helpful in the hands of a skilled technician and is the best initial imaging study in most children who are not obese. A CT of the abdomen and pelvis shows enhancement and dilation of the appendix in appendicitis. Figure 10-14 shows an appendix width of 17.1 mm; normal is < 6 mm. This test involves significant radiation exposure.

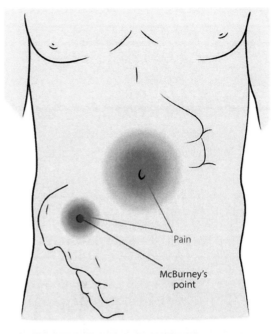

Figure 10-13: Typical location of appendix pain

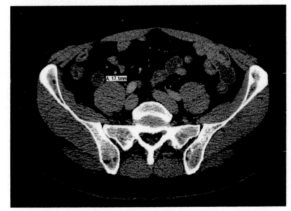

Figure 10-14: CT of inflamed appendix

Treatment

Treat with appendectomy. If the appendix is not ruptured, simply remove it, and patients generally can go home in 12–24 hours. If rupture has occurred, obtain intraoperative anaerobic and aerobic cultures in high risk patients, irrigate the peritoneal cavity, and place drains if abscesses are present. The 2010 American College of Emergency Physicians guidelines and the 2017 Surgical Infection Society guidelines suggest preoperative broad spectrum IV antibiotics in all children with appendicitis, even if they have not perforated. A single prophylactic dose is sufficient for nonperforated appendicitis; however, perforated appendicitis requires at least 7 days of antibiotics, which can be switched from IV to oral once the patient is improving clinically.

In some patients, perforation occurs days prior to presentation, and a palpable mass is noticeable in the RLQ. If the child is well without evidence of peritonitis, manage conservatively with antibiotic therapy and observation. If symptoms respond to the antibiotics, appendectomy can be done in 4–6 weeks. Do the surgery sooner if there is no response to the antibiotics.

Complications are rare today but can include wound infection and intraabdominal abscess.

NEUTROPENIC ENTEROCOLITIS

Neutropenic enterocolitis, commonly located in the cecum where it is called "typhlitis," is inflammation of the small or large bowel mainly seen during periods of neutropenia in patients who are being treated for leukemia. Overall, ~ 8% of patients with neutropenia develop neutropenic enterocolitis. It can also occur with other immunodeficiencies and after organ transplant. Neutropenic enterocolitis is dangerous in that the inflammation can progress rapidly to perforation and sepsis. Fever and RLQ pain can also suggest acute appendicitis. Abdominal x-ray sometimes shows bowel wall thickening or pneumatosis intestinalis. Most use CT to investigate.

Treat with bowel rest, IV fluids, and antibiotic therapy. Some recommend WBC transfusions. Almost all resolve without surgical intervention, unless perforation occurs. Once enterocolitis occurs, there is a high risk for recurrence with subsequent episodes of neutropenia.

INFLAMMATORY BOWEL DISEASE (IBD)

PREVIEW | REVIEW

- What are the 2 forms of inflammatory bowel disease?
- What are the differences between ulcerative colitis (UC) and Crohn disease regarding bowel involvement, tissue involvement, granulomas, and perianal disease?
- How do you diagnose UC?
- In which part of the gastrointestinal tract does Crohn disease most commonly occur?
- Which is more likely to cause weight loss and growth problems: Crohn disease or UC?
- Which is transmural: Crohn disease or UC?
- Which drugs are used for both the remission and maintenance of UC?
- Is surgical therapy curative for Crohn disease?

OVERVIEW

IBD is a chronic disorder affecting the digestive tract. There are 2 forms of IBD: **ulcerative colitis** (UC) and **Crohn disease**. UC involves only the mucosa of the colon while Crohn disease is a transmural inflammation and can occur anywhere along the digestive tract. Table 10-2 on page 10-26 provides a comparison of UC and Crohn disease.

Table 10-2: Comparison of Ulcerative Colitis and Crohn Disease		
Finding	Ulcerative Colitis	Crohn Disease
Bowel involvement	Colon only	Anywhere from mouth to anus
Pattern of lesions	Continuous, beginning distally and extending proximally	Skip lesions
Involvement of tissue	Mucosal only (generally)	Transmural disease
Granulomas likely	No	Yes
Weight loss	Less common	More common
Hematochezia	Common	Less common
Imaging studies	Colon dilation Loss of haustrations/"thumbprinting"	Skip areas String sign (luminal narrowing of small bowel) Mural thickening with dilatation
Perianal lesions	None	Common
Aphthous mouth ulcers	Rare	Common
Growth failure	Rare	Common
Risk of colorectal cancer	Yes	Yes, but not as high as with UC

ULCERATIVE COLITIS (UC)

In children, UC occurs less commonly than Crohn disease, and the mean age of diagnosis is 12 years, with a peak onset at adolescence. In UC, the inflammation is restricted to the **colon** and does not involve the small intestine. (Remember this with a simple mnemonic: **UC** = **u**nanimously **c**olon.) UC involves only the **mucosa**—mucosa that is contiguous without skip lesions. It starts in the rectum and extends proximally into the colon. See Figure 10-15 for colonic features of Crohn disease and UC.

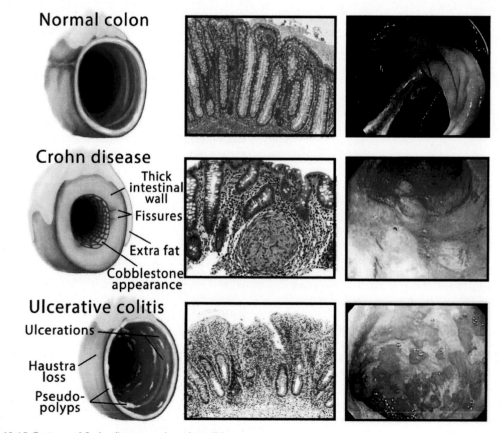

Figure 10-15: Features of Crohn disease vs. ulcerative colitis

Presentation

Patients classically present with abdominal pain and bloody diarrhea; however, at onset, many patients have only nonbloody diarrhea. The diarrhea is most common in the morning when arising and is often associated with tenesmus and urgency. Generally, the more severe the symptoms, the more severe the colonic involvement. Fever and arthralgia/arthritis are the most common extraintestinal findings. The arthritis is migratory, asymmetric, and mainly involves the hip and/or knee (large joints). Seronegative spondyloarthropathies, erythema nodosum (described as tender, red, oval nodules over the extensor surfaces of the legs; Figure 10-16), and pyoderma gangrenosum (Figure 10-17) can all occur. Primary sclerosing cholangitis occurs in ~ 3% of patients and sometimes presents before the colonic disease. There is also increased prevalence of deep vein thrombosis and pulmonary emboli.

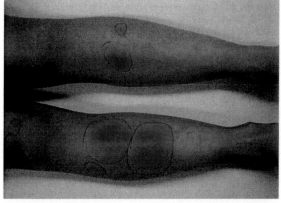

Figure 10-16: Erythema nodosum. Raised erythematous lesions that are subdermal and are commonly located on the shins.

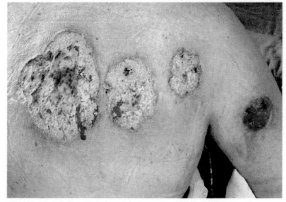

Figure 10-17: Pyoderma gangrenosum. Well-demarcated erythematous rim with central deep ulcer, often with a necrotic focus.

Diagnosis

Diagnosis is made by colonoscopy and upper endoscopy (to help differentiate between UC and Crohn disease) with characteristic endoscopic appearance and biopsies.

UC tends to involve a contiguous area of colon, beginning in the rectum and extending proximally. Involved mucosa is friable (bleeds when manipulated), erythematous, nodular, and often has mucus or pus oozing from it. Plain films can be done in an acutely ill child, but these are rarely helpful. With severe colitis, the colonic wall thickens from edema ("thumbprinting"). Colonoscopy for examination and biopsy is clinically indicated.

In children with UC, the histology from colon biopsies tends to show areas of chronic and acute inflammation, often with a mixed population of cells. The crypts in the wall of the colon are often distorted and full of small abscesses, signs of chronic inflammation. Granulomas are not present.

Colon Cancer

UC predisposes to colon cancer at an increasing rate that is correlated with the duration of active disease. After 10 years of active disease, the yearly risk of colon cancer is about 1%. Children and adolescents with UC should undergo colonoscopy with biopsy every 2 years after having the disease for 8 years. If dysplasia is found, colectomy is indicated.

CROHN DISEASE

Crohn disease is an inflammatory process that is **transmural**, involving the GI tract anywhere from mouth to anus. Bowel segments can be inflamed with intervening normal mucosal involvement, referred to as **skip lesions**. The terminal ileum is the most commonly involved site in patients with Crohn disease, with nearly 70% of pediatric patients also having some colonic involvement (usually the cecum and/or ascending colon). As with UC, the etiology of Crohn disease is still unknown. Aphthous ulcers are more common in Crohn disease and tend to parallel IBD activity. Extraintestinal manifestations are common and can precede the GI symptoms by years.

The prevalence of Crohn disease peaks in the mid-20s age group. In children, Crohn disease is seen most commonly in ages 10–18 years, with prevalence increasing with age, but there is now an increasing incidence of very-early-onset IBD (VEOIBD). VEOIBD has a higher prevalence among the Ashkenazi Jewish population.

Genetics are a major risk factor. If 1 parent is affected, the risk of a child having Crohn disease is ~ 1 in 8. If both parents are affected, the risk of having an affected child is ~ 1 in 3. Monozygotic twin studies show a very strong concordance for Crohn disease—far greater than for UC.

Presentation

Weight loss and growth failure are much more common with Crohn disease than with UC.

Abdominal pain and diarrhea are common. Anal fistulas and abscesses are seen in patients with Crohn disease (but not with UC!), but most patients do not have perianal disease. Other extraintestinal manifestations include mouth

GASTROENTEROLOGY

ulcerations, peripheral nondeforming arthritis, digital clubbing, renal stones, gallstones, erythema nodosum, uveitis (which can present independent of disease activity), and episcleritis, which often parallels IBD activity.

Crohn disease is transmural and can result in fistulous tracts as well as strictures. On microscopic examination, look for a chronic granulomatous inflammation involving all layers of the intestinal wall. On biopsy, **noncaseating granulomas** that contain multinucleated giant cells and epithelioid cells are pathognomonic for Crohn disease, although these are seen only 40% of the time.

Diagnosis

If the small intestine and the colon are both involved, Crohn disease is the diagnosis. What is difficult is when Crohn disease involves only the colon. In up to 15% of cases, patients are initially diagnosed as having indeterminate colitis or IBD-unspecified when no granulomas are seen microscopically. Colonoscopy with biopsy is the best means for diagnosis.

Colon Cancer

Crohn disease is much less likely than UC to induce colon cancer, but the rate of colon cancer is still 20× higher in patients with Crohn disease than in the normal population. The 2012 European Crohn's and Colitis Organization (ECCO)/ESPGHAN guidelines recommend patients undergo a colonoscopy after 8 years of disease and then regular surveillance every 1–3 years afterward, depending on the degree of colitis. Crohn patients without colitis do not need extra screening.

TREATMENT OF IBD

Treatment of IBD is similar for both Crohn disease and UC and primarily consists of immunosuppressant or antiinflammatory medications to prevent ongoing damage to the GI tract. Steroids, 5-ASA, immunomodulators like thiopurines and methotrexate, and biologics are the mainstay of treatment for both. The main difference is the use of surgical resection, which is still a last resort for both.

Steroids supply powerful immunosuppression and are used in acute exacerbations to induce remission. Do not prescribe for maintenance of remission because they can be quite dangerous if used for long periods of time. Long-term use causes significant side effects, including hyperglycemia, osteoporosis, osteonecrosis, myopathy, susceptibility to infection, cataracts, growth restriction, behavioral problems, acne, striae, and cushingoid appearance. Newer topical agents, such as budesonide and fluticasone, have much less adrenal-suppressive effects.

5-Aminosalicylic acid (5-ASA) can be used to both induce remission and maintain remission in mild-to-moderate cases of UC. Aminosalicylates have a topical effect and reduce inflammation in the lining of the intestine. There are various formulations, so select specific agent by release method and location of desired effect. Most patients with mild-to-moderate UC respond very well to 5-ASA. Large meta-analyses have shown that 5-ASA compounds are not as effective in Crohn disease. Nausea and headache are common side effects of the older agents.

Purine analogs 6-mercaptopurine (6-MP) and azathioprine are very effective in maintaining remission for moderate to severe disease (both UC and Crohn disease) but do not have a role in inducing remission. Purine analogs have cytotoxic and immunosuppressive properties and inhibit the proliferation and function of leukocytes. They have a very slow onset of action (~ 3 months). Severe complications are rare, but elevated transaminases and/or profound leukopenia. These medications are no longer recommended as 1st line agents, as there is a risk of hepatosplenic T-cell lymphoma, which mainly occurs in young males.

Methotrexate is an immunosuppressant agent that impairs DNA synthesis, inhibits cytokine production and causes T-cell apoptosis. Methotrexate is not routinely recommended for maintenance of remission for UC. It is used as a steroid-sparing agent for maintenance in Crohn disease when a patient is unable to use 6-MP or azathioprine, such as a male patient. It has potential toxicities, including bone marrow, kidney, and liver.

A **biologic agent** (including infliximab and adalimumab) is an IgG1 monoclonal antibody that is directed against tumor necrosis factor (a.k.a. tumor necrosis factor-α). It is effective at both inducing and maintaining remission. This is widely used in children with moderate-to-severe IBD who are steroid dependent or steroid refractory. Biologics are the treatment of choice in patients with fistulizing Crohn disease, which includes patients with perianal disease. The primary side effect is an allergic reaction to the chimeric protein. This can be immediate or a delayed serum sickness. Screen patients for TB, hepatitis, and varicella prior to starting a biologic agent due to TB reactivation.

Antibiotics are more commonly used with Crohn disease than with UC. Many providers use metronidazole and/or ciprofloxacin for fistulas and perianal abscesses. Side effects include nausea, appetite loss, and complaints of a metallic taste. Prolonged use can result in paresthesias, which can persist for years after stopping therapy. The therapeutic effect of antibiotics tends to fade with time; therefore, reserve antibiotic therapy for short-term use in the conditions indicated.

Nutritional therapy for Crohn disease requires a highly motivated patient who wishes to avoid alternative therapies. Unlike UC, Crohn disease responds to bowel rest. Recommend an elemental diet for 1 month, excluding other food. An elemental diet is an easily digestible formula consisting of amino acids, fats, sugars, minerals, and vitamins that is ingested or given via NG tube. Early relapse occurs if the diet is ended too soon. Once remission has occurred, recommend a cycle of elemental diet 1 out of every 4 months. Supplemental nocturnal NG feedings with elemental or polymeric formulas are used to reverse growth failure. Osteoporosis is also of significant concern in children with Crohn disease, and supplementation with calcium and vitamin D is recommended.

Surgery is "curative" in UC. Emergent surgery may be needed as a lifesaving procedure for uncontrollable massive bleeding, perforation, and toxic megacolon. Most often, though, surgery is done because of failure of standard medical therapy. Consider elective surgery in those with steroid dependence; intolerance of, or complications from, immunosuppressive therapy; or evidence of colonic dysplasia or cancer. A surgical pouch is created from the ileum to act as a stool reservoir. After surgery, pouchitis can occur, which is caused by bacterial overgrowth and resultant inflammation, causing diarrhea, lower abdominal pain, tenesmus, and sometimes hematochezia. Metronidazole or ciprofloxacin are usually given for an acute episode. Probiotics (typically VSL#3) are commonly prescribed for prevention of pouchitis.

Surgery does not cure Crohn disease, and the disease eventually recurs. Reserve surgery in these patients mainly for strictures or complications that fail to respond to medical management, such as massive hemorrhage, perforation, and fulminant colitis, as repeated resections can lead to short gut syndrome.

COLONIC POLYPS AND TUMORS

PREVIEW | REVIEW

- What is the difference in cancer risk between a solitary juvenile polyp and juvenile polyposis?
- What are the presenting symptoms of Peutz-Jeghers syndrome?
- Is there an increased risk of cancer in patients with Peutz-Jeghers syndrome?
- What does Gardner syndrome consist of?

OVERVIEW

A colorectal polyp is an overgrowth of cells into the lumen of the colon or rectum. The categories of colonic polyps include:

- **Inflammatory**—non-neoplastic with epithelial and inflammatory components
- **Hamartomatous**—polyps consisting of disorganized growth of tissue (This category includes solitary juvenile polyps, juvenile polyposis, Peutz-Jeghers syndrome, and *PTEN* syndromes.)
- **Adenomatous**—dysplastic polyps with malignant potential (This category includes familial adenomatous polyposis.)
- **Mixed**

Most polyps are asymptomatic but can present with rectal bleeding. Colonoscopy is the best method to detect and biopsy polyps. Treatment consists of removal during colonoscopy or surgical resection.

JUVENILE POLYPS AND JUVENILE POLYPOSIS

Juvenile polyps occur in ~ 1% of preschool children and account for the majority of all polyps in children. Juvenile polyps are benign inflammatory polyps, typically pedunculated hamartomata. The classic presentation is a child 2–10 years of age (peak age 3–4) who presents with intermittent, painless hematochezia with bowel movements. There is usually not a history of a familial polyp syndrome, and there are typically < 3–5 polyps. Solitary juvenile polyps of this type are not cancer prone. On the other hand, juvenile polyposis occurs when there are > 5 polyps, and these have a high, long-term risk of malignancy; affected individuals are 30× more likely to develop colorectal cancer.

Juvenile polyposis coli (involving only the colon) refer to polyps that are distributed throughout the colon. If a family member has already been diagnosed with juvenile polyposis, any other member who has even a single juvenile polyp is considered to also have juvenile polyposis.

Most children with unexplained rectal bleeding get a colonoscopy. It allows you to assess for the presence, number, and distribution of polyps, as well as the histologic data. Unless a large number of polyps are found, remove all polyps for histology. If you find a single rectosigmoid polyp with typical histology, no further evaluation is necessary. If ≥ 5 juvenile polyps are found, or if a juvenile polyp with adenomatous changes is found, perform colonoscopy every 6–12 months until no polyps are found; check every 2 years thereafter if no further polyps develop. Monitor children with 2–4 polyps with a repeat colonoscopy. For any child with polyps that show adenomatous changes, conduct further investigations.

PEUTZ-JEGHERS SYNDROME

Peutz-Jeghers syndrome (a.k.a. hereditary intestinal polyposis syndrome) is an AD disease (mutation of the *STK11* gene on chromosome 19p) with variable penetrance.

It presents with GI hamartomatous polyps and mucocutaneous hyperpigmentation of the lips and gums. The lesions are brown-black macules, 1–5 mm in diameter, and look like freckles (Figure 10-18 on page 10-30). They are almost universally on the lips and buccal mucosa and are less commonly found on the nose, hands, and feet. The lesions occur during infancy and childhood and fade during adolescence. Patients have multiple polyps throughout their GI tract. Most commonly affected is the small bowel, followed by the colon and the stomach. Rarely, polyps are found in the bronchi and GU tract. Histologically, they are distinguished from juvenile polyps by the presence of smooth muscle bands within the polyp.

GASTROENTEROLOGY

Figure 10-18: Hyperpigmented macules on lips of a patient with Peutz-Jeghers syndrome

About 1/3 of patients are diagnosed during childhood, but the mean age of onset of symptoms is ~ 22 years of age. The most common presentation is intermittent, colicky, abdominal pain with intestinal obstruction from intussusception, GI bleeding, and anemia. Nearly 50% of patients develop cancers outside of the colon during their lifetime, with the most common involving the breast, cervix, ovary, testicle, and pancreas; 2–13% develop colon cancer. Adenomatous changes are found in ~ 5% of Peutz-Jeghers polyps.

Diagnosis depends on finding the hamartomatous polyps, recognizing the skin lesions, and discerning a family history. Remove all large polyps, and perform surveillance endoscopy to continue removing additional polyps as they appear. Also, survey for other tumors, beginning in patients at 10 years of age or sooner if symptoms have already developed. Screen all 1st degree relatives regularly after 10 years of age.

SYNDROMES LINKED TO *PTEN* GENE MUTATIONS

PTEN Hamartoma Tumor Syndrome (PHTS)

PHTS includes Bannayan-Riley-Ruvalcaba syndrome (BRRS) and Cowden syndrome. The diagnosis of PHTS is made when a *PTEN* mutation is identified on chromosome 10. About 65% of patients diagnosed with BRRS and 85% of patients diagnosed with Cowden syndrome have a detectable *PTEN* gene mutation.

Bannayan-Riley-Ruvalcaba Syndrome

Bannayan-Riley-Ruvalcaba syndrome is characterized by macrocephaly, pigmented penile lesions, and hamartomatous intestinal polyps. The polyps present with rectal bleeding and sometimes abdominal pain. Additional findings include café au lait spots, lipomas, intellectual disability, and a lipid-storage abnormality. It most commonly results from mutations on the *PTEN* tumor suppressor gene.

Cowden Syndrome

Cowden syndrome is very rare and is characterized by having multiple hamartomata of the skin, mucous membranes, breast, and thyroid. These patients can have gastric, duodenal, and/or colonic polyps. Hyperkeratotic papillomas of the lips and tongue are characteristic. Cowden syndrome is most commonly caused by a mutation on the *PTEN* tumor suppressor gene on chromosome locus 10q22-23. These patients have an increased risk of breast cancer and nonmedullary thyroid cancer.

PROTEUS SYNDROME

Proteus syndrome is a rare disorder with hamartomatous polyps and hemihypertrophy, gigantism of the extremities, angiomas, pigmented nevi, and multiple lipomas or hamartomata. It results from a mutation in the *AKT1* gene, which is responsible for regulating cell growth and division. The defect is not inherited, but instead occurs randomly in 1 cell during fetal development. As the cells continue to divide, some will be affected and some will not (i.e., mosaicism). Remember this on an exam if they describe a patient with hemihypertrophy and hamartomata.

FAMILIAL ADENOMATOUS POLYPOSIS

Incidence

Familial adenomatous polyposis occurs in ~ 1/10,000 births and is due to mutations on chromosome locus 5q21-22. Most are autosomal dominant and due to mutation in the *APC* gene. Variable penetrance is often observed. A less common variant is autosomal recessive and is caused by mutations in the *MUTYH* gene. About 1/3 of the cases are due to a new mutation without a family history.

Patients present with > 100 GI adenomatous polyps, almost always involving the colon. Gardner syndrome (see Gardner Syndrome) is the most commonly described subset and is often tested on exams.

Gardner Syndrome

Gardner syndrome has a constellation of findings including adenomatous polyposis of the colon, small bowel, and stomach. Other findings include soft tissue tumors, extra teeth, osteomas, and congenital hypertrophy of the retinal pigment epithelium (CHRPE). Soft tissue tumors include desmoid tumors, sebaceous and epidermoid cysts, lipomas, and subcutaneous fibromas. Osteomas are usually found in the skull and mandible but can occur elsewhere also. Colon cancer risk is 100% if the colon is not removed; risk is much lower in other parts of the GI tract.

Diagnosis is established by finding hundreds of adenomatous polyps in the colon, with genetic testing by sequencing the *APC* gene to confirm.

Most authorities recommend yearly screening with colonoscopy, beginning between 10 and 12 years of age. Treatment with cyclooxygenase inhibitors has been shown to suppress polyp expression, and patients are maintained on sulindac (NSAID). Early colectomy is performed in a majority of patients, usually by the time they are young adults, and it prevents development of colonic adenocarcinoma. Patients are still at risk for malignant transformation of other tumors, especially those in the small bowel. Periodic endoscopic evaluation of the upper GI tract, as well as thyroid testing, is also recommended because of the increased risk of cancers in these areas.

CONGENITAL VENTRAL ABDOMINAL WALL DEFECTS

PREVIEW | REVIEW

- What is an omphalocele?
- If an omphalocele is present, should you suspect another congenital anomaly or is it likely an isolated event?
- What is a gastroschisis?

OCCURRENCE

Abdominal wall defects are varied in appearance and location. They are fairly rare, occurring in approximately 1/5,000 live births, and are always associated with some degree of malrotation.

OMPHALOCELE

An omphalocele is a ventral, **midline defect** in the abdominal wall at the umbilical region that can contain both hollow and solid visceral abdominal organs. Omphaloceles are larger than 4 cm and are covered by peritoneal **membrane** internally and amniotic membrane externally (Figure 10-19). In contrast, umbilical hernias are covered abdominal wall defects that are smaller than 4 cm and contain only intestine.

Approximately 50–75% of neonates with an omphalocele have an **associated congenital anomaly**, including thoracoabdominal syndrome (known as the pentalogy of Cantrell—defects of diaphragm, sternum, pericardium, and heart), lower midline syndrome, and Beckwith-Wiedemann syndrome. About 25% have major chromosomal abnormalities, including the trisomies.

Omphalocele presents as a central defect of the umbilical ring and has the abdominal contents inside a sac. The umbilical cord inserts into the sac. In ~ 1/2 of the cases, the sac contains the stomach, loops of small/large intestines, and liver. Giant omphaloceles present with large/ small intestines, liver, spleen, gonadal tissue, and bladder in the sac. Around 10–20% of omphaloceles rupture in utero and present more like gastroschisis, with thickened bowel covered in exudate. See Gastroschisis. Midgut volvulus is common in omphalocele.

Manage by keeping the infant warm and hydrated. Cover exposed omphalocele with a sterile bowel bag. Immediately begin IV antibiotics. Manipulate the bowel into a position so that circulation is well maintained. Nonoperative management is acceptable if the infant is too ill for surgery. Apply antiseptic agents, such as silver nitrate or povidone-iodine, to the omphalocele. These eventually become an eschar and epithelize, thus protecting the exposed organs. Once this has become granulated, you can place a skin graft, resulting in a ventral hernia, which can be repaired in the future. If primary surgical repair cannot be done, you can attempt a staged repair. Survival of infants with omphalocele is 75–95%; survival is usually affected by the associated congenital anomalies.

GASTROSCHISIS

Gastroschisis presents as a 2-cm to 5-cm **lateral defect** in the abdominal wall, just to the right of the umbilicus, with exposed (**no membrane!**) loops of small and large intestines that are short and thick due to an inflammatory reaction of the serosa (Figure 10-19). The solid visceral organs often are contained in the abdominal cavity, and the umbilical cord is normal. Gastroschisis is more common than omphalocele and often occurs with **midgut volvulus**; however, it is less likely, compared with omphalocele, to be associated with other congenital anomalies.

Initial management of gastroschisis is similar to that of omphalocele, with resuscitation, hydration, and temperature control. Most centers advocate placing the exposed intestines in a bowel bag immediately after delivery. For gastroschisis, surgery is mandatory and cannot be delayed. Primary surgical closure is frequently successful. Early postoperative complications include necrotizing enterocolitis and intestinal obstruction. The survival rate for gastroschisis is 95%.

Many children require bowel resection and end up with short bowel syndrome. Additionally, because the bowel is often fibrous and hypofunctioning from sitting freely in the amniotic fluid, many patients have poor motility or absorption of nutrients and may require parenteral nutrition.

Figure 10-19: (left) Omphalocele vs. (right) gastroschisis

GASTROENTEROLOGY

Table 10-3 provides a comparison of omphalocele and gastroschisis.

Table 10-3: Abdominal Wall Defects		
Feature	Omphalocele	Gastroschisis
Location	Central; midline; umbilical region	Lateral (almost always to the right) of the umbilicus
Covering membrane	Yes	No
Associations	Congenital anomalies	Midgut volvulus
Treatment	Staged surgery	Immediate surgery

ANORECTAL DISORDERS

PREVIEW | REVIEW

- True or false? Congenital anorectal disorders are usually isolated findings.
- Which chromosomal abnormality has an increased risk of imperforate anus?
- What are the 3 most common causes of rectal prolapse?
- What is the most common cause of rectal bleeding in children?

OCCURRENCE

Anorectal disorders occur in ~ 1/4,000 births and can be minor to severe. It is probably easiest to think of these based on gender because the defining characteristics of each disorder depend upon the sex of the patient. Generally, those disorders that cause severe deformity or absence of the sacrum result in serious abnormalities and lack of sphincter tone. Also, the absence of ≥ 2 vertebrae results in severe continence problems.

Congenital anorectal disorders are often part of other disorders, including the VATER and VACTERL disorders. VATER/VACTERL refers to **v**ertebral defects, **a**nal atresia, congenital heart defect, **t**racheo**e**sophageal fistula, **r**enal malformations, **l**imb (radial) dysplasia.

MALE ANORECTAL DISORDERS

Perineal Fistula

A perineal fistula presents with a small orifice on the perineum located just anterior to the center of the external orifice. Usually, it is close to the scrotum. Boys have a "bucket handle" malformation or "black ribbon" structure in their perineum that is a subepithelial fistula filled with meconium. Anal dimples are prominent. Less than 10% of those affected have other organ abnormalities. The defect can be repaired surgically without a colostomy.

Rectourethral Fistula

A rectourethral fistula is the most common anorectal defect in males. A rectourethral fistula occurs when the rectum communicates with the lower (bulbar) or upper (prostatic) part of the urethra. Most patients have a well-defined midline perineal groove and an anal dimple. This requires a protective colostomy during the newborn period, with complete surgical repair later in life.

Rectovesical Fistula

A rectovesical fistula occurs when the rectum communicates with the bladder neck. The sacrum is frequently absent. Bowel function is poor, and this requires a colostomy during the newborn period, followed by corrective surgery later in life.

FEMALE ANORECTAL DISORDERS

Perineal Fistula

As in boys, a perineal fistula is the simplest fistula found in girls; however, in girls, the small orifice is located close to the vulva. It does not require colostomy, unlike the other anorectal disorders that affect females.

Vestibular Fistula

Vestibular fistula is the most common anorectal defect in girls. In this instance, the rectum opens into the vestibule of the female genitalia immediately outside the hymenal orifice. The sacrum and sphincter tone are normal, and an anal dimple is present. A protective colostomy must be performed in the newborn period before definitive surgery can be done.

Persistent Cloaca

Persistent cloaca means that the vagina, rectum, and urinary tract meet and fuse as a common channel. There is a single orifice just behind the clitoris. The length can vary from 1-cm–10-cm. Those with short channels (< 3 cm) have a well-developed sacrum and good sphincter tone. Those with longer channels (> 3 cm) have a more complex defect and typically have a poorly defined sacrum and sphincter tone. Most girls with a cloaca have an abnormally large vagina filled with mucus (hydrocolpos). Perform a colostomy in the newborn period; 90% also have urologic abnormalities requiring emergent attention.

ANORECTAL DISORDERS PRESENTING SIMILARLY IN BOTH SEXES

Imperforate Anus (Anal Atresia) without Fistula

An imperforate anus occurs when the rectum is completely closed off and does not communicate with the anus or skin. On average, the rectum is found ~ 2 cm above the perineal skin. The sacrum is well developed, and the sphincteric mechanism is intact. Diagnosis is not always apparent on physical exam. The anus cannot be considered patent until the infant passes meconium. Eventual prognosis is good with an initial colostomy in the newborn period and eventual reparative surgery later. Defects located higher anatomically result in more long-term dysfunction. Children with trisomy 21 have a much higher incidence of imperforate anus than other children.

Rectal Atresia

Rectal atresia is one of the rarest anorectal abnormalities. Patients have a normal anal canal and a normal anus, so the defect is frequently found when the provider attempts to use a rectal thermometer on the patient. Obstruction is present ~ 2 cm above the skin level. A protective colostomy is necessary in the newborn period, followed by reparative surgery at a later date.

Rectal Prolapse

Rectal prolapse occurs when ≥ 1 layer of the rectum protrudes through the anus. Usually, it is only the mucosa that prolapses, and it presents as a red-purple, circular protrusion from the anus (Figure 10-20, A). It is common for a small amount of rectal mucosa to prolapse after normal defecation. If all layers prolapse, this is known as procidentia (rectal prolapse). Luckily, it is rare. It presents as a protrusion with circumferential folds due to the contractions of the circular musculature of the prolapsed rectum.

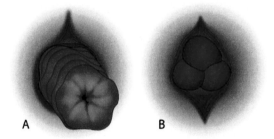

Figure 10-20: (A) Rectal prolapse and (B) external hemorrhoids

Mucosal prolapse is most common in those < 2 years of age because of the flat sacrum and weak pelvic floor muscles. (There have been reports of massive intestinal prolapse in children sitting on unprotected swimming pool drains!) Cystic fibrosis (CF) is always key to remember with rectal prolapse, but CF is not the most common cause—it actually comes in 3rd overall. Constipation is 1st, as this occurs from increased intraabdominal pressure, followed by infectious diarrhea (secondary to parasites or malabsorptive diseases). Other etiologies include various neuromotor disorders and celiac disease, and nearly 20% have no identifiable cause. Most mucosal prolapses reduce spontaneously, but the anus can gape open for up to an hour after reduction. Initial management includes manual reduction if spontaneous reduction does not occur. Some require surgical intervention (a rectopexy), but these are rare. Treat any underlying condition (e.g., constipation, diarrhea).

Hemorrhoids

Typically, internal hemorrhoids are painless and external hemorrhoids are painful when irritated. Although small, asymptomatic hemorrhoids are sometimes found incidentally on examination, the most common cause of symptomatic hemorrhoids is constipation with chronic straining. Other causes include an infection spreading to the hemorrhoidal veins, portal hypertension, or underlying Crohn disease.

Hemorrhoids are sometimes mistaken for rectal prolapse. You can distinguish them by noting that hemorrhoids do not involve the entire rectal mucosa and do not have a hole in the center of the bulging tissue (Figure 10-20, B).

Management is conservative and includes avoidance of straining with defecation, minimizing toilet time, increasing fluids and fiber to relieve constipation, and prescribing a stool softener. Warm-water sitz baths also alleviate symptoms.

Anal Fissures

Anal fissures are the most common cause of rectal bleeding in children of all ages. Anal fissures are slit-like tears of the anal canal, usually located on the posterior or anterior anal verge (Figure 10-21). In addition to blood, they cause pain with bowel movements. Frequently, fissures are due to the passage of large stools in a constipated infant or child. After the fissure heals, a small anal tag sometimes remains. Suspect Crohn disease in an older child if the anal fissure does not heal with stool softeners, warm sitz baths, and generous lubrication to the anal skin. Suspect sexual abuse if there are multiple anal fissures or signs of genital trauma.

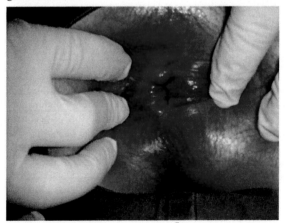

Figure 10-21: Anal fissure

Perianal Itching

Perianal itching (a.k.a. pruritus ani) is very common and is frequently due to perianal dermatitis or infection. *Candida* overgrowth commonly occurs after a course of antibiotics for otitis media or other infection. Other etiologies include atopic dermatitis, contact dermatitis, perianal streptococcal infection, and anal fissures. Pinworms and

GASTROENTEROLOGY

tapeworms also present with perianal itching. Some foods—including tea, coffee, chocolate, soft drinks, citrus, tomatoes, and chili—contain chemicals that irritate the skin or have histamine releasers. UTI can present in the younger child as itching.

Perianal strep infection, caused by group A β-hemolytic *Streptococcus* (*S. pyogenes*), presents as an "angry," bright red, confluent rash around the anal orifice and can spread throughout the entire perineal area. Diagnose by a perianal skin culture. Rectal bleeding can occur, and history may reveal a recent strep infection in the household. Occasionally, the affected child has a concomitant strep pharyngitis. Treat with oral penicillin. Topicals are ineffective.

HIRSCHSPRUNG DISEASE

PREVIEW | REVIEW

- What is the etiology of Hirschsprung disease?
- A term infant is 48 hours old and has not passed meconium. Is it necessary at this point to evaluate for Hirschsprung disease?
- How does enterocolitis present in infants with Hirschsprung disease?
- What is the gold standard procedure used to diagnose Hirschsprung disease?
- A biopsy shows histologic absence of what structures in a patient with Hirschsprung disease?

OCCURRENCE

Hirschsprung disease (a.k.a. congenital aganglionic megacolon) is given special attention here because it is the most common cause of lower intestinal obstruction in neonates! It occurs in 1/5,000 births and is due to the absence of enteric ganglionic neurons (aganglionosis) that begins at the anus and extends proximally for a varying distance. In 75% of those affected, aganglionosis is limited to the rectum and sigmoid; however, ~ 8% have total colon involvement, and an even smaller number have small intestinal aganglionosis as well. There are also occasional concerns in constipated adolescents and adults for the possibility of short-segment Hirschsprung disease.

The rectosigmoid form of the disease has a male predominance of 4:1. This form has a multifactorial or a recessive pattern of inheritance. There is a 7% risk that a sibling of an affected patient will have the disease. Racial differences are not noted. There is an increased association with Down syndrome, Bardet-Biedl syndrome, Smith-Lemli-Opitz syndrome, and Waardenburg syndrome.

PATHOGENESIS

Hirschsprung disease occurs in utero when neural crest cells fail to migrate from the craniocaudal region to the distal intestine between the 5th and 12th week of gestation. The earlier the arrest of migration, the longer the involved bowel segment. Various factors affect the migration of the neural crest cells, and experts believe that expression of these molecules is controlled by the *Hox* and *Sox* homeobox genes (sounds like a Dr. Seuss book!). Additionally, other unspecified factors also mediate the failure of the neural crest cells to develop and/or migrate properly.

Because of the loss of normal innervation of the rectum, there is an overexpression of extrinsic parasympathetic and sympathetic nerves in the lamina propria and muscularis mucosa. The overexpression of nerve activity causes the aganglionic segment, internal sphincter, and anal canal to remain constantly contracted, resulting in obstructive symptoms. The area proximal to the aganglionic segment is dilated and hypertrophied. (See Figure 10-22.)

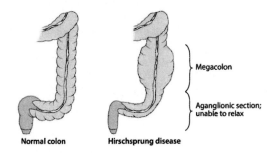

Figure 10-22: Hirschsprung disease

PRESENTATION

The diagnosis of Hirschsprung disease is usually made during the neonatal period (80–90% of patients), but some are not diagnosed until 3 years of age or later, with reports of patients diagnosed well into adulthood. 2 presentation types are noted:

1) Perinatally with intestinal obstruction (i.e., delayed passage of meconium, constipation, abdominal distention)

2) At 1 month of age with enterocolitis

90% of normal, full-term infants pass meconium within 24 hours, and 99% within 48 hours. In children with Hirschsprung disease, 94% fail to pass meconium within the first 24 hours. Therefore, evaluate for Hirschsprung disease in any term infant who does not pass meconium within 48 hours of birth.

Complete intestinal obstruction can occur in the newborn—or later in the older infant who has a history of only constipation. Intestinal obstruction is often accompanied by bilious vomiting, obstipation (inability to pass gas), and massive abdominal distention. No stool is found in the rectal vault.

The most severe complication of undiagnosed Hirschsprung disease is enterocolitis. This typically occurs during the 2nd to 4th weeks of life and is characterized by fever with explosive, foul-smelling stools. Bloody diarrhea is common, as is abdominal distention. X-ray shows dilated loops of bowel with air-fluid levels. The prognosis for enterocolitis is poor, and the mortality rate can be as high as 33%. The pathogenesis of enterocolitis is unknown, although it is thought to be due to overgrowth of colonic bacteria in an atonic distal colon. Delayed diagnosis is the contributing factor for many cases of enterocolitis. However, this complication can occur even after surgical correction for Hirschsprung disease.

DIAGNOSIS

If Hirschsprung disease is suspected, proceed quickly with rectal biopsy, which is the gold standard procedure for diagnosis. The longer it takes for a diagnosis to be made, the more likely enterocolitis will occur. The most commonly used tool is the suction rectal biopsy, a simple instrument that can be used on infants in the outpatient clinic.

Histologically, the diagnosis is based on the absence of any detectable ganglion cells in a biopsy containing adequate submucosa. If the diagnosis is still questionable, do a full-thickness rectal biopsy to look for aganglionosis in the submucosal and myenteric plexuses. Barium enema has been used in the past; however, due to low sensitivity and specificity for Hirschsprung disease, it is now used more often as an adjunct to biopsy to demonstrate a transition zone. Hirschsprung disease is suspected when bowel distal to the transition zone is narrowed, while bowel proximal to it is dilated.

Additionally, anorectal manometry is extremely accurate in the hands of those experienced with it. Failure of the internal anal sphincter to relax in response to distention of the rectum (rectosphincteric reflex) is diagnostic of Hirschsprung disease.

A syndrome with a similar presentation is meconium plugs. It is characterized by abnormal meconium consistency and occurs more frequently in infants with Hirschsprung disease, hypothyroidism, CF, and small left colon syndrome. (See the Neonatology section for more information.)

TREATMENT

Treatment is surgical. Surgical management of Hirschsprung disease usually encompasses 1 of 3 surgical techniques, all of which involve resection of the aganglionic bowel and then a reanastomosis of the proximal normal bowel to the normal anal canal. The differences depend on how the bowel is reconstructed. Most commonly, early surgical repair and reconstitution of the bowel is performed, although some specialists wait until the child is 6–12 months of age.

Immediate complications after surgery include stricture or leakage at the anastomotic site, as well as pelvic abscesses. Long-term dysfunction from Hirschsprung disease remains common. Many patients have ongoing difficulty with incontinence, and enterocolitis may still occur despite surgical correction.

Treat enterocolitis with IV fluids, broad-spectrum antibiotics, nasogastric decompression, and warm saline rectal washouts to help with colonic decompression. Once the patient is stable, perform a proximal colostomy.

DISORDERS OF THE EXOCRINE PANCREAS

PREVIEW | REVIEW
- What is Shwachman-Diamond syndrome?
- What are the commonly identified causes of acute pancreatitis in children?
- What is Cullen sign? Grey Turner sign?
- Which radiologic test is usually most helpful in diagnosing acute pancreatitis?
- What is the most common cause of chronic pancreatitis?

NOTE

Congenital disorders of the exocrine pancreas are almost always part of a generalized systemic disorder. Thankfully, 98% of the pancreatic functional reserve must be lost before pancreatic insufficiency develops.

CYSTIC FIBROSIS (CF)

CF, the most common cause of pancreatic insufficiency in children, is discussed in considerable detail in the Pulmonary Medicine section. Patients who are homozygous for Δ508, the most common mutation in the CFTR gene, have a very high risk for pancreatic insufficiency (60% of infants, 90% by 1 year of age).

SHWACHMAN-DIAMOND SYNDROME

Shwachman-Diamond syndrome, an AR disorder, is the 2nd most common inherited cause of exocrine pancreatic insufficiency in children. The lesion of the pancreas is acinar cell hypoplasia, with intact function of the pancreatic ducts. Shwachman-Diamond syndrome is also characterized by short stature, intermittent or persistent neutropenia, and skeletal abnormalities. Fetal hemoglobin levels are elevated in most patients. About 1/3 of affected boys develop myeloproliferative malignancies. Because of the neutropenia, recurrent infections are common. Pancreatic dysfunction is less severe than that seen in CF, and ~ 50% have improvement in pancreatic function over time. See the Hematology section for more information.

ACUTE PANCREATITIS

Causes

Acute pancreatitis is more common in children than previously thought. Many cases do not have a recognizable etiology but are probably due to an infectious cause, likely a virus.

Common causes of acute pancreatitis include:

- Biliary obstruction from gallstones (becoming much more common with increasing rates of adolescent obesity)
- Idiopathic (many of these are probably viral)
- Blunt abdominal trauma
- Multisystem disease

Less common causes include:

- Drugs such as didanosine (for HIV), valproate, asparaginase, and azathioprine
- Familial pancreatitis
- Congenital anomalies such as an annular pancreas
- Mumps (less commonly seen today) and other viruses
- Hemolytic uremic syndrome
- Diabetic ketoacidosis
- Kawasaki disease
- Bone marrow transplant
- Head trauma

CF is associated with chronic pancreatitis, although acute pancreatitis can occur. Alcohol has been increasingly recognized as a cause of acute pancreatitis in older adolescents.

Clinical Manifestations

Patients with acute pancreatitis typically present with epigastric abdominal pain and persistent vomiting. The abdominal pain commonly occurs in the midepigastric region and is described as steady and "boring into the back." Children flex their knees and hips and sit upright or lie on their side. The patient appears very uncomfortable and is irritable. Often, the abdomen is distended and tender to palpation. During the initial 24–48 hours, the pain increases along with the vomiting.

A severe form, **acute hemorrhagic pancreatitis** or necrotizing pancreatitis, is rare in children but is life threatening. The child is acutely ill with vomiting and abdominal pain. High fever and shock are common. Classic manifestations of acute hemorrhagic pancreatitis are **Cullen sign** (hemorrhagic bluish patchy discoloration around/near the umbilicus) and **Grey Turner sign** (hemorrhagic bluish discoloration of the flanks from retroperitoneal hemorrhage—"Turn to your side to see your flank!"). In this severe form, the pancreas becomes necrotic and eventually, without therapy, transforms into an inflammatory hemorrhagic mass. The mortality rate is > 50%.

Diagnosis

Patients with acute pancreatitis usually have laboratory, ultrasound, and/or radiographic evidence. Serum lipase levels tend to be highly sensitive and specific for acute pancreatitis if elevated > 4× the upper limit of normal (i.e., in the hundreds). Higher lipase levels indicate more severe pancreatic inflammation.

Ultrasound of the abdomen is the easiest and best imaging study in children because it can directly visualize the pancreas, showing peripancreatic fluid or an increase in pancreatic size, which supports the diagnosis of acute pancreatitis. Ultrasound can also show gallstones and choledochal cysts and help identify and follow abscesses and pseudocysts of the pancreas. CT is generally reserved for those cases in which ultrasound cannot delineate the anatomy well. See Figure 10-23, showing CT scan with a circle around a pseudocyst.

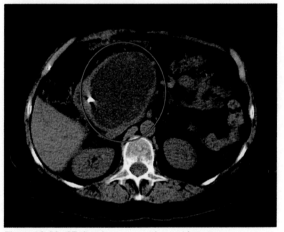

Figure 10-23: CT showing pancreatic pseudocyst

Additionally, magnetic resonance cholangiopancreatography (MRCP) is frequently used in children, especially those with complicated disease or a recurrent course. Endoscopic retrograde cholangiopancreatography (ERCP) can be helpful (both diagnostically and therapeutically) in rarer cases, such as a stone in the bile duct, autoimmune hepatitis, sphincter of Oddi dysfunction, and other anatomic biliary causes.

Treatment

Hospitalization is almost always recommended. Treatment consists of IV hydration, pain control, and fasting. Vigorous IV volume expansion is recommended (1.5× maintenance), and isotonic lactated Ringer's can improve some outcomes. Typically, parenteral narcotic pain medications are used, most often morphine, fentanyl, or hydromorphone. Monitor fluids and electrolytes, and replenish as necessary. Patients often have third spacing of fluid (e.g., peripheral edema, pleural effusions), but resist the urge to use diuretics like furosemide because these patients are still intravascularly dry! For those patients who are vomiting, NG suction can be helpful.

Low-fat feedings are often recommended, but evidence to support use in all patients is lacking. These can be started as soon as the patient is improving and desires to eat. In severe pancreatitis, postpyloric (i.e., jejunal) tube feedings with a semielemental formula are recommended very early in the course of therapy. Antibiotics are not recommended even for prophylaxis in necrotizing pancreatitis. Most patients respond after 2–4 days of therapy. If pancreatic pseudocysts occur, they typically resolve spontaneously; rarely, they require surgical or endoscopic drainage in conjunction with long term antibiotics.

CHRONIC PANCREATITIS

Chronic pancreatitis is rare in children but occurs when there is continuous destruction of the pancreatic gland with irreversible scarring of acinar and ductal cells and each exacerbation leads to additional damage. Some cases are due to hereditary pancreatitis, which is an AD disorder with incomplete penetrance, but most patients have idiopathic disease. Nearly 80% present before 20 years of age; the mean age of onset is 11 years. Often, there is a strong family history of pancreatitis. A subset of patients with chronic pancreatitis has a defect in the *PRSS1* gene for a trypsinogen protein that makes it hypersensitive to activation. Other defects in pancreatic regulatory proteins, such as the serine protease inhibitor (*SPINK1* gene), have now also been described. Some unique mutations in the *CFTR* (cystic fibrosis) gene have also been identified.

Intermittent/repeating episodes of chronic pancreatitis are usually mild to moderate and often resolve over 3–7 days. The frequency and severity of the episodes tend to decrease as the child ages. Acute or chronic episodes can be challenging to manage in these patients because they often have normal pancreatic enzymes. Treatment includes pancreatic enzyme replacement therapy (relieves pain in some by suppressing exocrine secretion) and nutrition. Pancreatic insufficiency occurs in up to 50% of cases, and DM occurs in ~ 25% of cases. Adenocarcinoma of the pancreas occurs in these patients with increased frequency.

DISEASES OF THE LIVER AND BILIARY TREE

JAUNDICE BEYOND NEONATAL PERIOD

Jaundice is the yellow discoloration of tissue due to deposition of bilirubin. Jaundice may be physiologic in infants or may be a sign of hemolysis, infections, or liver failure. Jaundice is classified as prehepatic, hepatic, or posthepatic. Prehepatic jaundice occurs when excess bilirubin overwhelms the ability of the hepatocyte to conjugate bilirubin. Hepatic jaundice occurs when there is failure of bile formation or excretion at the cellular level. Posthepatic jaundice occurs with interruption of bile drainage into the biliary system.

Eliciting a complete history with relevant details is important in ruling out important diagnoses. A full physical exam is mandatory because specific findings (e.g., Kayser-Fleischer rings in Wilson disease) will point you toward specific causes.

A full hepatic function panel with coagulation studies and a hepatitis panel need to be part of the initial evaluation. The bilirubin needs to be fractionated to distinguish between unconjugated and conjugated hyperbilirubinemia. Causes include:

- Unconjugated
  - Hemolysis
    - Hemoglobinopathies (i.e., sickle cell, thalassemia)
    - Enzyme defects (e.g., G6PD deficiency)
    - RBC membrane disorders (e.g., hereditary spherocytosis)
  - Inherited
    - Gilbert syndrome
    - Crigler-Najjar syndrome
- Conjugated
  - Infections
    - Hepatitis A, B, C, D, and E
    - EBV
    - CMV
  - Biliary tract disease
    - Choledochal cyst
    - Cholelithiasis/choledocholithiasis
    - Sclerosing cholangitis
    - Alagille syndrome
  - Drug-induced
  - Metabolic liver disease
    - Wilson disease
    - α_1-Antitrypsin deficiency
    - Dubin-Johnson syndrome
    - Progressive familial intrahepatic cholestasis
  - Autoimmune liver disease

A full abdominal ultrasound is essential in the workup; it is a valuable diagnostic tool when there is concern for vasculature or anatomic abnormalities. However, a liver biopsy is still considered to be the gold standard in diagnosing a cholestatic disorder.

CONGENITAL DISORDERS OF LIVER STRUCTURE

Liver Location Abnormalities

Situs inversus (left-sided liver) and heterotaxia (central liver) are relatively rare congenital anomalies. Either can occur with other anomalies, such as polysplenia or asplenia syndromes. Many of these patients have no functional difficulties.

GASTROENTEROLOGY

Congenital Anomalies of the Portal Vein

Congenital anomalies of the portal vein are frequently associated with cardiac and urinary system abnormalities. Portal vein thrombosis can have various etiologies:

- Umbilical infection
- Umbilical vein catheterization in the newborn period
- Pancreatitis
- Protein C, protein S, and antithrombin deficiencies
- The presence of anticardiolipin antibodies

Doppler ultrasound can be used to confirm portal vein abnormalities, frequently after the patient presents with splenomegaly or esophageal variceal bleeding.

Congenital absence of the portal vein is very rare.

CONGENITAL ANOMALIES OF THE BILIARY TREE

PREVIEW | REVIEW

- Which radiologic modality is useful for diagnosing choledochal cysts?
- What type of cancer is a patient still at risk for, despite surgical excision of a choledochal cyst?
- What is Caroli disease?
- What is Alagille syndrome?
- What are the cardiovascular findings seen with Alagille syndrome?

Extrahepatic Biliary Atresia

Most cases of extrahepatic biliary atresia are acquired, but up to 35% occur during the embryonic or fetal stage. These infants present with neonatal cholestasis and absence of bile duct remnants. Approximately 20% have other associated anomalies, including cardiac, GI, or GU systems. Pediatric liver transplantation is lifesaving. Extrahepatic biliary atresia is discussed in greater detail under Biliary Atresia on page 10-48.

Choledochal Cysts

Choledochal cysts are rare and are cystic dilatations of the biliary tree. There are 5 subtypes, with Type 1 being the most common. Asian girls are the most commonly affected group, especially Japanese girls. Nearly 40% present before 1 year of age, and an additional 35% present between 1 and 6 years of age. The classically described triad of abdominal pain, jaundice, and palpable RUQ mass occurs in only ~ 25%. Fever, nausea, vomiting, and pancreatitis are classic symptoms. Ultrasound shows both intrahepatic and extrahepatic biliary tree dilatation. MRCP can be useful for determining the anatomy.

Treatment for the cysts is aimed at early removal of the cysts and gallbladder, with reconstructive surgery based on the anatomic location of the cysts. Unfortunately, even after surgical correction, there is a high incidence of biliary malignancy in patients with choledochal cysts; rates are as high as 17.5%. Most are cholangiocarcinomata.

Structural Anomalies of the Gallbladder

Congenital absence of the gallbladder occurs in ~ 1/10,000 births and is of little clinical significance if it occurs in isolation. Frequently, though, absence of the gallbladder is associated with extrahepatic biliary atresia, imperforate anus, GU anomalies, bicuspid aortic valve, and cerebral aneurysms.

Hypoplastic gallbladders are more common and occur in ~ 1/3 of patients with CF. Additionally, hypoplastic malformations occur in trisomy 18.

Gallbladder duplication occurs in ~ 1/4,000 births.

Floating gallbladder occurs in 5% of the population. These gallbladders lack a peritoneal coat and are suspended and pendulous. This makes them more susceptible to torsion, which results in acute, severe RUQ pain with nausea and vomiting.

Congenital Hepatic Fibrosis

Congenital hepatic fibrosis is the most common abnormality of the ductal plate. The ductal plate forms at around 8 weeks of gestation and consists of hepatic precursor cells that remodel throughout fetal life to form the intrahepatic biliary tree. Congenital hepatic fibrosis usually occurs with AR polycystic kidney disease.

Neonates and infants present with abnormalities of the renal system, and older children and adults present with hepatic manifestations. The ductal plate abnormality results in dilated bile duct structures and portal tracts without interlobular ducts in the center. In children 5–13 years of age, this leads to portal hypertension and presents typically as hematemesis and/or melena due to esophageal varices. The bleeding can be life threatening and requires endoscopic intervention. On examination, the child has an enlarged liver, especially the left lobe, and splenomegaly. The liver transaminases are most often normal except for occasional mild elevations. The development of cholangitis is the greatest concern and the prime cause of mortality. Liver biopsy confirms the diagnosis.

Treatment can include portosystemic shunting for portal hypertension and antibiotic therapy for cholangitis. Liver transplantation is beneficial for those with chronic cholangitis or progressive hepatic dysfunction. Some with isolated congenital hepatic fibrosis do well and do not require specific therapy.

Caroli Disease

Caroli disease is another abnormality of the ductal plate and is due to a congenital dilatation of the larger, segmental intrahepatic bile ducts. If Caroli disease occurs in combination with congenital hepatic fibrosis, it is known as Caroli syndrome. Caroli disease and syndrome are autosomal recessive and present in adolescence or adulthood.

Patients present with recurrent cholangitis and abscesses. Liver biopsy can show the hepatic fibrosis, but further diagnosis of Caroli disease requires ultrasound, CT, ERCP, or percutaneous transhepatic cholangiography. These studies show dilatation of the hepatic bile ducts and enlargement of the major intra- and extrahepatic biliary passages.

Treat with antibiotics aimed at the cholangitis. If the disease is confined to 1 lobe, consider a partial hepatectomy. Sepsis is a frequent cause of death. Additional complications include cholangiocarcinoma and amyloidosis.

Alagille Syndrome

Alagille syndrome (a.k.a. arteriohepatic dysplasia, Watson-Miller syndrome, or syndromic duct paucity) is an AD disorder with variable penetrance that is caused by mutations in a single gene, *JAG1*, on chromosome 20p. It is rare, with an incidence of ~ 1/100,000 live births, and genetic testing for *JAG1* mutations can identify only 60–75% of patients.

Alagille syndrome is associated with peripheral pulmonic stenosis, vascular anomalies (including intracranial), occasionally tetralogy of Fallot, and neonatal cholestasis. Classically, patients present with chronic cholestatic liver disease with a paucity of small intrahepatic ducts, "butterfly" vertebrae, abnormal radius/ulna, posterior embryotoxon of the eye (a developmental abnormality marked by a prominent white ring of Schwalbe and iris strands that partially obscure the chamber angle), and characteristic facies. The facies of these children consist of a prominent forehead; moderate hypertelorism; a small, pointed chin; and a saddle or straight nose.

Most patients with Alagille have elevated conjugated bilirubin in the neonatal period. In about 1/2 of patients, hepatobiliary scans fail to show biliary excretion of tracer. Liver biopsy shows features consistent with chronic cholestasis and a reduced number of small bile ducts. Giant-cell transformation of hepatocytes can occur in neonates.

Most patients with Alagille syndrome have a benign course. Cholestasis usually resolves or improves over the 1st year of life, and most patients do not develop cirrhosis. Some infants have more severe, sometimes progressive, liver disease. Overall mortality approaches 25% and is typically due to cardiac disease, intercurrent infection, or progressive liver disease.

Do not perform Kasai portoenterostomy in infants with Alagille syndrome. Be aware also that children with Alagille are particularly prone to significant intracranial bleeding with even minor head trauma. This is regardless of their liver function and without a noticeable coagulopathy. Liver transplantation is performed for those with hepatic failure, severe growth failure, or intolerable itching (due to increased plasma bile acid levels) unresponsive to medical therapy.

LIVER TRAUMA

Blunt liver trauma ranges from a minimal parenchymal hematoma to massive organ disruption. The most common causes of hepatic injuries are motor vehicle accidents, falls, bicycle injuries, and child abuse. Suspect blunt hepatic injury in the presence of elevated liver enzymes and conjugated hyperbilirubinemia in a child with a history of trauma or in a suspected child abuse case. However, there is no correlation between the magnitude of the enzyme and bilirubin elevation and the severity of the trauma. The elevated levels usually decrease over 4–6 weeks. CT scan or radionuclide scintigraphy is used initially to identify the extent of trauma, and ultrasound can be used for follow-up exams. Prognosis is determined by the amount and extent of hemorrhage due to vessel injuries. The main cause of mortality from blunt hepatic trauma is due to injuries to the posterolateral aspect of the right lobe of the liver, involving the hepatic veins.

VIRAL HEPATITIS

PREVIEW | REVIEW

- How is hepatitis A transmitted from person to person?

- Which laboratory test is used to diagnose acute hepatitis A?

- What can be given to household contacts to prevent spread of hepatitis A once a case has been identified?

- How is hepatitis B transmitted?

- Which laboratory test indicates immunity to hepatitis B?

- Which laboratory test correlates with increased infectivity of the patient with hepatitis B?

- What is the window period for hepatitis B infection?

- Hepatitis B is associated with which autoimmune reaction?

- Once infected with acute hepatitis B, who is more likely to develop chronic hepatitis B—an infant or an adolescent?

- In adults, chronic hepatitis B is associated with which 2 serious conditions?

- Prior to 1992, what was a common mode of transmission of hepatitis C?

- Which is more likely to cause chronic hepatitis—hepatitis B or hepatitis C?

- Hepatitis C is associated with which vasculitides?

GASTROENTEROLOGY

- Which coinfection does hepatitis D require to cause infection?
- How is hepatitis E transmitted?
- In whom is hepatitis E most virulent?
- Can Epstein-Barr virus cause significant liver disease?

Viral hepatitis refers to inflammation of the liver caused by a virus. The most common causes include hepatitis A, hepatitis B, and hepatitis C viruses. These viruses can cause acute infection, resulting in nausea, abdominal pain, fatigue, and jaundice. In addition, hepatitis B and C can cause chronic infection that potentially leads to cirrhosis and hepatocellular carcinoma.

Hepatitis A

Hepatitis A is a single-stranded, nonenveloped RNA virus. It is easily transmitted via the fecal-oral route, generally among household and day care contacts. It can also be sexually transmitted. Food and water contaminated with hepatitis A virus (HAV), including seafood, have resulted in epidemics. There is no transplacental transmission! There are no carrier or persistent states, although occasionally there is prolonged cholestasis (with increased bilirubin and alkaline phosphatase) for up to 4 months. Incubation period is 15–50 days (Figure 10-24).

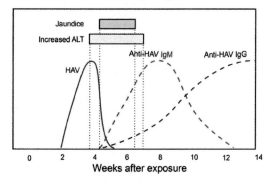

Figure 10-24: Hepatitis A serology timeline

Diagnosis of acute infection: high titers of IgM antibodies directed against the HAV (anti-HAV IgM) in serum. (IgG antibodies indicate only a previous infection.) The presence of the antibody in serum occurs 5–10 days after exposure and the shedding of hepatitis A in stool diminishes significantly within 7 days of symptom onset. Symptoms are unusual in young children but very common in adults (70%). Complications are rare—about 1% chance of fulminant hepatitis. Treatment is supportive.

Once a case has been identified, give the following groups prophylaxis:

- All household contacts
- Sexual partners
- Needle-sharing partners
- Day care and nursing home attendees and staff in close contact with a case

School, hospital, or workplace day-to-day contact does not warrant prophylaxis.

For prophylaxis, give either hepatitis A vaccine (HepA vaccine) or immunoglobulin (IG) in a dose of 0.02 mL/kg as soon as possible, preferably within 2 weeks of exposure. IG is good prophylaxis only against HAV. (Use hepatitis B immunoglobulin [HBIG] for hepatitis B [HBV].) HepA vaccine is the preferred prophylaxis for those ≥ 12 months of age, and IG is preferred for those < 12 months of age.

An inactivated HepA vaccine (Havrix and Vaqta) is given universally at 1 year of age in 2 doses, 6 months apart. Virtually all those completing the series develop protective levels of antibody to HAV (anti-HAV). Protection persists for up to 20 years in those who complete the series.

Even though the HepA vaccine is universally recommended in the U.S., many people did not receive it as a child. Be on the lookout for people who are at high risk for HAV infection or complications:

- High-risk sexual behavior or IV drug use
- Children > 2 years of age living in communities with high rates of HAV infection
- Chronic liver disease
- Travel to high-risk countries
- Patients with hepatitis B or C (because these patients are at risk of fulminant disease if they get hepatitis A)

Hepatitis B

Hepatitis B virus (HBV) is the only hepatitis virus composed of DNA. Worldwide estimations show that approximately 2 billion people have confirmation of past or present infection. The incubation period is 1–6 months (Figure 10-25). It is transmitted by sexual contact (the most common way in adolescents and adults), through contaminated body fluids and contaminated needles, and transplacentally.

Note: As you'll find in the "real world," we use the "anti-" and "Ab" terminology interchangeably (e.g., anti-HBc = HBcAb).

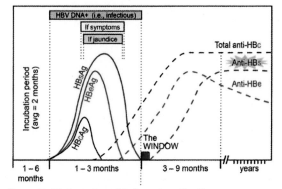

Figure 10-25: Acute hepatitis B serology timeline

Clinically, prodromal constitutional symptoms occur first and commonly resolve at the time jaundice becomes apparent. Occasionally (10–15%), the prodromal symptoms are serum sickness–like, with fever, arthritis, urticaria, and angioedema. This seems to be caused by circulating immune complexes (especially positive hepatitis B surface antigen [HBsAg+] complexed with anti-HBs) activating the complement system. With the onset of jaundice, the patient typically feels much better but can have liver swelling and cholestatic symptoms.

Know the 3 main antigenic markers in hepatitis B and their corresponding antibodies (follow along in Table 10-4):

1) **Hepatitis B surface antigen (HBsAg)**—If an asymptomatic patient has HBsAg in the serum, it means either the patient is a carrier or the patient has early hepatitis B—so initial action is only to follow closely. Once a patient is infected, neither vaccination nor HBIG helps. Finding IgG antibodies to the hepatitis B surface antigen (anti-HBs IgG) in the serum indicates past exposure to either HBV or the HepB vaccine and indicates immunity to the virus.

2) **Hepatitis B core antigen (HBcAg)**—HBcAg+ protein is the core particle (inner shell) of the virion. This protein is retained in the hepatocyte until it is covered with an HBsAg+ nucleocapsid outer shell, which then incorporates the DNA. Free HBcAg+ protein does not circulate in the serum. However, antibody to HBcAg appears early in the disease (initially IgM, then IgG) and persists for life, so anti-HBc IgG is the most reliable marker for previous exposure to HBV.

3) **Hepatitis B e antigen (HBeAg)**—HBeAg is a soluble protein made from the same gene as HBcAg; however, unlike HBcAg, which does not circulate in the serum, HBeAg is secreted from the hepatocytes and does circulate in the serum. HBeAg is a marker of actively replicating virus and, therefore, occurs with infectivity and liver inflammation. The presence of HBeAg is associated with a greater number of virions and greater HBV replication and thus with a higher chance of transmitting the infection. The hepatitis B antibody (anti-HBe) appears several weeks after the illness and means there is resolution of active viral replication. Detecting both HBsAg and HBeAg indicates active virions and high infectivity (more so than if the patient is HBsAg+ and HBeAg–). The tests for HBeAg and anti-HBe are often not available locally.

Once infected, the 1st marker detectable in the serum is the antigen HBsAg. This is followed by the appearance of antibody to the core antigen. In patients with acute HBV infection who do not go on to develop chronic disease, after HBsAg becomes undetectable, there is a period of several weeks before the anti-HBs antibody becomes detectable. This is called "the window," and anti-HBc IgM must be measured during this period to confirm acute hepatitis B.

Removal of HBV is T-cell mediated, and the only purpose of HBsAb is to prevent reinfection or initial infection with the use of vaccine, not to fight HBV infection once it has become established.

HBsAg	Anti-HBc	Anti-HBs	Interpretation
+	–	–	Acute infection
+	+	–	3 possibilities: 1) Acute infection (IgM anti-HBc) 2) Chronic hepatitis B (high ALT, IgG anti-HBc) 3) Asymptomatic carrier (normal enzymes, IgG anti-HBc)
–	–	+	2 possibilities: 1) Remote infection 2) Immunized
–	+	+	Remote infection
–	+	–	3 possibilities: 1) Window disease 2) Remote infection 3) False positive
+	+	+	More than 1 infection; e.g., patient who injects drugs or patient on dialysis with both acute and chronic hepatitis B (infected with different strains of hepatitis B).

Table 10-4: Hepatitis B Scenarios

ALT = alanine aminotransferase
Anti-HBc = hepatitis B core antibody
Anti-HBs = antibody to hepatitis B surface antigen
HBsAg = hepatitis B surface antigen
IgG = immunoglobulin G
IV = intravenous

HBIG (anti-HBs) provides some protection against HBV, although it appears to only decrease the severity of illness rather than protect the patient from disease. It is effective as prophylaxis when given within 24 hours after exposure if there is no history of vaccination in the past.

The 2 hepatitis B vaccines are composed of HBsAg. They are equally effective, and they are safe for pregnant patients. It is best if the hepatitis B vaccine (HepB vaccine) is given before the patient is exposed to HBV. The CDC recommends that newborns receive the 1st dose of HepB vaccine within 24 hours of birth. 95% of immunocompetent patients develop antibodies, whereas only ~ 50% of dialysis patients do. Because these vaccines are surface antigens, check for anti-HBs to ensure effectiveness after the course of vaccine has been given—there is no anti-HBc.

Hepatitis lab scenarios and serologic tests are listed in Table 10-4 and Table 10-5 on page 10-42.

Give HBIG and HepB vaccine to the newborn of a mother with hepatitis B. There is a 5–10% transplacental transmission of HBV. In high-prevalence areas (e.g., Alaska, northern Canada, other places with a high number of Asian immigrants), transplacental transmission is the main route of transmission. In low-prevalence areas, HBV is mainly acquired during adolescence and adulthood.

GASTROENTEROLOGY

| | | | | | | | | Table 10-5: Types of Viral Hepatitis and Their Serological Tests | | | | | | | | |

Disease Status	Anti-HAV IgM	Anti-HAV IgG	HBsAg	Anti-HBs IgG	Anti-HBc IgG	Anti-HBc IgM	HBeAg	Anti-HDV
Acute hepatitis A	+	–				–		
Previous HAV	–	+				–		
Acute HBV			+ early	–	–	+	+	–
Acute HBV window			–	–	–	+		– +++
Chronic active HBV			+	–	+	–	usually +	–
Remote HBV (immune)			–	+	+	–	–	–
Vaccinated (immune)	–		–	+	–	–	–	–
Acute hepatitis D (w/ acute HBV)			+ early	–	–	+	+	+
Acute hepatitis D (w/ CAH)			+	–	+	–	usually +	+

Anti-HBc = hepatitis B core antibody
Anti-HBs = antibody to hepatitis B surface antigen
CAH = chronic active hepatitis
HAV = hepatitis A virus
HBeAg = hepatitis B e antigen

HBsAg = hepatitis B surface antigen
HBV = hepatitis B virus
HDV = hepatitis D virus
IgG = immunoglobulin G
IgM = immunoglobulin M

If a person has possible blood exposure to a person with an acute HBV infection and the HBsAg is still negative, the CDC recommends giving that person HBIG, followed by a complete course of HepB vaccinations.

Note: Several months after an episode of hepatitis B, check for loss of HBsAg and HBV DNA to ensure that it has not become chronic.

Hepatitis B is strongly associated with **polyarteritis nodosa** (PAN), a necrotizing vasculitis of medium-size arteries. The surface antigen is found in 20–30% of these patients. It appears that the hepatitis B infection precipitates an autoimmune reaction resulting in PAN.

The likelihood of developing chronic hepatitis B, or persistence of the infection beyond 6 months, is inversely proportional to age. Chronic hepatitis B occurs in 90% of infants infected at birth, in 25–50% of children infected between 1 and 5 years of age, and in 5% of older children and adults who become infected. There is now universal preschool vaccination in the U.S. Overall, < 1% of patients with hepatitis B develop fulminant hepatitis, but ~ 5–7% develop chronic carrier states.

Chronic hepatitis B is a serious illness. In adults, especially those with high HBV levels, it often progresses to **cirrhosis** and is strongly associated with **hepatocellular cancer**. There have been poor results with liver transplantation so far, and chronic hepatitis B is not considered an indication for transplant. There are some treatment protocols with antivirals, interferons, and other agents. The goal of treatment is to achieve a nondetectable HBV DNA and seroconversion to HBeAb+.

Hepatitis C

Hepatitis C virus (HCV), a parenterally transmitted single-stranded RNA virus, is the most common bloodborne disease in the U.S. It is also the most common infectious cause of liver disease in the U.S. The prevalence of HCV infection in children is 0.1–0.2% compared to 1.8% in adults. Most HCV infections in the U.S. are Genotype 1, which happens to be less responsive to treatment.

In most instances, the source of the infection in individual patients is unknown. However, the following are risk factors for contracting hepatitis C:

• Illicit IV drug use
• Prison exposure
• High-risk sexual behaviors: STIs, prostitutes, > 5 sexual partners per year
• Blood transfusion and/or organ transplants before 1992
• Tattoos and body piercings
• Infants born to HCV-infected mothers

Although only 1% of adults with hepatitis B develop chronic disease, 70–80% of acute HCV infections become chronic. Also, hepatitis B has high viral counts, whereas hepatitis C has low viral counts. The low viral counts for hepatitis C are consistent with its more insidious nature:

• Only 25% of acute infections are symptomatic.
• HCV infection has an increased likelihood of becoming chronic.
• The chronic form has multiple clinical phenotypes. (25% are only carriers, 50% have no symptoms but have abnormal liver function tests [LFTs], and 25% have chronic active disease with symptoms.)

It is also consistent with the low rates of sexual transmission seen in monogamous couples: only 5% after 10–20 years. This is low but does occur, so recommend safe sex practices.

Needle-stick transmission rate from a known-infected patient is ~ 5–10%. Transplacental infection is < 5%.

Extrahepatic manifestations of hepatitis C include:

- Small vessel vasculitis with glomerulonephritis and neuropathy
- Mixed cryoglobulinemia: a small-vessel (leukocytoclastic) vasculitis with a rash consisting of "palpable purpura" or "crops of purple papules"
- Porphyria cutanea tarda (PCT; Figure 10-26)

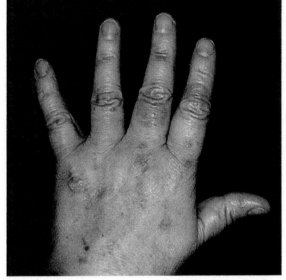

Figure 10-26: Porphyria cutanea tarda demonstrating chronic blistering skin lesions

Chronic hepatitis develops in 70–80% of patients infected with HCV—and ~ 25% of these get end-stage cirrhosis after 20–25 years. In addition, 1–4% of patients with cirrhosis develop **hepatocellular carcinoma** (HCC) each year. Chronic HCV infection has become the primary cause of adult liver transplants in the U.S. It must be assumed that many of these were infected during childhood.

Lab tests:

- In a person positive for anti-HCV, confirm positive antibodies with a RIBA (recombinant immunoblot assay) to exclude a false-positive test.
- For patients with a confirmed positive HCV by RIBA, check for active virus by ordering an HCV-RNA viral load. This is necessary because the anti-HCV does not confer immunity (unlike the HBV antibody).
- Within 2–4 months after an episode of hepatitis C, recheck for loss of HCV-RNA (via PCR) to ensure that it has not become chronic.

Past protocols for treatment relied on interferon and ribavirin, although the response rate was low. Beginning in 2015, several combinations of hepatitis C direct-acting antivirals have been developed, including:

- Elbasvir/grazoprevir (Zepatier)
- Ledipasvir and sofosbuvir (Harvoni)
- Sofosbuvir (Sovaldi)

These antivirals offer cure rates as high as 95% but are extremely expensive. Treatment for hepatitis C is consistently evolving. For the most recent recommendations, go to hcvguidelines.org.

There is no vaccine for hepatitis C.

Hepatitis D

Hepatitis D virus (HDV) is an RNA virus that requires a concomitant or previously existing HBV infection to become pathogenic. It is usually found among IV drug abusers and high-risk hepatitis B surface antigen (HBsAg) carriers. It typically does not make an acute HBV infection much worse; however, if acquired as a superinfection in an HBV carrier, the infection can be very severe, even fulminant, and increase the likelihood of the disease becoming chronic (either chronic active hepatitis [CAH] or cirrhosis). Immunity to hepatitis B implies immunity to hepatitis D. Diagnosis is by anti-HDV IgM.

See Table 10-5 for a review of the serologic tests done with hepatitis A, B, and D.

Hepatitis E

Hepatitis E is a single-stranded RNA virus that is spread through the fecal-oral route just like hepatitis A virus. Found in the Far East, Africa, and Central America, it frequently is due to contamination of water supplies after monsoon flooding.

Hepatitis E infection is acute and self-limited, with resolution occurring within 1–6 weeks. Like hepatitis A, hepatitis E has no known chronic form. Unlike hepatitis A, it carries a very high risk for fulminant hepatitis in the 3rd trimester of pregnancy—with a 20% maternal fatality rate. Think of acute hepatitis E infection in a returning traveler from an endemic area who presents with acute hepatitis and whose hepatitis A, B, and C serologies are negative.

Hepatitis G

Hepatitis G virus (HGV) is bloodborne, like HBV and HCV. The mode of transmission is not well defined but is similar to HCV. There is evidence of infection in 1.5% of blood donors. It causes < 0.5% of community-acquired hepatitis. There is no evidence that HGV causes chronic liver disease.

Differential Diagnosis

Epstein-Barr Virus (EBV)

EBV is a DNA virus that is transmitted by close person-to-person contact with infected secretions, most commonly saliva. EBV can cause infectious mononucleosis, which is characterized by fever, pharyngitis, and lymphadenopathy. Splenomegaly can occur and puts the patient at risk for splenic rupture. Liver involvement is common and presents with hepatomegaly, mild-to-moderate elevation of transaminases, and occasional jaundice. The liver disease tends to be mild and transient but can occasionally be severe and long lasting, particularly in those who are immunocompromised. A small number of patients can have fulminate liver failure. The normal course, however, is to document acute infection by serum EBV IgM and allow the disease to resolve on its own. The heterophile antibody test (Monospot) is often done acutely to diagnose EBV, but antibody testing is preferred, especially with liver involvement. Findings of EBV as an etiology for severe disease include a liver biopsy (rarely needed) showing portal and lobular inflammation with sinusoidal infiltration of mononuclear cells.

Provide supportive care and counsel patients to avoid contact sports if splenomegaly is present. Give a short course of prednisone to help alleviate the liver dysfunction if it is severe. Antiviral agents are not helpful in the treatment of EBV infection of the liver.

Cytomegalovirus (CMV)

In children and adolescents, CMV infection is usually asymptomatic but can cause a presentation similar to EBV-associated infectious mononucleosis, typically with mild hepatic involvement. The course is most often benign. Acute infection can be confirmed with CMV IgM (but this is rarely done). Treatment is supportive.

In neonates, CMV infection of the liver can be quite severe and resembles idiopathic neonatal hepatitis—which can eventually lead to cirrhosis. This is why testing for CMV infection is typically necessary only in pregnant patients presenting with mono-like symptoms.

Classic cytoplasmic inclusions in the biliary epithelium and hepatocytes occur in only 5% of those affected, but these are virtually pathognomonic when they are found.

Other Viruses

Parvovirus B19 rarely causes liver involvement, but recent case reports have implicated it as an etiology for fulminant liver failure, especially in infants. Mumps and measles (paramyxoviruses) can occasionally cause liver damage.

Final scenario on viruses and the liver: A patient presents with evidence of acute hepatitis. Which screening serologic tests do you order to determine if hepatitis A, B, or C is involved?

Answer:

- For hepatitis A: IgM HAV
- For hepatitis B: HBsAg, and IgM HBc
- For hepatitis C: anti-HCV antibody

These are the usual constituents of a viral hepatitis panel.

METABOLIC LIVER DISEASES

> **PREVIEW | REVIEW**
> - What is Gilbert syndrome?
> - How does Crigler-Najjar syndrome Type I differ from Crigler-Najjar syndrome Type II?
> - What is Dubin-Johnson syndrome?
> - How does α_1-antitrypsin deficiency present?
> - What are the eye findings in Wilson disease?
> - How do you diagnose Wilson disease?
> - How does progressive familial intrahepatic cholestasis-1 present?
> - What drug is associated with Reye syndrome?

Galactosemia, fructose intolerance, glycogen storage diseases, hereditary tyrosinemia, and disorders of fatty acid oxidation are discussed in the Metabolic Disorders section.

Glucuronosyltransferase Defects

Introduction

There are 3 disorders of bilirubin conjugation that result in varying levels of unconjugated hyperbilirubinemia. They are all the same disease (not enough uridine diphosphate [UDP]-glucuronosyltransferase) but have different mutations causing different enzyme levels:

1) Gilbert syndrome (mild deficiency; most common)
2) Crigler-Najjar syndrome Type II (CN II; mild-to-moderate deficiency in conjugation)
3) Crigler-Najjar syndrome Type I (CN I; severe deficiency in conjugation)

It is helpful to think of Gilbert syndrome, CN II, and CN I as points on a spectrum with mild, moderate, and severe deficiencies in conjugation of bilirubin. These are all due to mutations in *UGT1A1*, the gene that codes for UDP-glucuronosyltransferase, which conjugates bilirubin. These mutations lead to a less active, relative deficiency of UDP-glucuronosyltransferase and thus to less conjugating ability.

Gilbert Syndrome — Mild

Gilbert syndrome occurs in 2–10% of the population. It is often caused by a less severe mutation in *UGT1A1* or its promoter, resulting in lower levels of the bilirubin-conjugating enzyme UDP-glucuronosyltransferase. This results in a mild, indirect hyperbilirubinemia, usually < 5 mg/dL. It is often discovered incidentally when bilirubin is measured for some other reason (typically on a comprehensive metabolic panel). There is no associated hemolysis or hepatocellular damage. It usually becomes apparent during episodes of stress (like a viral illness) or fasting, when the patient becomes mildly jaundiced. No treatment is required, and no morbidity or mortality results from it. Infants with prolonged physiologic jaundice or breast milk jaundice often have polymorphisms in *UGT1A1* as well, and many can go on to have Gilbert syndrome later in life.

Crigler-Najjar Syndrome Type II — Moderate

Crigler-Najjar syndrome Type II results in partial activity (markedly reduced but not absent) of bilirubin UDP-glucuronosyltransferase. Hyperbilirubinemia of < 10 mg/dL is usual. It resolves with phenobarbital and other inducers of cytochrome P450, but phenobarbital is not recommended for long-term therapy due to its neurodevelopmental complications from prolonged use. Hyperbilirubinemia from this disorder does not require specific therapy and does not result in increased morbidity or mortality.

Crigler-Najjar Syndrome Type I — Severe

Crigler-Najjar syndrome Type I is more severe than Type II and is due to a complete absence of bilirubin UDP-glucuronosyltransferase activity. It presents in the newborn period with severe indirect hyperbilirubinemia and requires phototherapy and/or exchange transfusions. There is no conjugated bilirubin. Kernicterus is a major concern. DNA testing can confirm the diagnosis pre- and postnatally. The mainstay of treatment is phototherapy, although this is difficult to maintain in the long term. Liver transplant can be curative.

Dubin-Johnson Syndrome

Dubin-Johnson syndrome causes conjugated hyperbilirubinemia (unlike Gilbert syndrome and Crigler-Najjar syndrome, which are unconjugated hyperbilirubinemias) and is due to a deficiency in the *cMOAT/MRP2* gene, which encodes the canalicular transporter of conjugated bilirubin. It presents with mild conjugated hyperbilirubinemia of 3–8 mg/dL. It does not result in hepatocellular injury. It does not require specific therapy and does not result in increased morbidity or mortality.

α₁-Antitrypsin Deficiency

α₁-Antitrypsin deficiency, the most common genetic cause of metabolic liver disease in children, can cause progressive liver disease and occurs with an incidence of 1/2,000 live births. Suspect this diagnosis in any child with chronic liver disease. To diagnose, measure α₁-antitrypsin concentration and determine the alleles in the *Pi* locus

(and hence the phenotype). The 3 alleles occur in different frequencies and are helpful in determining risk of liver disease:

1) M: normal allele
2) S: mildly low α₁-antitrypsin
3) Z: severely low α₁-antitrypsin

Those with ZZ genotypes are most severely affected and have both lung and liver disease. Heterozygotes (MS or MZ) have an increased chance of lung and liver disease, especially with concurrent environmental exposure (e.g., smoking, alcohol use).

The liver disease can present as neonatal jaundice, juvenile cirrhosis, chronic hepatitis, or HCC. Cholestatic jaundice occurs in 10–15% of infants who are homozygous for the deficiency, and nearly 50% of infants who are homozygous have abnormal liver tests. Giant-cell hepatitis is the classic histologic finding in neonates. Periodic acid-Schiff (PAS)–positive staining of the liver is characteristic in patients > 12 weeks of age.

Treatment is nonspecific but includes fat-soluble vitamin supplementation and formula with MCT oil. Most infants with neonatal liver disease improve by 4 months of age for reasons that are unclear. A majority remain healthy throughout childhood. A few present later in life with cirrhosis or HCC. If patients progress to liver failure, liver transplant is curative.

Wilson Disease

Wilson disease is an AR disorder of copper metabolism that occurs with an incidence of ~ 1/100,000 to 1/500,000 births. The disease results from the excessive accumulation of **copper** in the eyes, liver, kidneys, and brain. This results in degenerative changes in the brain and liver and formation of **Kayser-Fleischer rings** in the cornea (Figure 10-27). These are copper deposits appearing as a golden-brown ring in the inner lining of the Descemet membrane and are almost always found in those with neurologic symptoms. In most cases, Kayser-Fleischer rings are identified only by seeing the copper deposits on slitlamp examination. The relevant gene is mapped to chromosome 13.

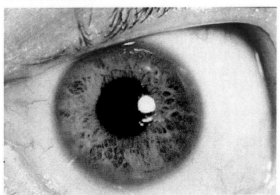

Figure 10-27: Kayser-Fleischer rings in Wilson disease

The disease begins with accumulation of copper in the liver. The clinical presentation varies widely. Most children do not present before 5 years of age; those who present in childhood usually do so with hepatic manifestations, including hepatomegaly and/or acute hepatitis. Hepatic insufficiency occurs later. Fulminant hepatitis rarely occurs before adolescence.

Adolescents can present with mostly neurologic and psychiatric dysfunction, which can include falling grades in school, behavioral changes, tremors, and slurred speech. If left untreated, dysarthria and dystonia eventually develop.

The Kayser-Fleischer rings are frequently absent in children who have only hepatic disease.

Suspect this disorder in children and adolescents with unexplained acute or chronic liver disease, neurologic symptoms of unexplained origin, acute hemolysis, psychiatric illness, behavioral change, Fanconi syndrome, or unexplained bone disease.

Know all the following regarding Wilson disease:

- Patients commonly present with hemolytic anemia.
- The best screening test is the serum ceruloplasmin level—but remember, it is not diagnostic. Most patients with Wilson disease have low ceruloplasmin levels. Ceruloplasmin is an acute phase reactant, so it can be falsely normal or elevated.
- 24-hour urinary copper is useful in diagnosis and monitoring treatment. Early in the disease, serum copper levels can be high, and 24-hour urinary copper excretion is increased, sometimes to 1,000 μg/day. (Normal urinary copper excretion is < 40 μg/day.)
- If you are still uncertain about the diagnosis, give a dose of D-penicillamine, which increases urinary excretion of copper to nearly 2,000 μg/day in those with Wilson disease.
- Liver biopsy is the gold standard for diagnosis and shows markedly elevated hepatic copper content—but you have to order the concentration level!

Screen family members of those with proven disease. This screening usually includes checking a serum ceruloplasmin and 24-hour urinary copper excretion. If abnormal, perform a liver biopsy.

Treat with copper-chelating agents, such as D-penicillamine, which normally leads to a rapid excretion of excess copper. With therapy, hepatic and neurologic functions improve, and Kayser-Fleischer rings disappear. If the patient cannot tolerate penicillamine, try triethylenetetramine dihydrochloride. Limit oral intake of copper to < 1 mg/day. Have patients avoid foods such as liver, shellfish, nuts, and chocolate. If the copper content of the local water supply is elevated, suggest a demineralizer.

Treatment is necessary for survival. For patients who already have fulminant liver failure or decompensated cirrhosis, liver transplant is necessary. Some recommend liver transplant for those with progressive neurologic disease, but this indication is controversial. In screened siblings who are asymptomatic with the disease, implement penicillamine therapy.

Hemochromatosis

Hemochromatosis is a disease of excessive storage of **iron**, mainly in the form of hemosiderin in the parenchymal cells of multiple tissues. It can result in abnormalities in the function and structure of the liver, heart, pancreas, skin, joints, gonads, and other endocrine organs.

There are 3 forms of this disease:

1) Hereditary hemochromatosis
2) Transfusion-induced hemosiderosis
3) Neonatal hemochromatosis

Hereditary hemochromatosis is most commonly due to a mutation in the *HFE* gene but has variable expression. This is not a disorder of childhood, but children can have elevated iron studies. Adults develop cirrhosis, diabetes mellitus (DM), and bronzing of the skin. (Hemochromatosis was called "bronze diabetes" in the past.) The diagnosis is confirmed with *HFE* mutation analysis. If families are screened, disease can be prevented in affected individuals by periodic phlebotomy, which in children is typically unnecessary until adolescence. Treatment consists of weekly phlebotomy until the ferritin level is decreased.

Transfusion-induced hemosiderosis occurs in those patients who repeatedly receive red blood cell transfusions. It most commonly occurs in those with congenital or acquired anemias who require frequent transfusions. (Look for a patient with sickle cell anemia and evidence of liver damage.) Monitor iron overload and treat with chelation therapy (e.g., deferoxamine).

Neonatal hemochromatosis is the most common identified cause of acute liver failure in the neonate. It is an acquired syndrome due to severe fetal liver damage, likely caused by maternal alloimmunity, and is associated with hepatic and extrahepatic (e.g., thyroid, pancreas, heart, salivary glands) deposition of iron. Mortality is > 90%. Liver failure can occur within hours of life, presenting with hypoglycemia, coagulopathy, and edema. Treatment is supportive.

Progressive Familial Intrahepatic Cholestasis (PFIC)

PFIC refers to a group of inherited disorders in which bile is not formed properly. PFIC1 (formerly known as Byler disease) and PFIC2 are characterized by normal serum gamma-glutamyl transferase (GGT) but with severe cholestasis. PFIC3 has elevated serum GGT levels (know this difference!).

PFIC1 usually presents between 3 and 6 months of age with conjugated hyperbilirubinemia and severe, unremitting pruritus—but remember: GGT is normal! It is due to a mutation in the *FIC1* gene on chromosome 18. Fat-soluble vitamin deficiencies (A, D, E, and K) are common, secondary to lack of available bile salts to facilitate absorption in the small intestine. These children have persistent diarrhea with fat malabsorption and protein loss. Poor growth is common. Cirrhosis develops in early childhood and requires liver transplant. Even after liver transplant, bouts of pancreatitis and diarrhea are still common.

PFIC2 is caused by a defect in the gene *FIC2*, which is located on chromosome 2 and this gene is a bile salt export pump. These children do not have pancreatitis or diarrhea, but they have prominent liver disease with normal GGT. It is most commonly seen in Middle Eastern Europeans.

PFIC3 differs from the other 2 PFIC diseases in that the cholestasis results in an elevated GGT. Jaundice is generally less prominent, but the pruritus is still severe. This type of PFIC actually is aggressive and progresses toward hepatic failure in the 1st few years of life.

Reye Syndrome

Reye syndrome is an acute liver disease with hyperammonemic encephalopathy. Although the etiology is not fully understood, it seems to be due to mitochondrial injury in conjunction with a viral illness, especially influenza or chickenpox. There is an association with aspirin (or salicylate) use, which led to the advisory against using aspirin in febrile children with an intercurrent viral infection. The incidence of Reye syndrome peaked in the 1960s and 1970s; it is very rare today.

Reye syndrome is characterized by vomiting and mental status changes that can rapidly progress to coma and death. Jaundice is not a specific finding of this disorder. An elevated ammonia level is the most common laboratory abnormality. Other lab findings include markedly elevated AST/ALT, hyperbilirubinemia (typically between 2 mg/dL and 3 mg/dL), and elevated lipase and amylase levels. The prognosis is determined by the neurologic rather than the hepatic findings, the latter of which frequently resolve over several days.

Treat by correcting metabolic abnormalities and minimizing intracranial hypertension. Any child diagnosed with Reye syndrome should be evaluated for an inborn error of metabolism defect.

DRUG-INDUCED LIVER INJURY (DILI)

PREVIEW | REVIEW

- What drug is administered to patients with acetaminophen toxicity in order to replenish glutathione stores?

Drugs are an important cause of liver injury; when it occurs, such injury is referred to as DILI (a.k.a. drug-induced hepatotoxicity). Acetaminophen is the most common cause of acute liver failure in the U.S. Its toxicity is dose dependent and due to shunting down a minor pathway that produces a toxic metabolite when the glucuronidation pathway is depleted. *N*-acetylcysteine replenishes glutathione stores and allows the liver to metabolize acetaminophen without generating toxic metabolites. There are nomograms that can be utilized to determine the risk of hepatotoxicity based on the time since ingestion and the measured metabolite level. In severe toxicity, emergent liver transplant may be required. Most cases occur in toddlers (accidental ingestion) or adolescents (intentional overdose). Look for co-ingestion, which is common and can make liver toxicity worse, especially if involving alcohol or iron. (See more on acetaminophen ingestion in the Emergency Medicine & Maltreatment Syndromes section.)

Idiosyncratic hepatotoxic reactions have been reported with many drugs, but a few are noted with great frequency. The most common offenders are antibiotics (amoxicillin/clavulanate, isoniazid, trimethoprim/sulfamethoxazole, fluoroquinolones, and macrolides) and antiseizure medications (ASM; e.g., phenytoin, valproic acid, carbamazepine). In most cases, other etiologies, such as viral or autoimmune, must be ruled out initially. Liver biopsy is sometimes helpful. The pattern is either hepatocellular (elevated AST/ALT) or cholestatic (elevated alkaline phosphatase or bilirubin), but it can also be mixed.

Oral contraceptives are associated with hepatic vein thrombosis (Budd-Chiari syndrome) and liver adenomas. Use of performance-enhancing androgens by adolescent athletes also increases the risk of liver toxicity.

Except for acetaminophen overdose, no specific therapy is useful for most liver toxicities. Usually, supportive care and stopping the offending agent are the only means to potentially reverse the course.

AUTOIMMUNE HEPATOBILIARY DISEASE

PREVIEW | REVIEW

- How do you diagnose autoimmune hepatitis?
- What is associated with primary sclerosing cholangitis?
- What is the best radiologic test to confirm primary sclerosing cholangitis?

Autoimmune Hepatitis (AIH)

AIH refers to a variety of diseases that affect the liver and frequently overlap with disorders that affect the bile ducts and other hepatic elements. The etiology of AIH is unknown, but it appears to have genetic features. It is likely that a viral infection or drug exposure initiates the disorder in those genetically susceptible. Other autoimmune comorbidities (e.g., Crohn disease, primary biliary cirrhosis, primary sclerosing cholangitis, autoimmune thyroiditis) are common. AIH tends to present with greater severity in children compared with adults, and > 50% of patients with AIH have cirrhosis at initial diagnosis.

GASTROENTEROLOGY

There are 2 main types of AIH:

- **Type I** is known as the classic form and affects females > males between 10 and 20 years of age and between 45 and 70 years of age. It is associated with the presence of anti-smooth muscle antibodies (ASMA) and/or antinuclear antibodies (ANA).
- **Type II** occurs in younger children (males = females) and is characterized by antibodies to the liver-kidney microsomal-1 (anti-LKM-1) and/or to a liver cytosol antigen (ALC-1). These children present with more severe liver disease than those in Type I.

Either of these 2 types can present in various ways. Most commonly, patients initially present with malaise, weight loss, and/or anorexia. Serious complications typically do not present until cirrhosis and portal hypertension have already occurred, and the child/adolescent presents with variceal bleeding. Jaundice can be quite variable. Always look for a family history of other autoimmune diseases, such as thyroiditis, arthritis, and IBD. Many older patients are diagnosed due to new onset of jaundice and are then found to have evidence of hepatitis on routine laboratory testing.

Diagnosis depends on finding the serum antibody markers in the face of elevated aminotransferases with an elevated total protein (due to hypergammaglobulinemia). Always evaluate for viral hepatitis, especially hepatitis C, which can lead to elevated ANA or LKM antibodies. Typically, you must perform a biopsy to show portal lymphoplasmacytic infiltrates that can extend to the surrounding hepatic lobule.

The 2010 American Association for the Study of Liver Diseases (AASLD) guidelines suggest beginning immunosuppression in all children with AIH at diagnosis. This consists of a combination of corticosteroids (usually on a taper to a low dose) and azathioprine or 6-MP (6-mercaptopurine). Liver transplant may be helpful in refractory cases, but AIH can recur in the transplanted liver, too.

Primary Sclerosing Cholangitis

Primary sclerosing cholangitis is a disease of unknown etiology that is characterized by chronic fibrosing inflammation of the intra- and extrahepatic bile duct. (Secondary sclerosing cholangitis has the same findings but is due to choledocholithiasis, postoperative stricture, toxin-induced bile duct injury, AIDS, or Langerhans cell histiocytosis.) Primary sclerosing cholangitis is associated with IBD (especially **ulcerative colitis**) and occasionally is ANCA (antineutrophil cytoplasmic antibody) positive, both of which indicate a possible immunologic etiology.

Clinical presentation is variable. Patients can be asymptomatic or have fatigue, jaundice, hepatosplenomegaly, or abdominal discomfort with itching. For some children, cirrhosis and portal hypertension are the 1st clues. Always consider primary sclerosing cholangitis in any child with IBD if there is evidence of hepatobiliary dysfunction (e.g., jaundice, elevated LFTs).

Laboratory testing shows elevated alkaline phosphatase and GGT (cholestatic pattern) in most patients. Low titers of anti-smooth muscle or anti-LKM antibodies may be present. Most experts perform MRCP prior to the more invasive ERCP, but the results are less precise. The best test to confirm the diagnosis is endoscopic retrograde cholangiography, which shows alternating normal strictures along with dilated portions of the biliary tree, known as "beading" (Figure 10-28). On histologic examination, the classic "onion-skin lesion" is pathognomonic but not common.

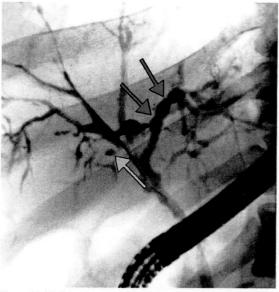

Figure 10-28: Primary sclerosing cholangitis. Green arrows show several strictures of the biliary tree, producing the characteristic beading, and the yellow arrow shows the outpouchings of dilated bile ducts.

Treat with endoscopic management of biliary strictures and supportive care for chronic liver disease if it is present. Recommend liver transplant if cirrhosis and portal hypertension have occurred.

BILIARY ATRESIA

PREVIEW | REVIEW

- What tests should be done quickly to diagnose extrahepatic biliary atresia?
- What procedure should be performed as soon as possible for extrahepatic biliary atresia?

Although biliary atresia is uncommon, it is nonetheless the most common reason for pediatric liver transplantation in the U.S. The cause is unknown. The condition leads to the destruction of bile ducts, progressing from extra- to intrahepatic, which in turn results in fibrosis, biliary cirrhosis, and eventual liver failure.

Clinically, cholestatic jaundice typically appears during the 2nd or 3rd week of life but can present at birth as well. Look for acholic (pale) stools and dark urine as clues to biliary atresia. Hepatomegaly is common. Laboratory evaluation reveals hyperbilirubinemia (both conjugated and unconjugated) and hypertransaminasemia. The gallbladder is frequently not seen on ultrasound.

These infants must be evaluated and treated quickly to increase the odds of a favorable outcome.

Do the following tests:

- Abdominal ultrasound can show an absent gallbladder but also is useful to rule out choledochal cyst or gallstones as a cause of extrahepatic obstruction.
- Hepatobiliary iminodiacetic acid (HIDA) scan can help determine whether any bile flows out of the liver and thus sometimes can rule out biliary atresia (but it is nonspecific—any cause of cholestasis can cause an abnormal HIDA).
- Liver biopsy—this will often show ductular proliferation, bile plugs, and portal fibrosis.
- Matrix metalloprotein-7 is a newer serum test that, when combined with a γ-glutamyl transferase, is a diagnostic biomarker for biliary atresia.
- If these tests are suggestive of biliary atresia, do an intraoperative cholangiogram, which is the gold standard for diagnosis. If this test is positive, the surgeon immediately can perform a Kasai portoenterostomy.

The Kasai procedure uses a piece of intestine as a drainage conduit for the liver, bypassing the malformed bile ducts. Typically, it must be done before 2 months of age to have a good chance of success. A successful Kasai procedure can delay the need for liver transplantation for many years.

Prognosis varies. In those in whom bile flow is not reestablished and jaundice never resolves, hepatic failure ensues, most often before 1 year of age. In a large majority of patients, however, bile flow is reestablished and jaundice slowly resolves over several months. In these patients, cirrhosis develops over time but much more slowly than it would without a Kasai procedure.

Ultimately, liver transplantation is required in all patients with biliary atresia. Only a small minority achieve apparent permanent drainage post-Kasai without progression of the disease in the liver itself.

After the Kasai procedure is performed, these children are at risk for ascending cholangitis and must be followed carefully for signs of fever and worsening jaundice. If a patient with biliary atresia presents with fever and rising bilirubin, assume they have ascending cholangitis and admit for blood cultures and empiric antibiotics (preferably something that covers both gram negatives and anaerobes, like piperacillin-sulbactam).

CHOLELITHIASIS

PREVIEW | REVIEW

- Which children are more likely to develop gallstones?

Cholelithiasis (gallstones) in healthy children and infants is likely more common than previously thought. Most are asymptomatic and found incidentally on radiologic studies. Follow these patients with periodic clinical and ultrasonographic surveillance.

If patients do have symptoms from cholelithiasis, they usually have the characteristic pain known as biliary colic. Classic symptoms of biliary colic include right upper quadrant pain (RUQ) pain, vomiting, and jaundice, without fever. These symptoms usually result from the digestive system's demand for bile causing the gallstone to transiently obstruct the cystic duct from the gallbladder or the common bile duct. Symptoms are especially common a few hours after fatty meals but can occur any time.

Certain factors predispose individuals to developing gallstones, including obesity, hemolytic disease (particularly sickle cell), chronic TPN, short bowel syndrome, DM, oral contraceptives, and pregnancy in adolescent females. Native Americans and Hispanics have a higher incidence of the disease. In the U.S., where there is increasing prevalence of obesity, rates of hospitalizations for pediatric cholelithiasis have also increased. The most common complication in children with cholelithiasis is pancreatitis due to an obstructing stone or stones in the common bile duct (choledocholithiasis).

Plain x-rays can reveal stones with high calcium content, but RUQ ultrasound is the best initial imaging study. If stones are picked up incidentally, many pediatricians recommend observation only. Cholecystectomy is recommended in patients with biliary colic, cholangitis, cholecystitis, or pancreatitis.

Gallstones are a common finding in adults, and many families ask if this is the cause of their child's abdominal pain. Even in children who do have gallstones, it is typically not the cause of pain. Routine removal of the gallbladder because of gallstones without evidence of obstruction is not generally recommended. Many clinicians order a radionuclide (HIDA scan to assess the gallbladder in a patient with biliary pain but without stones. A low gallbladder ejection fraction on a HIDA scan is the diagnostic finding for biliary dyskinesia. For more information on biliary dyskinesia, see Acute Cholecystitis.

ACUTE CHOLECYSTITIS

Acute cholecystitis is bacterial inflammation of the gallbladder; it can occur with or without stones (acalculous cholecystitis), although it rarely occurs in children at all. RUQ pain and tenderness on palpation of the gallbladder are common. If the pain worsens with inspiration, this is known as Murphy sign. Other things can cause similar pain, including hepatitis, hepatic abscess, Fitz-Hugh-Curtis syndrome (gonococcal perihepatitis), pancreatitis, appendicitis, pneumonia, pyelonephritis, and renal stones.

Most patients have an elevated WBC count with a left shift and mild increases in bilirubin and transaminases. Markedly elevated bilirubin, alkaline phosphatase, and/or

GASTROENTEROLOGY

GGT levels indicate obstruction of the biliary tree with a stone. Ultrasound is best to visualize stones or a thickened gallbladder. HIDA scan can demonstrate poor or no visualization in the presence of an inflamed gallbladder.

Children have a 30% complication rate, which includes perforation, abscess, and empyema. Most recommend hospital admission with IV fluids, antibiotics, and bowel rest. Perform cholecystectomy in patients with acute calculous cholecystitis.

Acalculous cholecystitis can be acute (< 1-month duration) or chronic. It appears to be caused by gallbladder stasis and/or ischemia. It presents acutely, similarly to calculous cholecystitis, except there are no visible stones. It occurs most commonly after a life-threatening illness, burn, or trauma. Manage with antibiotics and serial ultrasounds to follow for progression and complications. The chronic form is also known as **biliary dyskinesia**.

HYDROPS OF THE GALLBLADDER

PREVIEW | REVIEW

- Hydrops of the gallbladder can be seen in which conditions?

Hydrops of the gallbladder refers to an acute noncalculous, noninflammatory enlargement of the gallbladder. It can occur with Kawasaki disease, streptococcal pharyngitis, prolonged fasting, TPN, and immunoglobulin A vasculitis (IgAV; formerly Henoch-Schönlein purpura [HSP]). Patients complain of RUQ pain with a palpable mass. Fever, vomiting, and jaundice are common. Ultrasound shows a markedly dilated, stone-free gallbladder. Acute hydrops rarely requires cholecystectomy. If performed, a laparotomy will show a large, edematous gallbladder that contains white, yellow, or green bile. Treating the underlying condition usually results in the gallbladder returning to normal over several weeks.

TUMORS OF THE LIVER AND BILIARY TREE

PREVIEW | REVIEW

- What is the most common malignant liver tumor of childhood?
- Which laboratory test is elevated in children with hepatoblastomata?

Tumors of the hepatobiliary system are rare in children, comprising ~ 1–4% of all solid tumors. If they occur, they are most common in the right lobe of the liver. In children, benign tumors are seen much more frequently than malignant ones. The common benign tumors include hemangiomas, adenomas, focal nodular hyperplasia, and mesenchymal hamartomata.

Hepatoblastomata are the most common malignant liver tumors in children, most commonly presenting by 18 months of age. They are single masses found in infancy.

There is an increased risk of hepatoblastomata in patients with Beckwith-Wiedemann syndrome and familial adenomatous polyposis (FAP). The serum α-fetoprotein level is markedly elevated in these children and is useful for diagnosis and for monitoring after therapy (for recurrence). With complete resection and postoperative chemotherapy, survival rates approach 50%. Liver transplant has been used successfully when complete resection cannot be done.

For more information on liver tumors, see the Oncology section.

THE MEDSTUDY HUB: YOUR GUIDELINES AND REVIEW ARTICLES RESOURCE

For both review articles and current pediatrics practice guidelines, visit the MedStudy Hub at

medstudy.com/hub

The Hub contains the only online consolidated list of all current guidelines focused on pediatrics. Guidelines on the Hub are easy to find, continually updated, and linked to the published source. MedStudy maintains the Hub as a service to the medical community and makes it available to anyone and everyone at no cost to users.

FIGURE SOURCES

Figure 10-1: MedStudy illustration
Figure 10-2: DrM!KEY, CC BY-SA 3.0
Figure 10-3: Ahmed H. Al-Salem, CC0 1.0
Figure 10-6: MedStudy illustration
Figure 10-7: Ed Uthman, CC BY 2.0
Figure 10-9: Frank Gaillard, CC BY-SA 3.0
Figure 10-10: Kinderradiologie Olgahospital Klinikum Stuttgart, CC BY-SA 3.0
Figure 10-11: MedStudy illustration
Figure 10-12: Madhero88, CC BY-SA 3.0
Figure 10-13: MedStudy illustration
Figure 10-14: James Heilman, MD, CC BY-SA 3.0
Figure 10-16: James Heilman, MD, CC BY-SA 3.0
Figure 10-17: I, Monopol, CC BY-SA 3.0
Figure 10-18: Abdullah Sarhan, CC BY-SA 4.0
Figure 10-19: MedStudy illustration
Figure 10-20: MedStudy illustration
Figure 10-21: Jonathanlund, CC0 1.0
Figure 10-22: MedStudy illustration
Figure 10-23: James Heilman, MD, CC BY-SA 3.0
Figure 10-24: MedStudy illustration
Figure 10-25: MedStudy illustration
Figure 10-27: Herbert L. Fred, MD, Hendrik A. van Dijk, CC BY 3.0
The remaining figures are from the MedStudy archives.

GASTROENTEROLOGY

Pulmonary Medicine

SECTION EDITORS

Kimberly Jones, MD
Gratis Faculty, Associate Professor Pediatric Pulmonary
LSU Health Sciences Center
Pediatric Pulmonologist
Willis-Knighton Health Systems
Pediatric Pulmonary Specialists
Shreveport, LA

Eric Sherman, MD, MPH
Commander, 55th Medical Operations Squadron
Staff Physician - Pediatrics
U.S. Air Force Medical Service
Offutt Air Force Base, NE
Staff Physician
Pediatric Urgent Care and Pediatric Endocrinology
Children's Hospital & Medical Center
Omaha, NE

MEDICAL EDITOR
Lynn Bullock, MD
Colorado Springs, CO

Table of Contents

NORMAL RESPIRATION 11-1

DIAGNOSTIC TESTING 11-1
  LUNG VOLUMES AND PULMONARY
    FUNCTION TESTS 11-1
    Lung Volumes 11-1
    Flow-Volume Loops 11-2
    Bronchodilator Response and Challenge
      Testing 11-3
  PULSE OXIMETRY 11-3
    Causes of Hypoxemia 11-3
    Oxyhemoglobin Dissociation Curve 11-3
  BLOOD GAS ANALYSIS 11-4

VENTILATORY SUPPORT 11-4

NEONATAL STRIDOR 11-5
  NOTE 11-5
  LARYNGOMALACIA 11-5
  SUBGLOTTIC STENOSIS 11-5
  VOCAL CORD PARALYSIS 11-6
  LARYNGEAL ATRESIA / WEBS 11-6

CONGENITAL DISORDERS OF THE LOWER
  RESPIRATORY TRACT 11-6
  TRACHEAL DISORDERS 11-6
    Tracheal Agenesis 11-6
    Tracheal Stenosis 11-6
    Tracheomalacia and Bronchomalacia 11-6
  PULMONARY HYPOPLASIA 11-7
  CONGENITAL PULMONARY VENOLOBAR
    SYNDROME (SCIMITAR SYNDROME) 11-7
  PULMONARY ARTERIOVENOUS
    MALFORMATIONS (PAVMs) 11-7
  PULMONARY SEQUESTRATIONS 11-8
  BRONCHOGENIC CYSTS 11-8
  CONGENITAL PULMONARY AIRWAY
    MALFORMATION (CPAM) 11-8
  DIAPHRAGM MALFORMATIONS 11-9
    Congenital Diaphragmatic Hernia 11-9
    Eventration 11-9
    Accessory Diaphragm 11-9

NEUROMUSCULAR RESPIRATORY FAILURE 11-9

STRIDOR BEYOND THE NEONATAL PERIOD 11-9
  INFECTION 11-10
  PARADOXICAL VOCAL CORD
    DYSFUNCTION (VCD) 11-10

INFECTIONS OF THE UPPER
  RESPIRATORY TRACT 11-10
  NOTE 11-11
  LARYNGOTRACHEOBRONCHITIS (CROUP) 11-11
  EPIGLOTTITIS 11-11
  BACTERIAL TRACHEITIS 11-12

INFECTIONS OF THE LOWER
  RESPIRATORY TRACT 11-12
  BRONCHIOLITIS 11-12
    Respiratory Syncytial Virus (RSV)
      Immunoprophylaxis 11-12
  PNEUMONIA — GENERAL
    CONSIDERATIONS 11-13
  VIRAL PNEUMONIA 11-14

ACUTE BACTERIAL PNEUMONIA 11-14
  Streptococcus pneumoniae 11-14
  Streptococcus pyogenes 11-15
  Haemophilus influenzae 11-15
  Staphylococcus aureus 11-15
ATYPICAL PNEUMONIAS 11-15
  Mycoplasma pneumoniae 11-15
  Chlamydia pneumoniae 11-15
FUNGAL PNEUMONIAS 11-16
  Histoplasmosis 11-16
  Coccidioidomycosis 11-16
  Blastomycosis 11-16
  Allergic Bronchopulmonary
    Aspergillosis (ABPA) 11-16
RECURRENT PNEUMONIA 11-16
TUBERCULOSIS (TB) 11-17

ASTHMA 11-17
  OVERVIEW 11-17
  CLASSIFICATION 11-18
  COMORBIDITIES AND TRIGGERS 11-18
    Sinusitis 11-18
    Gastroesophageal (GE) Reflux 11-18
    Exercise 11-18
    The Difficult, Refractory Patient 11-19
  TREATMENT 11-19
    Corticosteroids 11-19
    Cromolyn Sodium 11-20
    Long-Acting Inhaled β_2-Agonists (LABAs) 11-20
    Combination Therapy 11-20
    Leukotriene Modifiers 11-20
    Tiotropium 11-20
    Theophylline 11-20
    Omalizumab 11-20
  ACUTE EXACERBATION 11-21
    Home Treatment 11-21
    Office Treatment 11-21
    Emergency Department (ED) Treatment 11-21
    Acute Severe Asthma 11-21

DDx OF WHEEZING 11-22

NONASTHMA CAUSES OF CHRONIC COUGH 11-22
  OVERVIEW 11-22
  COMMON CAUSES 11-22
    Foreign Body Aspiration 11-22
    Protracted Bacterial Bronchitis (PBB) 11-23
    Aspiration 11-23
    Upper Airway Cough Syndrome 11-23
  CRYPTOGENIC ORGANIZING
    PNEUMONIA (COP) 11-23
  BRONCHIOLITIS OBLITERANS (BO) 11-23
  BRONCHIECTASIS 11-24

SUDDEN INFANT DEATH SYNDROME (SIDS) 11-24

CYSTIC FIBROSIS (CF) 11-25
  OVERVIEW 11-25
  MANIFESTATIONS 11-25
    Respiratory Tract 11-25
    Gastrointestinal (GI) Tract 11-26
    Sweat Glands 11-26
    Reproductive Tract 11-26
  DIAGNOSIS 11-26

TREATMENT 11-27
   Cystic Fibrosis Centers.................................11-27
   Therapy for Pulmonary Disease in CF.............11-27
   Therapy for Gastrointestinal Disease in CF 11-28
COMPLICATIONS..11-28
   Pneumothorax...11-28
   Hemoptysis..11-28
   Pulmonary Hypertension 11-29
   Constipation / Rectal Prolapse 11-29
   CF-Related Diabetes....................................11-29

PRIMARY CILIARY DYSKINESIA (PCD) **11-29**

α₁-ANTITRYPSIN DEFICIENCY (AATD) **11-29**
   OVERVIEW 11-29
   DIAGNOSIS...11-30
   TREATMENT 11-30

HEMOPTYSIS..**11-30**
   OVERVIEW 11-30
   IDIOPATHIC PULMONARY
    HEMOSIDEROSIS (IPH) 11-30

INTERSTITIAL LUNG DISEASES (ILDs) **11-31**
   OVERVIEW 11-31
   LYMPHOCYTIC INTERSTITIAL
    PNEUMONIA (LIP) 11-31
   SARCOIDOSIS 11-31
   PULMONARY ALVEOLAR PROTEINOSIS...........11-32

THE LUNGS IN AUTOIMMUNE DISEASES............**11-32**
   OVERVIEW 11-32
   SYSTEMIC LUPUS ERYTHEMATOSUS (SLE)........11-32
   SCLERODERMA 11-32
   SJÖGREN SYNDROME 11-32
   GRANULOMATOSIS WITH
    POLYANGIITIS (GPA) 11-33
   ANTIGLOMERULAR BASEMENT MEMBRANE
    (Anti-GBM) DISEASE 11-33

**THE MEDSTUDY HUB: YOUR GUIDELINES
AND REVIEW ARTICLES RESOURCE**.................**11-33**

**APPENDIX — ASTHMA TREATMENT
REGIMENS**..**11-33**

FIGURE SOURCES **11-46**

NORMAL RESPIRATION

PREVIEW | REVIEW

- What is a normal respiratory rate for an infant 0–12 months of age?

Respiratory rate varies with activity and state (more during wakefulness than with sleep); therefore, a child's state should always be documented with recorded rate. To identify whether a child has tachypnea, it is best to count the respiratory rate for a minute when the patient is sleeping or at rest. The respiratory rate declines with age from birth to early adolescence, with the steepest decline in the first two years of life. An infant 0–12 months of age has a normal respiratory rate of 30–60 breaths per minute, whereas normal rates for a toddler 1–3 years of age are 24–40 breaths per minute. See Table 11-1 for normal respiratory rates by age.

Table 11-1: Normal Respiratory Rates

Age	Normal (breaths/minute)
0–12 months	30–60
1–3 years	24–40
4–5 years	22–34
6–12 years	18–30
13–18 years	12–16

DIAGNOSTIC TESTING

PREVIEW | REVIEW

- What is the pattern of FEV_1/FVC in patients with lower airway obstruction?

- What is vital capacity (VC)? Which smaller lung volumes are summed to make VC?

- What are the patterns of results of VC, total lung capacity, and residual volume in patients with restrictive lung disease?

- Characterize the differences in the flow-volume loops for obstructive and restrictive airway diseases. (See Figure 11-3 on page 11-2 and Figure 11-4 on page 11-2.)

- What is the 1st test performed in the evaluation of a patient with suspected asthma?

- When is the methacholine bronchoprovocation test performed?

LUNG VOLUMES AND PULMONARY FUNCTION TESTS

In your office, with spirometry, you can determine most of the lung volumes and capacities, expiratory flows, and flow-volume loops and also assess for a positive bronchodilator response. You can reliably accomplish this in most children ≥ 5 years of age.

Use a pulmonary function lab to determine:

- Total lung capacity (TLC) and residual volume
- DLCO (carbon monoxide diffusion capacity; a.k.a. transfer factor for carbon monoxide)
- Methacholine or other challenge test results

For the lung volumes discussed in the next topic, generally < 80% of predicted is abnormal and > 120% of predicted may also be significant.

When reviewing pulmonary function tests (PFTs), keep in mind the following:

- TLC is decreased in restrictive lung disease.
- Forced expiratory volume in 1 second (FEV_1) and the ratio of it to forced vital capacity (FEV_1/FVC) are used to assess for obstructive lung disease. Airway obstruction is diagnosed when the FEV_1/FVC is < 0.7 (70%).

Lung Volumes

Review the lung volumes diagram (Figure 11-1 on page 11-2). The lung is made of 4 basic functional volumes:

1) Residual volume (**RV**) = unused space
2) Expiratory reserve volume (**ERV**) = from full non-forced end-expiration to full forced end-expiration
3) Tidal volume (**TV**) = used in normal unforced ventilation
4) Inspiratory reserve volume (**IRV**) = from normal unforced end-inspiration to full forced end-inspiration

A "capacity" consists of ≥ 2 of these basic volumes and gives even more functional significance to them. For example, vital capacity (**VC**) is the volume you have available for breathing; VC = IRV + TV + ERV. The total lung capacity (**TLC**) additionally includes residual volume; TLC = VC + RV. Inspiratory capacity (**IC**) is the total capacity available for inspiration after passive exhalation; IC = IRV + TV. Functional residual capacity (**FRC**) is the capacity left in the lungs after passive exhalation; FRC = ERV + RV.

In restrictive disease, the TLC is decreased due to both a decreased VC and a decreased RV.

TLC is determined in the lab by helium dilution, nitrogen washout, or plethysmography. Use plethysmography for patients with airflow obstruction, as it can measure trapped gas volumes that are not as accessible by dilution or washout.

The tracing in Figure 11-1 on page 11-2 shows a forced expiration from maximum inspiration. The next diagram (Figure 11-2 on page 11-2) displays the differences in forced expirations for patients with normal, restrictive, and obstructive airways. This is an easy and important test, but you do not usually see it diagrammed this way.

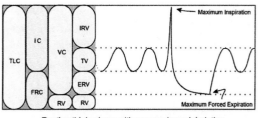
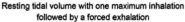

Resting tidal volume with one maximum inhalation
followed by a forced exhalation

Figure 11-1: Lung volumes

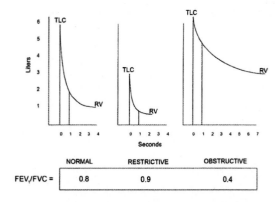

	NORMAL	RESTRICTIVE	OBSTRUCTIVE
FEV$_1$/FVC =	0.8	0.9	0.4

Figure 11-2: Forced expiratory volumes and FEV$_1$/FVC

Although the TLC cannot be determined from spirometry (must know the RV), you can determine the degree of obstruction by comparing the forced expiratory volume at 1 second (FEV$_1$) to the forced vital capacity in the ratio **FEV$_1$/FVC** (FVC = VC during a forced expiration).

In a patient with a normal lung, the FEV$_1$/FVC is ~ 0.8. It is always lower in a patient with airway obstruction, such as an asthmatic patient having an acute attack, but it can be normal or increased in a patient with restrictive disease—even though the VC is small—because this patient has no trouble getting air out. You must assure that a patient is giving good effort and performing spirometry correctly with adequate exhalation time or you may see lower values that appear similar to the pattern of restrictive lung disease.

A patient with asthma has reversible airway obstruction and, if not having an acute attack, can have a normal FEV$_1$/FVC.

Flow-Volume Loops

The diagrams of flow-volume loops shown below are a more common way of expressing airflow in the different lung diseases. Again, these flow-volume loops are derived from the spirometry data and are calculated and plotted by an attached computer, where the FEV$_1$/FVC is automatically determined. The *y* axis is flow rate.

Because we cannot determine RV from spirometry, we get most of our information by the shape of the loop. The exception is in restrictive disease. Although the shape is similar to normal, the VC (represented by [TLC – RV] or the loop width) is much smaller than normal.

Obstructive disease: Note that in Figure 11-3 increased expiratory airway resistance causes decreased expiratory flow rate. While the normal FEV$_1$/FVC = 80%, obstruction is defined as < 70%. (In severe obstruction, it can be much lower!) Additionally, there is a concave scooping of the tracing in the latter half of expiration. Causes of lower airway obstruction include asthma, bronchiectasis, and cystic fibrosis.

Restrictive disease: Notice that Figure 11-4 shows intrathoracic restrictive disease (e.g., parenchymal disease, interstitial lung disease) in which RV is always decreased. Extrathoracic restrictive disease states (e.g., obesity, neuromuscular weakness, kyphoscoliosis) can have a normal RV, but the shape and size are similar.

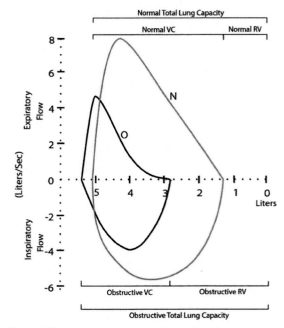

Figure 11-3: Normal vs. obstructive flow-volume loops

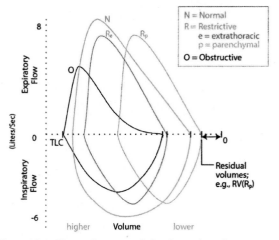

Figure 11-4: Obstructive vs. restrictive flow-volume loops

Bronchodilator Response and Challenge Testing

Bronchodilator response during pulmonary function testing is done for 2 reasons:

1) To determine if the obstruction is responsive to β-agonists. Before testing, withhold short-acting β2-agonists (SABAs) for 8 hours, ipratropium bromide for 24 hours, and long-acting bronchodilators for 48 hours.

2) To test for efficacy of the current asthma regimen. In this case, daily controller medications such as long-acting β-agonists (LABAs) are not withheld. If treated patients have a response to β2-agonists, it suggests they are not on an optimum regimen or are not taking it consistently or correctly.

Know that pre- vs. postbronchodilator spirometry is always the 1st test in the evaluation of a patient with suspected asthma. A bronchoprovocation challenge is done only when initial pre-/postspirometry testing is normal.

Methacholine or other bronchoprovocation-challenge testing is done in people with normal spirometry and intermittent asthma-like symptoms, or other symptoms suggestive of airflow obstruction, to determine if they have bronchial hyperreactivity. This test is often done in the workup of chronic cough (see Asthma on page 11-17) and occasionally in patients with cold air-induced exercise-related bronchospasm.

Inhaled methacholine (or histamine or cold air) is given to the patient in sequentially larger doses followed by spirometry monitoring for a drop in FEV_1. Know that a person with asthma can bronchoconstrict at a very low dose of the challenge irritant, whereas nonasthmatics do not. For methacholine, this is called the PC20 or the concentration at which FEV_1 drops ≥ 20%.

PULSE OXIMETRY

Pulse oximetry is a noninvasive measurement of oxygen (O_2) saturation in the blood. It estimates the hemoglobin saturation by measuring the difference of light absorption between oxygenated and deoxygenated hemoglobin. This test is useful in any setting where hypoxemia can occur. Limitations of pulse oximetry include the inability to differentiate between normal and abnormal types of hemoglobin, motion artifact, ambient light, poor perfusion, cold extremities, anemia, and nail polish.

Causes of Hypoxemia

Hypoxemia (low O_2 tension in the blood) can be caused by the following:

- **Ventilation-perfusion (V/Q) mismatch**—hypoxemia due to some alveoli with ↑V/↓Q and some with ↓V/↑Q. This is the major cause of hypoxemia in chronic lung diseases; responds well to 100% O_2 supplementation.
- **Right-to-left (R-to-L) shunting**—hypoxemia due to perfusion of nonventilated alveoli. Causes of R-to-L shunting, besides alveolar collapse, include intraalveolar filling (e.g., pneumonia, pulmonary edema), intracardiac shunt, and vascular shunt (e.g., an arteriovenous malformation).
- **Decreased alveolar ventilation**—seen with decreased tidal volumes or low respiratory rates; e.g., stopping breathing. This always has a high P_aCO_2 associated with the hypoxemia.
- **Decreased diffusion**—actually has little causal effect on hypoxemia at rest but can play a role in exercise-induced desaturations. It takes a tremendous amount of thickening of the alveolar-capillary interface to decrease diffusion of O_2. This occurs with interstitial lung diseases. Given that CO_2 diffuses more easily than O_2, there may not be a high P_aCO_2.
- **High altitude**—results in a reduced P_AO_2 (partial pressure of O_2 in the alveoli). The alveolar-arterial oxygen gradient is normal unless lung disease is also present.

Oxyhemoglobin Dissociation Curve

The oxyhemoglobin dissociation curve (or oxygen saturation curve; Figure 11-5) typically shows the percentage of O_2 saturation of hemoglobin (S_aO_2) for a certain partial pressure of oxygen (P_aO_2). It is the amount of O_2-saturated

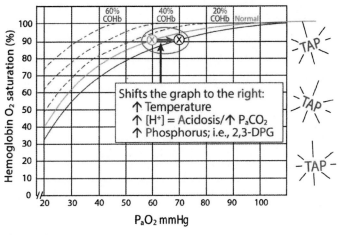

Figure 11-5: Oxyhemoglobin dissociation curve

hemoglobin that is important. You can see from the graph that, everything else being normal, a P_aO_2 of 60 mmHg results in an S_aO_2 of 90%.

The actual O_2 saturation of a particular hemoglobin (Hgb) molecule at a particular P_aO_2 is dependent on temperature, erythrocyte 2,3-DPG (2,3-diphosphoglycerate) level, and pH status. High or low levels of serum phosphorus cause an increased or decreased 2,3-DPG, respectively. The oxyhemoglobin dissociation curve shows the S_aO_2 for a certain P_aO_2—given variations in these 3 factors:

1) **T**emperature

2) **A**cidosis (H⁺ levels resulting in change in pH)

2) **A**cidosis (H^+ levels resulting in change in pH)

3) **P**hosphorus (2,3-DPG)

This gives us the mnemonic **TAP** for remembering what shifts the curve.

When the curve is shifted to the right, it reflects a decrease in Hgb affinity for O_2 (thus, a decreased O_2 uptake by the Hgb). Decreased affinity promotes off-loading of the O_2 to the tissues.

A shift to the left (with decreased levels of TAP) reflects an increased Hgb affinity for O_2 (thus, an increased S_aO_2 for a particular P_aO_2). Increased affinity promotes uptake of oxygen in the pulmonary circulation.

The blue line on the graph indicates what is called a "shift to the right," but it is more logical to think of it as a "shift down" in which, for a certain P_aO_2, the S_aO_2 is decreased. On the graph, at a P_aO_2 of 60 mmHg, the O_2 saturation decreases from 90% to 80% with this right shift.

Note that the TAP, TAP, TAP on the right of the graph is to remind you of the factors that shift the graph to the right—increased temperature and phosphorus, and acidosis.

Carbon monoxide (CO) binds tightly to Hgb, preventing O_2 from binding. Additionally, the binding of CO causes the other oxyhemoglobin (oxyHb) to bind even more tightly to O_2—shifting the curve to the left. The typical noninvasive saturation tests (e.g., pulse oximeter) do not distinguish between oxyHb and carboxyhemoglobin (COHb), so the oxyHb curve not only shifts to the left but also appears to quickly get 100% saturated. With severe CO poisoning, the majority of Hgb is saturated with CO, leaving little room for O_2. The red tracings show how the graph shifts to the left with increasing amounts of COHb.

Methemoglobin is produced when the iron in the Hgb molecule is oxidized from the ferrous (Fe^{2+}) to the ferric (Fe^{3+}) form, and the resulting methemoglobin molecule cannot hold onto O_2 or CO_2—with disastrous results to the tissues. Methemoglobin, like COHb, causes regular ferrous Hgb to hold much more tightly to O_2, thereby shifting the oxyHb dissociation curve to the left (or up for a set P_aO_2). Also, like COHb, typical bedside O_2 saturation tests cannot differentiate oxyHb from methemoglobin. The net result is a left shift of the oxyHb dissociation curve that climbs to 100% at lower P_aO_2 levels. Again, it is similar to the COHb effect but for different reasons.

Methemoglobinemia can be acquired (drugs) or hereditary. Clinical effects of methemoglobinemia vary by the level:

- > 25% = perioral and peripheral cyanosis
- 35–40% = fatigue and dyspnea begin
- > 60% = coma, death

Treat methemoglobinemia with removal of the cause, 100% O_2, and methylene blue (which causes rapid reduction of methemoglobin back to Hgb). Chronic, hereditary methemoglobinemia is best treated with 1–2 g daily of ascorbic acid due to its reducing potential.

Know that the typical pulse oximeter, which measures the absorption of 2 wavelengths of light, is inaccurate when there are significant levels of CO or methemoglobin. Also know that the O_2 saturation reported on an arterial blood gas analysis is a calculated value, not a measured one. In order to obtain true saturations of the different hemoglobins, blood must be inserted into a special CO-oximeter that uses a spectrophotometer to measure O_2 saturation and methemoglobin, COHb, and sulfhemoglobin levels.

Bottom line: Realize that the standard bedside pulse oximeter is not always helpful in CO poisoning and methemoglobinemia because the value is often falsely normal—you must order analysis for the carboxyhemoglobin or methemoglobin levels on fresh blood samples (venous or arterial).

BLOOD GAS ANALYSIS

Acid-base measurement and interpretation is covered in the Nephrology & Urology section.

VENTILATORY SUPPORT

PREVIEW | REVIEW

- What signs and symptoms indicate a child has acute respiratory failure needing ventilatory support?
- Does oxygen supplementation suffice for ventilatory support in a child with both low oxygen and high carbon dioxide levels?

A child with acute or impending respiratory failure needs appropriate ventilatory support. Look for symptoms of respiratory failure including complaints of not being able to breathe. On physical exam, you may note little or no air movement (when previously there may have been wheezing or crackles), retractions, nasal flaring, increased respiratory rate, looking anxious, and not wanting to lie down. More ominous signs can include cyanosis, extreme fatigue, and/or altered mental status with confusion or loss of consciousness. Note: A child with neuromuscular weakness can have progressive respiratory failure with few or no signs or symptoms.

Laboratory findings include oxygen (O_2) desaturation and elevated carbon dioxide (CO_2) levels with acute respiratory acidosis. Typically, you will see problems with oxygenation before changes in CO_2 gas exchange. In a person with chronic respiratory failure, the findings worsen, and the patient needs more support than baseline.

If the child is hypoxic and CO_2 gas exchange is not yet impaired, ventilatory support can start with use of supplemental O_2 by nasal cannula or face mask. If that does not improve oxygenation adequately, the child requires a step up to high-flow nasal cannula, bilevel positive airway pressure (biPAP) nasal ventilation, or intubation with positive pressure ventilation to deliver more O_2.

A child who has both low O_2 and elevated CO_2 levels needs more than just oxygen support. Even if O_2 supplementation improves saturation levels, the child is not ventilating adequately. Until the underlying condition improves, elevated CO_2 levels require either noninvasive support using biPAP or intubation with mechanical ventilation. Children requiring ventilation typically are in a monitored care unit (e.g., intensive care unit [ICU]) managed by subspecialists. Those who fail to improve can be considered for more invasive support, such as oscillatory ventilation or extracorporeal membrane oxygenation (ECMO). A critically ill child requiring high O_2 and/or ventilatory support is in a life-threatening situation; however, the child can often survive and return to baseline with proper management.

NEONATAL STRIDOR

PREVIEW | REVIEW

- What is the most common cause of stridor in the newborn?
- Which chromosomal abnormality is tested for in patients with glottic webs?

NOTE

Refer to Figure 11-6 as you review the causes of neonatal stridor. Most causes of neonatal stridor require direct visualization to make the diagnosis.

LARYNGOMALACIA

Laryngomalacia is the most common cause of stridor in the newborn. The laryngeal cartilage in some children is just not stiff enough, and inspiration causes significant luminal narrowing, resulting in inspiratory stridor. The stridor can occur at birth but is most commonly heard by 2 weeks of age. The stridor is more pronounced with agitation, feeding, and lying in a supine position. For most, close observation is sufficient, and the cartilage becomes more rigid with age. Most children outgrow the disorder by 12–24 months of age. In severe cases, feeding is often affected, and/or nighttime obstructive hypoxia occurs; these symptoms are sometimes alleviated by trimming the supraglottis.

Confirm the diagnosis by awake flexible laryngoscopy, which can be performed in the office setting.

SUBGLOTTIC STENOSIS

Subglottic stenosis can cause stridor and respiratory distress in the newborn or in the first few months of life. Milder cases may present as recurrent episodes of croup before 12 months of age. Infants with trisomy 21 (a.k.a. Down syndrome) have an increased incidence of congenital subglottic stenosis. Refer these patients to an otolaryngologist for diagnosis by direct laryngoscopy or bronchoscopy. Only treat stenosis that produces symptoms, and treat those cases as early as possible. Some cases require tracheostomy before surgery can be performed. Cases that occur later in life are acquired and

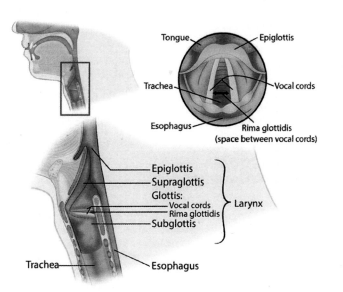

Figure 11-6: The larynx

can present with recurrent episodes of croup. Subglottic stenosis can develop after endotracheal intubation at any age, and the incidence increases with the length of intubation. These patients present with stridor and respiratory distress after a variable time period following extubation.

VOCAL CORD PARALYSIS

Vocal cord paralysis is caused by damage to the recurrent laryngeal nerve and can occur in one or both vocal cords. It can be seen in infants with other neurologic abnormalities (e.g., Arnold-Chiari malformation, posterior fossa tumor, hydrocephalus) or following birth trauma. During a difficult delivery, vocal cord paralysis can occur due to an injury of the recurrent laryngeal nerve caused by stretching the neck. Unilateral vocal cord paralysis may also be caused by intubation and is seen more commonly on the left because of the longer course of the recurrent laryngeal nerve on that side. Paralysis of one or both vocal cords can also occur as a complication of cardiothoracic and thyroid surgery or surgical repair of a tracheoesophageal fistula. Paresis (partial paralysis) can also occur. Affected infants have an absent or weak cry and are at risk for aspiration during feedings. Toddlers and children with vocal cord paralysis typically have a subdued, yet hoarse, raspy quality to their voices. Refer these patients to an otolaryngologist for diagnosis by awake fiberoptic nasopharyngoscopy. Treatment varies depending on the extent of involvement.

LARYNGEAL ATRESIA / WEBS

Laryngeal atresia is a rare condition due to failure of the larynx to recanalize by the 10th week of gestation. It remains blocked with cartilage or other tissue. Laryngeal atresia is usually incompatible with life, but with early prenatal diagnosis, the fetus may be able to survive with airway intervention by fetal ex utero intrapartum treatment (EXIT). This type of anomaly and similar abnormalities (e.g., laryngeal cysts) have been given the label of congenital high airway obstruction syndrome (CHAOS).

Partial recanalization during gestation results in laryngeal webs and occurs with abnormal development of structures in and around the laryngeal inlet of the developing embryo. Webs can present with abnormal voice or with stridor and respiratory distress. Glottic webs are identified by an otolaryngologist under direct laryngoscopy. In most cases, treatment options include incision or dilation. Tracheostomy is required for severe glottic webs. Webs can be seen in velocardiofacial syndrome (a.k.a. DiGeorge syndrome), which is identified by genetic testing for 22q11 gene deletions.

CONGENITAL DISORDERS OF THE LOWER RESPIRATORY TRACT

PREVIEW | REVIEW

- How does tracheal stenosis present?
- What is pulmonary venolobar syndrome (a.k.a. scimitar syndrome)?
- Why is bronchoscopy not useful in diagnosing pulmonary sequestrations?

TRACHEAL DISORDERS

Tracheal Agenesis

Tracheal agenesis is very rare and presents as 1 of 3 different types:

- **Type 1**—The proximal trachea is closed off, and the distal part communicates with the esophagus.
- **Type 2**—The bronchi meet in the midline and communicate with the esophagus through a fistula.
- **Type 3**—The trachea is absent, and both main bronchi communicate directly with the esophagus separately.

In all 3 types, infants present at delivery in severe respiratory distress with absent cry. Affected infants die shortly thereafter. Suspect this condition if the trachea cannot be intubated even though the larynx is visualized.

Tracheal Stenosis

Tracheal stenosis presents most commonly as a segmental stenosis and usually involves complete cartilaginous rings. It can occur anywhere along the trachea and can vary in length of involvement. Infants display severe retractions and dyspnea and have expiratory stridor. Also consider tracheal stenosis if a child presents with recurrent or prolonged croup. Bronchoscopy, computed tomography (CT), or magnetic resonance imaging (MRI) is used to confirm the diagnosis. Mild cases typically do not receive treatment, only observation, and improve as the airway grows. Management of symptomatic cases by an otolaryngologist includes balloon dilatation, resection of the stenotic portion, or slide tracheoplasty.

Tracheomalacia and Bronchomalacia

Tracheomalacia produces collapse of the trachea severe enough to cause airway obstruction. It can be a generalized or localized weakness of the tracheal wall. Bronchomalacia is the same disorder but in the bronchi. Tracheobronchomalacia involves both the tracheal wall and bronchi. The airway cartilage does not have adequate tone and collapses with breathing, resulting in airway obstruction and difficulty clearing secretions. Secondary malacia can occur from external compression from an aberrant vessel (vascular ring or sling). The resulting airway obstruction produces an expiratory stridor, as opposed to the inspiratory stridor heard with obstruction above the thoracic inlet such as laryngomalacia.

Tracheobronchomalacia is usually mild and self-limited and does not require specific therapy. It is sometimes found with other disorders such as tracheoesophageal fistula, cardiac abnormalities, and cervical/mediastinal masses. More severe cases require positive pressure ventilation to help stent the airways open. Severe tracheomalacia, particularly in infancy, sometimes requires tracheostomy.

PULMONARY HYPOPLASIA

Pulmonary hypoplasia is a common cause of neonatal death. Infants present at birth with respiratory distress and have severe hypoxemia and hypercarbia. Lung development is a complicated multifactorial process, and, if something in this process is disturbed, development can be severely affected.

Pulmonary hypoplasia is associated with oligohydramnios, as well as premature rupture of membranes, which leads to premature delivery. Premature infants vary in their lung function capacity depending on the degree of hypoplasia. The hypoplasia is due to a decrease in the number of alveoli with or without a decrease in the number of small airway branches.

Pulmonary hypoplasia can be bilateral or unilateral (e.g., in association with congenital diaphragmatic hernia). Prognosis depends on the severity of the pulmonary hypoplasia and the associated anomalies that typically coexist with or induce pulmonary hypoplasia. In severe cases, the lungs are too small and the infant dies. In less severe cases, the neonate is kept alive on mechanical ventilation or, rarely, ECMO until adequate lung growth occurs. Interestingly, some infants who appear to have markedly severe pulmonary hypoplasia improve dramatically within hours of being placed on mechanical ventilation.

CONGENITAL PULMONARY VENOLOBAR SYNDROME (SCIMITAR SYNDROME)

Congenital pulmonary venolobar syndrome is a rare disorder in which the pulmonary venous blood from all or part of the right lung returns to the inferior vena cava (IVC) just above or below the diaphragm. It is a left-to-right (oxygenated blood to deoxygenated blood) shunt. In the infantile form, abnormalities of venous drainage (e.g., hemianomalous pulmonary venous drainage to the IVC) can present as heart failure and/or pulmonary hypertension in the newborn period. A chest x-ray (CXR) may show the shadow of these veins as they course, giving a scimitar-like (Turkish sword) appearance (Figure 11-7). There is a worse prognosis if these infants present with heart failure, usually due to associated anomalies, including left-sided heart malformations.

Treatment is by transcatheter occlusion of aortopulmonary collaterals. Other treatment options include reimplantation of the vein or pneumonectomy. Mortality is high.

PULMONARY ARTERIOVENOUS MALFORMATIONS (PAVMs)

PAVMs (including pulmonary arteriovenous fistulas, aneurysms, and telangiectases) occur with several distinct congenital disorders. The most common cause (70%) is autosomal dominant **hereditary hemorrhagic telangiectasia** (HHT; a.k.a. Osler-Weber-Rendu syndrome). This disorder involves multiple abnormalities of the blood vessels in the skin, mucous membranes, and organs (e.g., lungs, liver, brain). By 20 years of age, 50% of patients have had episodes of epistaxis, although it can present at any age. PAVM in HHT is uncommon in childhood and increases in incidence with age. Many patients with PAVM are asymptomatic and are unaware of their risk of complications.

Large PAVMs cause problems due to R-to-L shunting of systemic venous blood directly into the pulmonary veins and left heart, leading to hypoxemia. Those with large-volume shunts present with dyspnea, bleeding with hemoptysis, and exercise intolerance. Heart failure is very uncommon because the blood flow is a "low-pressure" system. In those with persistent hypoxemia, polycythemia is common. Patients with PAVM are at increased risk of cerebral events such as stroke, transient ischemic attacks, and brain abscesses from paradoxical embolism.

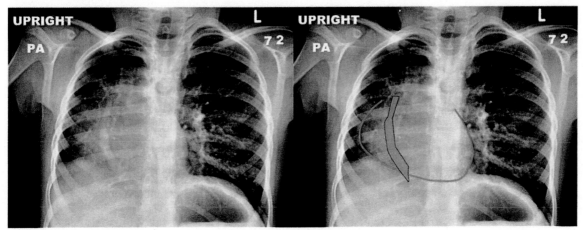

Figure 11-7: Congenital pulmonary venolobar syndrome; "scimitar" location in red

Both contrast echocardiograms and lung perfusion scans can be employed to confirm the abnormal R-to-L shunt at the level of the pulmonary vasculature in these patients. Starting in adolescence, patients with known HHT should have screening with contrast (bubble) echocardiogram for PAVM. A positive screening echocardiogram shows the appearance of bubbles in the systemic circulation and is confirmed with chest CT.

Treatment of symptomatic patients consists of pulmonary angiography and occlusion of the feeding arteries. Surgical removal of the fistulas is needed if they are large or if ablation is unsuccessful. PAVMs can recur and/or previously unrecognized PAVMs can enlarge.

PULMONARY SEQUESTRATIONS

Pulmonary sequestration is a mass of abnormal, non-functioning lung tissue isolated from the normal, functioning lung tissue and fed by systemic arteries. Pulmonary sequestrations can be either intralobar (contained within the normal visceral pleura) or extralobar (outside the normal lung with its own visceral pleura and venous drainage). It does not communicate with the tracheobronchial tree.

The **intralobar** form generally occurs in the lower lobes of each lung, most commonly in the posterior basal section of the left lower lobe. The intralobar form is usually isolated and is typically identified during childhood or adolescence.

The **extralobar** form is located just above or below the diaphragm, with almost all cases being on the left side. Other anomalies are common, including colon duplication, vertebrae abnormalities, and diaphragmatic defects. Most extralobar forms are diagnosed in infancy because of associated malformations.

Pulmonary sequestration is sometimes identified prenatally on ultrasound and often partially or completely regresses before delivery. A postnatal CT should always be done to confirm it has fully resolved.

Besides respiratory distress in infants, it is possible to see recurrent pneumonia, hemoptysis, or signs of infection. Older children may complain of severe pleuritic chest pain out of proportion to other findings. Some are asymptomatic and discovered as incidental findings on a CXR.

CXR or CT scan shows a dense mass in the lung or thorax, representing recurrent infection, cystic changes, or air-fluid levels. A Doppler ultrasound can help demonstrate the arterial supply and venous drainage. Bronchoscopy is not helpful because the sequestration is not connected to the normal airways. Surgical removal of the sequestered lobe is the treatment of choice.

BRONCHOGENIC CYSTS

Bronchogenic cysts result from abnormal budding of the tracheal diverticulum of the foregut before 16 weeks of gestation. They are the most common cysts in infancy and are typically single, unilocular, and on the right. Most bronchogenic cysts are filled with mucus. They can occur in the paratracheal, carinal, hilar, or paraesophageal area and most often are in the middle mediastinum. They do not communicate with the tracheobronchial tree. The paraesophageal cyst sometimes communicates with the esophagus.

The cyst can present as an isolated incidental finding of a middle or posterior mediastinal mass (that may have air-fluid levels) on a CXR, or it can present with respiratory distress because of compression of surrounding tissues. A bronchogenic cyst may also be prone to infection. Fever, chest pain, and productive cough are the most common presenting symptoms.

If the cyst ruptures, pneumothorax or hemoptysis can occur. Order a CT or an MRI to define the diagnosis. Cyst excision is curative in symptomatic cases. Excision is also the preferred treatment in asymptomatic patients because of a high likelihood of future symptoms and the potential for serious illness, including, rarely, malignant degeneration.

CONGENITAL PULMONARY AIRWAY MALFORMATION (CPAM)

CPAM (formerly congenital cystic adenomatoid malformation [CCAM]) is characterized by an adenomatoid proliferation of bronchioles that results in cysts rather than alveoli. These malformations result from abnormal branching of bronchioles during lung morphogenesis. Pregnancy may be complicated by hydramnios, pre-eclampsia, premature birth, and hydrops fetalis.

Lesions usually communicate with the normal tracheobronchial tree, though the connection can be constricted or anomalous. Blood supply is usually pulmonary arterial in origin. CPAM has been the most commonly diagnosed lung malformation in fetuses, accounting for 30–40% of all congenital lung diseases. CPAM is usually unilateral, affecting only 1 lobe of the lung.

Stocker's classification of CPAM has 5 types (0–4), based on cyst size and histopathologic findings. We will only discuss the most common one—Type 1 (50–70% prevalence). Type 1 consists of a single cyst or multiloculated large cysts that are variable in size, from 2 cm to 10 cm. They are seen at the bronchial and/or bronchiolar level. This type is localized, typically to part of a single lobe, and has the best prognosis.

Presentations vary. CPAM can appear with progressive respiratory distress in the neonatal period. The cysts become aerated and can progressively expand as the fetal lung fluid clears. Large lesions can compress the adjacent lung, and large cysts can cause mediastinal shift in young infants; this shift can regress with increasing age. Congenital diaphragmatic hernia with herniated bowel in the thorax may have an appearance similar to a CPAM. ~ 1/3 of CPAM cases appear after the neonatal period. Children or adults can present with recurrent pulmonary infections. A few cases of spontaneous pneumothorax have been reported. There is a rare risk of neoplastic and/or malignant transformation.

Almost all CPAMs can be detected in utero via ultrasonography (U/S) but may not be symptomatic at birth. Chest radiography is only 60% sensitive in asymptomatic infants with lesions noted at prenatal U/S. Thin-section chest CT is advised in asymptomatic infants with abnormal prenatal U/S findings to further define the abnormality. In an asymptomatic older child, a lesion may be found incidentally on chest radiograph.

If symptomatic, surgical excision is recommended. Elective excision is controversial for asymptomatic patients, such as those whose CPAM is detected prenatally. Reasons cited to perform surgery include preventing nonmalignant complications such as infection, allowing optimal lung growth of the remaining lung, and preventing malignant transformation. Bronchoalveolar carcinoma, pleuropulmonary blastoma, and rhabdomyosarcoma are known to have an association with CPAM. However, there is limited evidence regarding the natural history, and some elect to monitor the condition medically.

DIAPHRAGM MALFORMATIONS

Congenital Diaphragmatic Hernia

Lung hypoplasia can result from congenital diaphragmatic hernia. See Pulmonary Hypoplasia on page 11-7 and the Neonatology section for more information.

Eventration

Eventration is a marked elevation of the diaphragm. It is almost always congenital but can be acquired with an injury to the phrenic nerve (acquired during difficult instrumental delivery, insertion of a chest tube for pneumothorax, or cardiac surgery). It occurs more often in males, typically affects the left diaphragm, and can be partial or diffuse. Some children who have lung hypoplasia and compression of the lung bases are at risk for atelectasis, which increases risk of pneumonia. Infants can be asymptomatic or have tachypnea, dyspnea, retractions, and cyanosis.

Physical examination shows unilateral decrease in breath sounds. CXR shows elevation of the hemidiaphragm. Ultrasound or fluoroscopy confirms the diagnosis by showing minimal or paradoxical movement of the affected diaphragm. Usually, no treatment is needed, and the condition sometimes improves with time. Surgical plication is performed in cases that have significant respiratory compromise.

Accessory Diaphragm

An accessory diaphragm is rare and occurs when a fibromuscular band divides a hemithorax into 2 parts. (The right side is affected more often.) In most patients, it results in hypoplasia of the lung on the affected side, with resulting respiratory distress in the neonate. Older children tend to have recurrent infections. Lateral x-ray shows the accessory diaphragm. If it is symptomatic, surgery is needed to remove the accessory diaphragm.

NEUROMUSCULAR RESPIRATORY FAILURE

PREVIEW | REVIEW

- Muscle weakness from neuromuscular disease results in which specific problems that can lead to respiratory failure?

- What are some of the neuromuscular diseases that can cause respiratory failure?

Respiratory failure can result from certain neuromuscular diseases. Muscle weakness from such diseases can cause upper airway compromise, inspiratory muscle (i.e., diaphragm, intercostals, accessory) compromise, and/or expiratory muscle compromise. These result in problems with swallowing and secretion clearance, aspiration, mechanical obstruction of the upper airway, inadequate lung expansion resulting in hypoxemia from V/Q mismatch, and inadequate cough.

Some of the diseases that can cause respiratory failure include Guillain-Barré syndrome, myasthenia gravis, spinal muscular atrophy, muscular dystrophy, and cerebral palsy. For more information on these diseases, see the Neurology section.

STRIDOR BEYOND THE NEONATAL PERIOD

PREVIEW | REVIEW

- Describe the location of the obstruction based on inspiratory vs. expiratory stridor.

- What are the 2 main diagnoses to consider if a patient with acute-onset stridor also presents with high fever and rapid deterioration?

- True or false? Patients with vocal cord dysfunction respond to albuterol.

This topic covers stridor that occurs outside of the neonatal period. To review neonatal stridor, see Neonatal Stridor on page 11-5.

Stridor refers to a high-pitched sound caused by obstruction to airflow through a narrowed airway. Stridor is not a diagnosis. It is a symptom that signals an airway disorder. Inspiratory stridor occurs when the obstruction is at or above the subglottic area (portion of airway between vocal cords and thoracic cavity). (See Figure 11-6 on page 11-5). Expiratory stridor is heard when the obstruction occurs in the intrathoracic portion of the trachea. Since stridor signifies airway obstruction, immediate evaluation of the patient is needed to determine the cause. The acuity of onset and degree of stridor can help in the differential.

Acute onset with high fever and rapid deterioration can indicate:

• Epiglottitis
• Bacterial tracheitis

Acute onset without fever can indicate:

• Anaphylaxis
• Foreign body

Subacute onset can indicate:

• Croup
• Peritonsillar abscess
• Retropharyngeal abscess

Chronic onset can indicate:

• Laryngomalacia
• Tracheomalacia
• Subglottic stenosis
• Vascular ring

INFECTION

Unlike stridor in the neonatal period, which is due to structural abnormalities, stridor in older children is commonly caused by infection. Perform rapid assessment looking for hypoxia, nasal flaring, retractions, tachypnea/bradypnea, cyanosis, and worsening respiratory distress to identify patients who need resuscitation or direct laryngoscopy. If the patient is deemed stable, obtain a thorough history and physical. Typically, the diagnosis of croup is made clinically, and no further tests are needed. If the initial evaluation suggests a diagnosis other than croup, further workup can include complete blood count (CBC) looking for possible bacterial process, neck radiographs, chest radiographs, CT scan, and visualization of airway. Treatment depends on the cause of the stridor. See individual etiologies for treatment.

PARADOXICAL VOCAL CORD DYSFUNCTION (VCD)

Paradoxical VCD (a.k.a. inducible laryngeal obstruction) refers to an inappropriate, transient, and reversible narrowing of the larynx in response to external triggers. In patients with VCD, the vocal cords adduct (close) during inspiration instead of abducting or remaining open. See Figure 11-8.

The most common triggers are exercise, irritants (e.g., cigarette smoke), and emotional stress. VCD is more common in females and in patients with underlying psychiatric disorders (e.g., anxiety, obsessive compulsive disorder). Patients present with difficulty breathing, hoarseness, wheezing, and/or difficulty swallowing.

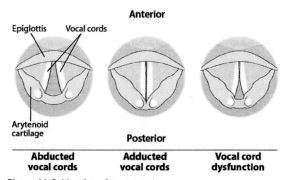

Figure 11-8: Vocal cord movement

Physical examination findings include stridor that is loudest over the anterior neck.

Because patients present with wheezing and difficulty breathing, VCD is frequently confused with asthma. However, patients with VCD do not respond to albuterol, and the difficulty breathing occurs during inspiration, not expiration. Also, patients with exercise-induced VCD develop symptoms during maximal exercise, while patients with asthma develop symptoms up to 20 minutes after exercise. In office, exercise challenge pulmonary function testing is not consistent with exercise-induced asthma, and symptoms often occur soon into exercise but are relieved with stopping the activity.

The gold standard for diagnosing VCD is laryngoscopy, which demonstrates adducted vocal cords during inspiration. Treatment often includes decreasing the exposure to airway irritants, speech and behavioral therapy, and relaxation exercises. Botulinum toxin can be used in patients who do not improve with speech therapy.

Exercise-induced VCD occurs exclusively during exercise and is associated with narrowing of the laryngeal airway at the glottic (vocal folds) or supraglottic level. Patients present with inspiratory stridor, cough, difficulty swallowing, and a hoarse voice during exercise. All symptoms resolve without intervention within 15 minutes of stopping exercise. Patients do not have symptoms at rest, and the symptoms do not improve with β-agonists therapy before or during exercise.

INFECTIONS OF THE UPPER RESPIRATORY TRACT

PREVIEW | REVIEW

• Which virus causes most cases of croup?
• What is the treatment for croup?
• What are the typical causes of epiglottitis?
• If you visualize a cherry-red epiglottis, what is your diagnosis?
• What is the treatment of epiglottitis?
• Which organism most often causes bacterial tracheitis?

NOTE

Refer to Figure 11-6 on page 11-5 as you review the causes of upper respiratory tract infections that can cause stridor.

LARYNGOTRACHEOBRONCHITIS (CROUP)

Croup typically occurs between 3 months and 3 years of age, with a peak around 2 years of age. Most episodes occur in fall and early winter. Most cases are due to parainfluenza virus Types 1 and 2. Sporadic cases can occur with other parainfluenza virus types, influenza virus, respiratory syncytial virus (RSV), measles, and other viruses.

Croup is predominantly a clinical diagnosis. The child is not terribly ill-appearing and presents with a low-grade fever, a high-pitched barking cough, and inspiratory stridor. Symptoms are typically worse at night or when the child is agitated. Neck x-ray can sometimes help exclude other etiologies and frequently shows subglottic narrowing at the cricoid cartilage (**steeple sign**; Figure 11-9).

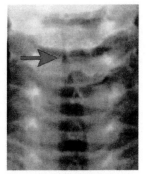

Figure 11-9: Steeple sign

Croup is commonly managed supportively with cool-mist humidifiers, using a shower to steam up the bathroom, and/or taking a child outside in the cool night air. If the child presents to the emergency department, most physicians give a single 0.6 mg/kg (max 10 mg) dose of oral (if possible; if not, then IM/IV) dexamethasone, which decreases the length and severity of the illness.

For moderate stridor at rest, moderate retractions, or more severe symptoms, in addition to giving dexamethasone, you can add nebulized epinephrine (5 mL of 1:1,000 L-epinephrine) or 0.05 mL/kg/dose (max 0.5 mL) of a 2.25% solution of racemic epinephrine diluted to 3 mL total volume with normal saline via nebulizer with 100% oxygen. The main problem with this therapy is the **rebound phenomenon**, a recurrence of symptoms after the medication has worn off (after ~ 2 hours). Therefore, observe children in the emergency department for at least 3–4 hours after therapy has begun. Hospitalize patients who require > 2 doses of nebulized epinephrine.

Spasmodic croup is typically a noninfectious croup in which the child wakes up in the middle of the night with symptoms of barking cough and mild-to-moderate stridor. The next day the child is asymptomatic, but the cycle repeats itself that night and possibly again over the next 2–3 nights. Spasmodic croup may or may not respond to cool mist or night air. Gastroesophageal reflux can be an important component. There can be mild signs of acute respiratory tract infection (coryza) but no fever; the child usually appears well otherwise.

Recurrent croup sometimes indicates a variant of asthma, in which case there is a positive bronchodilator response.

EPIGLOTTITIS

Epiglottitis is an infection of the larynx with rapid swelling of the epiglottis and increasing respiratory distress. It is now rare in developed countries because of widespread use of *Haemophilus influenzae* Type b vaccine, although the risk of invasive *H. influenzae* Type b disease is increased among unimmunized household contacts < 4 years of age. In the U.S., nontypeable *H. influenzae* is the most common cause of epiglottitis, followed by *Streptococcus pneumoniae*, *Streptococcus pyogenes* (a.k.a. group A β-hemolytic *Streptococcus* [GABHS]), and *Staphylococcus aureus*.

Epiglottitis typically affects children between 2 and 5 years of age. Patients present with abrupt onset of fever, sore throat, drooling, and stridor. Frequently, the child is very ill-appearing and apprehensive, sitting forward in a tripod position with the chin extended. It is differentiated from croup by its more rapid onset and toxic appearance.

Never use a tongue depressor on a symptomatic child—it can provoke airway spasm and life-threatening obstruction. Provide oxygen supplementation if necessary. Stay calm and keep the child calm. If respiratory failure is not imminent, the best next step is to seek the immediate help of an experienced pediatric anesthesiologist or otolaryngologist. The finding of a **cherry-red epiglottis** on laryngoscopy is diagnostic of epiglottitis (Figure 11-10).

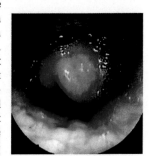

Figure 11-10: Epiglottitis

Besides airway management, treatment must include prompt antibiotic therapy, which typically includes an antistaphylococcal drug such as oxacillin, cefazolin, or clindamycin and either ceftriaxone or cefotaxime. Most of these children are bacteremic. When methicillin-resistant *S. aureus* (MRSA) colonization is high in the community, many use vancomycin as the antistaphylococcal agent.

Admit patients with epiglottitis to a closely monitored hospital unit.

Rifampin prophylaxis eradicates *H. influenzae* Type b from the pharynx in ~ 95% of carriers. In household contacts, it decreases the risk of invasive disease. Although there may be increased risk of secondary illness in childcare contacts, it is unlikely when all contacts are > 2 years of age.

BACTERIAL TRACHEITIS

Bacterial tracheitis is most often caused by *Staphylococcus aureus*. It can also be caused by pneumococcus *Moraxella catarrhalis*, nontypeable *H. influenzae*, and anaerobes. Bacterial tracheitis usually follows a viral upper respiratory infection (URI), such as croup due to parainfluenza virus Types 1 and 2, and does not involve the epiglottis. Because of the *H. influenzae* vaccine, bacterial tracheitis is more common than epiglottitis.

A child with tracheitis is typically < 3 years of age and presents very ill-appearing with high fever and a brassy, productive cough; however, the stridor/croup does not respond to usual treatment measures for croup, and the child's condition deteriorates rapidly. Intubation or tracheostomy is frequently required.

The majority of cases of bacterial tracheitis occur in previously healthy children in the setting of a viral respiratory tract infection. Most cases occur in the fall and winter, coinciding with the typical seasonal epidemics of parainfluenza, RSV, and seasonal influenza.

Treatment includes antibiotics, particularly nafcillin, aimed at *S. aureus*. Patients respond to therapy within 2–3 days; however, due to the continued edema from the tracheitis, most patients require an average of 10–14 days in the hospital. Vancomycin is used if MRSA is common in the community.

INFECTIONS OF THE LOWER RESPIRATORY TRACT

PREVIEW | REVIEW

- Which pathogen most commonly causes acute bronchiolitis?
- In children, the absence of which vital sign abnormality makes the diagnosis of pneumonia unlikely?
- When do you get a CXR in a child with fever?
- Are blood cultures routinely recommended in the management of outpatient pneumonia in children?
- Gram-positive diplococci seen in a sputum sample with a large number of PMNs and few epithelial cells most likely indicate which organism?
- What do you do about a pleural effusion in a child with recent pneumococcal pneumonia who clinically is responding to therapy?
- What do you do about pneumatoceles if they occur in *Streptococcus pyogenes* pneumonia?
- A patient with influenza develops a secondary bacterial pneumonia. Besides pneumococcus, which bacterial pathogen do you especially consider?
- What are the extrapulmonary manifestations of *Mycoplasma* infection?

- Name the geographical areas for histoplasmosis, coccidioidomycosis, and blastomycosis.
- If you see the words "San Joaquin Valley" in a test question, look for which fungus in the responses?
- A patient presents with worsening control of their asthma and an extremely high IgE level. What do you suspect as an etiology?
- How do you treat allergic bronchopulmonary aspergillosis?

BRONCHIOLITIS

Acute bronchiolitis is very common in infants and young children, especially during the winter and spring. It is most commonly due to respiratory syncytial virus (**RSV**), which is ubiquitous. Risk factors for severe RSV infection include secondhand smoke exposure, family history of asthma, crowded living conditions, lack of breastfeeding, and low birth weight. RSV can be spread by large-particle dispersion and through contact with fomites. Other etiologies include parainfluenza, human metapneumovirus, influenza virus, rhinovirus, coronavirus, and human bocavirus.

Frequently, affected infants and children < 2 years of age have a prodrome of low-grade fever, runny nose, and poor feeding before progressing to cough and wheezing. Symptoms peak around day 5. On physical examination, look for wheezing, crackles, stridor, retractions, hypoxia, or cough. CXR shows hyperinflation and is nonspecific. Rapid immunofluorescent and enzyme immunoassays for detection of viral antigens in nasopharyngeal specimens are available commercially and are generally reliable in infants and young children.

Treatment is supportive; hospitalization is reserved for patients who are hypoxemic, unable to feed, dehydrated, and/or toxic-appearing. β-Agonist therapy is not recommended for routine care in first-time wheezing related to bronchiolitis. Inhaled hypertonic saline (3%) is sometimes used as a mucolytic in hospitalized children. Corticosteroids and antibiotics are not recommended. Use ribavirin primarily in critically ill or immunocompromised children.

Infants can be severely affected and sometimes require intubation with mechanical ventilation, especially if they are premature.

Most infants are infectious for ~ 7 days, but some can have persistent shedding for 3–4 weeks or longer.

Respiratory Syncytial Virus (RSV) Immunoprophylaxis

RSV can affect the lower respiratory tract, causing bronchiolitis, bronchospasm, pneumonia, and acute respiratory failure—especially in infants and small children. Acquisition of RSV is not protective against subsequent exposures.

The 2021 *Red Book* by the American Academy of Pediatrics on RSV immunoprophylaxis recommends monthly palivizumab only for high-risk infants and children during the active season. In addition, during the COVID-19 pandemic, the AAP suggests administration of palivizumab for RSV prophylaxis in eligible infants outside of the typically recommended schedule if they live in regions with interseasonal RSV activity similar to that in a typical fall–winter season.

High-risk patients include:

- Infants and children < 24 months of age with chronic lung disease of prematurity who require medical therapy (e.g., diuretics, oxygen, systemic corticosteroids) within 6 months of the start of RSV season (Chronic lung disease of prematurity is defined as the requirement of oxygen for > 28 days in infants born at < 32 weeks of gestation.)
- Infants born at < 29 weeks of gestation in their 1st winter
- Children < 24 months of age with hemodynamically significant cyanotic and acyanotic congenital heart disease

Prophylaxis for infants who are immunocompromised or have significant pulmonary or neurologic problems that interfere with the ability to clear upper airway secretions is begun on a case-by-case basis. Once a child "qualifies" for initiation of prophylaxis at the start of the RSV season, continue prophylaxis until the end of the season, based on month of birth and gestational age, for up to 5 doses. Discontinue prophylaxis if an infant has an RSV infection requiring hospitalization.

PNEUMONIA — GENERAL CONSIDERATIONS

Clinical markers of pneumonia are not the same in infants and children as in adults, and the younger patients often do not present with the typical fever, cough, and productive sputum. Thus, various clinical guidelines have been developed to help us sort this out. The following information on diagnosing pneumonia refers to children ≥ 2 months of age. Infants < 2 months of age with pneumonia are discussed in the Neonatology and Infectious Disease sections.

First, consider whether the child has signs of respiratory distress:

- Tachypnea (See Table 11-1 on page 11-1 for normal respiratory rates by age.)
- Subcostal retractions
- Cough
- Crackles
- Decreased breath sounds

Note: The positive predictive values of these signs are best if the child has fever or cyanosis in addition to ≥ 2 of these signs.

Without the presence of fever, the negative predictive value of tachypnea is 97%. In other words, without fever, pneumonia is unlikely.

What about CXR?

CXR is recommended in the following:

- A child < 5 years of age has fever and high white blood cell (WBC) count of unknown source.
- There is clinical evidence of possible pneumonia, but the clinical findings are not clear-cut.
- Pleural effusion is suspected.
- Pneumonia is unresponsive to antibiotics.

Most studies have shown that CXR cannot distinguish between viral and bacterial pneumonia, and many studies have failed to show that CXR actually alters management decisions. (See Figure 11-11.)

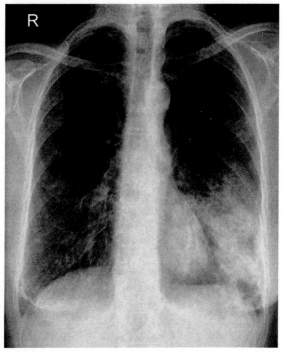

Figure 11-11: Left lower lobe pneumonia

What about WBC count and differential?

Most data shows that the likelihood of a bacterial cause increases as the WBC count increases above 15,000–20,000. A bacterial etiology is especially likely with WBCs this high and a fever > 102.2°F (39.0°C). But when do you order a WBC count? Consider a WBC count when the information available to you is insufficient to indicate antibiotic use.

If possible, in a child with severe disease, obtain a high-quality sputum specimen (< 10 squamous epithelial cells and > 25 polymorphonuclear neutrophils (PMNs)/low-power field suggests a purulent specimen), although this is often difficult. Sputum can be induced with a 3% hypertonic saline treatment. For mild or moderate disease, sputum studies are generally not necessary. In an immunocompromised patient or a child not responding to antibiotics, consider a lower respiratory culture obtained by flexible bronchoscopy, but you must take into account the risks of sedation. For children who are intubated, a tracheal aspirate can be obtained.

Blood cultures are not recommended as routine studies in the outpatient setting (the chance of a positive blood culture in this setting is < 5%), but they are recommended for inpatients with more severe pneumonia.

What about serologic testing, cultures, and polymerase chain reaction (PCR) testing?

Testing for specific pathogens, such as *Mycoplasma pneumoniae* or *Chlamydia pneumoniae* (formerly *Chlamydophila pneumoniae*), is not routinely recommended. Use other tests, such as viral cultures, viral antigens, and cold agglutinins, only when the result alters therapy.

Use of erythrocyte sedimentation rate and C-reactive protein are not recommended to diagnose pneumonia.

VIRAL PNEUMONIA

Pneumonia in children is most likely due to viruses. These include RSV, parainfluenza viruses, adenoviruses, rhinoviruses, influenza viruses, varicella virus, and rubeola (measles) virus. Clinically, children have a prodrome of URI-type symptoms, which is followed by a sudden onset of tachypnea, nonproductive and frequently paroxysmal cough, and low-grade fever. Physical findings consistent with pneumonia include dullness or decreased breath sounds, wheezing and crackles, or, in other cases, the lung examination can be normal except for tachypnea. CXR usually shows perihilar and parenchymal infiltrates.

Treatment is supportive, with fluids and oxygen if necessary. Specific viruses are discussed in the Infectious Disease section.

ACUTE BACTERIAL PNEUMONIA

Streptococcus pneumoniae

S. pneumoniae classically presents as an abrupt infection with high fever, chills, chest pain, and dyspnea, as well as blood-tinged sputum. (Remember: Pneumococci are gram-positive diplococci.) Children with pneumococcal pneumonia appear clinically ill and have tachypnea and tachycardia.

Physical examination shows dullness to percussion over the affected lung segment and diminished breath sounds. A pleural friction rub may be detected. Frank crackles may not be heard until later in the course of the illness.

Of major concern is the emergence of penicillin-resistant pneumococci; in some health care centers, it approaches 40–50% of cases. For outpatient therapy, use high-dose amoxicillin (80–100 mg/kg/day) for 7–10 days. For children with vomiting who are still well enough to return home, give IM ceftriaxone; then follow up the next day with oral outpatient therapy. For inpatient therapy, use a 2nd or 3rd generation cephalosporin. For those penicillin-allergic in either setting, consider a macrolide or cephalosporin (if no anaphylaxis to penicillin). Vancomycin can be used if macrolide resistance is high or if cephalosporins cannot be used.

Pleural effusions occur in 60% of cases. These are usually uncomplicated, sterile, and exudative. Empyema is a late complication. See Figure 11-12, an anteroposterior CXR showing right-sided pneumonia, and Figure 11-13, a large left-sided pleural effusion. Poor prognostic findings are leukopenia and shock; if both are present, mortality can approach 50%.

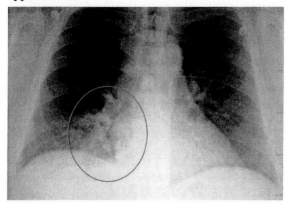

Figure 11-12: Right lower lobe pneumonia

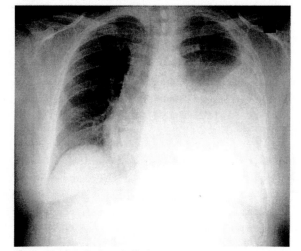

Figure 11-13: Left pleural effusion

Pleural effusions often persist for weeks and resolve without specific therapy. Later, if the child has recurrence of fever or symptoms with a persistent pleural effusion, perform appropriate studies (thoracentesis with cell count, pH, glucose, and bacterial culture) on the fluid to determine if empyema has occurred. Additional pleural fluid studies, including protein and LDH, can help in determining transudative vs. exudative effusion as discussed below.

Sterile effusions are turbid and free flowing within the chest and have a pH of > 7.3, glucose > 60 mg/dL, PMN count < 15,000 cells/μL, and negative microbiology. This contrasts with an empyema that is purulent in appearance, often loculated within the chest, and has a pH < 7.3, glucose < 40 mg/dL or pleural fluid:serum glucose ratio < 0.5, and LDH > 1,000 IU/L. Gram stain and culture may be positive. If empyema has occurred, closed suction drainage is often required.

Pneumococcal conjugate vaccines have decreased the incidence of invasive pneumococcal disease. Current recommendations are to administer PCV13 at 2, 4, 6, and 12–15 months of age. Also, a single dose of PPSV23 can be given at least 8 weeks later to children 2–18 years of age with immunocompromising conditions such as functional asplenia. A 2nd dose may be needed 5 years later for some conditions.

In patients who have not received PCV13 first, give the following vaccines 8 weeks prior to giving PPSV23:

• 2 doses of PCV13 to children 2–5 years of age or
• 1 dose to children 6–18 years of age

Streptococcus pyogenes

S. pyogenes (a.k.a. group A β-hemolytic *Streptococcus*) causes pneumonia usually after a rash disease such as rubeola, varicella, or scarlet fever. It can also occur sporadically without prior illness. *S. pyogenes* pneumonia presents abruptly with fever, chest pain, cough, and leukocytosis. Physical findings are similar to pneumococcal pneumonia. **Pneumatoceles** are common and disappear spontaneously but often take weeks to resolve. The most common complications from *S. pyogenes* pneumonia are **abscesses** and **empyema**.

Treat outpatients with oral penicillin/amoxicillin for 10–14 days. For hospitalized children, treat with IV penicillin. If empyema has occurred, closed suction drainage is usually necessary.

Haemophilus influenzae

Because *H. influenzae* vaccine use has become widespread, the incidence of *H. influenzae* pneumonia has decreased markedly. Findings are similar to pneumococcal pneumonia, although the course is more insidious. Outpatient therapy includes amoxicillin/clavulanate. Inpatient therapy is generally ceftriaxone or cefotaxime.

Staphylococcus aureus

S. aureus is much less common than pneumococcus and *S. pyogenes*, but it is very serious and frequently a fulminant cause of pneumonia. Infants with *S. aureus* pneumonia frequently develop pneumatoceles, pneumothoraces, **abscesses**, and empyema. The right lung is affected more often than the left.

Suspect *S. aureus* pneumonia in a patient with recent URI, chicken pox, or influenza who presents with abrupt onset of fever, tachypnea, tachycardia, and cyanosis. CXR showing distinct **pneumatoceles** is classic. Blood cultures are frequently positive.

Patients with suspected staphylococcal pneumonia require prompt hospitalization and treatment with nafcillin, or use vancomycin if there is high prevalence of methicillin-resistant strains (MRSA) in the community or if the patient has had recent hospitalization, indwelling catheter, or tracheostomy.

Pneumothoraces require decompression. Pneumatoceles are very common and appear 3–4 days into therapy. They require no specific treatment and usually resolve over time. Empyema requires closed suction drainage.

ATYPICAL PNEUMONIAS

Atypical pneumonias usually occur in children > 5 years of age. Patients typically have no sputum production, a nontoxic appearance, and a normal or slightly elevated WBC count. Atypical pneumonia often follows an upper respiratory infection and can be caused by *Mycoplasma*, *Chlamydia pneumoniae* (formerly *Chlamydophila pneumoniae*, Taiwan acute respiratory agent [TWAR]), *Chlamydia psittaci* (bird farmers), *Legionella*, *Histoplasma*, *Coccidioides*, and viruses. Other causes include Q fever and tularemia. Consider tularemia in patients who hunt or skin animals and are from Arkansas or Missouri. Think of Q fever if the patient lives around cattle or sheep—these animals are naturally infected; the causative organism, *Coxiella burnetii*, is not transmitted between humans.

Mycoplasma pneumoniae

Occurring year round, *M. pneumoniae* is a common cause of community-acquired pneumonias in children > 5 years of age and in adolescents. Having a 2- to 3-week incubation period, it spreads slowly (person to person). A prodrome of headache, fever, and pharyngitis is classic. It usually has an insidious onset, with the CXR often appearing worse than the symptoms suggest. Occasionally, it has a more acute onset and can mimic a pneumococcal pneumonia.

Extrapulmonary manifestations of *Mycoplasma* pneumonia include hemolytic anemia, splenomegaly, erythema multiforme (and Stevens-Johnson syndrome), arthritis, pharyngitis, tonsillitis, and neurologic changes—especially confusion. Diagnosis: Definitive is with an IgM antibody (think IgM-M-*Mycoplasma*), and suggestive is with a positive cold agglutinin titer (seen in up to 50% of cases with pneumonia).

Treat with a macrolide or doxycycline. Patients sometimes take a long time (> 6 weeks) to fully recover. Asymptomatic carrier state after infection can last for weeks to months.

Chlamydia pneumoniae

Chlamydia pneumoniae (formerly *Chlamydophila pneumoniae*, Taiwan acute respiratory agent [TWAR]) is increasingly recognized as a respiratory pathogen in children and adults. It causes epidemic pneumonia in older children and adolescents and is the cause of up to 10% of community-acquired pneumonias. Symptoms are similar to *Mycoplasma* pneumonia. Often, there is a biphasic illness: The patient presents with a sore throat negative for group A *Streptococcus*, and pneumonia develops 2-3 weeks later. Treat with a macrolide or tetracycline/doxycycline (not used in children < 8 years old).

FUNGAL PNEUMONIAS

Fungal infections occur less commonly than bacterial or viral infections. Unlike bacterial or viral infections, endemic fungal infections tend to occur in geographically distinct regions. See Figure 11-14. Learn more about fungal pneumonias in the Infectious Disease section.

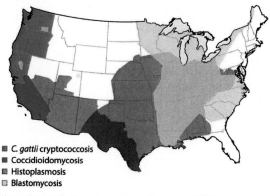

- ■ *C. gattii* cryptococcosis
- ■ Coccidioidomycosis
- ▨ Histoplasmosis
- ▢ Blastomycosis

Figure 11-14: Endemic fungal infection areas, 2019

Histoplasmosis

Histoplasmosis is common in endemic areas—the southern and midwestern U.S. Histoplasmosis is especially seen in the **Mississippi River** and **Ohio River valleys**. (Do not confuse this with "[San Joaquin] valley fever.") Think of histoplas**MO**sis (**M**ississippi, **O**hio). It is transmitted through soil contaminated with **bird** (including chickens) droppings and **bat** droppings. Most cases are asymptomatic, and a majority of residents in endemic areas have serologic evidence of past exposure.

With acute disease, the CXR shows hilar adenopathy and focal alveolar infiltrates. Heavy exposure ("epidemic," disseminating form) is suggested by a CXR revealing multiple nodules in addition to the hilar adenopathy. No treatment is indicated for acute pulmonary disease without complications. Use itraconazole for persistent disease > 4 weeks or if hypoxemia occurs in the acute setting. Disseminated disease requires amphotericin B. Urinary and serum antigen testing is useful in detecting disseminated disease.

Coccidioidomycosis

Coccidioides immitis infection (coccidioidomycosis; a.k.a. "valley fever") is endemic in the southwestern U.S.—the soil fungus is native to the San Joaquin Valley in California. Spores grow best in arid, desert-like climates. **Erythema nodosum** and **erythema multiforme** commonly occur in infected people. A typical presentation is a person with erythema multiforme and a history of travel to the southwestern U.S.

Diagnose with complement fixation titers.

The **self-limited** form generally does not require treatment and can leave thin-walled lung cavities. Treat with fluconazole and/or amphotericin B if there is severe disease, symptoms last > 2 months, or there is a high risk of disseminated disease.

Disseminated coccidioidomycosis is seen in immunocompromised and HIV patients. Individuals of African or Filipino descent are also at higher risk of severe illness. This is a fulminant disease with meningitis and with skin and bone involvement. Even with treatment (amphotericin B), it is frequently fatal.

Blastomycosis

Blastomycosis is uncommon and usually acquired in the central, southeastern, and mid-Atlantic states. Progression can be indolent to severe. No reliable skin test is available. CXR shows infiltrates that appear masslike. Sputum shows large, single, **broad-based budding** yeasts. Blastomycosis is more pyogenic than the other fungal infections—patients can have purulent sputum. In children, dissemination is typically to bone and skin.

Treatment for blastomycosis:

- Indolent—observe or prescribe oral itraconazole.
- Severe—prescribe amphotericin B. HIV patients require chronic suppression with itraconazole.

Allergic Bronchopulmonary Aspergillosis (ABPA)

ABPA is a rare condition caused by an allergic reaction to *Aspergillus* (usually *A. fumigatus*) in which there is immune complex deposition; there is usually a very high serum IgE. This allergy causes Type I (immediate wheal and flare; IgE-mediated) and Type III (> 4 hours out) reactions but not Type IV (delayed) reactions. Suspect ABPA in patients with asthma who have difficult-to-control or worsening asthma symptoms, are coughing up brownish mucous plugs, have recurrent infiltrates, and have peripheral eosinophilia. ABPA can also occur in patients with cystic fibrosis. Hemoptysis can also occur.

CXR and CT can show central mucus impaction and central bronchiectasis causing a "fingers in glove" appearing central infiltrate. Sputum may show branching hyphae (nonspecific). If there is only lung eosinophilia (no peripheral eosinophils), consider instead a chronic eosinophilic pneumonia. If the patient has immediate skin reactivity to *Aspergillus*, then an ABPA panel confirms the diagnosis with *Aspergillus*-specific IgE and IgG titers.

Treat ABPA with oral corticosteroids and itraconazole.

RECURRENT PNEUMONIA

Recurrent pneumonia is defined as ≥ 2 episodes within 1 year or 3 episodes within any time frame with radiographic clearing between episodes. Evaluation begins by obtaining a history with emphasis on foreign body aspiration, asthma, and symptoms of malabsorption (e.g., cystic fibrosis). In addition to respiratory rate and lung exam, physical exam requires special notice of nutritional status, neurologic exam, and presence of clubbing. There are 3 patterns on CXR that can help in the differential:

1) Recurrent infiltrates in the same location

2) Recurrent dense infiltrates in different locations

3) Recurrent interstitial infiltrates

Recurrent infiltrates in the same location can be due to pulmonary sequestration, bronchogenic cysts, foreign body aspiration, bronchiectasis, or a structural airway anomaly. Diagnosis is made by flexible bronchoscopy, chest CT, and/or MRI. Treatment for these lesions is typically surgical.

Recurrent dense infiltrates are usually caused by bacterial infections due to underlying causes. These underlying disorders can include asthma, cystic fibrosis, aspiration, primary ciliary dyskinesia, or immune dysfunction. Workup consists of CBC, PFTs, sweat test, HIV serology, and quantitative immunoglobulins. Further evaluation, including ciliary biopsy and additional immunologic testing, may be indicated. Management is appropriate antibiotic therapy and treatment of underlying condition.

Recurrent interstitial infiltrates result from viral infections and inflammatory disorders. Some conditions that cause recurrent dense infiltrates also cause recurrent interstitial infiltrates, including asthma, cystic fibrosis, and immune dysfunction. Other causes include GE reflux with aspiration, interstitial pneumonitis, and pulmonary hemosiderosis. Workup includes CBC, PFTs, HIV serology, quantitative immunoglobulins, and sweat test. In some cases, diagnosis requires lung biopsy. Management includes appropriate antibiotic therapy and treatment of underlying condition.

TUBERCULOSIS (TB)

Most infections caused by *Mycobacterium tuberculosis* in children and adolescents are asymptomatic. Most symptomatic children with TB present with pulmonary disease. Common symptoms are nonspecific and include cough, fever, and weight loss. Radiographic findings show opacification with hilar or subcarinal lymphadenopathy. Screening tests include the tuberculin skin test and the interferon-gamma release assays. Because laboratory confirmation is difficult to obtain in young children, the diagnosis is often based on the triad of:

1) close contact with infected person,

2) a positive screening test, and

3) suggestive radiographic or physical findings.

Treatment consists of multidrug therapy. See more on *M. tuberculosis* in the Infectious Disease section.

ASTHMA

PREVIEW | REVIEW
- Does having an abnormal sinus x-ray indicate bacterial infection in a child with asthma?
- What is the preferred treatment for the prevention of exercise-induced bronchospasm?
- What do asthma action plans provide for the families of children with asthma?
- When do you consider stepping down controller therapy in a child with asthma?
- What are some complications of prolonged use of systemic corticosteroids?
- What are some complications of prolonged use of inhaled steroids?
- Are long-acting β-agonists useful for rescue therapy in acute asthma attacks?
- What does adding erythromycin potentially do to a patient's theophylline level if their regimen already includes theophylline?
- Is omalizumab an appropriate therapy for a 6-year-old asthmatic child with mild disease?

OVERVIEW

Asthma is the most common chronic disease of childhood. Prevalence data shows increasing rates of asthma since the 1980s. It is more prevalent in African Americans of all ages and in boys of all races. Asthma is quite variable in its presentation and course. Reversible airway obstruction is the main pathologic problem, which is due to bronchial smooth muscle spasm, airway mucosa edema, bronchial mucus impaction, airway inflammation, and/or airway hyperresponsiveness. Reversibility is determined by performing spirometry before and after a bronchodilator is given. A 10–12% increase in FEV_1 following bronchodilator is consistent with a reversible obstruction.

Diagnosis begins with the history and physical examination. Common symptoms include recurrent wheezing, shortness of breath, chest tightness, exercise intolerance, mucoid vomiting, and chronic cough (common in patients with cough-variant asthma).

Various factors seem to trigger asthma attacks, including:

- Viral infection
- Cigarette smoke (including secondhand smoke)
- Exercise
- Allergen exposure
- Breathing cold, dry air
- Aspirin
- Aspiration
- Acid reflux

As many as 85% of exacerbations coincide with viral infection in school-age children and are the biggest risk factors for hospitalization. Physical examination during "normal" times may not show anything or can show only a prolonged expiratory phase. Wheezing, respiratory distress, tachypnea, and use of accessory muscles can be present during attacks. Office spirometry is used to document variable expiratory airflow obstruction. (See Figure 11-3 on page 11-2.)

The latest update (2020) to the asthma management guidelines from the National Asthma Education and Prevention Program: Expert Panel Report 3, Guidelines for the Diagnosis and Management of Asthma endorses the use of fractional exhaled nitric oxide (FeNO) in children ≥ 5 years of age in whom the diagnosis is uncertain despite history, physical exam, and spirometry testing. In addition, they recommend continued monitoring of FeNO (every 2–3 months) to monitor asthma control. (Nitric oxide helps to regulate pulmonary bronchial and vascular tone and is typically found in higher concentrations in exhaled air of people with asthma.)

Children who have recurrent wheeze during infancy continue to wheeze after 6 years of age ~ 15% of the time. Also, ~ 15% of children develop their 1st wheezing episode of asthma after 6 years of age.

CLASSIFICATION

Asthma is classified by severity as well as level of control. Determine severity at the initial visit. Assess the level of asthma control at every subsequent visit. The National Asthma Education and Prevention Program: Expert Panel Report 3, Guidelines for the Diagnosis and Management of Asthma, released in 2007, with edits in 2008 and a focused update in 2020, establish 3 age groups (0–4 years, 5–11 years, and ≥ 12 years of age). With increasing age, additional factors play a role in the classifications of severity and control.

Severity is classified as:

- Intermittent
- Mild persistent
- Moderate persistent
- Severe persistent

Control is classified as:

- Well controlled
- Not well controlled
- Very poorly controlled

Based on these classifications, you can determine treatment regimens. See Table 11-4 on page 11-35 through Table 11-10 on page 11-44 and Figure 11-18 on page 11-34 through Figure 11-21 on page 11-42 in the Appendix for details. Know this stepwise approach!

COMORBIDITIES AND TRIGGERS

Sinusitis

It is known that children with asthma have a high incidence of abnormal sinus x-rays. However, we know that a majority of these children likely do not have clinical bacterial sinusitis but rather simple acute rhinitis with an abnormal sinus x-ray. Therefore, having an abnormal sinus x-ray and asthma does not equate to needing antibiotic therapy. Pursue clinical diagnosis of sinusitis before initiating antibiotic therapy.

Gastroesophageal (GE) Reflux

GE reflux is sometimes a significant problem in the child with asthma. First, in the neonate, significant GE reflux can imitate asthma and lead to an incorrect diagnosis; second, in older children, significant GE reflux can exacerbate underlying asthma and initiate an acute attack. However, indiscriminate use of acid blockers in children with asthma who lack symptoms of reflux is of no benefit. Theophylline reduces lower esophageal sphincter tone, resulting in increased risk of GE reflux.

Exercise

Exercise causes bronchodilatation and an increase in expiratory flow rates in otherwise normal children as well as those with asthma. **Exercise-induced bronchospasm** describes the acute bronchoconstriction that occurs in some patients during or right after exercise. It is seen most commonly in adolescents who have no other signs or symptoms of asthma. They develop cough or difficulty breathing after 5–30 minutes of exercise (especially in cold, dry air), which typically resolves in 60 minutes. The pathophysiology of exercise-induced bronchoconstriction is complex but is likely triggered by hyperventilation. The increased respiratory rate leads to a decreased ability of the airway passages to humidify air adequately before it reaches the alveoli, which leads to osmotic changes in the airway surface and activation of mast cells. In addition, the cool air stimulates cholinergic receptors, leading to increased secretions and airway smooth muscle tone. The easiest way to diagnose this is with exercise challenge with pulmonary function testing.

Preferred treatment is pretreatment with an inhaled short-acting β-adrenergic agent (10–20 minutes before exercise), which usually prevents or reduces the severity of symptoms. An alternative treatment option is montelukast (a leukotriene receptor antagonist; requires days or even weeks to start working), but it is less desirable with the new (2020) FDA black box warning with concerns of neurobehavioral side effects associated with this drug. People with poorly controlled asthma are likely to have increased symptoms with activity due to limited lung function.

The Difficult, Refractory Patient

Think of **ICE** when you are presented with a patient who does not respond to routine therapies for asthma:

- **I**nhalation technique: problems with inhaled drug delivery
- **C**ompliance: poor adherence to the treatment plan
- **E**xacerbating factors: e.g., tobacco smoke exposure, GE reflux, sinusitis

Also consider pathologic causes of poor response (i.e., alternate diagnosis): cystic fibrosis, allergic bronchopulmonary aspergillosis, vocal cord dysfunction, hypersensitivity pneumonia, and sleep apnea.

~ 5% of children do not respond to standard therapy and require prolonged courses of corticosteroids to maintain a symptom-free period.

TREATMENT

The complete compendium of the National Asthma Education and Prevention Program: Expert Panel Report 3 comprehensive guidelines for asthma management, including its focused update from 2020, is available online. We've included the important figures and tables from the guidelines in the Appendix — Asthma Treatment Regimens. Be sure you know these perfectly! Treatment varies by age and is based on the symptoms the patient is having.

Let's review a few key points.

For intermittent or mild persistent asthma, treatment is straightforward:

- For **intermittent** asthma, no daily medication is recommended for any age group.
- For **mild persistent** asthma (symptoms occurring > 2×/week but not daily), use low-dose inhaled corticosteroid (ICS) as the preferred initial treatment for all age groups but an alternate option in those ≥ 12 years of age is the "as needed" use of ICS and short-acting β_2-agonist (SABA) concomitantly without the use of daily therapy.

If a low-dose ICS does not control symptoms, then the age of the child factors into treatment. For a child:

- ≤ 4 years of age, use a low-dose ICS and long-acting β_2-agonist (LABA) combination; preferred alternatives include low-dose ICS and montelukast or medium-dose ICS
- 5–11 years of age as well as ≥ 12 years of age, the preferred treatment option is low-dose ICS combined with an inhaled LABA

In the 2020 update, ICS and LABA combinations that utilize formoterol for the long-acting bronchodilator component are recommended for use as daily therapy as well as "as needed" use. This is referred to as single maintenance and rescue therapy (SMART), with the maximum number of inhalations per day being 12 puffs for patients ≥ 12 years of age and 8 puffs for patients 5–11 years of age. ICS-LABA combinations that contain salmeterol are not appropriate for SMART therapy and continue to require SABA for rescue therapy.

Know that in all patients who have an exacerbation, quick relief continues to include using a SABA (peak effect in 15 minutes, with duration of 4 hours). Oral or parenteral corticosteroids are also recommended, depending on response.

See Figure 11-18 on page 11-34 for management of asthma exacerbations in the hospital or emergency department setting.

Home peak flow monitoring can be a helpful adjunct to symptom monitoring in some patients to identify a change in control and to monitor response to therapy. It requires skill and effort to get reliable readings and can typically be performed by children ≥ 6 years of age. Consider use of peak flow for children with persistent asthma and observe the child doing the maneuver to determine if home monitoring is an option. Education is the key to preventing exacerbations as well as to getting exacerbations under control quickly. A written home asthma management (i.e., action) plan can help guide self-management. Families need to have a clear understanding of how and when to use asthma medicines, the skills to correctly deliver inhaled medication, and the knowledge of how to avoid or eliminate asthma triggers.

The primary goal is to get and keep the asthma under good control, which includes no or minimal daily (including nighttime) symptoms; no or minimal exacerbations; no limitations on daily activities; no missed school or work; minimal use of SABAs; and minimal-to-no adverse effects from therapy. If this goal is met, reassess in 3 months and determine if you can "step down" to a less-intense treatment regimen. If the symptoms are not being controlled, "step up" to a higher level of management to improve control.

Drug dosages are listed in Table 11-10 on page 11-44. For exams, you won't have to memorize specific dosages for most of the agents; in particular, you won't be responsible for remembering the "comparative" daily dosages for inhaled steroids.

Corticosteroids

Corticosteroids are the most effective antiinflammatory agents available for the treatment of asthma. They are formulated in oral, inhaled, and intravenous forms. Systemic (oral and IV) corticosteroids are used in acute asthma exacerbations that do not respond to the first couple of β-agonist treatments.

Unfortunately, long-term use of systemic formulations has many adverse effects:

- Suppression of the hypothalamic-pituitary-adrenal axis (See the next paragraph for clinical significance.)
- Immunosuppression
- Osteoporosis

- Cataracts
- Hyperglycemia
- Weight gain
- Thinning of the skin, bruises easily
- Abdominal striae
- Growth retardation

You must closely monitor patients on chronic oral steroids and be prepared to give stress corticosteroid (hydrocortisone) doses with fever, acute infection, surgery, or other significant physiologic stressors. These patients are not able to mount an appropriate adrenal response due to suppression of the hypothalamic-pituitary-adrenal axis.

Prolonged use of inhaled steroids may cause these findings/conditions:

- Oral candidiasis (thrush) is common and can be prevented by using a spacer (valved holding chamber) with metered-dose inhalers and rinsing the mouth after inhalation.
- Changes in growth velocity
- Dermal thinning and increased ease of skin bruising
- Cataracts (rare)
- Suppression of hypothalamic-pituitary-adrenal axis function (rare)

Cromolyn Sodium

Cromolyn sodium is an antiinflammatory medication that stabilizes mast cell membranes. Its mechanism of action is not well understood. It is no longer available as a metered-dose inhaler (MDI) but continues to be available for nebulization. It has a very good safety profile, with only occasional side effects of cough, dermatitis, myositis, and gastroenteritis. It is listed as an alternative; however, it is not preferred.

Long-Acting Inhaled β₂-Agonists (LABAs)

Salmeterol and formoterol are 2 inhaled agents that provide bronchodilatation for up to 12 hours. Formoterol has a faster onset of action than salmeterol. LABAs are not used as rescue therapy or as daily monotherapy. See Combination Therapy for more information.

Combination Therapy

Combination products containing inhaled corticosteroids (ICS) and long-acting bronchodilators work synergistically against inflammation and muscle dysfunction. There are currently 3 combination products available for use as asthma controllers:

- Fluticasone + salmeterol (Advair)
- Budesonide + formoterol (Symbicort)
- Mometasone + formoterol (Dulera)

Based on the 2020 focused update to the asthma management guidelines, combination therapy of an ICS with formoterol has been recommended to be preferred treatment for ages 5 years and up to be used as daily maintenance as well as rescue therapy. This is known as single maintenance and rescue therapy (SMART). Formoterol alone, without an ICS, is not recommended as a rescue therapy and is not recommended for daily monotherapy without the addition of inhaled corticosteroid. Combination inhalers containing an ICS corticosteroid along with salmeterol are not indicated for use with SMART.

Leukotriene Modifiers

The available leukotriene modifiers are montelukast and zafirlukast. They are biologically active fatty acids derived from the oxidative metabolism of arachidonic acid. They work by inhibiting the binding of leukotriene to receptors, thus reducing bronchoconstriction and inflammation. Montelukast has efficacy in preventing exercise-induced asthma. Neurobehavioral side effects (e.g., sleep disturbance, depression, aggression) have been reported in some patients with montelukast, and the FDA added a black box warning regarding the potential for these side effects in 2020.

Tiotropium

Tiotropium, a long-acting muscarinic agent, is approved for use in severe persistent asthma as an add-on controller therapy in patients ≥ 6 years of age who are not well controlled with ICS-LABA combination therapy. The most common side effects include dry mouth, constipation, and sore throat. It is not indicated for the treatment of acute bronchospasm.

Theophylline

Theophylline is a methylxanthine and requires serum monitoring of levels. (Serum concentrations of 5–15 μg/mL are considered optimal.) It has a slow onset of action and is not recommended for acute therapy.

Theophylline has a narrow therapeutic range and significant toxicity beyond that range. Toxicity usually presents with tachycardia, gastrointestinal symptoms, and behavioral effects. Drug-drug interactions can affect dosing: Oral contraceptives, erythromycin, ciprofloxacin, and cimetidine can increase serum blood levels, whereas phenobarbital and phenytoin can decrease serum theophylline levels.

Omalizumab

Omalizumab is an anti-IgE monoclonal antibody given intramuscularly to patients ≥ 6 years of age who have severe, difficult-to-control, allergic asthma. (In 2016, the FDA lowered the approved age of treatment with omalizumab from 12 years of age to 6 years of age.) The dose is based on weight and serum IgE level. Omalizumab works by blocking IgE receptors and reducing allergic reactivity. It takes time to work but, in some patients, allows weaning of chronic systemic or high-dose inhaled corticosteroids. Additional biologic modifier medications are now available for severe persistent patients, such as mepolizumab, reslizumab, and benralizumab that block IL-5, which is a key mediator in eosinophil activation. An additional modifier, dupilumab, blocks IL4 and IL13, both of which are responsible for airway inflammation. Mepolizumab is approved for patients 6 years of age and older with severe persistent eosinophilic asthma. Benralizumab and dupilumab are approved for patients 12 years of age and older. Reslizumab is the only IV formulation of currently approved biologics and is indicated for patients 18 years of age and older.

ACUTE EXACERBATION

It is a key focus for the physician, patient, and patient's family to respond early to an acute exacerbation of asthma, hopefully while the patient is still manageable at the office or at home.

With acute exacerbation, first determine the severity of the exacerbation; then determine whether to treat as an outpatient or have the patient go to the emergency department (ED).

If the patient goes to the ED, the 3 options of treatment are:

1) Treat and release
2) Prolonged intensive treatment as an inpatient
3) Transfer to the ICU

All asthma patients should have a specific written home care asthma action plan with treatment steps based on symptoms. This plan is individualized and codeveloped by you and your patient.

Home Treatment

Acute exacerbation of asthma starts with decreased airflow. Some patients have consistent associated symptoms with onset such as cough, shortness of breath, or wheezing. If the patient is able to consistently exhale with a strong effort, a peak flow meter is usually a good objective method to assess asthma severity. This works only if a baseline has already been established. The 2020 focused update recommendation for treatment for an acute exacerbation at home:

1) There are 2 medication options: Give ~ 2–4 puffs of a SABA or combination treatment of 1–2 puffs of ICS along with 2 puffs of a SABA. If the home plan includes prn ICS + SABA, dose ICS twice daily and SABA twice daily (but may need more frequently for the first 24–48 hours) for 3–4 days.

2) Reassess in 10–20 minutes; repeat 2 puffs of a SABA if necessary.

3) If good response, ensure any aggravating stimulus is removed; patient can continue self-care.

4) If incomplete response, give oral glucocorticoids, if this is part of the home plan.

5) If poor response or if initial symptoms are severe, send to the ED.

Office Treatment

SABA dosages can be doubled in the office setting and the treatment repeated up to 3 times total. Otherwise, management is similar to home treatment.

Emergency Department (ED) Treatment

With either home or office treatment, the decision to send the patient to the ED is based on high initial severity or lack of response to therapy. Most children with a moderate or severe exacerbation should be treated in the ED where they can be monitored closely and treated frequently.

Goals in the ED are:

• Determine severity.
• Reverse airflow obstruction: SABAs. (MDI with spacer has equal efficacy to nebulized treatments.) Give systemic glucocorticoids if obstruction is moderate to severe or if no response to SABAs.
• Correct hypoxemia (i.e., reverse obstruction, oxygen therapy).
• Prevent recurrence.

See Figure 11-18 on page 11-34 in the Appendix.

Acute Severe Asthma

The development of a severe asthma attack in which the patient is at risk of developing respiratory failure is acute severe asthma (a.k.a. status asthmaticus). These exacerbations can be slow in onset such as over several days, typically occurring in patients with severe and poorly controlled asthma, or rapid in onset often due to massive exposure of allergens or sensitivities to certain agents.

Pathologic exams in fatal asthma have shown mucous plugging mixed with inflammatory cells obstructing the airways. This obstruction leads to the gas exchange abnormalities of ventilation/perfusion (V/Q) mismatch. Prior history of intubation for asthma is the greatest single predictor of death. Additional risk factors for death from asthma include:

• Past history of sudden severe exacerbations
• Prior admission for asthma to an ICU
• ≥ 2 hospitalizations in the past year
• ≥ 3 emergency care visits for asthma in the past year
• Hospitalization or ED visit for asthma in the past month
• Use of > 2 canisters of SABA per month
• Current use of or recent withdrawal from oral systemic corticosteroids
• Difficulty recognizing airflow obstruction or its severity
• Comorbid conditions or serious psychosocial problems

These patients often present in extreme distress. They are unable to talk in complete sentences. They are unable to lie down. Drowsiness or confusion is an ominous sign. Physical exam should include evaluation for complications of severe asthma, including pneumothorax or pneumomediastinum.

The need for hospitalization is based on response to treatment, which includes the use of SABAs, anticholinergics, and steroids, as well as IV magnesium sulfate and O_2 to correct hypoxia. The decision to admit to the hospital and/or ICU is based on failure to respond to conventional therapies or interval worsening. Noninvasive ventilation is preferred and typically attempted prior to intubation except in extreme cases.

Mortality associated with severe acute asthma is significant with some estimates ranging from 1% to 10%. With the use of permissive hypercapnia, complications related to mechanical ventilation have lessened.

DDx OF WHEEZING

PREVIEW | REVIEW

- What are the most common causes of acute wheezing?

Wheezing is common in young children. ~ 30% have an acute wheezing episode before 3 years of age. It is usually associated with a respiratory illness. It is often called **reactive airway disease** when asthma is suspected but not yet diagnosed. Reactive airway disease is a general term used to describe a history of cough or wheezing; it does not indicate a specific diagnosis. Wheezing prevalence decreases with age and is ~ 13% by 10 years of age. The most common cause of both acute and recurrent wheezing is asthma.

Acute wheezing can be caused by:

- Asthma
- Bronchitis, bronchiolitis, tracheitis, or a combination
- Foreign body aspirated or lodged in esophagus

Chronic wheezing has many causes. The most common are:

- Asthma
- Allergies
- Gastroesophageal reflux
- Infections (e.g., URI, pneumonia, bronchitis, bronchiolitis)
- Obstructive sleep apnea

Bronchopulmonary dysplasia (BPD), which results from preterm birth, is a less common cause of wheezing. The more severe the BPD, the higher the risk of cognitive and motor neurodevelopmental problems. Long-term survivors are at increased risk of respiratory infections, asthma, and pulmonary hypertension. See the Neonatology section for more information on BPD.

There are many rare causes of chronic wheezing.

Rare structural causes of wheezing:

- Congenital vascular and tracheobronchial anomalies
- Mediastinal masses
- Cardiomegaly
- Tumor
- Vocal cord dysfunction

Rare functional causes of wheezing:

- Cystic fibrosis
- Heart failure
- Bronchiolitis obliterans
- Primary ciliary dyskinesia

Response to bronchodilators helps differentiate asthma from other causes of wheezing. Get a CXR on any child with chronic or recurrent wheezing or with an acute episode of wheezing that does not respond to bronchodilators.

NONASTHMA CAUSES OF CHRONIC COUGH

PREVIEW | REVIEW

- Is the CXR abnormal in all cases of foreign body aspiration?
- An adolescent presents having had 6 episodes of "bronchitis" that cleared up with antibiotics and then recurred in 1 or 2 months. What diagnosis do you entertain?
- Which viruses most commonly cause bronchiolitis obliterans (BO)?
- How do you definitively diagnose BO?

OVERVIEW

Cough is one of the most common complaints seen by the pediatrician and has many causes. A chronic cough is defined as a cough lasting > 4 weeks. Evaluation of a chronic cough consists of a detailed history, physical examination, CXR, and spirometry (if the child is able). Further investigation is determined based on findings from the initial evaluation.

COMMON CAUSES

Foreign Body Aspiration

Foreign body aspiration is at the top of the differential list if there is an abrupt onset of cough in a child while eating or playing. However, even without this history, chronic wet cough in a young child requires consideration of a foreign body aspiration because toddlers frequently place objects in their mouths. Fortunately, aspiration is infrequent. The most commonly aspirated objects are seeds, nuts, and peanuts. Other typical items include coins, hot dogs, grapes, small toys, balloons, jewelry, batteries, and firm vegetables. Organic materials most often lodge in the right main or left main bronchi, but objects can go pretty much anywhere. The child presents with a sudden onset of choking or coughing followed by expiratory wheezing, dyspnea, or stridor—often with asymptomatic intervals. For unwitnessed aspiration, there is a delay of the diagnosis for > 1 month in up to 20% of cases.

CXR is very helpful even though most of these items are radiolucent. Obstructive asymmetric hyperinflation is seen in nearly 66% of children who have bronchial foreign bodies; however, note that 10–25% have a normal x-ray.

For children who are cyanotic, cannot breathe, and cannot get the foreign body up, consider a variety of techniques. For infants < 1 year of age, most recommend turning the infant over (face down) and forcefully giving 5 back blows. For children > 1 year of age, the Heimlich maneuver (subdiaphragmatic abdominal thrusts) is the 1st intervention. Never do a blind finger sweep. This can cause the object to go further back (as well as put you at risk for the "bite off the doctor's finger" scenario in the uncooperative child).

If the initial maneuvers are unsuccessful, perform a "jaw thrust." If the foreign body can be visualized, attempt to remove it with a Magill or other large forceps. If this fails and the child is unconscious or not breathing, establish a surgical airway distal to the obstruction. Finally, if all the previous maneuvers fail or if the patient is stable, rigid bronchoscopy can be performed by an experienced endoscopist to remove the foreign body.

Protracted Bacterial Bronchitis (PBB)

PBB is now recognized as a common cause of cough in children. It presents with a chronic wet cough. Symptoms can be similar to asthma, but auscultation reveals rhonchi instead of wheezing. Rhonchi are continuous (inspiratory and expiratory) low-pitch noises with a snoring or gurgling quality due to secretions in the bronchi. Also, PBB does not respond to bronchodilators. The most common etiologies of PBB include nontypeable *Haemophilus influenzae*, *Streptococcus pneumoniae*, and *Moraxella catarrhalis*. Diagnosis is typically made clinically in a patient with prolonged wet cough who otherwise is well appearing. CXR is usually normal. Treatment is a 2- to 4-week course of amoxicillin/clavulanate or 2nd/3rd generation cephalosporin. Patients with recurrent PBB require investigation for underlying disorders such as cystic fibrosis and immune deficiencies.

Aspiration

Aspiration occurs when oral or gastric secretions are inhaled into the lungs. It is an unusual cause of cough in children unless there is an underlying neurologic/neuromuscular disorder or anatomic abnormality such as tracheoesophageal fistula. **GE reflux** can cause aspiration in some children, usually in those with neurologic disorders. See the Gastroenterology section for further discussion of fistula and GE reflux.

These patients can present with chronic cough, wheezing, apnea, and recurrent pneumonia. Suspect aspiration in patients with asthma symptoms who do not respond to standard treatment. Physical findings can include fever, tachypnea, wheezing, crackles, and respiratory distress. Initial workup includes CBC, pulse oximetry, and CXR. The CXR can show hyperinflation, diffuse infiltrates, consolidation, or peribronchial thickening. Additional testing can include sweat chloride test, screening for immune deficiencies, CT scan, barium esophagram, swallow tests, and esophageal pH monitoring.

Treatment of acute events typically requires a 2nd or 3rd generation cephalosporin in addition to conservative therapy. This consists of elevating the head of the bed; small, frequent meals; waiting 60–90 minutes between eating and bedtime; and modifying certain food consistencies. In some cases, medications are used and include prokinetic agents (e.g., metoclopramide), H_2-receptor antagonists, and/or proton pump inhibitors. Surgery is indicated for anatomical abnormalities.

Upper Airway Cough Syndrome

Upper airway cough syndrome (formerly postnasal drip syndrome) is seen in older children. It is caused by postnasal drip due to rhinitis and sinusitis. Patients can present with cough that worsens when lying down, sore throat, congestion, and sometimes ear pain. Treatment consists of antihistamines, decongestants, and nasal irrigation. Prescribe antibiotics if sinusitis is suspected. See more on acute sinusitis in the Ophthalmology & ENT section.

CRYPTOGENIC ORGANIZING PNEUMONIA (COP)

In patients with COP (formerly bronchiolitis obliterans with organizing pneumonia [BOOP]), the alveolar septa are thickened by a chronic inflammatory cell infiltrate, as well as Type II cell hyperplasia of the alveolar septa. In children, the cause is idiopathic, AIDS-related, or due to chemotherapy or complications following bone marrow transplant. Patients with COP frequently present with numerous episodes of "bronchitis" that respond to antibiotics and then recur. There are usually multiple cycles of bronchitis followed by antibiotics before you make a diagnosis. Corticosteroids are beneficial, and a positive response helps distinguish it from bronchiolitis obliterans. Diagnosis is confirmed by lung biopsy.

BRONCHIOLITIS OBLITERANS (BO)

BO occurs when small bronchi and bronchioles are obstructed by intraluminal masses of fibrous tissue. This can be caused by a variety of disorders, but in children it commonly occurs following a lower respiratory tract infection, particularly with adenovirus serotypes 3, 7, or 21. Children can become infected in utero or throughout childhood, but the highest incidence occurs between 6 months and 2 years of age. Children who have adenovirus pneumonitis have nearly a 33% risk of developing chronic lung disease. This increases to nearly 66% in some Native American populations! The incidence of BO has increased due to lung transplantation and graft-versus-host disease that is seen in bone marrow transplant.

Typically, the infant recovers from the acute viral illness, only to have persistent (> 60 days) respiratory symptoms. Signs and symptoms include tachypnea, chronic cough, wheezing, and/or crackles and can coincide with failure to thrive. BO results in hypoxemia and hypercarbia because of poor gas exchange. Pulmonary edema becomes common over time. You must perform a lung biopsy to confirm the diagnosis.

Treatment is supportive, with oxygen and avoidance of subsequent lung injuries. Treat pulmonary edema with diuretics. Adult data shows improvement with corticosteroids. If bronchiectasis is also present, airway clearance and secretion mobilization are useful.

Prognosis varies. Some children improve by 8–10 years of age. Others develop debilitating chronic lung disease with the potential for eventual respiratory failure and death. A minority develop a fulminant disease.

BRONCHIECTASIS

If a chronic wet cough persists after 4 weeks of antibiotic therapy, bronchiectasis needs to be considered. It is characterized by wet cough and wheezing.

Bronchiectasis refers to dilatation of the bronchi. The bronchi become damaged during an infection or inflammation and become distorted. Etiologies of bronchiectasis include cystic fibrosis, chronic aspiration, α_1-antitrypsin deficiency, dysmotile cilia syndromes, immune deficiencies, and allergic bronchopulmonary aspergillosis. Focal bronchiectasis can occur with retained foreign body or with severe infections such as tuberculosis, pertussis, measles, *Mycoplasma*, or adenovirus. It is usually irreversible. The diagnostic criteria for bronchiectasis (e.g., airway dilatation, bronchial wall thickening) are based on radiographic features of chest high-resolution computerized tomography (c-HRCT), which is the gold standard for diagnosis.

Bronchiectasis can be focal or generalized. Children present with a chronic productive cough and wheezing and have recurrent infections. Hemoptysis is rare in children. Clubbing of the fingers is very common (Figure 11-15). Affected children have an obstructive pattern on spirometry and a pattern of air trapping on lung volumes with a normal or increased total lung capacity, increased functional residual capacity, and a reduced vital capacity. Areas of ventilation-perfusion mismatch are common.

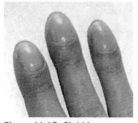
Figure 11-15: Clubbing

Treatment includes bronchodilators with airway clearance (i.e., bronchial hygiene). Sometimes, chronic antibiotic therapy is required to control colonization or prevent recurrent infections.

SUDDEN INFANT DEATH SYNDROME (SIDS)

PREVIEW | REVIEW

- Is apnea of prematurity a risk factor for sudden infant death syndrome (SIDS)?
- Which strategy has had the greatest impact on reducing incidences of SIDS?
- What are the infant risk factors for SIDS?
- Does maternal smoking during pregnancy increase the risk of SIDS?

SIDS is defined as the sudden death of an infant < 1 year of age that remains unexplained after an intensive review, including a thorough autopsy, examination of the death scene, and review of the clinical history. It is a diagnosis of exclusion. In the U.S., SIDS is the leading cause of death in infants 1–12 months of age. (Based on 2018 CDC data for infants 0–12 months of age, the leading cause of death is congenital anomalies, followed by prematurity-associated conditions, neonatal deaths due to maternal complications, SIDS, and unintentional injuries. See the Preventive Pediatrics section for details of causes of mortality for ages 0–19 years.)

Neither apnea of infancy nor apnea of prematurity is an independent risk factor for SIDS, but prematurity itself is a risk factor. Make sure that all caregivers know basic CPR.

The SIDS death rate has decreased markedly since implementation of the Safe to Sleep campaign (formerly the Back to Sleep campaign), which emphasizes placing infants on their backs to sleep.

SIDS usually occurs between 1 and 6 months of age, with a peak between 2 and 4 months of age. Boys are more commonly affected than girls. Evidence suggests that death can also occur while the infant is awake.

A higher incidence of SIDS is seen with:

- Prematurity
- Intrauterine growth restriction
- Winter months
- Hours between midnight and 8 a.m.
- Native American or African American ethnicity
- Secondhand smoke exposure after birth

Major maternal factors that increase the risk of SIDS:

- Young maternal age
- Smoking during pregnancy

There appears to be a slightly higher risk of SIDS in future siblings of SIDS infants. Breastfed infants have a lower risk, as do children who have received their immunizations.

For more information on sleep issues, see the Preventive Pediatrics section.

CYSTIC FIBROSIS (CF)

PREVIEW | REVIEW

- What is the mode of inheritance for cystic fibrosis (CF)?
- Which gene is responsible for CF?
- Which factor correlates best with survival in CF patients?
- What sinus and nasal findings commonly occur in CF patients?
- Early in CF, which bacterial organisms are most likely to cause pulmonary infection? What about later in CF?
- When does pancreatic insufficiency occur in CF?
- Which gastrointestinal findings are more common in CF?
- What is the abnormality of the sweat glands in patients with CF?
- What is the abnormality of the reproductive tract in males with CF?
- What is the laboratory test for diagnosing CF?
- Who should have a sweat test?
- How does newborn screening detect CF?
- How do you treat CF pulmonary exacerbations?
- Does the finding of a pneumothorax suggest more severe lung disease in a CF patient?
- Which vitamin deficiency do you consider in a CF patient who has hemoptysis with heavy bleeding and a history of easy bruisability?

OVERVIEW

CF is an autosomal recessive disorder, mainly affecting Caucasians, with a prevalence of 1 in 2,500 live births. It is the most common lethal genetic disease in Caucasians. Most cases are diagnosed by 2 years of age. It is characterized by:

- Elevated sweat chloride levels
- Persistent pulmonary infections
- Insufficiency of the exocrine pancreas

The genetics of CF involves a mutation of *CFTR* (the CF transmembrane receptor, or the CF gene) on the long arm of chromosome 7. The CF gene spans 256 kb. The most common mutation F508 del (also known as p.Phe508del) in the CF gene is a 3-base pair deletion that leads to the loss of a single phenylalanine at position 508. The F508del mutation is present in nearly 80% of all CF cases, but homozygosity for this mutation is only about 50%. There are nearly 2,000 other mutations identified at the CF locus! The resulting mutations cause abnormal ion transport across epithelial surfaces, including impermeable chloride channels and overactive sodium pumps. This results in viscid secretions in affected tissues and organs and further leads to blockage of ducts and air passages. The tissues most affected are the lungs, pancreas, intestinal mucous glands, liver, reproductive tracts, and sweat glands.

Median survival has increased from 10.6 years in 1966 to > 37 years today, and almost 1/2 of all CF patients in the U.S. now are adults. In addition to aggressive therapy and good nutritional status, exercise appears to be an important factor. The patient's level of fitness, even more than pulmonary function, correlates with longer survival.

MANIFESTATIONS

Due to extensive newborn screening, most patients are diagnosed with CF before becoming symptomatic. Before newborn screening became commonplace, most presented with meconium ileus, respiratory symptoms, and failure to thrive (FTT).

Respiratory Tract

CF patients universally have **pansinusitis**, which is a helpful clue in a young child with persistent disease. **Nasal polyps** can occur in up to 50% of patients with CF, and the finding of nasal polyps in a child < 12 years of age guides you to CF as a possible diagnosis. Eventually, **clubbing** of the digits occurs in almost every patient with lung disease.

Pulmonary disease is the leading cause of morbidity and mortality in patients with CF. The lower respiratory tract is normal at birth. However, over time—with recurrent airway inflammation, chronic viscid mucus production, and recurrent infection—the child develops **obstructive pulmonary disease**. Initially, you may diagnose the child as having recurrent cough and wheezing with recurrent bronchiolitis, asthma, or pneumonia. Eventually, hyperinflation and crackles occur with the development of chronic diffuse **bronchiectasis** (Figure 11-16 on page 11-26). Finding decreased forced expiratory flow (FEF_{25-75}) can indicate early obstructive disease. The obstructive component can later be evidenced by finding decreased FEV_1, decreased peak expiratory flow, and increased residual volume. Lung function testing is very helpful in following progression of the disease in the older child and adolescent.

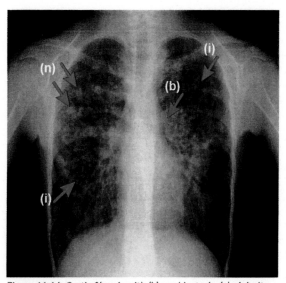

Figure 11-16: Cystic fibrosis with (b)ronchiectasis, (n)odularity, and (i)nterstitial disease

Most patients with CF have chronic **pulmonary infections** with acute exacerbations. Early in the disease, the bacteria most commonly responsible for exacerbations are *Staphylococcus aureus, Haemophilus influenzae,* and common gram-negative organisms, such as *Klebsiella.* Later, *Pseudomonas aeruginosa* becomes the predominant organism. The *Pseudomonas* in CF is characterized as being a more mucoid strain. Methicillin-resistant *Staphylococcus* aureus (MRSA) also has become an increasingly prominent pathogen in CF patients; nationwide incidence has increased to nearly 25%. Interestingly, infection outside the respiratory tract is unusual.

The rate of progression of lung disease is variable for each child. Worse prognosis results from secondhand cigarette smoke and recurrent viral infections. Pulmonary complications can include pneumothorax, hemoptysis, atelectasis, pulmonary hypertension, cor pulmonale, and respiratory failure.

Gastrointestinal (GI) Tract

Pancreatic insufficiency is present at birth in 50% of children with CF. Although 90% have signs/symptoms of pancreatic insufficiency by 9 years of age, diagnosis is often delayed in the 10% who do not have GI disease. Exocrine pancreatic insufficiency manifests with maldigestion of fats and proteins, which results in malabsorption, steatorrhea, fat-soluble vitamin deficiencies, and FTT.

Manifestations of fat-soluble vitamin deficiencies may include:

- Vitamin A—increased intracranial pressure, xerosis, and night blindness
- Vitamin D—rickets
- Vitamin E—hemolytic anemia in infancy, diminished reflexes, and muscle weakness
- Vitamin K—easy bruising and bleeding

~ 1/2 of patients with CF also develop endocrine-pancreatic dysfunction by adulthood, resulting in CF-related diabetes.

Patients with CF who present at birth (~ 10–20%) frequently do so with **bowel obstruction**, which is manifested by **meconium ileus**. In childhood, an additional 20–25% have distal intestinal obstruction syndrome (DIOS; a.k.a. meconium ileus equivalent). ~ 20% have **rectal prolapse** during early childhood. **Intussusception** occurs much less frequently than the above manifestations in CF, but CF is one of the more common causes of intussusception in children > 1 year of age. Other GI disorders found with increased frequency in CF patients are gastroesophageal reflux, constipation, cholelithiasis, focal biliary cirrhosis, and nonspecific steatosis of the liver. Liver cirrhosis is common; however, secondary liver failure is rare in CF. Portal hypertension and its complications affect 5–15% of patients.

Sweat Glands

Sweat glands in CF patients produce a very high salt content, which is a hallmark of the diagnosis. Sodium and chloride concentrations in a CF patient's sweat are > 60 mEq/L (normal is < 40 mEq/L). Infants can develop severe hyponatremia. Because of these findings, the sweat test is very helpful in diagnosing CF, even today with molecular genetics.

Reproductive Tract

Males with CF have atresia of the vas deferens, which results in obstructive azoospermia and **sterility**. Males can have children by using in vitro methods. Females have thick cervical mucus, which also results in **decreased fertility**. Because of poor nutrition and/or chronic illness, many children with CF have **delayed puberty**.

DIAGNOSIS

Diagnosis requires a 2-pronged approach:

1) At least 1 of the following is required:
   - Typical features of CF (e.g., pulmonary disease, exocrine pancreas deficiency, salt loss in sweat, male infertility)
   - CF in a sibling
   - Positive newborn screening test
2) Plus, 1 of the following is required:
   - Positive sweat test (e.g., > 60 mEq/L of sweat chloride)—best initial test!
   - Identification of 2 CF mutations known to cause CF
   - Abnormal nasal transepithelial potential difference measurement

Because there are > 1,000 mutations, it is still common for CF to be diagnosed with the sweat test. Sweat tests using quantitative iontophoresis done in CF care centers accredited by the Cystic Fibrosis Foundation are reliable. Infants ≥ 2 weeks of age are tested; those > 2 kg and born at > 36 weeks of gestation are typically able to produce adequate sweat. Those tests done outside a reliable testing center have a high risk for false-positive and false-negative results. There are numerous reasons for false-positive results (> 60 mEq/L) but only 3 for false-negative (< 40 mEq/L): laboratory error (most common), edema due to hypoproteinemia, and rare CF mutations that do not result in sweat gland abnormalities. Who should have a sweat test? Obviously, if FTT, steatorrhea, and chronic pulmonary disease are present, it is an easy decision. However, be suspicious of certain other findings; these are listed in Table 11-2. Many of these findings are keyword clues to get you looking for CF. Be suspicious!

Table 11-2: Reasons to Consider Sweat Testing
Gastrointestinal pearls for testing:
• Meconium ileus
• Rectal prolapse
• Prolonged neonatal jaundice
• Chronic diarrhea
• Steatorrhea
Respiratory pearls for testing:
• Nasal polyps
• Pansinusitis
• Chronic cough
• Recurrent wheezing
• *Staphylococcus aureus* pneumonia
• Finding *Pseudomonas* in throat, sputum, or bronchial cultures
Miscellaneous pearls for testing:
• Digital clubbing
• Family history of cystic fibrosis
• Failure to thrive
• "My baby tastes salty"
• Male infertility

You can identify CF mutations by using blood, buccal brushings, or chorionic villus sampling. Most commercial labs look for 25–100 of the most common mutations, which can account for ~ 95% of all patients with CF. However, we know that 4% of the Caucasian population is heterozygous for the CF mutation, so finding 1 mutation does not rule in or rule out CF.

The nasal potential difference test measures the bioelectric voltage difference across nasal epithelium and is done only in a few CF care centers.

Newborn screening for elevated blood immunoreactive trypsinogen (IRT) has become routine in all states and the District of Columbia. It has few false negatives, but > 90% false positives. Depending on the state, if the IRT is abnormal, it is repeated or the blood is sent for mutation analysis using PCR testing for the most common mutations (F508del in particular). It is possible that a child with CF can be missed with newborn screening; so, if you have a clinical suspicion with any child, obtain a quantitative pilocarpine iontophoresis sweat test to confirm diagnosis.

TREATMENT

Cystic Fibrosis Centers

Survival is greatest in children followed in care centers accredited by the Cystic Fibrosis Foundation.

Therapy for Pulmonary Disease in CF

Airway clearance is a core therapy to manage and prevent airway obstruction. It is done using postural drainage and percussion and/or a percussive vest. In older children, devices generating positive expiratory pressure can also be used. Airway clearance is routinely directed at all pulmonary segments at least 1–4 ×/day with increased frequency during exacerbations.

Exercise is beneficial, particularly aerobic activities such as swimming and jogging. Exercise can also help stimulate appetite.

Inhalational therapy can include bronchodilators, antibiotics, and mucolytic agents (i.e., *N*-acetylcysteine, 7% hypertonic saline, recombinant human DNase). These agents are of uncertain benefit; thus, each must be taken on a case-by-case basis.

The use of **prophylactic macrolide therapy** (azithromycin 1×/day, 3×/week) to reduce inflammation decreases exacerbations, decreases hospitalizations, improves pulmonary function, and results in small increases in weight. Additionally, high-dose ibuprofen is being used by some CF care centers because of its antiinflammatory effects.

Corticosteroids have been shown to be beneficial in some trials but have obvious side effects and drawbacks. Although inhaled corticosteroids benefit those who have asthma as well, they are not recommended for routine use in all CF patients.

Antibiotics have probably provided the greatest benefit in prognosis. Treatment of exacerbations with antistaphylococcal (e.g., nafcillin, cefazolin, vancomycin) and antipseudomonal (e.g., piperacillin-tazobactam, or cefepime, plus ciprofloxacin or tobramycin) drugs is paramount. Once *Pseudomonas* is established, it is almost impossible to get rid of it. However, there is some success in temporary eradication of newly acquired *Pseudomonas* using inhaled tobramycin. It is particularly bad if a mucoid form establishes itself. Quinolone use in CF is widespread, and data to date has not shown significant bony or cartilage abnormalities.

Use of antibiotics varies from CF care center to center and patient to patient, but 3 general categories prevail:

1) Use of continuous (often cycled) prophylactic antibiotics (inhaled or oral) with the addition of IV antibiotics for acute exacerbations

2) No antibiotics except with exacerbations

3) Aggressive antibiotics (oral, aerosol, or IV) based on sputum cultures, for 2–3 weeks every 1–2 months for patients with any evidence of pulmonary disease

In many CF care centers, oral antibiotics are given at the 1st sign of pulmonary exacerbation. Aerosolized antibiotics, typically tobramycin or aztreonam, can be useful as therapy to keep *Pseudomonas* colonization from causing an exacerbation or to treat in the midst of an acute exacerbation. IV antibiotics are indicated when the patient either does not respond to outpatient therapy or else presents with a moderate-to-severe exacerbation.

Antibiotic choices include:

- The aminoglycosides (frequently tobramycin is used followed by gentamicin or amikacin)
- Semisynthetic antipseudomonal penicillins (e.g., ticarcillin, ticarcillin-clavulanate, piperacillin-tazobactam)
- Imipenem or meropenem
- Ceftazidime
- Aztreonam
- Quinolones
- Colistin (rarely)

IV therapy is continued until the patient has clinically improved or reached a new plateau of functioning. This generally takes 2–3 weeks; however, it can take longer.

The 1st therapy targeting the basic cellular defect, ivacaftor (Kalydeco), is available for patients ≥ 2 years of age. It is a targeted **CFTR function potentiator** for individuals with *G551D* and several other similar gating-type mutations. A combination of ivacaftor and lumacaftor (Orkambi; **CFTR corrector**) is used to treat the most common cause of *CFTR* mutation, which is 2 copies of *F508del*. It is approved for patients ≥ 2 years of age. It works by correcting the misfolded CFTR protein. Patients have demonstrated improved lung function with the combination drug. The dosage is 2 tablets every 12 hours taken with fatty foods.

End-stage lung disease, the most common cause of death in CF, is an indication for **bilateral lung transplantation**. CF is the top reason for lung transplantation in children.

Therapy for Gastrointestinal Disease in CF

Growth with normal weight-to-height ratio is an important prognostic factor in keeping CF patients' lung function healthy. Thus, nutritional efforts are aggressive in helping these patients gain weight and encouraging them with sound nutritional guidance. Use of **pancreatic enzyme replacement** is a cornerstone of therapy for pancreatic insufficiency (PI). Dosages of enzymes must be titrated to the individual patient. H_2 blockers can enhance the bioavailability of the enzymes. Supplementation with **fat-soluble vitamins** A, D, E, and K is necessary for those with PI. Most patients with CF require 100–150% of the recommended dietary allowances for their age, even with control of malabsorption. For those patients who have difficulty gaining weight, a high-fat diet and oral nutritional supplements can be beneficial. Some patients cannot keep up with the daily intake needed to gain weight and require nighttime enteral feeds to provide enough calories.

COMPLICATIONS

Pneumothorax

Pneumothorax (Figure 11-17) occurs in ~ 10% of CF patients and can be a common cause of chest pain. Small pneumothoraces often resolve with bedrest and oxygen therapy, but some require chest tube placement. A majority of patients have recurrence. Having a pneumothorax is typically a poor prognostic sign that suggests severe lung disease. Prevention of recurrences is aided by using open thoracotomy through a small subaxillary incision, excision of apical blebs, stripping the apical pleura, and manual abrasion of the remaining accessible pleura. A caveat is that some transplant centers view surgical or chemical ablation of pleura as a relative contraindication for lung transplant; as noted under Therapy for Pulmonary Disease in CF on page 11-27, CF is the top reason for lung transplantation in children.

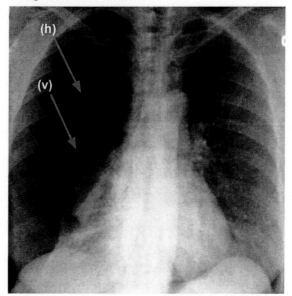

Figure 11-17: Right pneumothorax with (h)yperlucency and (v)isceral pleura

Hemoptysis

Hemoptysis involving blood-streaked sputum is quite common with bronchiectasis due to CF, particularly during pulmonary exacerbations. Massive hemoptysis is defined as acute bleeding of > 240 mL within 24 hours or recurrent bleeding of > 100 mL daily for several days. Pulmonary complication guidelines (2010) from the Cystic Fibrosis Foundation recommend suspension of all chest physiotherapy in the event of massive hemoptysis. Massive hemoptysis occurs in only about 5–10% of patients and is rarely significant enough to require transfusions or other interventions. If hemoptysis occurs, it is usually due to infection. Treat the exacerbation with IV antibiotics and other routine management.

CF patients can have malabsorption of fat-soluble vitamins, so consider vitamin K deficiency if there is hemoptysis; this often occurs with other signs of abnormal blood loss such as melena, mucosal bleeding, and easy bruisability. Such a deficiency can be seen with CF-related liver disease and in those with pancreatic insufficiency not taking vitamin K supplementation.

Pulmonary Hypertension

Pulmonary hypertension with the development of cor pulmonale and enlargement of the right ventricle is seen in late CF. Heart failure with peripheral edema and hepatomegaly are poor prognostic signs and usually indicate survival of < 8 months. Standard therapy of oxygen, fluid restriction, and diuretics is beneficial; do not use digitalis unless there is accompanying left ventricular dysfunction. Combined heart-lung transplant is sometimes used in CF patients with cor pulmonale and severe lung disease.

Constipation / Rectal Prolapse

Abdominal complaints are common in patients with CF. Constipation is a recurrent complaint. Chronic constipation can lead to DIOS or to rectal prolapse, so institute active therapy to relieve constipation. Lactulose and polyethylene glycol 3350 are used to prevent chronic constipation. If DIOS occurs, treat with oral polyethylene glycol with added electrolytes (if obstruction has not yet occurred) or hyperosmolar enemas, such as meglumine diatrizoate. Rectal prolapse can typically be reversed with gentle manual pressure and control of malabsorption.

CF-Related Diabetes

Another complication of CF that is more common with age is CF-related glucose impairment and diabetes mellitus. While patients usually do not develop acute ketoacidosis, their inability to properly use glucose contributes to malnutrition and increased infection risk. Insulin, rather than carbohydrate restriction, is indicated for those with significant hyperglycemia, given the high caloric demands and concurrent pancreatic insufficiency. 2010 guidelines from the Cystic Fibrosis Foundation recommend annual oral glucose tolerance testing for CF patients ≥ 10 years of age.

PRIMARY CILIARY DYSKINESIA (PCD)

PREVIEW | REVIEW

- What is Kartagener syndrome?

The prevalence of PCD is ~ 1:15,000 to 1:20,000 and is caused by ciliary abnormalities, including aplasia, akinesia, and dyskinesia. Most cases of PCD have an autosomal recessive inheritance pattern. Normally, cilia beat synchronously at 7–22×/second. Any impairment with the beat or the synchrony can result in poor mucociliary clearance and subsequent recurrent episodes of upper and lower respiratory tract infections. In addition, other features include bronchiectasis, otitis media, and male infertility. There are numerous mutations that can cause the disorder, but half of the patients with PCD have **Kartagener syndrome**. Kartagener syndrome occurs when one or both dynein arms of the cilia are absent. It presents with recurrent infections (i.e., sinusitis, otitis, pneumonia), bronchiectasis, situs inversus totalis, and reduced male fertility. It can be sporadic or familial in character and is autosomal recessive.

Rule out cystic fibrosis with a negative sweat test. Definitive diagnosis of PCD can be challenging and requires referral to specialized centers with expertise on this disease. There are different tests to assess ciliary motility, ciliary ultrastructure (sample is obtained from nasal or bronchial brush biopsy), nasal nitric oxide measurement, mucociliary clearance, and genetic defects. Genetic studies are recommended.

Treatment of these syndromes is the same as for bronchiectasis, consisting of chest physiotherapy and occasionally requiring antimicrobial treatment in the presence of bacterial overgrowth.

Prognosis is good for those with cilia-related symptoms; most have a normal lifespan despite frequent respiratory infections.

α_1-ANTITRYPSIN DEFICIENCY (AATD)

PREVIEW | REVIEW

- Which liver abnormalities are seen in children with α_1-antitrypsin deficiency (AATD)?
- Which pulmonary abnormalities are seen with AATD?

OVERVIEW

AATD rarely causes pulmonary symptoms in children, and it typically does not manifest until the 5th decade of life. Like most enzyme deficiency disorders, it is autosomal recessive. Parents are frequently asymptomatic carriers, and the family history is often negative for the disease.

Suspect homozygous AATD in nonsmokers with early-onset **emphysema** with lower lobe predominance. Know that ~ 15% of persons with the homozygote Pi^{ZZ} phenotype also get **progressive liver fibrosis** and **cirrhosis**—the manifestation most likely to be seen in children. With this type of cirrhosis, as with cirrhosis of any cause, there is an increased incidence of **hepatoma**.

Heterozygotes have no increase in pulmonary disease unless the individual smokes—in which case pulmonary disease can present similarly to homozygotes.

See the Gastroenterology section for more information.

DIAGNOSIS

Test patients with persistent airflow obstruction on spirometry. Additional features that lead clinicians to test for severe AATD include:

- Emphysema in a young individual (≤ 45 years of age)
- Emphysema in a nonsmoker or very light smoker
- Emphysema characterized by predominant basilar changes on the chest radiograph
- A family history of emphysema and/or liver disease
- Clinical findings or history of panniculitis
- Clinical findings or history of unexplained chronic liver disease

Testing includes measurement of α_1-antitrypsin levels by rocket immunoelectrophoresis, radial immunodiffusion, or nephelometry. Patients with lower serum or plasma α_1-antitrypsin levels then undergo genetic testing.

TREATMENT

Treatment is with IV α_1-antitrypsin. When the emphysema is severe, refer for lung transplantation.

HEMOPTYSIS

PREVIEW | REVIEW

- What are the common causes of hemoptysis in children?
- What is diagnostic for a pulmonary source of hemoptysis?

OVERVIEW

Hemoptysis is the presence of blood in the sputum or the spitting up of blood. It is rare in children ≤ 6 years of age because they generally swallow their sputum.

The most common causes in children are:

- Infection
- Foreign bodies
- Bronchiectasis (especially CF associated)

Rarer causes include:

- Immunoglobulin A vasculitis (IgAV; formerly Henoch-Schönlein purpura [HSP])
- Granulomatosis with polyangiitis (GPA)
- Antiglomerular basement membrane (anti-GBM) disease (Anti-GBM disease involving both kidneys and the lungs is termed Goodpasture syndrome; additional information on Goodpasture syndrome is available in the Nephrology & Urology section.)
- Systemic lupus erythematosus
- Congenital heart and lung defects
- Neoplasm
- Arteriovenous malformation (AVM)

- Hemangioma
- Trauma
- Pulmonary embolism
- Idiopathic pulmonary hemosiderosis (IPH)

The 1st step in management is to stabilize the patient and intubate if needed. Evaluate by localizing the bleeding source if possible. Is it gastrointestinal in origin (look for coffee-ground appearance or food)? Or, is it respiratory tract in origin (bright red or rust colored, "frothy," or mixed with sputum)? Check the mouth and nasal passages for any lacerations or lesions.

Other history/signs/symptoms that are helpful in determining the etiology:

- Clinical findings or history of unexplained chronic liver disease
- Fever or chills: pneumonia, lung abscess
- Drug use: cocaine, smoking
- Microscopic hematuria: GPA or Goodpasture syndrome
- Skin telangiectasia: pulmonary AVM (with hereditary hemorrhagic telangiectasia [HHT])
- Recurrent nosebleeds: HHT or GPA
- Previously healthy child with wheezing and cough: foreign body
- Clubbing: chronic lung disease (e.g., cystic fibrosis) or congenital heart disease

Do a chest radiograph in the initial evaluation; however, up to 33% of patients have a normal CXR. Bronchoscopy with bronchoalveolar lavage (BAL) is the next step after bleeding is controlled; the finding of **hemosiderin-laden macrophages** is diagnostic for a pulmonary source of bleeding—they usually appear 3 days after bleeding. If the BAL is positive or there are suspicious findings on CXR, proceed to chest CT with contrast (or CT angiography). An echocardiogram is recommended in cases of pulmonary hemorrhage. If the echocardiogram is normal, look for pulmonary-renal syndromes, bleeding abnormalities, or suspect IPH (see Idiopathic Pulmonary Hemosiderosis (IPH)). Lung biopsy is done in most children with diffuse alveolar hemorrhage.

Management of most cases of hemoptysis is supportive because a majority of cases with mild hemoptysis resolve spontaneously and do not recur. Treat massive hemoptysis with hemostasis and embolotherapy. This requires specialist intervention. Other therapy depends on the underlying cause.

IDIOPATHIC PULMONARY HEMOSIDEROSIS (IPH)

Hemosiderosis is rare, but it appears in the blueprint for ABP exam topics; so, we cover it briefly. Recurrent pulmonary bleeding (alveolar hemorrhage in particular) can eventually cause pulmonary hemosiderosis. When no underlying etiology for repeated hemorrhages occurs, it is called IPH.

Children usually present before 10 years of age with either abrupt hemoptysis or a progressive course of anemia, dyspnea, fatigue, and recurrent cough. Most patients present with iron deficiency anemia. There can be a restrictive pattern on lung function testing with the development of pulmonary fibrosis. Sputum or BAL show hemosiderin-laden macrophages.

Perform lung biopsy to confirm diagnosis and to exclude other specific pathology. Other conditions to be excluded include vasculitis, granulomatous lung disease, or auto-immune disease.

Use systemic corticosteroids in acute episodes and chronically for patients with regular symptoms. However, the response varies, so if there is not a good response, use other immunosuppressants. Children generally have a more rapid course and poorer prognosis than adults.

INTERSTITIAL LUNG DISEASES (ILDs)

PREVIEW | REVIEW

- What does the CXR characteristically show in sarcoidosis?
- What does the biopsy of an affected bronchial wall in sarcoidosis show?
- True or false? Erythema nodosum is a poor prognostic indicator in sarcoidosis.
- In a patient with pulmonary alveolar proteinosis, hypoxemia is often due to what?

OVERVIEW

ILDs encompass a number of disorders that injure the alveoli and surrounding tissues, resulting in interference of gas exchange. This injury is followed by wound healing that results in fibrosis. Many types of ILD also involve inflammation. ILD causes a restrictive pattern of lung physiology and diffuse infiltrates on CXR.

LYMPHOCYTIC INTERSTITIAL PNEUMONIA (LIP)

LIP (a.k.a. lymphoid interstitial pneumonia) is the most commonly described ILD in children. Pathogenesis is unknown, but it appears to have 2 causes:

- An exaggerated response to inhaled antigens in a child with another autoimmune dysfunction
- As a result of a primary infection with a virus such as HIV or Epstein-Barr virus (EBV)

LIP, as an exaggerated immune response, is seen in many autoimmune diseases.

LIP is commonly seen in children with a perinatally acquired HIV infection—with over 25% of these children developing it, usually at 2–3 years of age. LIP is considered an AIDS-defining illness in children. It is thought to be associated with EBV and human T-cell lymphotrophic virus Type 1 (HTLV-1). An alternate hypothesis is HIV-induced proliferation of bronchus-associated lymphoid tissue (BALT).

Patients with LIP present with dyspnea, cough, and fever. CXR shows a bibasilar infiltrate.

Treatment is supportive with oxygen, immunosuppressives (typically corticosteroids), and cytotoxic drugs as necessary.

SARCOIDOSIS

Sarcoidosis is a chronic multisystem disorder of unknown origin that affects young adults and, rarely, children. It is characterized pathologically by noncaseating epithelioid cell granulomas in affected organs, particularly lungs and thoracic lymph nodes.

CXR findings are variable. Usually, there is bilateral hilar and/or mediastinal adenopathy +/− reticulonodular or alveolar infiltrates. Hilar adenopathy alone or in combination with parenchymal infiltrates is found in 40–60% of children with sarcoidosis. Hilar adenopathy disappears as the disease progresses, as illustrated in Table 11-3. PFTs are either normal or show restrictive +/− obstructive mechanics. The serum angiotensin-converting enzyme (SACE) level is nonspecific and not used for diagnosis, although it can sometimes be helpful in monitoring disease progression (controversial). If the SACE level was previously elevated during active disease and low when inactive, it can be useful in determining if the disease is once again active. Hypercalcemia, hypercalciuria, and hypergammaglobulinemia can be seen.

Table 11-3: Radiographic Staging of Sarcoidosis	
Stage	**Chest X-Ray Findings**
0	Clear lung fields, no adenopathy
I	Bilateral hilar adenopathy
II	Adenopathy + parenchymal infiltrates
III	Diffuse parenchymal infiltrates
IV	Fibrosis, bullae, cavities

Sarcoidosis is a diagnosis of exclusion. It is imperative to exclude the other granulomatous diseases, including hypersensitivity pneumonitis, berylliosis, and infectious diseases caused by mycobacteria and fungi. Do a biopsy and obtain material for histologic examination and culture. The best method for diagnosing sarcoidosis is by fiberoptic bronchoscopy with transbronchial or bronchial wall biopsies showing **noncaseating granuloma**.

Associated **erythema nodosum** indicates a good prognosis! Perform a slitlamp exam on all patients with sarcoidosis to look for asymptomatic **uveitis**, which can lead to blindness.

Overall, 75% of sarcoid patients recover without treatment. In rare cases, it progresses to pulmonary hypertension or pulmonary fibrosis. Treat severe disease with corticosteroids. Although corticosteroids do not induce remission, they help to decrease the symptoms and improve PFTs. Inhaled corticosteroids decrease the respiratory symptoms and are an alternative to systemic corticosteroids for disease that primarily affects the bronchi.

Indications for systemic corticosteroids:

- Involvement of eyes
- Heart conduction abnormalities
- CNS involvement
- Severe pulmonary symptoms
- Severe skin lesions
- Persistent hypercalcemia

Other medications used to treat severe disease include methotrexate and hydroxychloroquine. Consider lung transplant for patients with end-stage lung disease.

PULMONARY ALVEOLAR PROTEINOSIS

In children, most cases of pulmonary alveolar proteinosis result from a genetic or acquired defect in surfactant metabolism (including surfactant protein mutations, lysinuric protein intolerance, and granulocyte-macrophage colony-stimulating factor [GM-CSF] receptor mutations), leading to a buildup of proteinaceous material in the airways.

Similar to cases in adults, acquired causes include infections, malignancies, immunodeficiencies, and exposure to inhaled chemicals or minerals, such as in silicosis.

Severity of cases can range from severe respiratory failure in neonatal forms to chronic ILD in older children. Poor weight gain, fatigue, chronic cough with gelatinous sputum, and exercise intolerance are common. Often, patients are hypoxemic from a large R-to-L shunt because gas exchange is impaired secondary to clogged alveoli.

Diagnosis is usually confirmed with open lung biopsy, which shows intact alveolar walls and alveoli that are filled with fatty material.

Treatment depends on the underlying cause: If severe, a whole-lung lavage is done under general anesthesia to remove proteinaceous material. Some patients experience long-term resolution, while others have recurrent problems. GM-CSF treatment may restore proper alveolar macrophage function.

THE LUNGS IN AUTOIMMUNE DISEASES

PREVIEW | REVIEW

- Which collagen vascular disease causes pulmonary hypertension out of proportion to the pulmonary disease noted?
- Which laboratory test is positive in many patients with granulomatosis with polyangiitis?

OVERVIEW

Systemic inflammatory disease that clinically affects the lungs is rare in the pediatric setting. However, when present, it can indicate high morbidity and mortality in this population, and pulmonary disease is the predominant initial clinical presentation in some patients. More information on the following disorders is found in the Rheumatology and Nephrology & Urology sections.

SYSTEMIC LUPUS ERYTHEMATOSUS (SLE)

SLE causes painful pleuritis +/– effusion and diffuse atelectasis. It sometimes induces diaphragmatic weakness, therefore resulting in orthopneic dyspnea out of proportion to the CXR findings, although the CXR sometimes shows an elevated diaphragm. SLE also occasionally causes hemoptysis similar to that in IPH. SLE affects both lung and pleura more frequently than any other collagen vascular disease (60%), while scleroderma affects the lung alone more than any other collagen vascular disease (100%! but no pleural changes).

SCLERODERMA

Scleroderma is a rare autoimmune disorder that, in children, most often has only skin involvement. Systemic scleroderma is uncommon and affects internal organs. Scleroderma has 2 lung effects:

1) Interstitial fibrosis (See Interstitial Lung Diseases (ILDs) on page 11-31.)

2) Intimal proliferation

Scleroderma-caused intimal proliferation in the pulmonary artery causes pulmonary hypertension out of proportion to the pulmonary disease. So, it is the **intimal proliferation**—not the ILD—that causes the real pulmonary problem in scleroderma patients. In addition, these patients often get pneumonia.

SJÖGREN SYNDROME

Sjögren syndrome is a chronic autoimmune disorder that is rare in children. It can cause desiccation of the airways and is also associated with LIP. For a more detailed discussion, refer to the Rheumatology section.

GRANULOMATOSIS WITH POLYANGIITIS (GPA)

GPA is a systemic vasculitis with **necrotizing granulomas** that affects both the upper respiratory tract (nose and sinuses) and the lower respiratory tract (with pulmonary vasculitis).

GPA can also cause necrotizing glomerulonephritis, although the disease is sometimes limited to the lungs.

Remember: sinus, lungs, kidneys. Consider GPA in any exam question scenario focusing on a patient with purulent nasal discharge, epistaxis, and/or signs of a glomerulonephritis with hematuria. The patient is typically not dyspneic and can have a nonproductive cough or hemoptysis.

c-ANCA (cytoplasmic antineutrophil cytoplasmic antibody; thought to be a destructive autoantibody) is used as an ancillary test for diagnosis. It is ~ 90% sensitive and 90% specific. When positive in a patient with GPA, the offending antibody is virtually always c-ANCA (96%), whereas in polyarteritis, it is usually p-ANCA.

Confirm diagnosis by either a nasal membrane biopsy or an open lung biopsy. Do not diagnose by kidney biopsy due to invasiveness and because it does not always show the granulomas. Treatment of GPA is cyclophosphamide with or without corticosteroids.

ANTIGLOMERULAR BASEMENT MEMBRANE (Anti-GBM) DISEASE

Anti-GBM disease (a.k.a. Goodpasture syndrome; see the Nephrology & Urology section for additional information) tends to present in young adult males with a male-to-female ratio of 3:1. Lung disease is the same as IPH, but Goodpasture syndrome also affects the kidneys. Typically, there is no frank hemorrhage, but often there is hemoptysis that precedes renal abnormalities. Think of this disease if the patient presents with dyspnea, hemoptysis, iron deficiency anemia, and glomerulonephritis, but without the upper airway signs that are seen in GPA.

Symptoms are due to anti-GBM antibodies, which result in linear deposition of **IgG** and **C3** on alveolar and glomerular basement membranes.

Like patients with IPH, patients with Goodpasture syndrome can also have iron deficiency anemia. These patients are usually ANCA negative. Definitive diagnosis is made with renal biopsy demonstrating **anti-GBM antibodies**.

Treat with immunosuppressives and plasmapheresis. If the patient has severe pulmonary hemorrhages, nephrectomy may help.

THE MEDSTUDY HUB: YOUR GUIDELINES AND REVIEW ARTICLES RESOURCE

For both review articles and current pediatrics practice guidelines, visit the MedStudy Hub at

medstudy.com/hub

The Hub contains the only online consolidated list of all current guidelines focused on pediatrics. Guidelines on the Hub are easy to find, continually updated, and linked to the published source. MedStudy maintains the Hub as a service to the medical community and makes it available to anyone and everyone at no cost to users.

APPENDIX — ASTHMA TREATMENT REGIMENS

The source for all figures and tables in the Appendix (Table 11-4 on page 11-35 through Table 11-10 on page 11-44 and Figure 11-18 on page 11-34 through Figure 11-21 on page 11-42) is The National Asthma Education and Prevention Program: Expert Panel Report 3, Guidelines for the Diagnosis and Management of Asthma—released in 2007, with edits in 2008 and a focused update in 2020.

For a discussion of factors that can affect theophylline levels, see Theophylline on page 11-20.

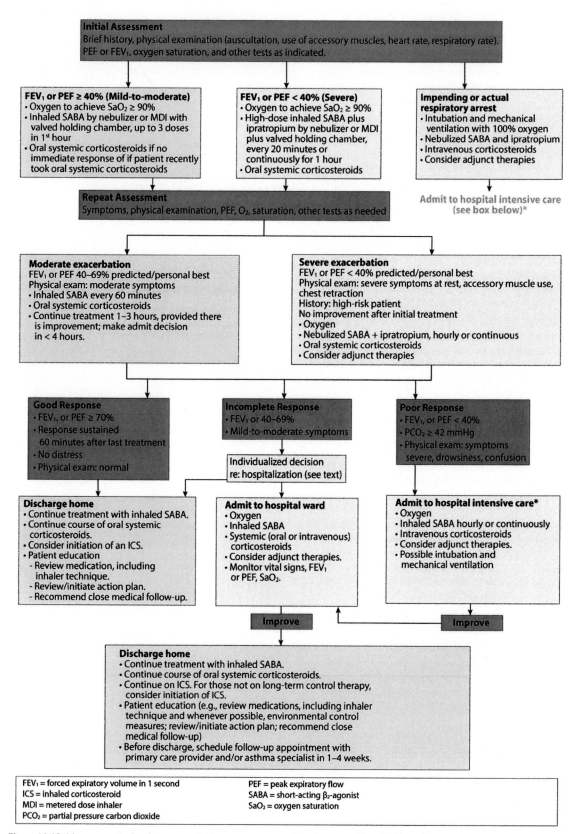

Figure 11-18: Management of asthma exacerbations—emergency department and hospital-based care

Table 11-4: Classifying Asthma Severity and Initiating Treatment in Children 0-4 Years of Age

Components of Severity		Classification of Asthma Severity			
		Intermittent	Persistent		
			Mild	Moderate	Severe
Impairment	Symptoms	≤ 2 days/week	> 2 days/week but not daily	Daily	Throughout the day
	Nighttime awakenings	None	1–2×/month	3–4×/month	> 1×/week
	β$_2$-agonist use (not preventive of exercise-induced bronchoconstriction)	≤ 2 days/week	> 2 days/week but not daily	Daily	Several times per day
	Activity limits	None	Minor limitation	Some limitation	Extremely limited
Risk	Exacerbations requiring OSC	0–1×/year	≥ 2 exacerbations in 6 months requiring OSC or ≥ 4 wheezing episodes/year lasting > 1 day and risk factors for persistent asthma		
Recommended Step for Initiating Therapy (See Figure 11-19 on page 11-36 for treatment steps.)					
		Step 1	Step 2	Step 3, and consider short course of OSC.	
		In 2–6 weeks, depending on severity, evaluate level of asthma control that is achieved. If no clear benefit is observed in 4–6 weeks, consider adjusting therapy or alternative diagnoses.			

OSC = oral systemic corticosteroids

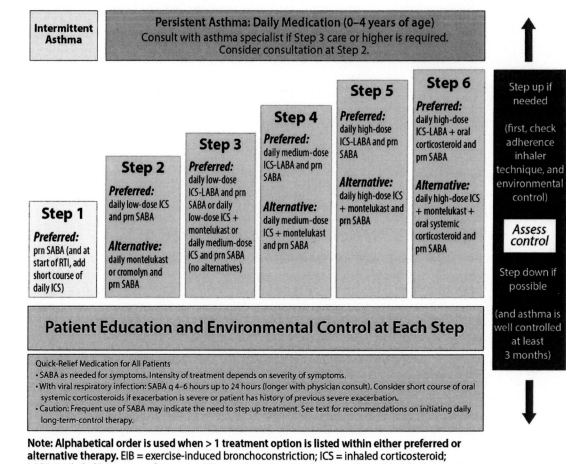

Note: Alphabetical order is used when > 1 treatment option is listed within either preferred or alternative therapy. EIB = exercise-induced bronchoconstriction; ICS = inhaled corticosteroid; LABA = inhaled long-acting β₂-agonist; RTI = respiratory tract infection; SABA = inhaled short-acting β₂-agonist

Figure 11-19: Stepwise approach for managing asthma in children 0–4 years of age

Table 11-5: Assessing Asthma Control and Adjusting Therapy in Children 0–4 Years of Age

Components of Control		Classification of Asthma Control		
		Well Controlled	**Not Well Controlled**	**Very Poorly Controlled**
Impairment	Symptoms	≤ 2 days/week	> 2 days/week	Throughout the day
	Nighttime awakenings	≤ 1×/month	> 1×/month	> 1×/week
	β₂-agonist use (not preventive of exercise-induced bronchoconstriction)	≤ 2 days/week	> 2 days/week	Several times per day
	Activity limits	None	Some limitation	Extremely limited
Risk	Exacerbations requiring OSC	0–1×/year	2–3×/year	> 3×/year
	Treatment-related adverse effects	Medication side effects can vary in intensity from none to very troublesome and worrisome. The level of intensity does not correlate to specific levels of control but should be considered in the overall assessment of risk.		
Recommended Action for Adjusting Therapy (See Figure 11-19 for treatment steps.)				
		• Maintain current treatment. • Follow up regularly at 1–6 months. • Consider step down if well controlled for at least 3 months.	• Check adherence, inhaler technique, environmental factors, and comorbid conditions. • Step up (1 step) and reevaluate in 2–6 weeks. • If no clear benefit in 4–6 weeks, consider alternative diagnoses or adjusting therapy. • For side effects, consider alternative treatment options.	• Consider short course of oral systemic corticosteroids. • Step up (1–2 steps) and reevaluate in 2 weeks. • If no clear benefits in 4–6 weeks, consider alternative diagnoses or adjusting therapy. • For side effects, consider alternative treatment options.

OSC = oral systemic corticosteroids

Table 11-6: Classifying Asthma Severity and Initiating Therapy in Children 5–11 Years of Age						
Components of Severity			**Classification of Asthma Severity**			
			Intermittent	**Persistent**		
				Mild	**Moderate**	**Severe**
Impairment	Symptoms		≤ 2 days/ week	> 2 days/week but not daily	Daily	Throughout the day
	Nighttime awakenings		≤ 2×/month	3–4×/month	> 1×/week	Often 7×/week
	β₂-agonist use (not preventive of exercise-induced bronchoconstriction)		≤ 2 days/ week	> 2 days/week but not daily	Daily	Several times per day
	Activity limits		None	Minor limitation	Some limitation	Extremely limited
	Lung function:	FEV₁	> 80% > 85%	80%	60–80%	< 60%
		FEV₁/FVC	Normal FEV₁ between exacerbations	> 80%	75–80%	< 75%
Risk	Exacerbations requiring OSC		0–1×/year	≥ 2 in 1 year		
Recommended Step for Initiating Therapy (See Figure 11-20 for treatment steps.)						
			Step 1	Step 2	Step 3 low-dose ICS-LABA option, and consider short course of oral systemic corticosteroids.	Step 3 low-dose ICS-LABA option, or Step 4, and consider short course of oral systemic corticosteroids.
			In 2–6 weeks, evaluate level of asthma control that is achieved and adjust therapy accordingly.			

FEV₁ = forced expiratory volume in 1 second
FVC = forced vital capacity
ICS = inhaled corticosteroids
OSC = oral systemic corticosteroids

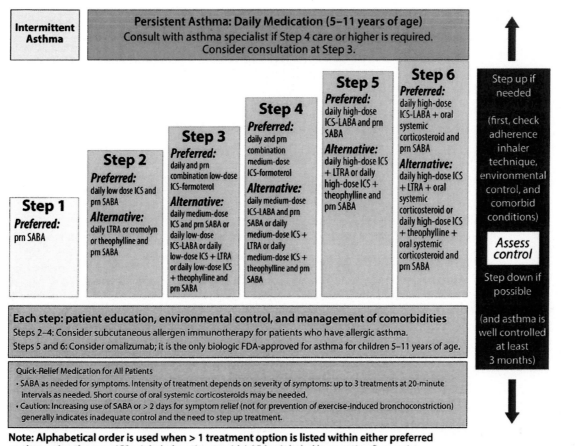

Intermittent Asthma

Persistent Asthma: Daily Medication (5–11 years of age)
Consult with asthma specialist if Step 4 care or higher is required.
Consider consultation at Step 3.

Step 1
Preferred:
prn SABA

Step 2
Preferred:
daily low dose ICS and prn SABA

Alternative:
daily LTRA or cromolyn or theophylline and prn SABA

Step 3
Preferred:
daily and prn combination low-dose ICS-formoterol

Alternative:
daily medium-dose ICS and prn SABA or daily low-dose ICS-LABA or daily low-dose ICS + LTRA or daily low-dose ICS + theophylline and prn SABA

Step 4
Preferred:
daily and prn combination medium-dose ICS-formoterol

Alternative:
daily medium-dose ICS-LABA and prn SABA or daily medium-dose ICS + LTRA or daily medium-dose ICS + theophylline and prn SABA

Step 5
Preferred:
daily high-dose ICS-LABA and prn SABA

Alternative:
daily high-dose ICS + LTRA or daily high-dose ICS + theophylline and prn SABA

Step 6
Preferred:
daily high-dose ICS-LABA + oral systemic corticosteroid and prn SABA

Alternative:
daily high-dose ICS + LTRA + oral systemic corticosteroid or daily high-dose ICS + theophylline + oral systemic corticosteroid and prn SABA

Step up if needed

(first, check adherence inhaler technique, environmental control, and comorbid conditions)

Assess control

Step down if possible

(and asthma is well controlled at least 3 months)

Each step: patient education, environmental control, and management of comorbidities
Steps 2–4: Consider subcutaneous allergen immunotherapy for patients who have allergic asthma.
Steps 5 and 6: Consider omalizumab; it is the only biologic FDA-approved for asthma for children 5–11 years of age.

Quick-Relief Medication for All Patients
• SABA as needed for symptoms. Intensity of treatment depends on severity of symptoms: up to 3 treatments at 20-minute intervals as needed. Short course of oral systemic corticosteroids may be needed.
• Caution: Increasing use of SABA or > 2 days for symptom relief (not for prevention of exercise-induced bronchoconstriction) generally indicates inadequate control and the need to step up treatment.

Note: Alphabetical order is used when > 1 treatment option is listed within either preferred or alternative therapy. ICS = inhaled corticosteroid; LABA = inhaled long-acting β₂-agonist; LTRA = leukotriene receptor antagonist; SABA = inhaled short-acting β₂-agonist

Figure 11-20: Stepwise approach for managing asthma in children 5–11 years of age

Table 11-7: Assessing Asthma Control and Adjusting Therapy in Children 5–11 Years of Age					
Components of Control			**Classification of Asthma Control**		
			Well Controlled	**Not Well Controlled**	**Very Poorly Controlled**
Impairment	Symptoms		≤ 2 days/week	> 2 days/week	Throughout the day
	Nighttime awakenings		≤ 1×/month	≥ 2×/month	> 2×/week
	β_2-agonist use (not preventive of exercise-induced bronchoconstriction)		≤ 2 days/week	> 2 days/week	Several times per day
	Activity limits		None	Some limitation	Extremely limited
	Lung function:	FEV_1 or PF	> 80%	60–80%	< 60%
		FEV_1/FVC	> 80%	75–80%	< 75%
Risk	Exacerbations requiring OSC		0–1×/year	≥ 2/year	
	Reduction in lung growth		Evaluation requires long-term follow-up.		
	Treatment-related adverse effects		Medication side effects can vary in intensity from none to very troublesome and worrisome. The level of intensity does not correlate to specific levels of control but should be considered in the overall assessment of risk.		
Recommended Action for Adjusting Therapy (See Figure 11-20 on page 11-39 for treatment steps.)					
			• Maintain current treatment. • Follow up regularly in 1–6 months. • Consider step down if well controlled for at least 3 months.	• Check adherence, inhaler technique, environmental factors, and comorbid conditions. • Step up at least 1 step and reevaluate in 2–6 weeks. • For side effects, consider alternative treatment options.	• Consider short course of oral systemic corticosteroids. • Step up 1–2 steps and reevaluate in 2 weeks. • For side effects, consider alternative treatment options.

FEV_1 = forced expiratory volume in 1 second
FVC = forced vital capacity
OSC = oral systemic corticosteroids
PF = peak flow

Table 11-8: Classifying Asthma Severity and Initiating Treatment in Children ≥ 12 Years of Age						
Components of Severity			**Classification of Asthma Severity**			
			Intermittent	Persistent		
				Mild	**Moderate**	**Severe**
Impairment Normal FEV$_1$/ FVC: • 8–19 years 85% • 20–39 years 80% • 40–59 years 75% • 60–80 years 70%	Symptoms		≤ 2 days/week	> 2 days/week but not daily	Daily	Throughout the day
	Nighttime awakenings		≤ 2×/month	3–4×/month	> 1×/week but not nightly	Often 7×/week
	β$_2$-agonist use (not preventive of exercise-induced bronchoconstriction)		≤ 2 days/week	> 2 days/week but not daily and not more than 1× on any day	Daily	Several times per day
	Activity limits		None	Minor limitation	Some limitation	Extremely limited
	Lung function:	FEV$_1$	Normal FEV$_1$ between exacerbations: > 80%	> 80%	60–80%	< 60%
		FEV$_1$/FVC	Normal	Normal	Reduced by 5%	Reduced by > 5%
Risk	Exacerbations requiring OSC		0–1/year	≥ 2/year		
Recommended Step for Initiating Therapy (See Figure 11-21 on page 11-42 for treatment steps.)						
			Step 1	Step 2	Step 3 and consider short course of oral systemic corticosteroids.	Step 3 and 4 and consider short course of oral systemic corticosteroids.
			In 2–6 weeks, evaluate level of asthma control that is achieved and adjust therapy accordingly.			

FEV$_1$ = forced expiratory volume in 1 second
FVC = forced vital capacity
OSC = oral systemic corticosteroids

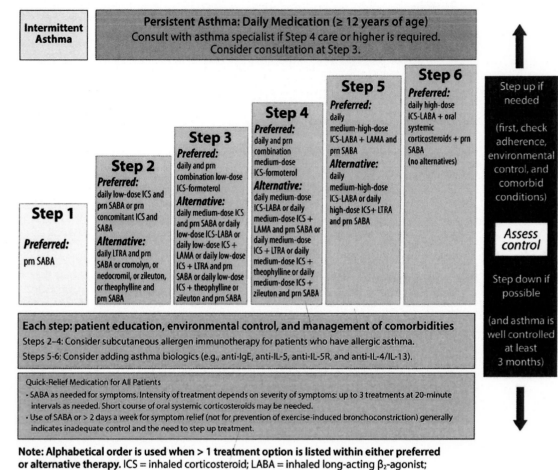

Intermittent Asthma

Persistent Asthma: Daily Medication (≥ 12 years of age)
Consult with asthma specialist if Step 4 care or higher is required.
Consider consultation at Step 3.

Step 1

Preferred:

prn SABA

Step 2

Preferred:
daily low-dose ICS and prn SABA or prn concomitant ICS and SABA

Alternative:
daily LTRA and prn SABA or cromolyn, or nedocromil, or zileuton, or theophylline and prn SABA

Step 3

Preferred:
daily and prn combination low-dose ICS-formoterol

Alternative:
daily medium-dose ICS and prn SABA or daily low-dose ICS-LABA or daily low-dose ICS + LAMA or daily low-dose ICS + LTRA and prn SABA or daily low-dose ICS + theophylline or zileuton and prn SABA

Step 4

Preferred:
daily and prn combination medium-dose ICS-formoterol

Alternative:
daily medium-dose ICS-LABA or daily medium-dose ICS + LAMA and prn SABA or daily medium-dose ICS + LTRA or daily medium-dose ICS + theophylline or daily medium-dose ICS + zileuton and prn SABA

Step 5

Preferred:
daily medium-high-dose ICS-LABA + LAMA and prn SABA

Alternative:
daily medium-high-dose ICS-LABA or daily high-dose ICS + LTRA and prn SABA

Step 6

Preferred:
daily high-dose ICS-LABA + oral systemic corticosteroids + prn SABA
(no alternatives)

Step up if needed

(first, check adherence, environmental control, and comorbid conditions)

Assess control

Step down if possible

(and asthma is well controlled at least 3 months)

Each step: patient education, environmental control, and management of comorbidities
Steps 2–4: Consider subcutaneous allergen immunotherapy for patients who have allergic asthma.
Steps 5-6: Consider adding asthma biologics (e.g., anti-IgE, anti-IL-5, anti-IL-5R, and anti-IL-4/IL-13).

Quick-Relief Medication for All Patients
· SABA as needed for symptoms. Intensity of treatment depends on severity of symptoms: up to 3 treatments at 20-minute intervals as needed. Short course of oral systemic corticosteroids may be needed.
· Use of SABA or > 2 days a week for symptom relief (not for prevention of exercise-induced bronchoconstriction) generally indicates inadequate control and the need to step up treatment.

Note: Alphabetical order is used when > 1 treatment option is listed within either preferred or alternative therapy. ICS = inhaled corticosteroid; LABA = inhaled long-acting β₂-agonist; LTRA = leukotriene receptor antagonist; SABA = inhaled short-acting β₂-agonist

Figure 11-21: Stepwise approach for managing asthma in children ≥ 12 years of age

Table 11-9: Assessing Asthma Control and Adjusting Therapy in Children ≥ 12 Years of Age

Components of Control		Classification of Asthma Control		
		Well Controlled	**Not Well Controlled**	**Very Poorly Controlled**
Impairment: Use the ACT to assess.	Symptoms	≤ 2 days/week	> 2 days/week	Throughout the day
	Nighttime awakenings	≤ 2×/month	1–3×/week	≥ 4×/week
	Activity limits	None	Some limitation	Extremely limited
	β$_2$-agonist use (not preventive of exercise-induced bronchoconstriction)	≤ 2 days/week	> 2 days/week	Several times per day
	Lung function: FEV$_1$ or PF	> 80%	60–80%	< 60%
	Validated questionnaires	ACT ≥ 20	ACT = 16–19	ACT ≤ 15
Risk	Exacerbations requiring OSC	0–1/year	≥ 2/year	
	Reduction in lung function	Evaluation requires long-term follow-up.		
	Treatment-related adverse effects	Medication side effects can vary in intensity from none to very troublesome and worrisome. The level of intensity does not correlate to specific levels of control but should be considered in the overall assessment of risk.		
Recommended Action for Adjusting Therapy (See Figure 11-21 for treatment steps.)				
		• Maintain current step. • Follow up regularly every 1–6 months to maintain control. • Consider step down if well controlled for at least 3 months.	• Check adherence, inhaler technique, environmental factors, and comorbid conditions. • Step up 1 step and reevaluate in 2–6 weeks. • For side effects, consider alternative treatment options.	• Consider short course of oral systemic corticosteroids. • Step up 1–2 steps and reevaluate in 2 weeks. • For side effects, consider alternative treatment options.

ACT = asthma control test
FEV$_1$ = forced expiratory volume in 1 second; ;
OSC = oral systemic corticosteroids
PF = peak flow

Table 11-10: Usual Dosages for Long-Term Control Medications in Children			
Medication / Dosage Form	**0–4 Years of Age**	**5–11 Years of Age**	**Comments**
Systemic Corticosteroids			
Methylprednisolone 2, 4, 8, 16, 32 mg tablets	0.25–2 mg/kg daily in single dose in a.m. or every other day as needed for control	0.25–2 mg/kg daily in single dose in a.m. or every other day as needed for control	(Applies to all 3 corticosteroids) • For long-term treatment of severe persistent asthma, administer single does in a.m. either daily or on alternate days. (Alternate-day therapy may produce less adrenal suppression.) • Short courses or "bursts" are effective for establishing control when initiating therapy or during a period of gradual deterioration. • There is no evidence that tapering the dose following improvement in symptom control and pulmonary function prevents relapse. • Patients receiving the lower dose (1 mg/kg/day) experience fewer behavioral side effects (Kayani and Shannon 2002), and it appears to be equally efficacious (Rachelefsky 2003). • For patients unable to tolerate the liquid preparations, dexamethasone syrup at 0.4 mg/kg/day may be an alternative. Studies are limited, however, and the longer duration of activity increases the risk of adrenal suppression (Hendeles 2003).
Prednisolone 5 mg tablets, 5 mg/5 cc, 15 mg/5 cc	Short-course "burst": 1–2 mg/kg/day, maximum 30 mg/day for 3–10 days	Short-course "burst": 1–2 mg/kg/day, maximum 60 mg/day for 3–10 days	
Prednisone 1, 2.5, 5, 10, 20, 50 mg tablets; 5 mg/cc, 5 mg/5 cc			
Long-Acting β₂-Agonists (LABAs)			
Salmeterol DPI 50 mcg/blister	Safety and efficacy not established in children < 4 years of age	1 blister q 12 hours	• Salmeterol should not be used for symptom relief or exacerbations. • Formoterol and salmeterol should be used only with ICS. • Decreased duration of protection against exercise-induced bronchoconstriction may occur with regular use. • Most children < 4 years of age cannot provide sufficient inspiratory flow for adequate lung delivery. • Do not blow into inhaler after dose is activated. • Each capsule is for single use only; additional doses should not be administered for at least 12 hours. • Capsules should be used only with the inhaler and should not be taken orally.
Formoterol DPI 12 mcg/single-use capsule	Safety and efficacy not established in children < 5 years of age	1 capsule q 12 hours	
Combined Medication			
Fluticasone/ Salmeterol DPI 100 mcg/50 mcg, 250 mcg/50 mcg, 500 mcg/50 mcg HFA 45 mcg/21 mcg, 115 mcg/21 mcg, 230 mcg/21 mcg	Safety and efficacy not established in children < 4 years of age	DPI: 1 inhalation bid HFA: 2 puffs bid	• There have been no clinical trials in children < 4 years of age. • Most children < 4 years of age cannot provide sufficient inspiratory flow in DPI device for adequate lung delivery. • Do not blow into inhaler after dose is activated.
Budesonide/ Formoterol HFA MDI 80 mcg/4.5 mcg, 160 mcg/4.5 mcg	Safety and efficacy not established	2 puffs bid	• There have been no clinical trials in children < 4 years of age. • Currently approved for use in youths ≥ 12 years of age. Dose for children 5–12 years of age based on clinical trials using DPI with slightly different delivery characteristics (Pohunek et al. 2006; Tal et al. 2002; Zimmerman et al. 2004).

Table 11-10: Usual Dosages for Long-Term Control Medications in Children (Continued)

Medication / Dosage Form	0–4 Years of Age	5–11 Years of Age	Comments
Mometasone furoate/formoterol HFA 100 mcg/5 mcg, 200 mcg/5 mcg	Not indicated in children < 12 years of age	Not indicated in children < 12 years of age	Indicated for ≥ 12 years of age; 2 puffs bid
Cromolyn			
Cromolyn MDI 0.8 mg/puff	Safety and efficacy not established	2 puffs qid	• A 4- to 6-week trial may be needed to determine maximum benefit. • Dose by MDI may be inadequate to affect hyperresponsiveness. • One dose before exercise or allergen exposure provides effective prophylaxis for 1–2 hours. Not as effective as inhaled β₂-agonists for exercise-induced bronchoconstriction. • Once control is achieved, the frequency of dosing may be reduced.
Leukotriene Receptor Antagonists (LTRAs)			
Montelukast 4 mg or 5 mg chewable tablet 10 mg tablet (for ≥ 14 years of age) 4 mg granule packets	4 mg qhs (1–5 years of age)	5 mg qhs (6–14 years of age)	• Montelukast exhibits a flat dose-responsive curve. • No more efficacious than placebo in infants 6–24 months (van Adelsberg et al. 2005) • For zafirlukast, administration with meals decreases bioavailability; take at least 1 hour before or 2 hours after meals.
Zafirlukast 10 mg tablet	Safety and efficacy not established	10 mg bid (7–11 years of age)	• Monitor for signs and symptoms of hepatic dysfunction.
Methylxanthines			
Theophylline Liquids, sustained-release tablets, and capsules	Starting dose 10 mg/kg/day; usual maximum: • < 1 year of age: 0.2 (age in weeks) + 5 = mg/kg/day • ≥ 1 year of age: 16 mg/kg/day	Starting dose 10 mg/kg/day; usual maximum: 16 mg/kg/day	• Adjust dosage to achieve serum concentration of 5–15 mcg/mL at steady-state (at least 48 hours on same dosage). • Due to wide interpatient variability in theophylline metabolic clearance, routine serum theophylline level monitoring is essential. • For a discussion of factors that can affect theophylline levels, see Theophylline on page 11-20.

Dosages are provided for those products that have been approved by the U.S. Food and Drug Administration or have sufficient clinical trial safety and efficacy data in the appropriate age ranges to support their use.

DPI = dry powder inhaler
HFA = hydrofluoroalkane (inhaler propellant)
ICSs = inhaled corticosteroids
MDI = metered-dose inhaler

FIGURE SOURCES

Figure 11-1: MedStudy illustration
Figure 11-3: MedStudy illustration
Figure 11-5: MedStudy illustration
Figure 11-6: MedStudy illustration
Figure 11-7: JVinocur, CC BY-SA 3.0
Figure 11-8: MedStudy illustration
Figure 11-10: 韓濤孝志, CC BY-SA 3.0
Figure 11-11: Hellerhoff, CC BY-SA 3.0
Figure 11-12: James Heilman, MD, CC BY 3.0
Figure 11-13: Clinical Cases, CC BY-SA 2.5
Figure 11-14: CDC
Figure 11-15: Jerry Nick, MD
Figure 11-18: MedStudy illustration
The remaining figures are from the MedStudy archives.

Neurology

SECTION EDITOR

Daniel Freedman, DO
Assistant Professor, Department of Neurology
Dell Medical School
University of Texas at Austin
Austin, TX

MEDICAL EDITOR

Lynn Bullock, MD
Colorado Springs, CO

Table of Contents

CONGENITAL ANOMALIES OF THE CENTRAL NERVOUS SYSTEM (CNS) 12-1
NEURAL TUBE DEFECTS (NTDs) 12-1
Factors that Influence NTD Risk 12-2
Spina Bifida 12-2
Encephalocele...12-3
Anencephaly 12-4
SYRINGOMYELIA 12-4
HYDROCEPHALUS 12-4
What Is Hydrocephalus? 12-4
Anatomy Review 12-4
Noncommunicating vs. Communicating
Hydrocephalus...12-5
Basic Plumbing 12-5
Causes...12-5
Symptoms and Signs 12-5
Diagnosis...12-6
Treatment 12-6
CHIARI MALFORMATION................................12-6
KLIPPEL-FEIL SYNDROME 12-7
MIGRATIONAL ANOMALIES 12-7
POLYMICROGYRIA 12-7
LISSENCEPHALY 12-7
SCHIZENCEPHALY...12-7
HOLOPROSENCEPHALY 12-8
AGENESIS OF THE CORPUS CALLOSUM 12-8

CEREBRAL PALSY (CP) 12-9
DEFINITIONS 12-9
ETIOLOGY 12-9
The Bottom Line..12-9
Neonatal Encephalopathy 12-9
Asphyxia 12-9
Low Birth Weight...12-9
Congenital Malformations...........................12-9
Infection 12-9
TYPES OF CP...12-9
Spastic...12-9
Dyskinetic 12-10
Ataxic..12-10
Hypotonic..12-10
Mixed Forms of CP.......................................12-10
SEIZURES AND INTELLECTUAL DISABILITY 12-10
DIAGNOSIS OF CP...12-10
TREATMENT OF CP 12-10

CHOREA 12-10

CEREBROVASCULAR DISEASES 12-11
OVERVIEW 12-11
CLINICAL FEATURES......................................12-11
DIFFERENTIAL DIAGNOSIS 12-11
ISCHEMIC STROKE..12-12
Cardiac Disorders 12-12
Prothrombotic Disorders 12-12
Sickle Cell Disease 12-12
Moyamoya Disease 12-12
Cervicocephalic Arterial Dissection 12-12
CNS Vasculitis..12-13
Metabolic Etiologies 12-13
Neonatal Cerebral Infarction 12-13
Ischemic Stroke Treatment 12-13
HEMORRHAGIC STROKE 12-13
CEREBRAL VEIN THROMBOSIS 12-14

INJURY / TRAUMA TO THE CENTRAL AND PERIPHERAL NERVOUS SYSTEMS 12-15
OCCURRENCE...12-15
SCALP INJURIES..12-15
Lacerations 12-15
Hematomas..12-15
SKULL FRACTURES...12-15
PARENCHYMAL INJURIES...............................12-16
Cerebral Contusion 12-16
Diffuse Axonal Injury 12-16
Epidural Hematoma......................................12-16
Subdural Hematoma 12-17
Epidural vs. Subdural Hematoma on Imaging....12-17
SPINAL CORD INJURY....................................12-17
COMMON PERIPHERAL NERVE INJURIES 12-18
Brachial Plexus..12-18
Sciatic Nerve Injury 12-18

CRANIAL NERVE (CN) ABNORMALITIES 12-18
CN REVIEW 12-18
FACIAL NERVE PALSY 12-19
MARCUS GUNN PHENOMENON 12-19

SEIZURE DISORDERS 12-20
OCCURRENCE...12-20
GENERALIZED SEIZURES 12-20
Mechanism / Characteristics.......................12-20
Tonic-Clonic Seizures...................................12-20
Myoclonic Seizures 12-21
Juvenile Myoclonic Epilepsy (JME) 12-21
Absence Seizures...12-21
Atonic or Akinetic Seizures..........................12-22
FOCAL SEIZURES 12-22
Occurrence..12-22
Focal Aware Seizures 12-22
Focal Seizures with Impaired Awareness 12-22
Treatment 12-22
INFANTILE SPASMS 12-22
LENNOX-GASTAUT SYNDROME......................12-23
POSTTRAUMATIC SEIZURES 12-23
NEUROCUTANEOUS SYNDROMES 12-23
OTHER SEIZURE TYPES 12-24
Photosensitive Epilepsy...............................12-24
Rasmussen Syndrome 12-24
Gelastic Seizures 12-24
SEIZURE MANAGEMENT 12-24
DRUG THERAPY AND SIDE EFFECTS...............12-24
Valproate (Valproic Acid).............................12-25
Carbamazepine..12-25
Phenytoin..12-25
Ethosuximide...12-25
Phenobarbital..12-25
Oxcarbazepine...12-25
Lamotrigine..12-26
Levetiracetam..12-26
Topiramate...12-26
Vigabatrin..12-26
Therapeutic Drug Monitoring of Antiseizure
Medications (ASMs) 12-26
COMMON EPILEPSY QUESTIONS...................12-26
When Do You Stop Therapy? 12-26
What Are the Teratogenic Effects of
These Drugs?...12-26
What About Breastfeeding?.........................12-26

STATUS EPILEPTICUS.....................................12-26
NEONATAL SEIZURES 12-27
FEBRILE SEIZURES..12-28

HEADACHE...**12-29**
OVERVIEW 12-29
ETIOLOGIES..12-29
PRIMARY HEADACHE DISORDERS 12-29
   Tension Headaches 12-29
   Migraine Headaches..................................12-29
   Cluster Headaches.....................................12-31
   Chronic Headaches 12-31
ORGANIC HEADACHES...............................12-31
   Idiopathic Intracranial Hypertension (IIH) 12-31
CT / MRI EVALUATION OF HEADACHES 12-32

NEUROMUSCULAR DISEASES **12-32**
OVERVIEW 12-32
SPINAL MUSCULAR ATROPHY (SMA) 12-33
DUCHENNE MUSCULAR DYSTROPHY (DMD) ...12-33
BECKER MUSCULAR DYSTROPHY 12-34
MYASTHENIA GRAVIS..................................12-34
GUILLAIN-BARRÉ SYNDROME.......................12-34
CHARCOT-MARIE-TOOTH DISEASE 12-35
BOTULISM..12-35
TRANSVERSE MYELITIS................................12-35
MULTIPLE SCLEROSIS (MS)...........................12-36

ATAXIA **12-36**
OVERVIEW 12-36
ACUTE CEREBELLAR ATAXIA OF CHILDHOOD..12-37
FRIEDREICH ATAXIA....................................12-37
ATAXIA TELANGIECTASIA.............................12-38

OTHER DISEASES OF THE CENTRAL NERVOUS
  SYSTEM (CNS) **12-38**

THE MEDSTUDY HUB: YOUR GUIDELINES
  AND REVIEW ARTICLES RESOURCE.................**12-38**

FIGURE SOURCES **12-39**

CONGENITAL ANOMALIES OF THE CENTRAL NERVOUS SYSTEM (CNS)

PREVIEW | REVIEW

- What agent can be taken before pregnancy to reduce the risk of neural tube defects?
- Describe spina bifida occulta.
- What can a patch of hair located at the lower back indicate?
- What is the usual therapy for spina bifida occulta?
- Which meningoceles require immediate surgical intervention?
- What is the difference between a noncommunicating and a communicating hydrocephalus?
- In older children, what is the most common, nonspecific symptom of hydrocephalus?
- When increased intracranial pressure occurs due to hydrocephalus, which cranial nerves are likely affected?
- What are the appropriate studies to diagnose hydrocephalus in newborns, older infants, and children?
- What are the common symptoms of Chiari malformation Type I?
- Which type of Chiari malformation is most commonly diagnosed at birth?
- What is the treatment for asymptomatic Chiari malformation Type I?
- What is the Klippel-Feil syndrome triad?
- Differentiate between neuronal migrational anomalies.
- How is agenesis of the corpus callosum inherited?
- Use of what illicit drug by pregnant women has been noted to increase the risk of agenesis of the corpus callosum?

NEURAL TUBE DEFECTS (NTDs)

The embryonic neural tube eventually develops into the brain and spinal cord. The order of events for neural tube formation includes (Figure 12-1 and Figure 12-2):

- Neural plate forms day 17 postconception
- Invaginates day 18 to form a groove
- Neural tube formed by end of 3rd gestational week
- Cranial end (anterior neuropore) closes first by day 24
- Caudal end (posterior neuropore) closes by day 25

If there is a problem with the closure at any point, an NTD results. There is an approximate incidence of 1 NTD per 1,000 births (0.1%). If the cranial portion of the neural tube fails to close, anencephaly or encephalocele results. If the caudal portion fails to close, meningocele, myelomeningocele, or spina bifida occulta manifests. An **elevated maternal serum α-fetoprotein** level between 16 and 18 weeks of gestation identifies infants at high risk for NTDs.

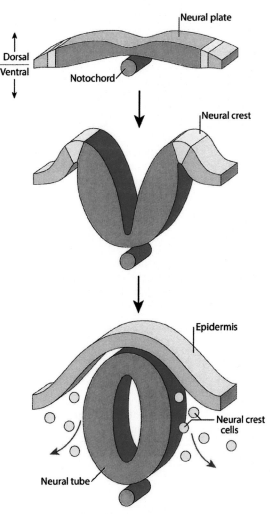

Figure 12-1: Neural tube basics

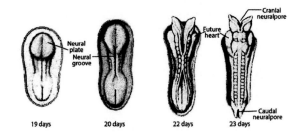

Figure 12-2: Neural tube formation

Factors that Influence NTD Risk

Periconceptional **folic acid** supplementation prevents ≥ 50% of NTDs, including spina bifida and anencephaly. The posterior neuropore closure occurs by day 28 of conception (even before pregnancy is confirmed). Hence, folic acid supplementation must start before conception and continue through the first 12 weeks of gestation. Most recommend that all females of childbearing potential take 0.4–0.8 mg of folic acid daily. Advise a woman with a previously affected child with spina bifida, or a woman on antiseizure therapy, to take 4 mg of folic acid daily, starting 1 month before attempting conception and continuing through the 1st trimester. Certain drugs increase the risk of an NTD—especially **valproic acid**, which increases the incidence of NTDs (from 0.1% to 1–2%). Thus, it is especially important to make sure that postpubertal females taking valproic acid or other antiseizure medications (ASMs; a.k.a. antiepileptic drugs, anticonvulsants) are prescribed supplemental folic acid.

Spina Bifida

Spina bifida is a congenital defect in which a portion of the neural tube does not form properly, resulting in a defect in the vertebrae. This occurs within 28 days postconception. There are 3 forms of spina bifida, based on the severity of the presentation:

1) Spina bifida occulta (mild effects, if any; most common [10–20% of population!])
2) Meningocele (moderate severity; rare)
3) Myelomeningocele (very severe; more common [1–2 per 1,000 births])

Symptoms vary, depending on the type of spina bifida and the level of the lesion, but can include motor and/or sensory defects in the lower body, loss of bladder and bowel control, scoliosis, hydrocephalus, learning disabilities, and hip, leg, and foot deformities.

Spina Bifida Occulta

Spina bifida occulta, also known as closed spinal dysraphism, is very common (~ 10% of population) and rarely causes any problems. It consists of a midline defect of the spinous processes without protrusion of the spinal cord or meninges. The underlying vertebral defect is "occult" because it is covered with skin and is not obvious. Some cases of spina bifida occulta have an overlying cutaneous marker—including patches of hair, lipoma, skin-color changes, or a dimple or dermal sinus in the midline of the lower back—indicating abnormal neuroectodermal differentiation and marking the underlying defect (Figure 12-3). Symptoms can include constipation, leg weakness, and neurogenic bladder. Some patients may be asymptomatic and are diagnosed only because of the overlying cutaneous abnormality. The vertebrae typically involved are L5 and S1. Although ultrasound of the spine is easier to obtain, MRI of the spine is the imaging modality of choice because its increased sensitivity provides a more complete evaluation of abnormalities (e.g., tethered cord). For symptomatic patients, surgical treatment is often warranted. Asymptomatic patients need close monitoring to evaluate for development of neurologic or urologic problems.

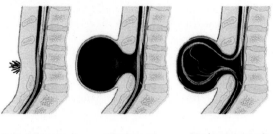

Spina bifida occulta   Meningocele   Myelomeningocele

Figure 12-3: Types of spina bifida

A dermoid sinus often occurs in association with spina bifida occulta; it presents as a small skin opening leading into a narrow duct below the skin. It sometimes has protruding hairs, a hairy patch, or a vascular nevus on the surface. Dermoid sinuses can occur in the lumbar region (indicating meningoceles) or in the occipital region (indicating encephaloceles). Sometimes, the sinuses pass through the dura and result in recurrent infections such as recurrent bacterial meningitis.

Occasionally, spina bifida occulta occurs with other spinal cord problems, including syringomyelia (see more under Syringomyelia on page 12-4), diastematomyelia (split spinal cord), or a tethered cord—a stretched spinal cord with an abnormally low terminal position, usually due to fatty or fibrous tissue adhering the filum to the bony canal (Figure 12-4).

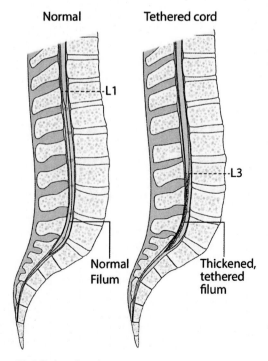

Normal   Tethered cord

L1

L3

Normal Filum

Thickened, tethered filum

Figure 12-4: Tethered cord

Meningocele

A meningocele is the rarest of the 3 types of spina bifida (1/5,000 births); it is a herniation of the meninges—but not the spinal cord—through a defect in the posterior vertebral arches (see Figure 12-3). Usually the spinal cord itself is in normal position. On transillumination along the vertebral column in a patient with a meningocele, you find a fluctuant midline mass, typically in the lower back. Most meningoceles are well covered with skin and pose no urgent problem.

You can delay surgery in children with completely normal neurologic examinations and complete full-thickness skin covering of the meningocele. This allows for full radiologic review for possible tethered spinal cord, lipomas, or diastematomyelia (splitting of the spinal cord due to complete or incomplete sagittal division by an osseous or fibrocartilaginous septum). Technically, the surgery is also easier when the child is larger and the skin is less fragile.

Children with cerebrospinal fluid (CSF) leaking from the meningocele or with incomplete skin covering need immediate surgical repair to prevent meningitis.

The meningocele sometimes occurs anteriorly and projects into the pelvis through a defect in the sacrum. If it increases in size, this protrusion can cause constipation and bladder dysfunction.

Myelomeningocele

Occurrence

Myelomeningocele (a.k.a. meningomyelocele; see Figure 12-3) is the most severe type of spina bifida and is usually just called spina bifida. It results when the posterior neuropore fails to close properly (see Figure 12-2 on page 12-1) and occurs in ~ 1/1,000 to 2/1,000 births. Risk increases with an increased number of affected siblings. With 1 previously affected child, the risk in subsequent siblings increases to 2–3%; with 2 previously affected children, the risk in subsequent siblings increases to 10%.

Clinical Findings

A myelomeningocele involves the nerve roots, spinal cord, meninges, vertebral bodies, and skin. It can be located anywhere along the neuraxis but most commonly affects the lumbosacral region.

The extent and degree of neurologic deficit depend on the level of the meningomyelocele. As a general rule, the lower the lesion is along the spine, the less severe are the neurologic deficits. Lesions located farther up the spine have progressively more severe lesions, with the most severe and extensive neurologic manifestations occurring in the lower thoracic region—above which neurologic manifestations decrease. Location in the upper thoracic or cervical areas actually cause minimal neurologic manifestations.

Example 1: A low, sacral-region myelomeningocele is likely to cause bowel and bladder incontinence and numbness of the perineal area but no motor dysfunction.

Example 2: With a high lumbar myelomeningocele, the infant is likely to have bowel and bladder incontinence as in example 1 but lower extremity flaccid paralysis with no deep tendon reflexes, no response to touch or pain in the lower extremities, and postural abnormalities (e.g., clubfeet, hip subluxation) due to lack of appropriate movement in utero.

Myelomeningoceles cause a downward displacement of the brain stem and cerebellar tonsils down into the spinal column—a condition known as **Chiari** malformation Type II (a.k.a. Arnold-Chiari malformation; see Chiari Malformation on page 12-6). This, in turn, causes an obstruction to normal CSF flow, resulting in **hydrocephalus** ~ 85% of the time. See Hydrocephalus on page 12-4.

Treatment

Treatment involves a multidisciplinary team, with the pediatrician frequently acting as coordinator. Delay in repair of the myelomeningocele for a few days is possible if there is no CSF leak. After repair, many infants require a ventricular shunt for hydrocephalus. Pay special attention to the genitourinary system and bladder catheterization because **neurogenic bladder** is common and easy to miss! For patients with lesions at L3 or lower, ~ 80% will walk, either with or without bracing of some type.

Prognosis for survival is generally good, with ~ 15% mortality rate; most deaths occur before 4 years of age. Approximately 75% of survivors have normal intelligence, but many, especially those with hydrocephalus, have learning difficulties.

Encephalocele

An encephalocele is a herniation of the brain, its coverings, or both, through a skull defect; 75% of the time, it is in the occipital region. Encephalocele occurs with an incidence of 1/10,000 births in the U.S. but still is less common than anencephaly in its total incidence due to the high number of spontaneous and elective abortions in anencephaly. Males and females are equally affected.

The herniated sac of materials can contain meninges, CSF, or dysplastic neural tissue. The size of the sac does not correlate with the amount of brain tissue present; transillumination gives a better assessment. If just meninges are in the sac, many do well, with normal development and no central nervous system (CNS) defects. Obviously, significant brain tissue involvement correlates with poor neurologic outcome.

Use MRI to determine the extent of brain tissue in the encephalocele. Confirm prenatal diagnosis by ultrasound and/or an elevated α-fetoprotein. However, if the defect is covered by skin/scalp, the level can be normal.

Treatment: prompt surgical removal of the sac and closure of the defect.

NEUROLOGY

Anencephaly

Anencephaly occurs when the anterior neural tube (neuropore) fails to close, which normally happens by 24 days postconception. See Figure 12-2 on page 12-1. Anencephaly results in both cerebral hemispheres being absent and usually no hypothalamus. The resulting hypoplastic pituitary gland causes failure of end-organ development–leading, for example, to adrenal insufficiency. Large parts of the cranium are sometimes missing, typically the occipital bones but also sometimes the frontal and parietal bones. Associated malformations of the face and eyes are common.

Anencephaly, which is an invariably lethal condition, occurs with an incidence of ~ 1/10,000 live births (~ 375/year; this rate underestimates the actual rate due to spontaneous and elective abortions). Girls are affected more often than boys and Caucasians more commonly than African Americans.

Suspect anencephaly prenatally if you find elevated maternal serum levels of α-fetoprotein—which is found in open neural tube defects. Fetal ultrasound confirms the diagnosis.

SYRINGOMYELIA

Syringomyelia is relatively rare and presents as a paracentral cavity, known as a syrinx, in the spinal cord. The syrinx can be localized or involve multiple segments, especially in the cervical spine. If the lesion extends up to the brainstem, it is known as syringobulbia. There is a strong association with **Chiari malformation Type I** (see Chiari Malformation). Syrinx is also seen fairly frequently in association with lumbar myelomeningocele (spina bifida).

Symptoms depend on where the syrinx is located. Wasting of the small muscles of the hand, sensory deficits of the arms, or absence of deep tendon reflexes in the upper extremities is commonly seen with cervical syrinx. Damage to crossing sensory fibers (lateral spinothalamic tracts) results in bilateral loss of pain and temperature sensation, leading to trophic ulcers of the fingertips. Respiratory problems in sleep are also common in those with syringobulbia.

MRI makes the diagnosis (Figure 12-5). Isolated clinically significant syringomyelia is treated with shunting. Posterior fossa decompression is helpful in those patients who also have Chiari malformation Type I.

HYDROCEPHALUS

What Is Hydrocephalus?

Hydrocephalus is defined as an excessive volume of intracranial CSF with ventricular dilatation. Hydrocephalus is not a specific disease but rather describes a diverse group of disorders that result from impaired circulation and CSF absorption or, rarely, from increased CSF production (which is usually caused by a choroid plexus papilloma).

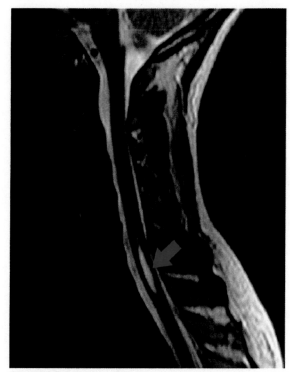

Figure 12-5: Syringomyelia

The absorption of CSF is inhibited by either mechanical or functional blockage of the flow of fluid along its typical path. With this blockage, there is increased pressure in and distention of the ventricular system.

Anatomy Review

The choroid plexus in each of the 4 ventricles produces CSF.

Let's review the normal anatomy of how the ventricular system connects (Figure 12-6):

Fluid moves through the ventricular system like the internal plumbing of a building. It starts in the choroid plexus of the paired lateral ventricles and then flows → paired foramina of Monro → single midline 3rd ventricle → aqueduct of Sylvius → midline 4th ventricle → 3 exit openings: paired lateral foramina of Luschka and a midline foramen of Magendie → spinal subarachnoid space → intracranial subarachnoid space over the cerebral convexities → absorbed into the venous sinuses via the arachnoid granulations.

In the spinal subarachnoid space, the fluid flows toward the head.

Most of the CSF is absorbed by the arachnoid granulations (over the convexities) and in the spinal subarachnoid space. Less fluid is absorbed by the ependyma of the ventricular system. In an adult, the normal CSF volume is 150 mL, with 25% within the ventricular system; in an infant, the total CSF volume is ~ 50 mL. In adults, CSF can be formed at a rate of 20 mL/hour. Thus, we know that CSF is turned over 3–4 times a day. The CSF production rate is less in infants and young children, but few studies have been done to adequately document the rate.

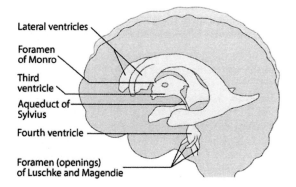

Figure 12-6: Ventricular system

Noncommunicating vs. Communicating Hydrocephalus

Hydrocephalus can be either noncommunicating or communicating. Noncommunicating (a.k.a. obstructive hydrocephalus) refers to the type of hydrocephalus in which the fluid in the ventricles does not communicate with CSF in the spinal subarachnoid spaces or in the basal cisterns.

Noncommunicating hydrocephalus is due to a blockage of CSF flow somewhere in the ventricular system, typically in the foramina of Monro, the aqueduct of Sylvius, or the 4th ventricle and its outlets. A communicating (nonobstructive) hydrocephalus is due to blockage of CSF absorption (occurs outside of the ventricular system), wherein the ventricular fluid communicates with the spinal subarachnoid space and basal cisterns. Typically, the "plumbing" is OK, but there is an issue with absorption at the arachnoid granulations due to scarring from various causes, such as bacterial meningitis and intracranial bleed. In the absence of shunting procedures, the complete blockage of CSF and the complete inability to absorb CSF are incompatible with life.

Basic Plumbing

Obstruction of CSF flow is the most common cause of hydrocephalus. Think of hydrocephalus as a plumbing problem and review the "plumbing" noted in Figure 12-6—because the ventricular system dilates and expands proximal to the blockage. For example: If one foramen of Monro is obstructed, the lateral ventricle on that side will dilate. If the aqueduct of Sylvius is obstructed, will the 4th ventricle be enlarged? No, because that ventricle is after the obstruction. In communicating hydrocephalus (remember this is outside the ventricular system), the entire ventricular system is dilated!

Causes

There are many causes of hydrocephalus. The most common causes of **communicating hydrocephalus** are meningitis and subarachnoid hemorrhage. Meningeal leukemia reduces resorption of CSF. Communicating

hydrocephalus can develop from an infection of the CNS—especially bacterial meningitis and viral meningoencephalitis. Hydrocephalus from intrauterine infection such as cytomegalovirus (CMV), rubella, toxoplasmosis, and syphilis is also possible. These infections cause an inflammatory reaction of the ependymal linings of the ventricular system and the meninges of the subarachnoid space, resulting in decreased ability to absorb CSF. Another important cause is posthemorrhagic hydrocephalus, arising mostly because of a perinatal intraventricular hemorrhage (IVH; especially in extremely low birth weight babies). The blood in the subarachnoid space can cause fibrosing arachnoiditis, leading to hydrocephalus.

Noncommunicating hydrocephalus results in the occlusion of the CSF pathway and can be either acquired (e.g., posterior fossa tumors) or congenital. An example is obstruction in the aqueduct of Sylvius, which can occur with congenital aqueductal stenosis. There is also an X-linked genetic form of congenital hydrocephalus due to aqueductal stenosis (seen in boys), most often due to mutations in the L1 cell adhesion molecule (*L1CAM*) gene. Additionally, there are numerous named syndromes that can occur with noncommunicating hydrocephalus.

The **Dandy-Walker malformation** consists of a posterior fossa cyst that is continuous with the 4th ventricle, partial or complete absence of the cerebellar vermis, and hydrocephalus. The **Chiari malformation Type I** occurs when the cerebellar tonsils are displaced down into the cervical spinal canal (below the foramen magnum), and the flow of spinal fluid can be impaired in the posterior fossa, leading to hydrocephalus. The **Chiari malformation Type II** is due to displacement of the 4th ventricle, the cerebellar vermis, and lower medulla below the level of the foramen magnum and is associated with hydrocephalus, spina bifida, and meningomyelocele. See Chiari Malformation on page 12-6 for additional information.

Acquired causes that obstruct the intraventricular pathway include brain tumors, intraventricular clots, abscess, and vein of Galen malformation.

Excessive CSF production is rare and often caused by functional choroid plexus papillomas and carcinomas. Surgical removal is often curative of the hydrocephalus; however, because of the highly vascular nature of the tumor, the associated bleeding causes communicating hydrocephalus as a result of poor absorption of the CSF into the venous system. If a tumor obstructs a foramen of Monro or the 4th ventricle, it also causes a noncommunicating hydrocephalus.

Symptoms and Signs

Many of the symptoms and signs are due to the underlying cause of the hydrocephalus. Much depends on the rate of CSF accumulation and the progression of the hydrocephalus. If accumulation is slow, few symptoms are initially apparent, whereas rapidly progressive ventricular dilatation produces symptoms quickly. Headaches are the most common, nonspecific symptom in older

© 2021 MedStudy

NEUROLOGY

children. Hydrocephalus often presents with early-morning headaches along with nausea and vomiting. Personality and behavior changes are typical. In infants and young children, excessive head growth is noticeable on serial examinations. Without treatment, frontal bossing with dilated scalp veins eventually develops. If either the midbrain or the brain stem is involved, lethargy and drowsiness can occur. Increased intracranial pressure can result in papilledema and extraocular muscle palsies, especially involving 2 cranial nerves: CN 3 and CN 6. Lower extremity spasticity, growth disturbances, early pubertal development, or fluid/electrolyte disorders also can occur.

In all ages, as hydrocephalus worsens, bradycardia, systemic hypertension, and altered respiratory rates occur if brainstem function is affected. This is known as **Cushing triad**. Setting-sun sign occurs when upward gaze is impaired due to pressure on the midbrain, and the sclera above the iris becomes visible.

Diagnosis

In the absence of symptoms, for infants, routine and serial head circumference measurements showing marked increase in size steer you toward the diagnosis.

For confirmation, ultrasound (through the open anterior fontanelle) typically is performed in newborns to avoid ionizing radiation, whereas CT or MRI is diagnostic in older infants and children (Figure 12-7). It is also possible to diagnose intrauterine hydrocephalus with fetal ultrasound or fetal MRI.

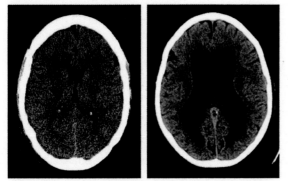

Figure 12-7: Axial CT—(left) normal vs. (right) hydrocephalus

Treatment

Treat the underlying condition if possible. Surgical therapy is the most effective treatment for hydrocephalus. Usually, you use a mechanical shunt system to circumvent the obstruction. (We're back to plumbing!) A catheter is placed in the lateral ventricle and connected by a 1-way valve system that opens when the pressure in the ventricle exceeds a predetermined baseline level. The valve typically is placed under the scalp, in the postauricular area. Then the distal end is placed in the right atrium (a ventriculoatrial shunt, which is used less commonly today) or into the peritoneal cavity (ventriculoperitoneal shunt,

which most often is used today). If the shunt becomes obstructed or nonfunctioning, hydrocephalus can recur and symptoms will reappear. Shunt revision is likely necessary.

Besides the mechanical problems, shunts can become infected and result in ventriculitis. Shunt infection can be subtle or severe. Children present with fever, seizures, and/or other hydrocephalus symptoms (as indicated previously) if the shunt malfunctions. The most common organism responsible (> 50% of occurrences) is *Staphylococcus epidermidis*, which usually responds only to vancomycin. Other organisms include *S. aureus* (~ 33%), *Escherichia coli* and other gram negatives, diphtheroids (*Propionibacterium acnes* and *Corynebacterium jeikeium*), and strep species.

CHIARI MALFORMATION

Chiari malformation is a hindbrain abnormality in which there is downward (caudal) displacement of the brainstem and cerebellum. (Do not confuse this with Budd-Chiari syndrome, which is a hepatic blood flow obstruction.)

There are 3 types, classified by the degree of displacement:

Type I: The cerebellar tonsils or vermis are pushed down below the level of the foramen magnum (Figure 12-8). Generally, > 0.5-cm displacement is considered significant. Type I has a strong association with **syringomyelia** (see Syringomyelia on page 12-4). Type I lesions can become symptomatic at any time between infancy and adulthood, but most are asymptomatic and are often found incidentally on imaging. Symptoms occur due to dysfunction of lower cranial nerves, the brainstem, and/or the spinal cord. These symptoms can include dysphagia, vertigo, sleep apnea, ataxia, headache, and neck pain. Spinal cord dysfunction often presents as weakness, spasticity of the extremities, sensory loss, and, occasionally, bowel and bladder dysfunction.

Central sleep apnea is a rare cause of sleep apnea in children and can be associated with neurosurgical abnormalities, such as Chiari malformation. Unlike obstructive sleep apnea, central sleep apnea involves pauses in ventilation due to an absence of respiratory effort, typically caused by an abnormality in the breathing center in the brainstem. The abnormality can be due to a primary lesion (e.g., congenital central hypoventilation syndrome) or secondary lesion (e.g., Chiari malformation, hydrocephalus, tumor, prior infection). The workup for central sleep apnea is polysomnography to make the initial diagnosis and then MRI to evaluate the etiology.

Arnold-Chiari malformation (a.k.a. Chiari malformation **Type II**): This malformation occurs when the 4th ventricle and lower medulla are pushed down below the level of the foramen magnum—more than with Type I. This blocks the outflow of CSF, and 85% of these patients have hydrocephalus. As previously mentioned, virtually all **myelomeningoceles** have a Chiari malformation Type II. As noted above, syringomyelia is sometimes seen in

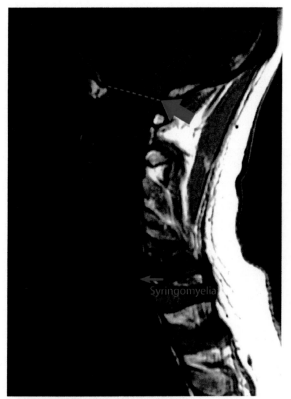

Figure 12-8: Syringomyelia with Chiari Type I

Type II, most often in the cervical or thoracic region but can occur at any level of the spinal cord.

Children with Chiari malformation Type II usually are diagnosed at birth, and the symptoms relate to lower cranial nerve dysfunction due to cervicomedullary kinking with the displacement. Patients with Chiari malformation Type II have symptoms like those in Type I, but they have the added burden/symptoms of the accompanying hydrocephalus and myelomeningocele. Other brain imaging findings, including variable cortex malformations, are seen with Type II.

Type III (rare): Herniation of the cerebellum occurs through a cervical spina bifida defect.

Treatment: For asymptomatic Chiari malformation Type I, no treatment is necessary. Surgery, including suboccipital decompressions with or without cervical laminectomies, is indicated for Types II and III and for symptomatic Type I malformations. Polysomnograms and swallowing studies are often used to evaluate the degree of brainstem dysfunction prior to surgery.

KLIPPEL-FEIL SYNDROME

Klippel-Feil syndrome is characterized by the congenital fusion of various vertebral segments. It can be inherited as an autosomal dominant (AD) or autosomal recessive (AR) trait. Clinically, it is characterized by a triad of short neck, low posterior hairline, and limited range of neck motion. See the Musculoskeletal & Sports Medicine section for more information.

MIGRATIONAL ANOMALIES

Migrational anomalies refer to abnormalities in which parts of the brain are completely missing, partially missing, or not developed.

POLYMICROGYRIA

Polymicrogyria is a common disorder of neuronal migration where multiple small gyri (or cerebral folds) are formed. It accounts for 20% of all cortical malformations. The cerebral cortex has an irregular, sometimes pebble-like appearance. There can be focal, bilateral, or diffuse areas of polymicrogyria. There are many causes, including intrauterine ischemic injuries, intrauterine infection-like CMV, genetic. It is seen in association with genetic syndromes (e.g., Aicardi syndrome, Zellweger spectrum syndrome) and other cortical malformations, such as schizencephaly. Symptoms vary widely depending on the severity and location of the malformation. Developmental delays, intellectual disability, spasticity, microcephaly, and early seizure onset are common in patients with diffuse malformations.

LISSENCEPHALY

Lissencephaly (a.k.a. agyria) is caused by defective neuronal migration during embryonic development, causing a smooth cerebral surface with thickened cortical mantle and a lack of cerebral folds (gyri) and grooves (sulci). Luckily, it is rare. Infants who survive to delivery have failure to thrive, microcephaly, marked developmental delay, and often severe epilepsy. Some are blind. Approximately 15% occur in association with **Miller-Dieker syndrome** (due to deletions of part of chromosome 17) and present with prominent forehead, bitemporal "hollowing," anteverted nostrils, prominent upper lip, and micrognathia. CT or MRI shows a smooth brain without sulci and with an abnormally thick cortical ribbon (gray matter along the outer edge of the brain; Figure 12-9).

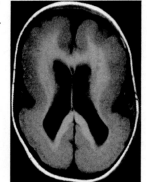

Figure 12-9: Lissencephaly

Treatment consists of antiseizure medications to manage the seizures and supportive care for feeding difficulties and impaired motor functioning. These patients die early, rarely reaching 10 years of age.

SCHIZENCEPHALY

Schizencephaly (literally translated as "split brain") is the occurrence of unilateral or bilateral clefts within the cerebral hemispheres. CT or MRI is diagnostic and shows the clefts (Figure 12-10 on page 12-8).

NEUROLOGY

Infants with bilateral clefts usually have severe epilepsy, microcephaly, severe intellectual disability, and spastic quadriparesis. Those with unilateral clefts often have focal epilepsy and hemiplegic cerebral palsy. Treatment consists of antiseizure medications and physical therapy.

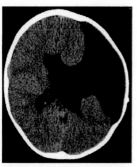

Figure 12-10: Schizencephaly

HOLOPROSENCEPHALY

Holoprosencephaly (literally translated as "whole forward brain") refers to a disorder in the development of the brain itself due to a defective cleavage of the prosencephalon (i.e., forebrain or cerebral cortex, basal ganglia, thalamus, hypothalamus). This results in failure of the formation of 2 cerebral hemispheres (Figure 12-11). It is most often seen with **trisomy 13**, but many different genetic mutations and teratogens also can cause it.

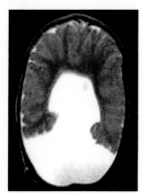

Figure 12-11: Holoprosencephaly

Facial anomalies are common, with flat midface and nasal bridge, hypotelorism, medial cleft lip, and single maxillary central incisor. Severe cases sometimes include cyclopia (single central eye) and/or cebocephaly (malformation of the head in which there is a defective or absent nose and close-set eyes; Figure 12-12). Cases with such severe facial abnormalities also typically have severe brain abnormalities, and most are stillborn or die shortly after birth. Many also have diabetes insipidus, panhypopituitarism, visual problems, and epilepsy.

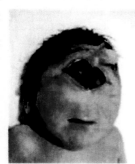

Figure 12-12: Holoprosencephaly facial abnormalities

AGENESIS OF THE CORPUS CALLOSUM

The corpus callosum is a white matter tract that connects the 2 cerebral hemispheres. Absence of the corpus callosum can be inherited as an X-linked dominant or recessive trait or as an AD trait. It can also be seen in conjunction with trisomy 8 and trisomy 18.

Agenesis of the corpus callosum occurs in a wide variety of disorders, with similar severity variations. Some are asymptomatic and have normal intelligence, while others have severe intellectual disability.

MRI shows widely separated frontal horns with the 3rd ventricle very high between the lateral ventricles. Figure 12-13 shows a close-up view of the absence of the corpus callosum, and Figure 12-14 shows a normal corpus callosum.

Figure 12-13: MRI with agenesis of corpus callosum

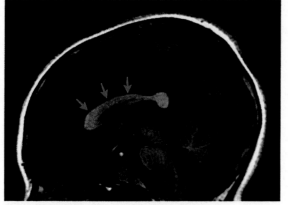

Figure 12-14: MRI with normal corpus callosum

Aicardi syndrome (a disorder of girls due to its X-linked dominant inheritance) is a triad of agenesis of the corpus callosum, infantile spasms, and chorioretinopathy (e.g., chorioretinal lacunae).

Maternal cocaine use has been linked to agenesis of the corpus callosum. Diagnosis is possible from about 20 weeks of gestation by ultrasound.

Treatment is supportive and based on the clinical manifestations.

NEUROLOGY

CEREBRAL PALSY (CP)

PREVIEW | REVIEW

- Describe cerebral palsy (CP). Does it also involve sensory abnormalities?
- True or false? Birth asphyxia is the major cause of CP.
- How does spastic CP present?
- Where is the brain abnormality located that causes dyskinetic CP?

DEFINITIONS

CP is a static encephalopathy and refers to a group of disorders that occur due to a CNS insult during early development that results in chronic, nonprogressive afflictions of movement, posture, and tone. The insult can occur before birth, during birth, or shortly after delivery. CP refers only to motor deficits but frequently is seen in conjunction with seizures, intellectual disability, and learning disabilities.

Static encephalopathy refers to a state of cerebral dysfunction after an insult of limited duration. The key word is static, which means the lesion does not progress and sometimes even improves with time.

The prevalence of CP is estimated to be ~ 2/1,000 to 4/1,000 live births.

There are 5 types of CP:

1) Spastic (70%)
2) Dyskinetic (15%)
3) Ataxic (5%)
4) Hypotonic (7%)
5) Mixed (3%)

ETIOLOGY

The Bottom Line

Know that causes of CP are multifactorial. None of the following factors, either alone or in combination, has been shown to account for more than a fraction of the total number of cases of CP.

Neonatal Encephalopathy

Brain injury can occur due to hypoxia, ischemia, asphyxia, and/or acidosis. Preterm infants often show weakness of the lower extremities (diplegic CP) because the hypoxic damage involves the periventricular white matter where the descending motor fibers for the lower extremities are closer to the ventricles. The radiologic correlate of this injury is **periventricular leukomalacia**. Diffuse hypoxic-ischemic encephalopathy (HIE) can lead to spastic quadriparesis (spastic weakness of all 4 limbs). HIE is usually diffuse but on occasion is focal.

Asphyxia

Most providers once believed that asphyxia during labor and delivery was a major cause of CP, but now it is considered the cause of a very small percentage of cases (< 10%). A tight nuchal cord resulting in birth asphyxia is the only factor that has a high clinical correlation with development of CP.

Low Birth Weight

There is an increased risk of CP in infants with low birth weight, but the correlation is not linear or absolute. About 10% of infants weighing < 1,500 g develop CP. Conversely, of all those born with CP, only 10–28% weigh < 1,500 g at birth. However, a large percentage of children with spastic diplegia have low birth weight. (Spastic diplegia is a type of CP that includes bilateral spasticity, with the lower extremities more severely affected.)

Studies have shown that magnesium sulfate given to women in preterm labor reduces the incidence and severity of cerebral palsy, but it does not affect mortality.

Congenital Malformations

The presence of congenital malformations increases the risk of CP. It is known that ~ 20% of children with CP have a major, noncerebral malformation (e.g., cardiac, renal anomalies). Plus, having a congenital malformation increases the risk of perinatal asphyxia, a known risk factor for CP.

Infection

Infection accounts for ~ 15% of the total spastic CP cases in children with normal birth weight. Infection generally results in a much higher incidence of spastic quadriplegia than the diplegic or hemiplegic subtypes. (Hemiplegia means paralysis affecting one half of the body, though "-plegia" is often used interchangeably with "-paresis" to mean weakness.)

TYPES OF CP

Spastic

Spastic CP presents with upper motor neuron signs, including weakness, hypertonicity with contractures, and hyperreflexia with clonus (rhythmic contractions and relaxations initiated by stretch reflex). Know: Because spastic CP involves upper motor neuron signs, abnormal reflexes, such as extensor plantar response, are typically seen in these children. The upper motor neuron effects of spastic CP can manifest as hemiplegia, quadriplegia, or spastic diplegia (legs with more spasticity than the arms). Spastic diplegia most commonly presents in preterm infants with a history of IVH and subsequent periventricular leukomalacia, hence its association with low birth weight infants.

NEUROLOGY

Dyskinetic

Dyskinetic CP refers to the presence of impaired, uncontrolled, and purposeless movements of the axial and/or appendicular muscles that disappear during sleep. The abnormal pathology is in the basal ganglia. The most common type of dyskinetic CP is **choreoathetosis**. Chorea is the rapid, jerky motion of proximal muscle groups of the arms, legs, and face (see Chorea), whereas athetosis refers to slow, irregular writhing movements of the arms, legs, face, neck, and torso. The movements become much more exaggerated with emotion or with intentionally trying to control the movements. Generally, these children have truncal twisting, facial grimacing, and extreme rigidity of their arms and legs, all of which are due to the continual, simultaneous contraction of the agonist and antagonist muscle groups.

Dystonic CP is the 2nd category of dyskinetic CP, and these patients tend to be more severely affected. An important cause of dystonic CP is neonatal bilirubin encephalopathy (kernicterus). Persistent neonatal reflexes are often present.

Ataxic

Ataxic CP occurs when there is damage to the cerebellum and its pathways. It results in dysfunction of coordination and gait. These children have a wide-based gait. They cannot perform finger-to-nose pointing well. An important cause of ataxic CP is malformation of the cerebellum. This type is rare and is a diagnosis of exclusion. It does not result in neurologic or functional decline, familial ataxia, foot deformities, or sensory deficits; if these do occur, another diagnosis is more likely.

Hypotonic

The child with hypotonic CP has decreased control of the head and often has floppy arms and legs. This is often noticed in early infancy by the head hanging down when being pulled into a sitting position (excessive head lag on pull-to-sit maneuver). Hypotonic CP typically is seen with damage to the cerebellum. Most children with hypotonic CP end up having other subtypes of CP. Intelligence is often normal, but some patients have difficulty attaining normal cognitive development and motor skills milestones.

Mixed Forms of CP

Mixed forms of CP occur usually with a combination of spasticity and choreoathetosis. Additionally, athetosis and ataxia can occur.

SEIZURES AND INTELLECTUAL DISABILITY

Seizures occur in ~ 25–40% of children with CP. Children with hemiplegia most commonly have seizures (due to their cortical damage), whereas those with the dyskinetic form have < 10% incidence of seizures, which is easily understood because most of their injury is to the basal ganglia. Most seizures begin between 2 and 6 years of age.

Intellectual disability occurs in 25–75% of children with CP. It is most common in mixed CP and least common in dyskinetic and ataxic types. It is important to anticipate visual, hearing, and speech disorders in these children.

DIAGNOSIS OF CP

Diagnosis depends on clinical findings. The key: serial examinations showing a static (nonprogressive) disorder. Note, though, that the spasticity and other abnormal tone or movement patterns often clinically evolve over time despite a static injury. If progression is occurring, you must consider a progressive encephalopathy, especially metabolic disorders. Ultrasound of the newborn and MRI of older children are helpful in delineating CNS involvement. An electroencephalogram (EEG) helps confirm clinically suspected seizures but does not differentiate among various etiologies.

TREATMENT OF CP

Rehabilitation with physical and occupational therapy is the cornerstone of treatment. Proper stretching and positioning to reduce contractures and assistance with improving gait are paramount. You can control seizures with a variety of agents (Table 12-1 on page 12-24).

Spasticity often is improved with the use of diazepam, dantrolene sodium, or baclofen. Intramuscular botulinum toxin has been used in areas of local spasticity to inhibit release of acetylcholine from motor nerve terminals. Surgery with selective dorsal rhizotomy—in which abnormal, afferent dorsal rootlets of L2 to S2 are cut—has been shown to be effective in children with lower extremity spasticity but normal upper extremity function.

CHOREA

PREVIEW | REVIEW
- Define chorea.
- What is the most common cause of chorea in children?

Chorea is a movement disorder characterized by the rapid, discrete, jerky motion of proximal muscle groups of the arms, legs, and face. Frequently, athetosis (which refers to slow, irregular, continuous writhing movements of the arms, legs, face, neck, and torso) also occurs in the same patient. The movements are present at rest, become much more exaggerated with emotion or with intentionally trying to control the movements, and disappear with sleep. Depending on the etiology, chorea is sometimes the only manifestation or can be accompanied by other symptoms.

Most cases of childhood chorea are acquired. The most common is **Sydenham chorea**, which is a clinical manifestation of acute rheumatic fever (ARF; see the Cardiology section). Sydenham chorea can sometimes be the only manifestation of ARF, but patients should still receive chronic antibiotics per the American Heart Association's 2009 acute streptococcal pharyngitis treatment guidelines. Systemic lupus erythematosus is another cause (see the Rheumatology section). Toxins and drugs (e.g., oral contraceptive pills, metoclopramide) can also cause chorea. There are many different causes of primary chorea, and it can be transmitted by AD, AR, or X-linked inheritance.

Determining the etiology of chorea requires a thorough history (including age of onset, progression, and recent infections or toxin exposure), family history, and physical exam. Acute or subacute onset points to an infectious, autoimmune, or toxic cause, whereas a chronic and progressive presentation typically means a neurodegenerative etiology. Lab tests for antideoxyribonuclease B and antistreptolysin O titers are useful to screen for recent group A strep infection. Antinuclear antibodies and antiphospholipid antibodies are helpful in screening for autoimmune etiologies. If a hereditary cause is suspected, genetic testing is available for many primary causes.

Secondary chorea usually resolves with treatment of the underlying cause, whereas there is no effective treatment for primary chorea. Regardless of the cause, dopamine receptor blockers can control the severity of the choreiform movements.

CEREBROVASCULAR DISEASES

PREVIEW | REVIEW

- What is a common presentation for stroke in a child < 2 years of age?
- What central nervous system event can occur in children with congenital heart disease?
- The presence of antiphospholipid antibody is a risk factor for what event?
- True or false? Children with sickle cell disease can have MRI evidence of prior stroke without symptoms.
- Describe Moyamoya disease.
- What is the most common cause of central nervous system vasculitis?
- Which virus has been shown to be a risk factor for causing infarcts in the basal ganglia or internal capsule?
- In which cerebral artery location do most neonatal infarcts occur? Are these usually embolic or thrombotic in character?
- What is the most common presentation for an infant with neonatal cerebral infarction?

- What is the most common cause of intracranial bleed?
- Saccular aneurysms are associated with which diseases?
- In neonates, how do most cerebral vascular thrombotic events present? In older children?

OVERVIEW

The incidence of childhood stroke ranges from 3/100,000 to 25/100,000 in various population-based studies.

About 50% of these are **ischemic strokes**: 75% of ischemic strokes are arterial, and 25% are a result of sinovenous thrombosis. Within the pediatric age group, about 1/3 of the ischemic strokes occur in neonates. Stroke is nearly 10× more common in neonates overall compared with infants and children. It occurs most frequently in preterm infants (approximately 1 in 140 live births).

Hemorrhagic stroke occurs as frequently as ischemic stroke; hemorrhagic strokes can occur from bleeding into ischemic strokes or from rupture of intracranial arteries. Strokes in children usually are due to congenital or genetic factors—not due to atherosclerosis, which is the most common cause in adults.

CLINICAL FEATURES

Clinical presentation of cerebrovascular diseases in children varies, depending on the age of the child:

- Strokes in utero can present as early-onset hand dominance (at < 1 year of age) or hemiplegic CP.
- Perinatal strokes most commonly present acutely with focal neonatal seizures and mental status changes; the focal neurologic deficits do not show up for weeks to months.
- Most cerebral infarctions in newborns occur in full-term infants, whereas hemorrhage—particularly IVH—is more common in preterm infants.
- In children < 2 years of age, most strokes present with seizures and hemiparesis.
- Older children present with an acute focal neurologic deficit, with or without seizures.

DIFFERENTIAL DIAGNOSIS

Acute hemiplegia is often due to stroke, but 3 other diagnoses need to be considered in children:

1) **Transient postictal hemiparesis** (Todd paresis) generally lasts < 24 hours but can last for several days and sometimes has EEG activity consistent with seizures or postictal state (focal EEG slowing). It is a neuronal exhaustion phenomenon. By definition, MRI never shows an acute infarction.

2) **Complex migraine** can occur with a severe headache, with focal deficits lasting hours—even up to 1 week. Family history is usually positive for hemiplegic migraine. MRI is negative for infarction.

3) **Alternating hemiplegia of childhood** is a rare disorder, generally beginning in children < 2 years of age. The hemiplegia lasts for minutes to hours, with weakness fluctuating between the 2 sides for each attack. Seizures are common but do not occur during the period of weakness. Most children have progressive neurologic or developmental deterioration. The etiology is genetic.

ISCHEMIC STROKE

Cardiac Disorders

Congenital heart disease complications cause ~ 25% of pediatric ischemic strokes. Most are due to embolic phenomena from the heart or shunted through the heart. Suspect embolic disease if multiple ("showering") infarcts are found on MRI/CT.

Emboli from endocarditis can be infectious or noninfectious. Approximately 50% of strokes in children occur within 3 days of catheterization or cardiac surgery. Strokes occur in 5–10% of children who undergo the Fontan procedure and in 5% with valve replacement surgery without anticoagulation. Tetralogy of Fallot and transposition of the great vessels also predispose children to stroke.

Prothrombotic Disorders

Abnormality in prothrombotic factors increasingly is recognized as an important cause of pediatric strokes, although its impact as a single primary risk factor is unknown. One of the more frequent disorders in this group is an acquired **antiphospholipid antibody**, including anticardiolipin antibody and lupus anticoagulant. Acquired deficiencies also can occur due to oral contraceptives, nephrotic syndrome, and liver disease.

Activated protein C (APC) resistance (Factor 5 Leiden) is the most common inheritable cause of venous thrombosis; in older children, it also is known to cause arterial thrombosis. APC resistance can cause strokes and hemiplegic CP in neonates. For the hereditary deficiencies, APC resistance is more frequent than deficiencies of protein C, protein S, or antithrombin, which are some of the other causes of ischemic stroke. Test for a hypercoagulable disorder in all children with ischemic stroke who do not have sickle cell disease. Thrombophilia evaluation in the acute stroke setting may not produce accurate test results for protein and homocysteine levels; therefore, these tests should be repeated during follow-up care.

Sickle Cell Disease

Sickle cell disease is responsible for ~ 10% of pediatric strokes, which include ischemic strokes, hemorrhagic strokes, or transient ischemic attacks (TIAs). As a single risk factor, sickle cell disease is the most common cause of strokes in children. In infants and younger children with sickle cell disease, ischemic stroke is more likely, whereas hemorrhagic stroke is more prevalent in adults with the disease. Genotype SS has the highest incidence of stroke among the sickle hemoglobinopathies.

Children 2–5 years of age with sickle cell disease have the highest incidence of stroke, but stroke is rare in a sickle cell patient < 2 years of age. Higher concentrations of hemoglobin F do not lower the risk of stroke.

Approximately 20% of children with sickle cell disease have MRI/CT evidence of stroke but no recognizable clinical symptoms ("silent strokes"). Ischemic strokes are rarely fatal, but hemorrhagic strokes have a mortality rate of > 25%. Recurrence of strokes is very common within the first 3 years. Follow chronic transfusion protocols to prevent recurrences. Use transcranial Doppler ultrasound to predict which children with sickle cell disease are at increased risk (mean blood flow > 200 cm/second in either the internal carotid or middle cerebral artery). As in any sickle cell–related vasoocclusive emergency, the acute treatment is exchange transfusion.

Moyamoya Disease

Moyamoya disease is a chronic, occlusive, cerebrovascular disease that can be a primary disease or secondary to sickle cell disease, neurofibromatosis Type 1, trisomy 21, and cranial irradiation. Moyamoya is a Japanese term meaning "puff of smoke," which refers to the extensive collateral vessels resulting from prior occlusions of arteries around the circle of Willis, as seen on cerebral angiography (Figure 12-15). CT or MRI without angiography may show evidence of prior strokes. Treatment consists of revascularization surgery.

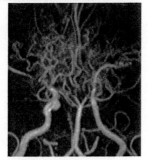

Figure 12-15: Moyamoya

Cervicocephalic Arterial Dissection

Cervicocephalic arterial dissection occurs in 2.5/100,000 children each year. The most commonly affected arteries are the internal carotid arteries. Spontaneous dissections occur, such as in patients with connective tissue disorders, but a common cause is secondary to trauma from neck movements or deceleration injuries. In children, look for focal cerebral symptoms with ipsilateral headache, neck, or eye pain. With internal carotid artery dissection, Horner syndrome (miosis, ptosis, and anhidrosis) and transient monocular blindness are seen more commonly in adults than children.

Dissections of the internal carotid or vertebral arteries are best diagnosed with cerebral angiography. Magnetic resonance angiography (MRA) can be useful for cervicocephalic arterial dissection. Treatment is anticoagulation for extracranial dissection; however, for intracranial vessel dissections, anticoagulation is contraindicated because of the increased risk of subarachnoid hemorrhage.

CNS Vasculitis

Bacterial meningitis is the most common cause of CNS vasculitis. Infarction is found in ~ 25% of children with bacterial meningitis and is typically a venous infarct secondary to retrograde thrombophlebitis. Tuberculosis can cause arterial infarcts.

Chickenpox has been shown to be a risk factor for childhood stroke, with cases occurring in children < 10 years of age. The infarcts affect the basal ganglia or internal capsule and usually occur within 9 months of the chickenpox rash. Some retrospective studies indicate that up to 1/3 of children 2–10 years of age with ischemic stroke had postvaricella vasculopathy occurring weeks to months after uncomplicated varicella infection.

CNS lupus has a 6% incidence of CNS vasculitis in adults but < 2% in children. **Inflammatory bowel disease** has about a 3% risk of CNS vasculitis in children.

Childhood primary angiitis of the CNS causes inflammation of the blood vessels in the brain. Etiology is unknown but presents with arterial stroke. More information on childhood primary angiitis of the CNS is found in the Rheumatology section.

Takayasu arteritis is rare in the U.S., but 5–10% of affected Asian females develop strokes. Immunosuppression is the treatment of choice. See the Rheumatology section for more information.

Cocaine and **diet pill use** increase the risk of vasculopathy and vasospasm.

Metabolic Etiologies

Metabolic etiology of stroke is rare in children but can be due to Fabry disease and homocystinuria, both of which can cause vascular occlusion. **Fabry disease** is caused by deficiency of α-galactosidase, which creates an accumulation of ceramide trihexoside in vascular endothelium that, in turn, leads to arterial narrowing, ischemia, and eventual infarction. **Homocystinuria** causes injury to vascular endothelium, which leads to thrombus formation.

Measure serum homocysteine levels in all children with ischemic stroke because data shows that homocysteine levels in these patients are elevated for a large variety of genetic and environmental etiologies. These etiologies include vitamin deficiencies; renal disease; drugs, such as phenytoin and theophylline; cigarettes; and hypothyroidism.

MELAS is a syndrome of **m**itochondrial **e**ncephalopathy, **l**actic **a**cidosis, and **s**troke-like episodes. MELAS typically presents in children 5–15 years of age. More on metabolic causes of stroke can be found in the Metabolic Disorders section.

Neonatal Cerebral Infarction

Neonatal cerebral infarction has an increased prevalence compared with older children. Most neonatal cerebral infarctions occur in full-term infants, but some preterm infants also can be affected. It is estimated to occur in 1/4,000 infants.

Most neonatal cerebral infarctions are embolic and occur in the distribution of the middle cerebral artery. The placenta appears to be the source for some of these emboli. Other causes include prothrombotic disorders (see Ischemic Stroke) and acute, severe hypertension.

The most common presentation for infants with neonatal cerebral infarction is **focal seizures** within the first 3–4 days of life.

MRI is the best diagnostic study for strokes in neonates. Early on, there are usually only subtle changes, but over time the infarct becomes more apparent on MRI. MRI with diffusion-weighted imaging picks up the lesion earlier than regular MRI and helps date the stroke.

Aim management at treating any confounding, underlying causes, and treat seizures with antiseizure medications. Monitor closely for motor and speech issues throughout the first few years of life.

Ischemic Stroke Treatment

Acute treatment of ischemic stroke remains controversial because pediatric trial data for recanalization therapies (e.g., intravenous tissue-type plasminogen activator [tPA], endovascular thrombectomy) is lacking. Based in part on the success of thrombectomy in highly selected adult ischemic stroke patients, the American Stroke Association's 2019 guideline states it is reasonable to consider limiting thrombectomy acute intervention for pediatric patients meeting these criteria:

- Persistent disabling symptoms (pediatric NIH Stroke Scale score ≥ 6)
- Imaging confirmed large vessel occlusion confirmed by radiographic imaging
- "Larger children" due to concerns about catheter and vessel size
- Management supported by neurologists experienced in treating children with stroke
- Intervention performed by an endovascular surgeon experienced in treating children and adult stroke patients

HEMORRHAGIC STROKE

Hemorrhagic stroke in children is as prevalent as ischemic stroke. Bleeding of normal vessels occurs due to head trauma or coagulopathies; abnormal vessels bleed because of vascular malformations or aneurysms. Bleeding can be subarachnoid, intraparenchymal, or both.

Subarachnoid hemorrhage presents with "the worst headache of my life," followed by findings of meningeal irritation and increased intracranial pressure. Children with **intraparenchymal bleeding** present with headache, focal neurologic findings, seizures, and mental status changes. Large bleeds frequently cause coma. Neonates can present with seizures, refusal to feed, lethargy, and vomiting.

Acute bleeds are easily detected on a noncontrast CT scan. Head trauma is the most common cause of intracranial bleeding and is very typical in abusive head trauma (AHT; formerly "shaken baby" syndrome). Coagulopathies are the next most common cause of bleeding; however, trauma is generally a precipitating event—although the trauma can be very minor.

Vascular malformations are arteriovenous, cavernous, venous angiomas, or capillary telangiectasias.

Arteriovenous malformations (AVMs) are abnormal collections of arteries and veins without the normal intervening capillary bed. Smaller AVMs appear with focal seizures, whereas those with large AVMs present with headache, focal neurologic findings, intracranial bruit, and seizures. AVMs require embolization or surgical removal and, if large enough, can be fatal with rupture.

Cavernous malformations are collections of thin-walled vessels with only a single layer of endothelium—and nothing else. Recurrent bleeding is typical, which can cause seizures, but the lesions are rarely life-threatening. Enhanced MRI can detect these quite easily.

Venous angiomas (a.k.a. developmental venous anomaly) are the most common vascular malformation. Most children with these malformations are asymptomatic, but some present with seizures. CT or MRI shows the lesions. Even when symptomatic, venous angiomas rarely require surgery, and in fact, surgery sometimes increases the severity and frequency of symptoms.

Capillary telangiectasias typically are asymptomatic and therefore incidental findings on neuroimaging performed for other reasons. These lesions consist of small capillaries that are dilated and contain no smooth muscle or elastic fibers. Treatment is not warranted.

Saccular aneurysms typically are asymptomatic and less common than AVMs. They are seen in conjunction with coarctation of the aorta, polycystic kidneys, Ehlers-Danlos syndrome, and Marfan syndrome. Usually, the aneurysms arise from the internal carotid artery or anterior cerebral artery. These aneurysms, although generally asymptomatic, can cause acute subarachnoid hemorrhage, which results in the "worst-headache-of-my-life" scenario described above. If subarachnoid hemorrhage occurs, surgery is the treatment of choice.

CEREBRAL VEIN THROMBOSIS

Cerebral vein thrombosis is an important cause of stroke in infants and children. Its incidence is estimated to be 0.67/100,000 children a year. Neonates are affected most commonly. Symptoms depend on which vessel is occluded.

Superior sagittal sinus thrombosis leads to obstruction of cerebrospinal fluid (CSF) absorption and causes increased intracranial pressure (ICP). (See Noncommunicating vs. Communicating Hydrocephalus on page 12-5.) The cortical veins from the superior surface of each cerebral hemisphere drain into the superior sagittal sinus. Patients present with headache, papilledema, nausea, vomiting, and cranial nerve (CN) 6 palsy.

The superior sagittal sinus empties into the right lateral sinus. In the preantibiotic era, **right lateral sinus thrombosis** was very common with otitis media and mastoiditis. Cranial nerves frequently were affected. It is still one of the causes of pseudotumor cerebri, characterized by papilledema and CN 6 palsy, which result from increased intracranial pressure. For more details, see Idiopathic Intracranial Hypertension (IIH) on page 12-31).

Cavernous sinuses drain blood from the orbits, middle cerebral veins, and the anterior undersurface of the brain; the cavernous sinuses then drain into the internal jugular veins via the petrosal sinuses. **Thrombosis of the cavernous sinuses** results in proptosis, chemosis, and uni- or bilateral ophthalmoplegia. Thrombosis of the cavernous sinuses occurs most commonly due to infection of the paranasal sinuses, face, nose, or mouth.

In neonates with any of these cerebral venous thromboses, seizures are the most common clinical presentation. For older children, headache and vomiting are most frequent symptoms.

Risk factors for cerebral venous thrombosis typically include prothrombotic conditions (e.g., estrogen-containing contraception in teenagers), infection, and dehydration (especially in neonates and infants).

CT scan is normal initially in 40% of patients. Contrast is usually required; "the empty delta sign" occurs after contrast is injected and presents as a filling defect of the superior sagittal sinus. MRI with magnetic resonance venography (MRV) is the best method of diagnosis. If MRV is not readily available, CT venogram (CTV) also is a sensitive diagnostic tool.

Management is controversial. In adults, data suggests anticoagulation is beneficial even in hemorrhagic lesions. Data on children is minimal but appears to parallel the adult data. Neurologic morbidity can be seen in up to 30–60% of patients with cerebral vein thrombosis, with mortality seen in ~ 10% of affected children. Pursue aggressive treatment of underlying dehydration and infection in all patients, regardless of age. Management of increased ICP and monitoring for vision loss are recommended. In rare situations, endovascular thrombolysis or thrombectomy can be considered.

INJURY / TRAUMA TO THE CENTRAL AND PERIPHERAL NERVOUS SYSTEMS

PREVIEW | REVIEW

- In what area(s) of the skull does a fracture most commonly occur in children?
- What type of fracture is indicated by bilateral "raccoon eyes"?
- When would you do a CT scan with bone windows instead of plain skull x-rays in a child < 3 years of age with suspected skull fracture?
- How are most uncomplicated linear skull fractures managed?
- When do pond fractures of the skull require surgical elevation?
- What type of fracture is indicated by otorrhea and rhinorrhea?
- Which type of basilar skull fracture requires observation in the hospital?
- Under what conditions are you most likely to see diffuse axonal injury?
- Describe an epidural hematoma.
- What is the classic presentation of a child with epidural hematoma?
- How does early herniation present in a child with epidural hematoma?
- What are the most common causes of spinal injury in children?
- What is the most common cause of peripheral nerve injury in an infant?
- How does Erb palsy (a.k.a. Erb paralysis, Duchenne-Erb palsy) present?
- How does Déjerine-Klumpke palsy present?

OCCURRENCE

Accidents account for 40% of all pediatric deaths, making them the leading cause of pediatric mortality overall. Head injury makes up a good proportion of these accidents. The incidence of head trauma in children 0–19 years of age is 2/1,000, with 1/10,000 of those dying from their head trauma. Boys have an incidence 2× that of girls. In children < 4 years old, falls rank as the leading cause of head injury. In older children, motor vehicle accidents and sports-related injuries are the leading causes of head injury.

SCALP INJURIES

Lacerations

Scalp lacerations lead to marked and alarming bleeding because of the rich anastomotic blood supply of the scalp as well as the limited ability of the vessels to constrict in the dense connective tissue layer. Large lacerations heal very well, and infection is rare. Primary closure is best, but if conditions prevent immediate intervention, you can delay it for 8–12 hours without increasing the risk of infection.

Hematomas

Hematomas of the scalp are common in children, but they are usually not very large and absorb within 2–3 days. If a galeal laceration occurs, it often permits bleeding from above to permeate the subgaleal connective tissue layer and results in a quick-forming, extensive swelling that is of enormous size. The swelling occurs because there is no limiting membrane to prevent its spread. Close galeal lacerations > 0.5 cm with sutures. Cephalohematomas occur in newborns and some older children; these are discussed in the Neonatology section.

SKULL FRACTURES

Skull fractures vary in size, shape, and location. They can occur as isolated events but, unfortunately, present more commonly with underlying cerebral injury. More information on skull fractures is found in the Emergency Medicine & Maltreatment Syndromes section.

> 80% of skull fractures are **simple linear** or **diastatic** fractures. Linear fractures most commonly involve the parietal area while diastatic fractures typically involve the lambdoid suture.

Children < 1 year of age have craniums that are not well calcified; thus, bones can be displaced inward without an actual break and produce what is known as a "**ping-pong**" or "pond" fracture.

Depressed skull fractures often have corresponding underlying cerebral injury. They result from significant force over a small area. The depressed portion of bone can penetrate underlying brain tissue. This can also cause intracranial hemorrhage. Sometimes a bony defect is felt on palpation of affected area. This type of skull fracture carries a higher incidence of seizures and infection.

Basilar skull fractures cause separation of the occipital bone, leading to direct brain injury, disruption of venous structures, and significant bleeding in the posterior fossa. The prognosis is generally poor, with significant risk of permanent sequelae. Manifestations that suggest a basilar skull fracture include:

- Bilateral orbital ecchymoses ("raccoon eyes" or black eyes)
- Posterior auricular ecchymoses (Battle sign)
- Tympanic membrane discoloration if the petrous bone of the middle fossa is involved
- Cerebrospinal fluid (CSF) otorrhea and rhinorrhea
- Air collected in the intracranial cavity (pneumocephalus) implies fractures through the paranasal sinuses

NEUROLOGY

In all children < 3 years of age, skull x-rays are usually done for all but trivial head injury. If you suspect an underlying intracranial lesion, order a CT scan with bone windows.

Suspect underlying lesions in any of the following:

- Depressed or comminuted skull fracture
- Loss of consciousness lasting more than a few seconds
- Altered mental status or irritability
- Bulging fontanelle
- Focal neurologic signs or deteriorating neurologic condition
- Recurrent vomiting
- Nonimpact seizures in children < 6 months of age

Use skeletal surveys and cervical spinal films in trauma situations or if abuse is suspected, and make sure to immobilize the cervical spine to protect the spinal cord from injury until the spine is stable.

Children who have partially recovered by the time they make it to the emergency department typically have few signs on examination. Most of these patients can be managed at home if observed 6–8 hours after injury, which is the time interval for most acute intracranial bleeds to develop.

Simple linear fractures do not require specific therapy; advise parents not to restrict the child's normal activities. Repeat skull x-ray in 3 months to show union. Most fractures heal within 6–12 months. A late complication of linear fracture is a leptomeningeal cyst, which results from dural laceration, especially in the parietal area. The cyst can result in projection of the arachnoid membrane into the fracture site, with brain herniation causing bone erosion of the overlying skull over months or years. This complication is suggested by late onset of focal seizures, focal neurologic signs, and occasionally a visible and palpable skull deformity. Skull x-rays are diagnostic, showing bony erosion over a prior fracture site. Nearly 50% occur in children < 1 year of age and 90% occur in children < 3 years of age.

Ping-pong or pond fractures do not typically require surgical elevation unless they are depressed > 0.5 cm. Observe most pond fractures regularly for 3 months.

Consult neurosurgery for depressed skull fractures to determine if surgical elevation is needed. Mild depressed fractures without intracranial hematoma can be observed.

Hospital observation is needed for basilar skull fractures that result in otorrhea or rhinorrhea. Plugging or irrigating the ear or nose is contraindicated. Antibiotics are not recommended prophylactically. CSF commonly stops draining within 7 days. If it does not, consider closed-system spinal fluid drainage from the lumbar subarachnoid space. If this fails, surgery may be indicated. Watch for signs of CNS infection because risk of meningitis is high if the CSF leak continues after 7 days. Suppress coughing and sneezing because the associated Valsalva maneuver often worsens CSF leaks.

PARENCHYMAL INJURIES

Cerebral Contusion

Cerebral contusions, usually located on the surface, are ecchymoses of the brain. Contusions can result in focal neurologic findings. Contusions can occur directly under the blunt trauma (**coup**) or can be distant from the site of impact, as in an acceleration-deceleration injury (**contrecoup**). For example, a blow to the occiput can cause frontal or temporal lobe injury, depending on the direction of the force.

Order CT to make the diagnosis. Then observe with frequent neurologic assessments.

Treatment is supportive and depends on the severity of swelling. Sometimes medications to reduce cerebral swelling and/or surgical intervention are needed.

Diffuse Axonal Injury

Diffuse axonal injury is seen most commonly with acceleration-deceleration injuries from motor vehicle accidents. The gray matter and white matter have different densities, so force results in different acceleration and deceleration for each tissue, causing shearing of the white matter, typically at the gray-white matter junction. In the absence of brain contusion, axonal injury is frequently responsible for prolonged alteration in alertness level and cognitive function. Use MRI to confirm axonal injury.

Treatment is supportive and, if needed, includes medications to reduce swelling in the brain. Surgery is not indicated in diffuse axonal injury.

Epidural Hematoma

Epidural hematoma is a hemorrhage that occurs between the skull and the dura and is confined by the suture lines because the dura is adhered to the skull (Figure 12-16). On a CT scan, the hematoma is biconvex or lentiform (Figure 12-17).

It most commonly occurs with 1 of the following:

- Temporal bone fracture, which causes a tear of the middle meningeal artery
- Tear in the bridging veins or dural sinuses (more common in children)

The scenario is classic. Whether in your practice or on an exam, look out for a child who is unconscious by trauma, regains consciousness over several hours (i.e., has a lucid interval), and then worsens. Epidural hematomas of arterial origin can grow rapidly—and acutely raise intracranial pressure, which results in hypertension, bradycardia, and a progressive decline in mental status. Focal seizures may occur. Because the pressure increase is so rapid—and frequently is asymmetric in character—the cerebral contents shift away from the lesion, possibly resulting in herniation of the tip of the temporal lobe and compression of the midbrain with resulting death. Early herniation is characterized by a dilated pupil ipsilateral to the hematoma,

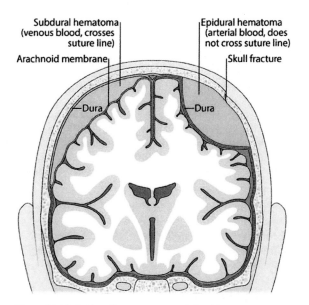

Figure 12-16: Epidural hematoma vs. subdural hematoma

progressing to a complete CN 3 palsy and a contralateral hemiplegia (opposite to the lesion). In late stages, both pupils become fixed and dilated, respiration is slow and irregular, and hypotension and tachycardia develop.

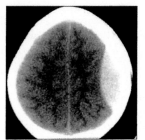

Figure 12-17: Epidural hematoma

Treatment is surgical intervention. Untreated, mortality is ~ 100%.

Subdural Hematoma

Subdural hematomas result from bleeding between the dura and the arachnoid membrane (Figure 12-16). They are common in children < 1 year of age. On neuroimaging, a subdural hematoma is concavoconvex or crescent-shaped and is not confined by the suture lines (Figure 12-18). Acute presentation occurs within 3 days of the trauma; subacute, from 3 days to nearly 3 weeks later; and chronic, > 3 weeks afterward. Acute lesions are usually arterial and require emergent care. Abusive head trauma (formerly "shaken baby" syndrome) is the most common cause of chronic subdural hematomas in infants and toddlers.

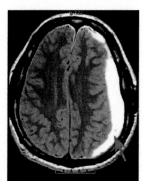

Figure 12-18: Subdural hematoma

External signs of trauma are frequently missing if the trauma is due to shaking. Retinal hemorrhages are a strong indication of child abuse. Children may present with lethargy, irritability, and vomiting. Failure to thrive also may occur in abused children. In severe cases, coma, seizures, and focal neurologic signs can be present. Note: Subdural empyema, which is a complication of bacterial meningitis, also presents as a chronic subdural collection.

Seek neurosurgical consultation. Necessity of neurosurgical intervention depends on the acuity of the bleeding, clinical manifestations, and neuroimaging features, such as presence of midline shift. When surgery is indicated, often craniotomy with evacuation of the hematoma is performed. Contrast subdural hematoma to epidural hematoma where surgical intervention is always indicated. Outcome largely depends on the cause and neurologic condition at presentation.

Epidural vs. Subdural Hematoma on Imaging

See Figure 12-16. Epidural bleeds (Figure 12-17) are restricted by the dural attachments to the skull, causing the classic biconvex appearance on imaging. In contrast, subdural bleeds (Figure 12-18) are free to extend across suture lines and cause a more linear concave finding.

SPINAL CORD INJURY

Spinal injuries can occur in children. The most common causes are motor vehicle crashes, falls, and swimming pool injuries (diving). In neonates, trauma during delivery is the most common etiology.

Younger children (< 3 years of age) have an increased proportion of cervical and upper thoracic spine injuries, as well as a higher frequency of spinal cord injury without radiographic abnormalities (SCIWORA). This was first described in the pre-MRI era when plain films and CT scan were the only available modalities. Today, MRI of the spinal cord usually reveals existing abnormalities, and prognosis correlates with the degree of defect seen.

Spinal cord injury ranges from whiplash—in which the spine is hyperextended or overflexed with musculoskeletal symptoms—to complex severing or infarction of the cord.

In newborns, use the Galant reflex to help determine the extent of damage in the thoracic cord. In this reflex, scratch the paraspinal region to elicit incurvation of the spine toward the side of the stimulus; with injury, the reflex is absent at that level.

"Spinal shock" is a period of flaccidity and areflexia; it can occur after an acute injury, coupled with autonomic dysfunction of blood vessel tone below the level of the cord injury, causing hypotension and shock. After 2 weeks, it progresses to varying degrees of spasticity and hyperreflexia. Generally use spinal MRI to delineate the problem.

Intravenous methylprednisone is not endorsed by major guidelines due to the limited evidence of improved neurologic outcomes. Never manipulate cervical spine injuries to reduce a fracture.

NEUROLOGY

COMMON PERIPHERAL NERVE INJURIES

Brachial Plexus

Birth trauma is the most common cause of peripheral nerve injury. The brachial plexus has points of fixation to the 1st rib medially and the coracoid process of the scapula laterally. Forced abduction of the arm stretches the nerves under and against the coracoid and can result in stretching, avulsing, or compressing the lower plexus. Lateral deviation of the head and depression of the shoulder results in similar constriction to the upper plexus. Injuries of this type can occur with breech or cephalic deliveries.

Risk factors include macrosomia, use of forceps, shoulder dystocia, and gestational diabetes; ~ 50% are due to shoulder dystocia.

Most patients make a full recovery. Initial treatment consists of observation and appropriate positioning. Physical therapy is sometimes used. Surgery is indicated after 3 months of no improvement.

Erb Palsy

Upper brachial plexus injuries are the most common peripheral nerve injuries. When C5, C6, and occasionally C7 nerve roots are involved, it is referred to as Erb palsy (a.k.a. Erb paralysis, Duchenne-Erb palsy).

The infant presents with a sagging shoulder, an arm that hangs limp in internal rotation, and a flexed wrist ("waiter's tip position"; Figure 12-19). If the phrenic nerve is involved, the infant can also have unilateral diaphragmatic paralysis that presents with asymmetric chest expansion and decreased oxygenation.

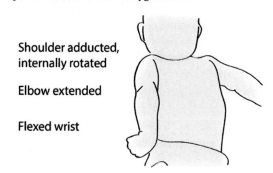

Shoulder adducted, internally rotated

Elbow extended

Flexed wrist

Figure 12-19: Erb palsy

Symptoms are due to paralysis of the supinator, deltoid, biceps, brachioradialis, and extensor carpi radialis muscles. The biceps tendon reflex is absent. The triceps reflex is present if C7 is not involved. Sensory examination is normal.

Treatment involves placing the arm in abduction and external rotation; > 90% of infants have a full recovery within 3 months. Those who do not improve with conservative management need evaluation for possible surgical repair.

Déjerine-Klumpke Palsy

Lower brachial plexus injuries (C8–T1) show more sensory (ulnar side of the hand) and vasomotor involvement, with paralysis of the extensors of the forearm, flexors of the wrist, and intrinsic muscles of the hand. The classic presentation of Déjerine-Klumpke palsy (a.k.a. Klumpke palsy) is the "claw hand" with extension of the metacarpophalangeal joints and flexion of the proximal and distal interphalangeal joints. If the 1st thoracic root is involved, Horner syndrome (ptosis and miosis on ipsilateral side) is likely. Injury occurring with Horner syndrome has an overall worse long-term motor outcome.

Treat by splinting the forearm and wrist in a neutral position. Most recover in 3–6 months but do not improve as much as those with upper plexus root injury. Surgery with microvascular techniques is often beneficial in cases that are severe or do not resolve.

Sciatic Nerve Injury

Sciatic nerve injury is most commonly iatrogenic with intramuscular (IM) injections. IM injections during infancy are contraindicated in the intragluteal area; they must be used with extreme caution in older children.

Complete sciatic paralysis produces total foot paralysis and loss of leg flexion. It also results in flail footdrop, absence of ankle jerk reflex, and sensory loss of the leg below the knee, except for the medial portion. Knee jerk is preserved. Most patients are managed conservatively with pain control and physiotherapy. Consider surgery in infants and in patients with severe deficits that do not improve in 3 months.

CRANIAL NERVE (CN) ABNORMALITIES

PREVIEW | REVIEW

- What are some causes of facial nerve palsy?
- What is Möbius syndrome?
- What is Marcus Gunn phenomenon, and what causes it?

CN REVIEW

CN 1 is the olfactory nerve and responsible for the sense of smell. It usually is not assessed in the clinical setting.

CN 2 (optic) carries visual impulses from the eye to the occipital cortex via the optic tracts and, thus, does not control ocular motility. Optic nerve testing includes visual acuity, visual field testing, color vision, and pupillary reaction to light. Fundus examination is an important tool to evaluate many pathologies of the optic nerve. The optic nerve constitutes the afferent limb of the pupillary reflex arc and functions in conjunction with efferent (motor) nerves, which travel with CN 3 to cause pupillary constriction on exposure to light.

CN 3 (oculomotor), CN 4 (trochlear), and CN 6 (abducens) are responsible for extraocular movements. The oculomotor nerve is responsible for most of the movement of the eyeball. Function of the oculomotor nerve is assessed in conjunction with the trochlear and abducens nerves, which are also responsible for controlling eyeball mobility. The trochlear nerve innervates only the superior oblique muscle, allowing the eye to look down. The abducens nerve controls the lateral rectus muscle, permitting lateral movement of each eye. The oculomotor nerve controls the muscles that allow motion in all other directions—medial rectus looks medially; inferior rectus looks down; superior rectus looks up; and inferior oblique looks up. The mnemonic **SO4–LR6–All the Rest 3** is sometimes helpful in interpreting clinical findings during extraocular muscle testing (superior oblique–CN 4; lateral rectus–CN 6; "all the rest" of the muscles innervated by CN 3). Also remember, the recti muscles cause movement in the same direction as their name (superior rectus looks up; inferior rectus looks down), whereas oblique muscles cause movement in the opposite direction (superior oblique looks down; inferior oblique looks up). Because CN 3 also innervates the muscle that raises the upper eyelid, oculomotor dysfunction also causes ptosis of the lid on the affected side.

CN 5 (trigeminal) provides sensation to the ophthalmic, maxillary, and mandibular regions of the face. It provides motor function to the temporalis and masseter muscles, causing teeth clenching and movement of jaw from side to side, respectively. It is also responsible for the sensory portion of the corneal reflex; the motor portion is provided by CN 7 (facial). In addition to its role in the corneal reflex, CN 7 is responsible for facial symmetry and expression and for carrying taste sensations from the anterior 2/3 of the tongue.

CN 8 (vestibulocochlear) is responsible for hearing and balance.

CN 9 (glossopharyngeal) and CN 10 (vagus) are considered together because they travel together and have some overlapping function. They are responsible for innervating the pharynx and palate. When normal, the uvula is midline and the palate and uvula rise symmetrically when the patient says "Ahh." Both CN 9 and CN 10 are involved in the gag reflex. CN 9 provides taste for the posterior 1/3 of the tongue. CN 10 provides sensory, motor, and autonomic functions of viscera (e.g., glands, digestion, heart rate).

CN 11 (spinal accessory) innervates the sternocleidomastoid and trapezius muscles that help control head movement.

CN 12 (hypoglossal) controls the intrinsic muscles of the tongue.

FACIAL NERVE PALSY

Facial nerve (CN 7) palsy can be congenital or acquired. **Bell's palsy**, caused by dysfunction of the facial nerve after exiting from the pons, accounts for approximately half of the cases of facial nerve palsy. The pathogenesis of Bell's palsy is believed to be viral but may also be postinfectious immune-mediated demyelination. HSV is the likely cause in most cases, followed by herpes zoster. Other causes include Lyme disease, trauma, and neoplasms.

Congenital facial nerve palsy can be due to trauma to the peripheral (extracranial) facial nerve or due to cranial nerve nucleus abnormalities, often referred to as **Möbius syndrome**. It is caused by hypoplasia or agenesis of the facial nucleus and/or nerve and is accompanied by CN 6 (abducens) abnormalities causing ocular abduction impairment. Other cranial nerves can also be involved. Affected infants have an expressionless, dull appearance and are unable to smile, frown, suck, grimace, or blink. If the ipsilateral abducens nerve is involved in acquired palsy, a brainstem lesion is possible due to the close proximity of the abducens nucleus to the facial nerve and nucleus.

The initial feature of the neuritis typically is pain or tingling in the ear canal ipsilateral to the subsequent facial palsy. The palsy has explosive onset and becomes maximal within hours. It typically involves 1 side of the face but occasionally can be bilateral. There can be drooling, pain of the jaw or behind the ear on the affected side, decreased tearing, inability to close the eye, and taste disturbance.

Diagnosis is made in many cases by history and physical examination. If symptoms last more than 6 weeks or there is concern of underlying etiology, further workup is needed. This can include Lyme serology, electrodiagnostic studies, and imaging studies.

If a cause is found, such as Lyme disease or otitis, treat the underlying disorder. For Bell's palsy, oral steroids are given either alone or combined with antiviral medication (e.g., acyclovir) due to the association of facial nerve palsy and HSV infection. If the patient cannot close the eye completely, artificial tears during the day and ointment with patching at night is prescribed. Most patients with Bell's palsy recover completely.

In the case of bilateral lower motor neuron–type facial weakness or if the patient experiences a second episode, more testing is warranted, including MRI scan with contrast (to look for tumors and other infiltrative disease processes), lumbar puncture, and tests for Lyme disease, sarcoidosis, and HIV.

MARCUS GUNN PHENOMENON

Marcus Gunn (jaw-winking) phenomenon is characterized by simultaneous eyelid blinking during sucking jaw movements as the child contracts the pterygoid muscle. The disorder is due to abnormal innervation of the trigeminal and oculomotor nerve—namely, aberrant innervation of the ipsilateral levator muscle of the eyelid by the mandibular branch of the trigeminal nerve. It is sporadic and typically unilateral but rarely can occur bilaterally. The eyelid droops with jaw movement to the ipsilateral side and elevates when the jaw is moved to the contralateral side. Levator function is variable, the upper eyelid crease is present, and there may be associated strabismus. Children with Marcus Gunn must be monitored for amblyopia, refractive errors, or strabismus. Although usually a benign phenomenon, surgical intervention is necessary when the associated ptosis is severe or causes amblyopia.

SEIZURE DISORDERS

PREVIEW | REVIEW

- What is the most common type of seizure in childhood?
- How do myoclonic seizures classically present?
- Name the disorder that presents with morning myoclonic jerks and with onset between 8 and 20 years of age.
- Define absence seizures.
- How do many focal aware seizures present?
- What locations of the body are affected in focal aware seizures?
- Define focal seizures with impaired awareness.
- Describe a "jackknife" flexor spasm.
- What is the long-term prognosis for an infant with infantile spasms?
- In the U.S., what are the various therapeutic options for infantile spasms?
- Define Lennox-Gastaut syndrome.
- With a traumatic head injury, what risk factors increase the likelihood of posttraumatic seizure disorder in children?
- What is Rasmussen syndrome?
- Know the preferred drugs for seizure disorders in Table 12-1 on page 12-24!
- Why is valproate avoided in young children?
- Which antibiotic should be avoided with carbamazepine use?
- Describe the pharmacokinetics of phenytoin.
- What is the drug of choice for absence seizures?
- Should you use phenobarbital in older children?
- Which drugs increase the risk of neural tube defects in infants of pregnant women on these medications?
- Is it okay for a woman on antiseizure medications (ASMs) to breastfeed?
- Define status epilepticus.
- What are some causes of neonatal seizures?
- In neonatal seizures, what should be the 1st thing to check before treatment?
- What drugs are best for treating neonatal seizures?
- How long do you continue ASMs in an infant with uncomplicated neonatal seizures?
- What is the major contributing risk factor for a febrile seizure?
- Is family history important in febrile seizures?
- What are the indications for a lumbar puncture in neonates with suspected febrile seizures?
- Is an electroencephalogram necessary to evaluate a simple febrile seizure?
- Do simple febrile seizures cause brain damage?
- A child has had 2 simple febrile seizures in the past 6 months. Does the child need an ASM to prevent the seizures from recurring?
- What risk factors make a recurrent febrile seizure more likely?

OCCURRENCE

Seizures have multiple etiologies, including abnormal electrolytes (e.g., Na^+, Ca^{2+}, Mg^{2+}), metabolic disturbances (glucose and acid-base problems), CNS infections, trauma, and others. On the other hand, **epilepsy** refers to recurrent seizures, typically unprovoked. (Epilepsy is defined as having 2 or more unprovoked seizures at least 24 hours apart.) About 1% of children have 1 afebrile seizure by 14 years of age, and 0.4–0.8% have epilepsy by 11 years of age.

GENERALIZED SEIZURES

Mechanism / Characteristics

Generalized epilepsy is the most common type in children and involves diffuse abnormal electrical activity from both cerebral hemispheres from the beginning of the seizure. Generalized epilepsy makes up about 50% of all epilepsies in childhood.

Certain characteristics are classic for seizures in generalized epilepsy:

- Abrupt onset
- Loss or alteration of awareness
- Variable bilateral symmetric motor activity associated with changes in muscle tone
- No warning of the attack; no aura
- Epileptiform activity that is bilateral and synchronous (shown on EEG)

Tonic-Clonic Seizures

Generalized tonic-clonic seizures (formerly grand mal seizures) are the classic form of generalized-onset seizures. Note: The combined tonic-clonic event is rare in infancy but can occur in early childhood—due to the commonality of simple febrile seizures, which are generalized tonic-clonic in nature. Besides febrile seizures, most seizures in younger-age children (≤ 2 years old) are either tonic or clonic in character.

The **tonic** phase occurs first, with loss of consciousness simultaneous with marked, sustained contractions of the entire musculature. With these movements, the eyes deviate conjugately upward. During this phase, there is pupillary dilation, salivation, diaphoresis, and increased blood pressure. Urinary incontinence is common. The tonic phase usually lasts 10–20 seconds. It is followed by the **clonic** phase, which is a series of rhythmic muscle jerks of the limbs that interrupts the sustained, tonic muscular spasm. The clonic phase usually lasts 30–60 seconds.

After the seizure, in the postictal period, the child slowly regains full consciousness and is typically confused and sleepy for a few minutes to several hours. Once fully awake, the child may complain of headache and muscle aches but otherwise cannot remember the seizure event.

Myoclonic Seizures

Myoclonic seizures are classically defined by:

- Short duration (< 1–2 seconds)
- Rapid muscle contractions, often in 1 limb, but can involve bilateral extremities or trunk
- Isolated or repetitive jerks
- Likelihood of the patient falling (if severe and involving the axial muscles)
- Preservation of awareness

Myoclonic seizures can be isolated or occur with absence attacks. Myoclonic seizures often occur in children with generalized epilepsies. Myoclonic seizures can also be a symptom of progressive neurodegenerative genetic diseases that cause progressive cognitive and functional decline, worsening seizures, and early death. These conditions collectively are referred to as **progressive myoclonic epilepsy** (PME). Examples of PME include Lafora body disease and myoclonic epilepsy with ragged red fibers (MERRF).

Myoclonic seizures are best treated with valproate, levetiracetam, benzodiazepines, lamotrigine, or other broad-spectrum antiseizure medications (ASMs; a.k.a. antiepileptics, anticonvulsants).

Juvenile Myoclonic Epilepsy (JME)

JME is a subtype of generalized epilepsy and is characterized by:

- Morning myoclonic jerks (often with dropping of items in hands)
- +/− History of absence seizures
- Generalized tonic-clonic seizures occurring just after awakening or during sleep
- Normal intelligence
- Family history of similar seizures
- Onset at 8–20 years of age

Seizures increase with sleep deprivation, stress, or alcohol use. EEG shows generalized epileptiform discharges with fast (4–6 Hz) polyspike and slow wave pattern, which is often triggered by photic stimulation. Valproate is the drug of choice. If valproate is contraindicated or undesirable (especially in postpubertal girls due to increased risk of neural tube defects if pregnancy occurs), levetiracetam or lamotrigine are alternative 1st line options. The seizures typically respond well to medications; however, this is usually a lifelong condition and long-term ASMs are required.

Absence Seizures

Absence seizures (formerly petit mal seizures) are characterized by:

- Episodes of extremely short lapses in awareness (10–20 seconds)
- Absence of aura
- Amnesia during the episodes
- Short duration (rarely longer than 10–20 seconds)
- Abrupt onset and end (frequently in mid-conversation or activity)
- Staring and behavioral arrest (with possible flickering of the eyelids or eye rolling or mouth automatisms)
- No postictal period

Atypical absence seizures additionally can have:

- Brief jerks of the eyelids and limbs
- Transient change in postural tone (increase or decrease)
- Pupillary dilation
- Skin-color changes
- Tachycardia

Atypical absence seizures are not associated with auras, hallucinations, or postictal abnormalities.

Absence seizures can be confused with focal seizures with impaired awareness, but focal seizures often last longer (usually > 30 seconds), have auras, and have slow return to awareness postictally.

Absence seizures most commonly are seen with **childhood absence epilepsy**, which occurs in children 4–12 years of age. These seizures can occur many times in a day. Occasionally, the staring is unnoticed. Sometimes the child presents with symptoms of attention-deficit/hyperactivity disorder (ADHD) or with scholastic difficulties. Hyperventilation for 3–4 minutes usually provokes an absence seizure; do this routinely during EEG to help make this diagnosis. EEG shows a characteristic **3-Hz generalized spike and wave** discharge.

Those affected have normal intelligence and normal neurologic examination. Treat with ethosuximide. Alternatives include valproate or lamotrigine. Note that carbamazepine can worsen absence seizures. Prognosis is excellent and > 90% of patients become seizure free with treatment. Remission occurs by 12 years of age.

Atonic or Akinetic Seizures

An atonic seizure (a.k.a. drop attack) has the following characteristics:

- Sudden and complete loss of tone in the limbs, neck, and trunk muscles (without warning)
- Typically brief in duration
- Loss of awareness
- Complete awareness returning very quickly after the attack
- 1 or more myoclonic jerks sometimes occurring immediately before muscle tone is lost

Atonic seizures are more common in children with epileptic encephalopathies (e.g., Lennox-Gastaut syndrome) and are frequently difficult to treat.

FOCAL SEIZURES

Occurrence

Focal seizures are less common in children than adults but still make up 40–45% of childhood seizures. Children rarely have a definable "focal" lesion responsible for their focal seizure and many children have normal neuroimaging. Etiologies include idiopathic focal epilepsy syndromes, brain malformations (cortical dysplasias) and gliosis (related to remote injury). Only a minority of patients have focal seizures due to stroke (acute or remote), brain tumors, or AVMs. Children with Sturge-Weber syndrome typically have an ipsilateral leptomeningeal angioma, which causes a contralateral focal seizure.

The most common focal epilepsy in childhood is **benign (childhood) epilepsy with centrotemporal spikes** (BECTS or CECTS), also known as benign rolandic epilepsy. Affected children are usually elementary school age and tend to have focal hemifacial or extremity seizures shortly after going to sleep or just before or after waking up. Focal seizures during the night or upon awakening account for 75% of the seizures seen in this epilepsy syndrome. Hypersalivation and dysarthria also can be seen, and many children retain awareness during the seizure. Secondary nighttime generalized tonic-clonic seizures (formerly grand mal seizures) occur in upwards of 50% of patients and are often the first indication of the underlying seizure disorder. Most children outgrow this form of epilepsy within 2 years or, at the latest, by puberty. EEG classically shows bilateral centrotemporal spikes. Many clinicians do not treat benign rolandic epilepsy with antiseizure medications (ASMs) if the episodes are infrequent and occur only at night. If you choose to start ASMs, carbamazepine or oxcarbazepine is preferred. Long-term prognosis is excellent.

Focal Aware Seizures

Focal aware seizures (a.k.a. focal seizures without impairment of consciousness and formerly called simple partial seizures) refer to seizures in which the patients can still interact with their environment without loss of consciousness. They can vary greatly in symptoms and signs and can be focal motor (from the precentral gyrus), focal adversive (from the mesial frontal lobe), or focal somatosensory (from the parietal lobe) in character. They usually last 10–20 seconds. Focal motor findings are the most common and include asynchronous clonic or tonic movements that tend to involve the face, neck, and extremities. Aura, chest discomfort, or headache tend to occur. Complex emotional or hallucinatory phenomena are common, especially in seizures arising from the temporal lobe. There is no postictal confusion. Focal aware seizures are followed sometimes by **Todd paralysis**, a transient paralysis of the affected body part lasting for minutes or hours.

Focal Seizures with Impaired Awareness

Focal seizures with impaired awareness (a.k.a. focal seizures with impaired consciousness and formerly called complex partial seizures) have variable symptoms but usually include alterations in consciousness, unresponsiveness, and automatisms. Automatisms are repetitive, purposeless, undirected, and inappropriate motor activities. Commonly, automatisms include repetitive lip smacking, swallowing, chewing, or fidgeting of the fingers or hands. Prior to the seizure, an aura is common, and children sometimes report a sense of detachment or depersonalization, forced thinking, visual distortions, or hallucinations. Feelings of intense emotion or fear also can occur. The type of aura (e.g., visual, auditory) gives important clues about the location of the seizure focus. Postictally, patients are confused and recover awareness slowly. During the postictal period, these children may act aggressively or angrily to objects or persons that are in their way; this behavior does not occur as a manifestation of the seizure itself.

Treatment

The drugs of choice for treatment of focal epilepsy are carbamazepine, oxcarbazepine, or phenytoin. Levetiracetam is approved as adjunctive therapy in children ≥ 4 years of age. Resective epilepsy surgery is also an option for children with focal epilepsy that is intractable to ASMs.

INFANTILE SPASMS

Infantile spasms are a unique type of seizure occurring in infants and children < 1 year of age. A majority have spasms at 3–7 months of age (< 10% present after 2 years of age). The classic spasm is the **"jackknife" flexor spasm** (a.k.a. salaam attack and Blitz-Nick-Salaam-Krämpfe). These children have sudden, simultaneous flexion of their neck and trunk, with flexion and adduction of their extremities. Some children have extensor spasms or a combination of flexion and extension (mixed). The spasms are brief and usually occur in clusters with several spasms occurring during a single cluster. The number of clusters varies from a few to too numerous to count (> 100). The spasms frequently are initiated or aggravated by transitions from sleep to wakefulness. Most children also have developmental regression with the onset of infantile spasms.

A very abnormal EEG in children with infantile spasms is known as **hypsarrhythmia**—high-voltage, irregular, slow waves that are asynchronous, occur over all head regions, and are intermixed with spikes from multiple foci.

Cerebral dysgenesis, genetic and metabolic/genetic disorders (e.g., phenylketonuria, tuberous sclerosis, trisomy 21), intrauterine infections, and hypoxic-ischemic brain damage are the most commonly identified etiologies. Up to 30% of cases are caused by tuberous sclerosis.

Infantile spasms resolve over time even without specific therapy; however, most surviving children have severe intellectual disability and other types of seizure disorders (most typically **Lennox-Gastaut syndrome**; see Lennox-Gastaut Syndrome). Mortality is ~ 20%. Those with previously normal development and without known preceding neurologic abnormalities (idiopathic cases) or those without a known cause for developmental delays and neurologic abnormalities prior to onset (cryptogenic cases) often have a better prognosis. Successful treatment of infantile spasms possibly improves the long-term prognosis.

West syndrome is a severe epilepsy syndrome that includes the triad of infantile spasms, intellectual disability, and hypsarrhythmia.

Spasms are refractory to traditional antiseizure therapy. The 3 most efficacious treatments for infantile spasms are intramuscular adrenocorticotropic hormone (ACTH), oral prednisolone, and oral vigabatrin. Response usually occurs within 2 weeks of starting therapy. The main adverse effects of ACTH and prednisolone include hypertension, irritability, and infection. Additionally, the mode of administration (intramuscular) of ACTH and its cost become important considerations prior to initiating therapy. Vigabatrin has a black box warning of permanent visual field deficits; this medication requires physicians to register in a special program to prescribe it. It is the drug of choice for use in infantile spasms with coexistent tuberous sclerosis. A variety of antiseizure drugs have been used in affected neonates who do not respond to ACTH, prednisolone, or vigabatrin—but usually with only partial, if any, improvement in symptoms. Pyridoxine (vitamin B_6) is sometimes effective.

LENNOX-GASTAUT SYNDROME

Lennox-Gastaut syndrome refers to a varied group of symptoms with multiple seizure types (e.g., generalized tonic-clonic seizures, absence seizures, atonic seizures, tonic seizures), intellectual disability, and a characteristic EEG pattern. EEG has generalized, bilaterally synchronous, sharp and slow wave complexes, occurring in a repetitive fashion in long runs at ~ 1.5–2.5 Hz (a.k.a. "slow spike and wave"). (Compare Lennox-Gastaut syndrome to childhood absence epilepsy, which has 3 Hz spike and wave discharges, and to juvenile myoclonic epilepsy, which has "fast" spike and wave complexes at 4–6 Hz.)

The syndrome does not have a specific etiology but can be due to any cause of diffuse encephalopathy, including genetic epilepsy, cerebral malformation, perinatal asphyxia, head injury, anoxic encephalopathy, or infection. Approximately 30% are idiopathic; 25–40% have a history of infantile spasms.

Seizures usually begin in the first few years of life and are refractory to medications. Younger children have atonic, tonic, and atypical absence seizures, whereas older children have tonic-clonic seizures. Most children have ≥ 2 different kinds of seizures on a daily basis.

Prognosis is poor, with most children having seizures into adulthood. Drug therapy is empiric at best, with valproate, lamotrigine, felbamate, and topiramate available. Rufinamide (Banzel) and clobazam (Onfi) are approved as adjunctive therapy in those ≥ 4 years and ≥ 2 years of age, respectively. Cannabidiol is FDA-approved for treatment of seizures associated with Lennox-Gastaut syndrome.

POSTTRAUMATIC SEIZURES

Head trauma can result in seizures at any age. The seizures can occur as a coinciding reaction to the brain trauma (impact seizures), within 1 week after the injury (early posttraumatic seizures), or months to years after the injury (late posttraumatic seizures or posttraumatic epilepsy). The risk of a seizure disorder after a head injury is directly related to the severity of the head injury. The greatest risk is seen with intracerebral hematoma, cerebral contusion, or unconsciousness lasting > 24 hours. Those children with mild head injury and momentary unconsciousness without skull fracture or neurologic deficit have no increased risk of later seizures.

NEUROCUTANEOUS SYNDROMES

Neurocutaneous syndromes are a broad group of disorders involving both the nervous system and the skin, which have a common embryologic origin from the ectoderm.

Neurofibromatosis Type 1 (NF1) is the most common neurocutaneous syndrome, with a prevalence of ~ 1/3,000 in the general population. These patients classically have café au lait spots and small benign tumors, called neurofibromas, that grow on the skin and nerves. A low percentage (4–6%) of these patients have epilepsy.

Tuberous sclerosis is the neurocutaneous syndrome in which epilepsy is most frequently seen. It is the 2nd most common neurocutaneous disorder (with a prevalence of ~ 1/6,000 in the general population), and 80–90% of these patients have epilepsy, with most presenting at ≤ 12 months of age. As noted in Infantile Spasms, the initial presenting symptom of many of these patients is infantile spasms.

These 2 disorders are covered more thoroughly in the Genetics section.

Sturge-Weber patients usually have a birthmark called a port-wine stain (capillary angioma) in the periorbital area. 10–20% of these patients also have an ipsilateral (typically) leptomeningeal angioma that can cause seizures, weakness on the contralateral side of the body, or developmental delay. Some also develop glaucoma. Neuroimaging may show leptomeningeal angiomatosis, hemispheric intracranial calcification, and underlying cerebral atrophy. Unlike tuberous sclerosis and NF1, Sturge-Weber syndrome does not affect other areas of the body.

OTHER SEIZURE TYPES

Photosensitive Epilepsy

Intermittent or flickering light—especially strobe lights, sunlight through trees, or video games—rarely provokes myoclonic seizures with or without absence or generalized tonic-clonic seizures (formerly grand mal seizures). Almost always, photic-induced seizures begin between 8 and 19 years of age. Some children self-induce the attacks by waving their hand in front of their eyes. EEG shows bilateral, synchronous, spike-wave discharges that are irregular in occurrence. This is an uncommon presentation of epilepsy in children.

Treatment usually involves limiting the provoking stimulus; dark glasses are helpful in some children. For drug therapy, valproate is considered the best.

Rasmussen Syndrome

Many believe Rasmussen syndrome (chronic focal encephalitis) is caused by an immunologic process involving only 1 hemisphere of the brain. About 70% have a history of infectious or inflammatory illness themselves or in a family member. Initially, the seizures are generalized but soon become focal, unremitting, and limited to 1 part or side of the body. Eventually, hemiparesis, diminished intelligence, and hemianopia occur. Over time, there is evidence of unilateral cerebral atrophy on MRI. The disease is not fatal but deteriorates to a stable, often devastating, neurologic deficit.

Medical therapy is disappointing—especially ASMs. Corticosteroids and immunologic therapies show evidence of benefit, but more studies are needed. A modified hemispherectomy or focal cortical excision usually improves symptoms markedly and is the recommended treatment for Rasmussen syndrome.

Gelastic Seizures

Gelastic seizures occur in children and present as pathologic (and often mechanical and mirthless) **laughter** without an appropriate reason for laughing. They are usually focal in nature and most commonly found in patients with **hypothalamic hamartomas**.

SEIZURE MANAGEMENT

Management of epilepsy includes the following:

- Evaluation
  - EEG
  - MRI, if focal seizure
  - Genetic testing, if appropriate
- Education
  - First aid for seizures (e.g., rolling child on side to prevent aspiration)
  - Possible triggers (e.g., infection, lack of sleep)
  - Seizure precautions (e.g., water safety, leave bathroom door unlocked when taking bath, bike helmet)
  - Folic acid for teenage females who are taking antiseizure medications (ASMs)
- ASMs
  - Rescue plan—rectal diazepam
  - Maintenance (See Table 12-1.)

DRUG THERAPY AND SIDE EFFECTS

Review the preferred drugs for seizure disorders in Table 12-1. There has been a move away from the 1st generation ASMs due to long-term side effects, such as osteoporosis, as well as significant drug-drug interactions. Many 1st generation ASMs (e.g., phenytoin, carbamazepine) induce liver enzymes. This effect can decrease levels of concomitantly administered medications (especially chemotherapeutic agents). In girls who take birth control pills, enzyme induction tends to result in contraceptive failure. In addition, the dose of levonorgestrel should be doubled for those on enzyme-inducing seizure medications who need to take emergency contraception. Valproate, on the other hand, is a liver enzyme inhibitor but typically is not used in patients of child-bearing age due to its increased risk of neural tube defects. Table 12-2 lists some important side effects for common ASMs.

Table 12-1: Preferred Drugs for Seizure Disorders	
Type of Seizure	**Preferred Drug**
Focal seizures (with and without impaired awareness) and secondary generalized seizures	Oxcarbazepine or carbamazepine
Absence seizures	Ethosuximide or valproate
Idiopathic/primary generalized tonic-clonic seizures (formerly grand mal seizures)	There are many options; refer to the next topics on drug therapy.
Infantile spasms	ACTH or vigabatrin (Vigabatrin is recommended if patient has tuberous sclerosis.)

Table 12-2: Side Effects of Antiseizure Medications

Drug	Possible Side Effects
Valproate	Teratogen; hyperammonemia; dose-related thrombocytopenia; weight gain, tremor
Carbamazepine	Leukopenia; hepatotoxicity; syndrome of inappropriate antidiuretic hormone secretion (SIADH), resulting in hyponatremia
Phenytoin	Hirsutism; gum hypertrophy; ataxia; Stevens-Johnson syndrome
Ethosuximide	Abdominal pain; skin rash; liver dysfunction; leukopenia
Phenobarbital	Severe behavioral changes; impairment of cognition; only use in infants
Oxcarbazepine	Ataxia; nystagmus; hyponatremia
Lamotrigine	Stevens-Johnson syndrome
Levetiracetam	Irritability; aggression
Topiramate	Slowing of cognition; metabolic acidosis; glaucoma
Vigabatrin	Permanent visual field deficits

Valproate (Valproic Acid)

Use valproate for generalized tonic-clonic, absence, atypical absence, and myoclonic seizures. There is an increased risk of severe valproate-associated hepatotoxicity in children < 3 years of age who have underlying metabolic disorders, in some cases leading to death. If possible, use another drug for this age group; if not possible, order a metabolic screen before starting valproate and follow with liver function tests after starting it. More common side effects include weight gain, hair loss, hyperammonemia, and dose-related thrombocytopenia (associated with viral infections). Less common side effects include pancreatitis.

Valproate has an increased risk of teratogenicity vs. other ASMs (especially with respect to risk of neural tube defects). Remember that neural tube closure occurs within the first 2 weeks of a missed period! Hence, this drug is best avoided in postpubertal adolescent girls. On the other hand, never stop ASMs if a patient becomes pregnant, because there is a significant risk of fetal damage if the patient suffers a breakthrough seizure.

Valproate interacts with carnitine and decreases carnitine serum levels. L-carnitine is used to treat valproate toxicity and is also sometimes given as a supplement, especially in children < 2 years of age.

Carbamazepine

Carbamazepine is useful for focal seizures, with or without secondary generalized seizures. It is avoided in patients with absence seizures and other generalized epilepsies because it can precipitate convulsions. Serious but rare side effects include severe leukopenia and hepatotoxicity during the initial 4 months of therapy. It also can cause syndrome of inappropriate antidiuretic hormone secretion (SIADH) with a potential side effect of hyponatremia. Other side effects include dizziness, drowsiness, and diplopia. Avoid erythromycin because it elevates carbamazepine levels.

Phenytoin

Phenytoin is not typically used in children due to its zero-order kinetic metabolism, which makes achieving therapeutic levels difficult in chronic dosing; toxicity or underdosing is common. When used, it works best for focal seizures, with and without secondary generalization.

The potential side effects of phenytoin include hirsutism, gum hypertrophy, ataxia, skin rash, Stevens-Johnson syndrome, nystagmus, drowsiness, and blood dyscrasias. The IV formulation also causes skin burns if extravasated (due to very basic pH) and can induce hypotension.

Phenytoin has an important role in management of status epilepticus, especially in its phosphorylated form (fosphenytoin), which has a lower potential for local tissue reaction and can be infused at a faster rate. For further information, see Status Epilepticus on page 12-26.

Ethosuximide

Ethosuximide is the drug of choice for absence seizures. Side effects include abdominal pain, skin rash, liver dysfunction, and leukopenia. It is not used for any other seizure types and does not reliably treat major motor (convulsive) seizures in patients.

Phenobarbital

Phenobarbital is useful for generalized tonic-clonic seizures and focal seizures; it also has a role in management of status epilepticus. Phenobarbital most commonly is used in neonates and infants. Do not use phenobarbital in older children because many patients have severe behavioral changes or impairment of cognition while on the drug. It typically is very sedating and causes hepatotoxicity.

Oxcarbazepine

Oxcarbazepine is approved as adjunctive and monotherapy for focal seizures in children 4–16 years of age. Side effects include somnolence, vomiting, ataxia, rash, and nystagmus. Hyponatremia is seen in 1–5% of patients who take oxcarbazepine. (See the discussion of its sister drug in Carbamazepine.)

NEUROLOGY

Lamotrigine

Lamotrigine is approved for focal seizures, generalized seizures of Lennox-Gastaut syndrome, and primary generalized tonic-clonic seizures in children > 2 years of age. The agent has a black box warning for Stevens-Johnson syndrome, with an incidence of 8/1,000 in pediatric patients.

Levetiracetam

Levetiracetam is approved as adjunct therapy for focal seizures with impaired awareness in children ≥ 4 years of age, primary generalized tonic-clonic seizures in children ≥ 6 years, and juvenile myoclonic epilepsy in children ≥ 12 years. It has no significant drug-drug interactions. Except for behavioral adverse effects (e.g., irritability, aggression) in ~ 10% of patients, it is reasonably well tolerated. Because it is renally excreted, administer 50% of normal dose in patients with low glomerular filtration rate (GFR).

Topiramate

Topiramate is used for both focal and generalized seizures. Advise caution for children with a history of kidney stones. Side effects include slowing of cognition, metabolic acidosis, and acute angle-closure glaucoma. It is also used in the treatment of migraines.

Vigabatrin

Please refer to Infantile Spasms on page 12-22.

Therapeutic Drug Monitoring of Antiseizure Medications (ASMs)

Drug levels can be measured commercially for some of the ASMs, especially carbamazepine, phenytoin, ethosuximide, phenobarbital, and valproate. However, serum drug levels should not be used in isolation to guide therapy because therapeutic ranges can vary for individual patients. Some patients may achieve good seizure control at an apparently "low" serum level while others may require high levels. The titration of medications should balance seizure control and adverse effects experienced by the patient, with drug levels used only as a guide. Serum drug levels are helpful to diagnose drug toxicity, assess noncompliance, and monitor drug-drug interactions.

COMMON EPILEPSY QUESTIONS

When Do You Stop Therapy?

Neurologically normal children with idiopathic epilepsy, whose seizures come under control readily and whose current EEGs are normal or near normal, are typically tapered off therapy after being seizure free for 2 years. Certain epilepsy syndromes, such as juvenile myoclonic epilepsy, need lifelong treatment.

What Are the Teratogenic Effects of These Drugs?

Pregnant women taking ASMs have a 2–3× greater risk of having an infant with congenital abnormalities. The most common major malformations are cleft lip/palate, neural tube defects (e.g., spina bifida), and cardiac anomalies. Valproate increases the risk of neural tube defect by 1.5% and carbamazepine by 0.5–1.0%. The risk of malformation may be greater in mothers taking more than one ASM compared with those taking only one. The neural tube defect risk can be decreased with folic acid intake before pregnancy. As neural tube development occurs even before pregnancy is discovered, all girls who are taking ASMs and of child-bearing age should be supplemented with folic acid. Generally, most practitioners recommend not using valproate or carbamazepine during child-bearing age and limiting treatment to a single ASM during pregnancy, if possible.

Minor anomalies include nail hypoplasia, hypertelorism, low-set ears, prominent lips, and nasal bridge abnormalities. Use of valproate during pregnancy has been associated with increased risk of cognitive impairment and autism in the offspring.

In addition, almost all drugs cause or promote a hemorrhagic diathesis in newborns that is not necessarily prevented by vitamin K at birth. Many providers recommend giving oral vitamin K phytonadione (20 mg/day) to pregnant women in the last month of pregnancy.

All this notwithstanding, a woman on ASMs still has a 90–95% chance of having a healthy baby.

What About Breastfeeding?

Breastfeeding is not contraindicated; encourage mothers to breastfeed. The only problem is with phenobarbital and primidone, which sometimes cause poor sucking or excessive drowsiness in the infant.

STATUS EPILEPTICUS

Status epilepticus is defined as repeated seizures without regaining awareness or a seizure prolonged for at least 5 minutes.

The seizures can be characterized as one of the following:

- Convulsive (tonic-clonic)
- Nonconvulsive (absence or focal)
- Focal (epilepsia partialis continua)
- Subclinical (electrographic status epilepticus)

Underlying disorders, such as sepsis, meningitis, trauma, or encephalopathies, are common. Morbidity is most affected by hypoxia, hypotension, and hyperthermia—therefore, you must control these quickly and effectively. Airway, breathing, and circulation (referred to as the ABCs) must be the 1st priority. Give high-flow oxygen, insert an oral airway, and obtain IV access. Blood pressure is usually elevated in status epilepticus and does not require circulatory support.

Always rule out reversible causes of seizure, especially in a patient who is not known to have epilepsy. In younger children presenting with status epilepticus, obtain a capillary blood glucose level and chemistries at the initiation of treatment. Electrolyte abnormalities can cause seizures, and these do not stop or respond to ASMs until electrolytes are stabilized. Checking levels of ASMs helps detect noncompliance in patients with a known seizure disorder.

For treatment of status epilepticus, benzodiazepines are the 1st line treatment. Slowly infuse an IV dose of diazepam (0.3–0.5 mg/kg, not to exceed 10 mg) or lorazepam (0.05–0.1 mg/kg, up to 4 mg). A rectal gel formulation of diazepam is available, which is often used as part of the acute seizure plan by parents prior to arrival to the emergency department. Repeat the dose of benzodiazepine if seizures persist. 2nd line medications include fosphenytoin at a dose of 20 mg/kg (maximum dosage: 1,500 mg), levetiracetam of 60 mg/kg (maximum dosage: 4,500 mg), or valproic acid of 40 mg/kg (maximum dosage: 3,000 mg). Phenobarbital is an alternative; give 15–20 mg/kg IV, and repeat if seizures continue. Be sure to monitor vital signs. Be prepared to intubate and provide ongoing respiratory support (i.e., ventilator in an ICU) whenever you give IV benzodiazepines or phenobarbital.

If there is still no improvement, general anesthesia with endotracheal intubation is required. Midazolam has been used in continuous infusion in some instances. Other drugs used in this setting include continuous infusion of propofol, ketamine, or pentobarbital.

NEONATAL SEIZURES

Neonatal seizures are different from those that occur in older children. Neonatal seizures usually have an identifiable cause, and the immature brain augments the initiation, maintenance, and propagation of the seizure activity. The incidence is estimated to be 0.5–2/100 live births. In newborn intensive care units, the incidence is much higher—nearly 10%.

Neonates can have seizures with or without EEG changes. Neonates sometimes also have unusual movements, such as jitteriness or tremor movements, which are sometimes misidentified as seizures.

Seizures in neonates have varied etiologies:

- **Hypoxic-ischemic encephalopathy:** This occurs from perinatal complications is the most common cause of seizures in the newborn.
- **Intraventricular hemorrhage (IVH):** This mainly affects premature infants, and those with IVH typically have focal or multifocal clonic seizures.
- **Hypoglycemia:** In the term newborn, hypoglycemia is defined as having a glucose level < 30 mg/dL in the first 72 hours of life and < 40 mg/dL thereafter. In preterm infants, < 20 mg/dL is the cutoff. The absolute effect of hypoglycemia is confounded by other factors; therefore, treat all seizing infants with glucose.
- **Hypocalcemia:** For infants with birth weight

> 1,500 g, hypocalcemia is defined as calcium level < 8 mg/dL; for very low birth weight infants, the cut off is < 7 mg/dL. Causes include prematurity, infants of diabetic mother, hypoxic-ischemic encephalopathy (HIE), and hypoparathyroidism (e.g., DiGeorge syndrome; see the Genetics section for more information).

- **Infections:** Infections of the CNS make up ~ 10% of the etiologies for neonatal seizures. Every infant who has a seizure needs a lumbar puncture to rule out meningitis. Most infections are bacterial, and 1/3 are viral in origin (including HSV, CMV, enterovirus, and rubella). Toxoplasmosis is an infection caused by the parasite *Toxoplasma gondii* and can cause seizures. Chorioretinitis suggests CMV or toxoplasmosis. EEG findings in herpes are characteristic, with periodic lateralized epileptiform discharges found in older children but typically not in infants. Of note, an HSV-PCR is the diagnostic study of choice for herpes encephalitis, although there is a significant false-negative rate and repeat testing is sometimes required. Intracranial calcifications often are seen in CMV or toxoplasmosis but not until later in life.
- **Congenital malformations of the brain:** Obviously, if the brain is not formed correctly—e.g., in holoprosencephaly, schizencephaly—seizures are likely.
- **Inborn errors of metabolism (IEM):** Several rare inborn errors of metabolism, such as urea cycle defects and aminoacidopathies, can present with neonatal seizures. Suspect an IEM in a neonate with seizure onset after the first few days of life (after establishment of feeds) without any perinatal risk factors. Also suspect IEM when seizures do not respond to conventional ASMs. Metabolic workup should be considered in these neonates. Pyridoxine-dependent epilepsy is a rare but treatable cause of neonatal seizures, and an empirical trial of IV pyridoxine (vitamin B6) is recommended in neonates with refractory seizures without an apparent cause.
- **Familial neonatal seizures:** Benign neonatal seizures have been described in some families. The condition appears to be autosomal dominant, associated with a mutation in potassium-channel genes. The seizures are clonic and begin within the 1st week of life. EEGs taken at the time of the seizures show focal and generalized patterns; interictal EEGs are commonly normal. Usually the seizures eventually stop; however, 15% of patients develop epilepsy.
- **Benign neonatal seizures** (nonfamilial): These infants typically are born at term with good Apgar scores following a normal pregnancy and delivery. The incidence of benign neonatal seizures peaks at 4–6 days of life (referred to as "fifth day fits"). Seizures are most often clonic and may be unifocal or multifocal in nature. The neurologic examination before seizures and interictally is normal, as is the workup (including metabolic studies, neuroimaging, EEG, and cerebrospinal fluid analysis). Usually, there is no family history of neonatal seizures or postneonatal epilepsy.

Benign neonatal seizures are a diagnosis of exclusion. In general, benign neonatal seizures completely resolve within 24–48 hours of onset. Long-term ASM is not required, and prognosis is excellent.

Be sure that the infant is having true seizures and not some other neurologic activity or event. Before starting drug treatment for neonatal seizures, identify whether there is an electrolyte abnormality and, if so, treat that quickly. One nonepileptic condition that can be confused with neonatal seizures is benign neonatal sleep myoclonus. This is asynchronous myoclonic activity during the early stages of sleep. The episodes occur only during sleep and stop when the baby is awakened. ASM is not indicated.

Treat infrequent or transient seizures with diazepam 0.1–0.5 mg/kg IV or lorazepam 0.1 mg/kg IV. If seizures do not stop, occur more often, or are more severe, give phenobarbital 20 mg/kg IV, with a repeat dose as needed. A typical maintenance dose of phenobarbital is 3–5 mg/kg/day. If phenobarbital is not effective, give fosphenytoin 20 mg/kg IV slowly over 20 minutes, with ECG monitoring. It is worth keeping in mind that benzodiazepines (diazepam and lorazepam) in newborns are not always effective, which is likely due to GABA receptor activation that can lead to excitation at this developmental stage. With all of these medications, be prepared to intubate and provide ongoing respiratory support.

When do you stop therapy? Most neonatal seizures resolve by 1 month of age. Most pediatricians stop ASMs before or shortly after discharge from the hospital (e.g. within 1–3 months of seizure onset) if the neurologic examination and EEG are normal.

FEBRILE SEIZURES

Febrile seizures occur in children between 6 and 60 months of age with fever. To meet the definition, there must not be intracranial infection or inflammation, and the child must not have experienced a prior seizure in the absence of fever. The febrile seizure is considered simple if the seizure lasts < 15 minutes, is nonfocal (including both the seizure itself and the neurologic exam), and does not recur within a 24-hour period. 80% of patients meet these criteria. A complex febrile seizure has focal findings, lasts ≥ 15 minutes, or recurs within 24 hours.

Febrile seizures are very common. 2–5% of children experience at least 1 febrile seizure before 5 years of age, and 50% of these occur before 18 months of age. Maximum height of fever is the major contributing risk factor for febrile seizure; the higher the temperature, the higher the risk. Other risk factors include family history, attendance at day care, and the winter season. Most children with febrile seizures are developmentally and neurologically normal. Certain common infections, particularly roseola (human herpesvirus 6) and *Shigella* infection, result in a higher incidence of febrile seizures.

Family history is very important; ~ 40% of those affected have at least one 1st or 2nd degree relative who has had a febrile seizure. In some families, the predilection is so strong that an AD mode of inheritance is suspected.

History and physical examination are very important to identify the focus of the fever, if possible, and to rule out other potential etiologies for the seizure. In young children, this often requires a lumbar puncture.

The 2011 AAP febrile seizures guidelines recommend lumbar puncture in the following situations:

- In the presence of meningeal signs and symptoms
- In children 6–12 months of age whose immunization status is unknown or who are not or incompletely immunized for *Haemophilus influenzae* or *Streptococcus pneumoniae*
- In those who are on antibiotics (because antibiotics can mask the clinical manifestations of meningitis)

No workup is required in cases when history and physical examination clearly point to febrile seizure. Do not routinely order CT or MRI. An EEG is essentially useless in the evaluation of simple febrile seizures.

Simple febrile seizures do not damage the brain. Most of these resolve very quickly and do not require special intervention. Ensure a clear airway and give oxygen if available. Intubation is not necessary.

Children with febrile status epilepticus are a completely different entity, falling into the complex febrile seizure category. These children can sustain brain damage from an attack that lasts > 30 minutes. Treat these children as though they have conventional status epilepticus (see Status Epilepticus on page 12-26).

What about prevention of future febrile seizures? Do not give ASMs to children with simple febrile seizures, even if they recur. Antipyretics and tepid baths have not been shown to prevent febrile seizures. Rectal diazepam is approved for use in children who have frequent febrile seizures and often is used by parents to abort attacks in those with recurrent prolonged episodes.

Who is at risk for recurrence? Generally, it's children who have:

- Their 1st seizure before 12 months of age
- History of a 1st degree relative with febrile seizures
- History of seizure with only a modest temperature elevation (< 104.0°F [< 40.0°C])
- Suffered a seizure after having the fever for only a very short duration

Note: Children whose 1st simple febrile seizure occurs when they are < 12 months of age have a 50–60% chance of recurrence.

About 65% of children with febrile seizures have only 1 episode. Of the 35% of children who experience a recurrence, < 10% have 2 or more additional seizures.

Approximately 1–2% of children with simple febrile seizures eventually develop epilepsy (not too different from the general population), but this development is likely genetic in nature and not due to structural damage arising from the febrile seizures. Alternatively, as many as 5–10% of children who have had complex febrile seizures are eventually diagnosed with epilepsy.

HEADACHE

PREVIEW | REVIEW

- What are the 3 main groups of headaches in children?
- What is the most common type of headache in children?
- Know the criteria for pediatric migraines.
- What is the best treatment for acute symptoms of cluster headaches?
- What are 3 causes of organic headaches?
- What are the warning signs of an organic headache, and what is the preferred imaging modality?
- What is the hallmark of idiopathic intracranial hypertension (IIH; formerly pseudotumor cerebri)?
- What are risk factors for developing IIH?
- When should you order an MRI in a child with headache?

OVERVIEW

Headaches are the most common recurrent pain syndrome in children and can be divided into 3 main groups: tension, migraine, and organic. Tension headaches are by far the most common, followed by migraines. The average age of onset is ~ 7 years. In children < 7 years of age, headaches occur somewhat more frequently in males, whereas they occur equally among males and females between 7 and 11 years of age and far more frequently in females during adolescence.

ETIOLOGIES

Headaches in children and adolescents are common and typically benign. Causes of primary headache:

- Infection is the most typical cause of headache seen in the emergency department (due to viral meningitis, pharyngitis, otitis media, or sinusitis; it also can be caused by fever, likely due to vasodilation).
- Primary headaches
  - Tension (dull, nonpulsating tightness of head or neck; no nausea or vomiting)
  - Migraine (severe, pulsating, throbbing; scotomas, sensitivity to light and noise, nausea and vomiting)
  - Cluster (a series of relatively short, highly painful, strictly unilateral headaches occurring in clusters of ≥ 5 from 1×/day to 5×/day; uncommon in children < 10 years old; sharp, stabbing)
- Emotional factors such as stress and anxiety

Serious causes of headache are:

- Infection (i.e., viral encephalitis, bacterial meningitis, orbital abscess)
- Tumor (usually chronic and progressive). Most have additional symptoms, such as nausea, vomiting, ataxia, or visual problems.
- Intracranial hemorrhage from trauma (subdural or epidural hematoma) or spontaneous (usually subarachnoid hemorrhage). Most also have neurologic findings such as abnormal eye movements or partial paralysis.
- CO poisoning (often with flulike symptoms, fatigue, altered mental status)
- Hypertensive encephalopathy (rare in children and adolescents)

PRIMARY HEADACHE DISORDERS

Tension Headaches

Tension (stress) headaches are due to muscle contraction, are infrequent in the morning hours, and typically become more severe as the day progresses. They present as a pressing, dull, persistent tightness, often described as a band around the head. Pain is generally bilateral and most often distributed in the frontal region, less commonly in the occipital area or over the vertex. It is generally less intense compared with a migraine. Nausea and vomiting are uncommon; pain sometimes resolves within 30–60 minutes or persists for several days. Investigate the possibility of an underlying emotional cause, such as bullying, poor self-esteem, or depression. And remember that heavy backpacks (all too typical) also can lead to tension headaches.

Migraine Headaches

Migraines were once thought to be due to vascular disturbances, but the current understanding suggests a primary neuronal dysfunction and abnormalities in neurotransmitters like serotonin and calcitonin gene–related protein. Migraines can be spontaneous or induced by psychological stress, foods (e.g., chocolate, cheese, monosodium glutamate), or other factors.

An aura is a temporary, progressive neurologic dysfunction followed by complete recovery. Auras are common in adults but relatively rare in children. Typically, an aura in children involves visual, sensory, or speech deficits.

Diagnostic Criteria

The 3rd edition (2018) of the International Classification of Headache Disorders (ICHD-III) differentiates between pediatric migraine criteria from that of adults by modifying the time, location, and symptoms:

- Shorter duration (2–72 hours instead of 4–72 hours)
- Less definitive location (bilateral instead of just unilateral)
- Symptoms of photophobia and phonophobia can be inferred from behavior (i.e., going into a dark, quiet room) instead of verbal affirmation from the child.

Pediatric migraine without aura is defined as at least 5 attacks that:

- Last between 2 and 72 hours
- Include at least 2 of the following:
  - Bilateral or unilateral location
  - Pulsating
  - Moderate-to-severe pain
  - Pain made worse with activity
- Have at least 1 associated symptom:
  - Nausea/vomiting
  - Photophobia/phonophobia

Pediatric migraine with aura:

- At least 2 attacks with the following features:
  - Gradual development of autonomic aura
  - Aura that is fully reversible
  - Aura present < 1 hour
  - Headache within 1 hour of aura
- 1 or more fully reversible aura symptoms (visual, sensory, speech, motor, brainstem, or retinal)
- At least 2 of the following characteristics:
  - At least 1 aura symptom spreads gradually over ≥ 5 minutes or ≥ 2 symptoms occur in succession, or both.
  - Each individual aura symptom lasts 5–60 minutes.
  - At least 1 aura symptom is unilateral.
  - The aura is accompanied, or followed within 60 minutes, by headache.
- Migraine with aura is less common in children than it is in adults.

Unusual forms of migraine headache include:

- **Basilar artery migraine:** Occurs more commonly in adolescent girls and presents with vertigo, syncope, and dysarthria. Some also have visual alterations and loss of consciousness.
- **Hemiplegic migraine:** The child has weakness on 1 side of the body with or without aphasia. This can last hours or even days! Some families have this with AD inheritance. This is different from alternating hemiplegia of childhood, which presents with paroxysmal, repeated episodes of hemiplegia lasting minutes to days; results in intellectual decline; and occurs in those < 18 months of age.
- **Ophthalmoplegic migraine:** An abnormality of eye movements. CN 3 is typically affected, and CN 4 or CN 6 less commonly so.
- **Confusional migraine:** Presents as a profoundly confused state that lasts for hours.
- **Benign paroxysmal vertigo of childhood** (BPVC): A self-limited condition (though symptoms may last 2–3 years), thought to be a precursor to migraine. It causes sudden episodes of vertigo in children, usually between 1 and 4 years of age. The attacks last a few minutes and can be distinguished from seizures by the maintenance of alertness during the episode, the lack of a postictal state, and the reproducible signs and symptoms (e.g., nystagmus, worsening vertigo with head movements). A family history of migraine usually is present. Many children with BPVC develop migraine later in life.
- **Abdominal migraine:** Recurrent attacks of midline abdominal pain, characterized as moderate to severe, lasting 2–72 hours, and associated with vasomotor symptoms, nausea, and vomiting. It occurs without headache.
- **Cyclic vomiting:** Recurrent attacks of nausea and vomiting, usually with predictable time intervals; it may be associated with pallor and lethargy.

Treatment

Treatment is 2-pronged: Alleviate pain in acute attacks and prevent further attacks.

For **abortive therapy** during acute attacks, use ibuprofen. For adolescents with migraine, the 2019 American Academy of Neurology (AAN) Practice Guidelines Update for acute treatment of pediatric migraines recommends that clinicians prescribe sumatriptan/naproxen, zolmitriptan, sumatriptan, rizatriptan, or almotriptan to reduce headache pain. Rizatriptan is approved for children 6–17 years of age. Triptans are contraindicated in patients with a history of transient ischemic attack (TIA), stroke (or other vascular disease), migraine with brainstem aura, or hemiplegic migraine; therefore, clinicians should consider referral to a headache specialist for further management of these patients. Antiemetics also should be considered in patients with prominent nausea or vomiting. Nonmedical treatments often are useful (but less specifically) and include applying ice packs, muscle relaxation techniques (e.g., use of shoulder rolls), and/or allowing the patient to lie down or go to a dark, quiet place to rest.

Chronic prevention (prophylaxis) is indicated when headaches occur 3–4 times per month or are prolonged or debilitating. Topiramate is approved for prevention of migraines in adolescents 12–17 years of age. Although most data is anecdotal, other frequently used agents include cyproheptadine, valproate (≥ 10 years of age), calcium channel blockers, propranolol, and amitriptyline. Nonpharmacologic treatment includes avoidance of triggers, not skipping meals, adequate sleep, avoidance of caffeine/sodas, adequate water intake, and cognitive behavioral therapy (CBT).

In 2017, results from the Childhood and Adolescent Migraine Prevention (CHAMP) trial showed no significant differences in headache frequency or related disability over a 24-week period in those taking amitriptyline, topiramate, or placebo. Those taking the active drugs had more adverse events. This study has prompted a discussion about the role of prophylactic agents. However, the 2019 AAN Practice Guideline Update for the Prevention of Pediatric Migraine recommends engaging in shared decision making regarding short-term trials of treatment options—including topiramate, propranolol, and amitriptyline—in combination with CBT.

Cluster Headaches

The term "cluster headache" is derived from the periodicity of the headaches. They can occur up to several times per day for a few weeks before remitting. Daily attacks occur at the same hour each day in 50% of patients. The pain is strictly unilateral, severe (described as an "ice pick" or "hot poker"), and is supraorbital, retroorbital, or temporal in location. It peaks quickly (within 5–10 minutes) and resolves in 1–2 hours. In about 50% of cases, headache predictably occurs within 2 hours after falling asleep. In contrast to migraines, individuals with cluster headaches are restless, move constantly, or rock back and forth with pain. Also, unlike migraines, ipsilateral autonomic symptoms (ptosis, miosis, lacrimation, eye redness, rhinorrhea, and congestion) typically occur.

Cluster headaches are rare in children < 10 years of age but become increasingly common between 10 and 20 years of age. Boys are affected much more than girls (3:1 to 4:1).

The 1st line treatment for cluster headaches includes oxygen and triptans. Inhalation of oxygen at 6 L/min for 15 minutes is usually rapidly abortive, acting to inhibit neuronal activation in the trigeminocervical complex. Triptans, including intranasal spray or subcutaneous injections, also are effective as 1st line therapy. Octreotide, intranasal lidocaine, and ergot drugs are alternative options for patients who do not improve with oxygen or cannot tolerate triptans. After a patient experiences the 1st of what will likely become a cluster headache, you can institute prophylactic treatment. Verapamil is the drug of choice; other agents sometimes used include lithium, glucocorticoids, and topiramate. Glucocorticoids sometimes are used acutely while waiting for verapamil to take effect. Taper medications after the cluster headache is over.

Chronic Headaches

Chronic daily headache is defined as headache that occurs > 15 days a month for > 3 months and is not due to organic pathology. Chronic daily headache encompasses 5 subtypes of daily headache:

1) Chronic migraine
2) Chronic tension-type headache
3) Medication overuse headache
4) New daily persistent headache
5) Hemicrania continua

In children 12–14 years of age, the overall prevalence is ~ 1.5%, and it is more common in girls than boys. Most adolescents with chronic daily headache have chronic tension headache or chronic migraine (66% and 7%, respectively). Medication overuse has been reported in 20–36% of adolescents with daily headache and is an independent predictor of chronic daily headache persistence. Major depression is another independent predictor. Nonmedical therapies such as acupuncture, massage, improved diet, exercise, and fitness also have a role in long-term management.

ORGANIC HEADACHES

Organic headaches are usually diffuse and generalized and result from:

- Structural abnormalities
- Metabolic diseases
- Infectious etiologies

Severity and frequency generally increase over time, and they respond poorly, if at all, to over-the-counter analgesics. Headaches due to an **intracranial tumor** or other mass lesion frequently awaken the child from sleep or occur soon after awakening. They often are associated with vomiting, which may offer temporary improvement of pain. Further physical examination and laboratory and/or radiologic studies are critical to revealing the etiology (Table 12-3). MRI is the preferred modality, but CT can also be used. Treatment should involve addressing the underlying problem if possible.

Table 12-3: Organic Headache Warning Signs
Nocturnal awakening from headache
Absence of family history of migraine
Papilledema
Confusion
Abnormal neurologic examination
Growth abnormalities
Nuchal rigidity
Headache worsened by cough, micturition, or defecation
Recurrent, localized headache
Persistent vomiting, especially early morning or upon awakening
Progressive increase in headache frequency or severity
Lethargy
Personality change
Pulsatile tinnitus

Idiopathic intracranial hypertension (formerly pseudotumor cerebri) often presents with signs and symptoms that suggest an organic headache. It has been associated with the use of doxycycline or tetracycline (headache in an adolescent being treated for acne) and hypervitaminosis A (i.e., headache in an adolescent taking multiple vitamin preparations or being treated with vitamin A analogs, such as retinoic acid). This disorder also is associated with obesity and the use of oral contraceptives. For more information, see Idiopathic Intracranial Hypertension (IIH).

Idiopathic Intracranial Hypertension (IIH)

IIH (formerly pseudotumor cerebri) is a condition in which there is increased intracranial pressure (ICP) for no apparent reason. It is more common in obese females between 15 and 45 years of age. Although less likely, it can occur in younger children. The hallmark sign of IIH is papilledema.

NEUROLOGY

Symptoms of IIH include:

- Headache
- Visual obscurations (brief episodes of blindness)
- Tinnitus
- Photopsia (seeing light flashes)
- Retrobulbar pain
- Diplopia

These symptoms are not specific to IIH; therefore, other causes such as tumor or infection must be ruled out.

Risk factors for IIH are:

- Obesity
- Drugs: tetracycline, excessive vitamin A, growth hormone
- Systemic diseases: primary adrenal insufficiency (a.k.a. Addison disease), sleep apnea, lupus

IIH is diagnosed by physical examination, MRI, and lumbar puncture. On exam, papilledema is noted. It is usually bilateral and symmetric. Visual-field testing shows whether there is any visual loss. In advanced cases, there can be restriction of visual fields, leading to tunnel vision. A cranial nerve (CN) 6 (abducens) palsy can be seen and is unilateral or bilateral. Perform MRI with magnetic resonance venography (MRV) to rule out other etiologies of intracranial hypertension, such as tumor, abscess, cerebral venous sinus thrombosis, or obstructive hydrocephalus. If MRI is negative, perform lumbar puncture to detect elevated opening pressure (> 25 cm H_2O), which is essential to the diagnosis. MRI may show signs of increased pressure, such as flattening of the back of the eyeball, enlarged optic nerve sheaths, intraocular protrusion of the optic nerve head, and a partially empty sella. The cerebrospinal fluid (CSF) chemistry and cytology are otherwise normal.

Diagnosis is made when all of the following modified Dandy criteria are met:

- Signs and symptoms of increased ICP
- No abnormal neurologic findings on exam (except for visual field and oculomotor findings)
- Increased ICP with normal cerebrospinal fluid composition
- No etiology found on imaging study
- No other cause found for increased ICP

If left untreated, vision loss can result. Aim treatment at relieving the patient's symptoms and preventing vision loss, including discontinuing offending agents (e.g., vitamin A) and treating underlying diseases (e.g., primary adrenal insufficiency). IIH often is treated with medications, but sometimes surgery is required. Treat with carbonic anhydrase inhibitors, diuretics, and migraine medications. If the symptoms are still not relieved with these measures, surgery is indicated. The 2 main surgical procedures performed include optic nerve fenestration and CSF shunting.

CT / MRI EVALUATION OF HEADACHES

Red flags requiring CT or MRI for a child with a headache:

- Occipital headaches (These are rare in children and usually have a structural cause.)
- Unexplained academic decline or behavioral changes
- Abnormal neurologic signs
- Fall-off in growth
- Headache that awakens the child from sleep
- Early morning headaches with increase in frequency and severity
- Headache with focal seizure
- Papilledema
- Migrainous headache, followed by a seizure
- Headache with vomiting in the absence of a family history of migraine
- Cluster headaches
- Any child < 3 years with chief complaint of headache
- Brief coughing episode resulting in headache
- Increasing or "crescendo" headaches
- Persistent focal headaches
- Increase in head circumference
- Increase in severity of headache with Valsalva maneuver

NEUROMUSCULAR DISEASES

PREVIEW | REVIEW

- What are the 4 types of spinal muscular atrophy?
- What is a common presentation for a boy with Duchenne muscular dystrophy (DMD)?
- How is DMD diagnosed?
- How does juvenile myasthenia gravis present?
- How is myasthenia gravis diagnosed?
- How does Guillain-Barré syndrome classically present?
- What is helpful about a lumbar puncture in Guillain-Barré syndrome?
- How do infants with botulism present?
- How do older children with botulism present?
- How are older children with botulism treated?
- What is transverse myelitis?
- How does multiple sclerosis present in childhood?

OVERVIEW

Weakness is a presenting symptom in the neuromuscular diseases. It is defined as the diminished capacity to purposefully move muscles against resistance. Known causes are upper motor neuron disorders, lower motor neuron disorders, neuromuscular junction disorders, and myopathies. Upper motor neuron weakness refers to lesions occurring along the axons from the brain, through the spinal cord, and to (but not including) the anterior horn cell. Lower motor neuron weakness includes lesions occurring from within the anterior horn cell, the peripheral nerve, the neuromuscular junction, or the muscle.

Upper motor neuron symptoms usually affect large muscle groups and include weakness, hypertonia, clonus, spasticity, hyperreflexia, and a positive Babinski sign. Atrophy is mild if present, and there is an absence of fasciculations and fibrillations. Some causes are intracranial hemorrhage, stroke, CNS trauma, CNS tumor, and transverse myelitis.

Lower motor neuron symptoms tend to affect small groups of muscles and include weakness, muscle atrophy, fasciculations, fibrillations, hypotonia, and hyporeflexia. Causes include infections, Guillain-Barré syndrome, botulism, myasthenia gravis, and rhabdomyolysis.

Lab tests to look for infection or inflammatory processes can be helpful. Neuroimaging usually is performed for acute symptoms. Genetic tests are available for many of the hereditary causes. Nerve conduction velocity tests can show a reduction in affected nerves, but 80% of the nerve fibers must be involved to yield a positive test. Some conditions require a muscle or nerve biopsy.

SPINAL MUSCULAR ATROPHY (SMA)

SMA is the 2nd most common lethal AR disorder. (Cystic fibrosis is the most common.) The gene is located on chromosome 5q. Patients with SMA present with hypotonia, weakness of the intercostal muscles, muscle atrophy, and fasciculations. The responsible lesion causes degeneration of the anterior horn cells and, sometimes, also the bulbar nuclei. Muscle weakness is symmetric, with the proximal muscles affected to a greater degree. The legs are affected more commonly than the arms. Because this degeneration affects only the anterior horn cell (motor neurons), no sensory or intellectual deficits are noted.

There are 4 types of SMA in children:

- **Type 0** (prenatal SMA) presents with onset in utero leading to arthrogryposis, polyhydramnios, intrauterine growth restriction (IUGR), and pulmonary hypoplasia.
- **Type 1** (Werdnig-Hoffmann disease, or severe infantile SMA) is the most severe and presents at < 6 months of age with hypotonia and weakness, difficulty feeding, and tongue fasciculations. Most patients die by 2 years of age due to respiratory failure.
- **Type 2** (intermediate or chronic infantile SMA) occurs in up to 1/15,000 births. Infants appear healthy at birth and achieve initial normal milestones, but these milestones are lost by 2 years of age. The majority of affected children die by 12 years of age. Weakness can be static for long periods and then progresses with intercurrent illness.

- **Type 3** (Kugelberg-Welander disease, or juvenile SMA) presents between 2 and 17 years of age, and the child becomes unable to walk or stand unaided. The degree of deficit correlates with the age of onset of symptoms—the earlier the onset, the greater the deficit. These patients have a normal lifespan.

Gene mutation screening allows diagnosis of 95% of SMA cases; the defect is in the *SMN1* gene found on chromosome 5q13. Creatine kinase is normal. Traditionally, management has been aimed at aggressive respiratory, nutritional, and orthopedic interventions. These interventions remain important aspects in the care of patients with SMA. However, the introduction of disease-modifying therapies, such as intrathecal nusinersen (an antisense oligonucleotide) and onasemnogene abeparvovec (a viral vector gene replacement therapy), has made early diagnosis critically important.

DUCHENNE MUSCULAR DYSTROPHY (DMD)

DMD is the most common form of muscular dystrophy. It occurs in ~ 1/3,000 male births and is an X-linked recessive disorder; thus, the mother is usually a carrier, but up to 30% of cases occur as spontaneous mutations. DMD is caused by a mutation in the dystrophin gene and results in absent or deficient dystrophin protein.

Boys present between 2 and 6 years of age with frequent falling, a waddling gait, and toe walking. Classic things to look for on an exam: a child with **calf muscle pseudohypertrophy** and the **Gowers sign**—using arms to climb up the legs when rising from a seated position on the floor. Affected boys generally lose the ability to walk by 12 years of age. Respiratory muscle weakness corresponds to gross motor weakness. Eventually, respiratory secretions cannot be handled, and aspiration/infection commonly occurs. Cardiomyopathy also is a component of DMD.

If DMD is clinically suspected, measuring creatine kinase level is the next step. It will be elevated in patients with the disease. Serum alanine transaminase (ALT) and aspartate transaminase (AST) levels also may be elevated due to muscle breakdown. Diagnosis is confirmed by identifying a mutation of the *DMD* gene. Muscle biopsy is typically only used to confirm the diagnosis in patients whose genetic testing is negative.

Management is largely supportive. Scoliosis begins before loss of muscle function and progresses rapidly once the child is in a wheelchair. Long-term care is an issue, and respiratory failure is a common cause of death. There is evidence to support the use of glucocorticoids (prednisone or deflazacort) to delay wheelchair use. In 2016, the FDA approved the use of eteplirsen, an antisense oligonucleotide, in patients with DMD who have certain mutations.

BECKER MUSCULAR DYSTROPHY

Becker muscular dystrophy resembles DMD in many aspects but tends to follow a less severe course with a later onset of symptoms. It is an X-linked recessive disease that leads to defective dystrophin production but not a total absence of the protein. The disease primarily affects proximal muscles, and creatine phosphokinase (CPK) levels are typically elevated. Cardiomyopathy is also a component of Becker muscular dystrophy. By definition, these patients retain ambulatory abilities after 15 years of age. Life expectancy can be into the 4th or 5th decade. Diagnosis and management are the same as they are for DMD.

MYASTHENIA GRAVIS

Myasthenia gravis is rare in children but still is the most common primary disorder of neuromuscular transmission. In patients with this disease, the postsynaptic receptors for acetylcholine are reduced in number, resulting in the postjunctional membrane being less sensitive to acetylcholine. Almost all adolescents who develop myasthenia gravis have autoantibodies that attack the acetylcholine receptor (AChR), thereby reducing the number of AChRs over time. These autoantibodies also fix complement. They probably originate in the thymus, where there are clusters of myoid cells expressing AChR.

There are 3 types of myasthenia gravis in children:

1) Transient **neonatal** myasthenia gravis occurs when the newborn is exposed to transplacental passage of maternal acetylcholine receptor antibodies (AChR-Ab). The child does not make these antibodies endogenously. The neonate presents within 72 hours of birth with hypotonia, weak cry, difficulty feeding, facial weakness, and palpebral ptosis. Respiratory compromise occurs due to aspiration and progressive respiratory muscle weakness. Neonatal myasthenia resolves in 2–6 weeks, after the maternal antibodies clear.

2) **Congenital** myasthenia gravis constitutes several different genetic diseases with variable age of onset. This disorder occurs as a result of structural or physiologic dysfunction of transmission across the neuromuscular junction. Those affected do not have circulating antibodies to the AChR.

3) **Juvenile** myasthenia gravis is an acquired autoimmune disorder and affects girls more than boys, usually after 10 years of age. Circulating autoantibodies to AChRs are found in 80–90% of affected children. The disease progresses gradually, with worsening muscle weakness, fatigability, and respiratory compromise. Muscle weakness is exacerbated by repetitive muscle use. Ocular muscles are involved, resulting in ptosis and ophthalmoplegia.

Diagnosis of myasthenia gravis is made by demonstrating AChR-Ab. Most patients who are AChR-Ab positive have thymic abnormalities, including hyperplasia or thymoma. Also test for antibodies to the muscle-specific receptor tyrosine kinase (MuSK). MuSK antibodies are present in 38–50% of those with generalized myasthenia gravis who are AChR-Ab negative. Because 6–12% of patients are seronegative for both antibodies, EMG with repetitive-stimulation studies looking for electrodecrement can be helpful.

Treat with oral anticholinesterase medications (e.g., pyridostigmine); these increase the concentration of acetylcholine at the receptor site and can result in muscarinic (e.g., abdominal cramping, diarrhea, salivation) and nicotinic (e.g., fasciculations, muscle cramping) side effects. Most patients require immunosuppression at some point as well. Thymectomy induces remission in as many as 50–60%. Finally, plasmapheresis or IV immunoglobulin (IVIG) is beneficial for short-term amelioration of worsening symptoms.

GUILLAIN-BARRÉ SYNDROME

Guillain-Barré syndrome (acute inflammatory demyelinating polyradiculoneuropathy) is a disorder that frequently is presented on exams. The immune response typically is directed toward the myelin of peripheral nerves, resulting in demyelination and blockage of nerve impulses. Look for a child with acute paralysis, beginning with weakness of the legs, followed by increasing areas of ascending paralysis. It can progress to involve the respiratory muscles and the cranial nerves. Sensory losses are rare and restricted to the vibratory and position sense. Tendon reflexes are also absent. The Babinski sign is downgoing (normal). Less commonly, there can be autonomic instability, blood pressure problems (hypo- and hypertension), and ataxia. Bladder function is usually normal.

The etiology of Guillain-Barré is unknown, but antecedent infections frequently occur, especially *Campylobacter jejuni* (up to 30% of cases), *Mycoplasma*, and Epstein-Barr virus (EBV).

Differential diagnoses include tick paralysis, toxic neuropathies, porphyria, botulism, transverse myelitis, and poliomyelitis. Transverse myelitis can be distinguished from Guillain-Barré syndrome, even in the presence of spinal shock, because patients with Guillain-Barré do not have a sensory level.

Lumbar puncture can be helpful and frequently shows elevated protein levels as high as 100–150 mg/dL with a spinal WBC < 10 cells/μL (**cytoalbuminologic dissociation**). Nerve conduction studies show slowing and/or decreased amplitudes, depending on the subtype.

Treatment is supportive because the condition resolves over time, but close monitoring in an ICU setting usually is required for more severe disease due to the potential for respiratory compromise. Plasmapheresis and IVIG may improve recovery time. Steroids have not shown any benefit. Permanent sequelae can occur in ~ 15% of patients. The course usually progresses for up to 4 weeks and then resolves over the next 2–4 weeks. Most children are ambulatory within 6 months after onset of symptoms. Avoid antihypertensive medications due to the acute autonomic instability, which can induce severe hypotensive crisis.

CHARCOT-MARIE-TOOTH DISEASE

Charcot-Marie-Tooth disease, also called hereditary motor sensory neuropathy, is an inherited neuropathy that is caused by a variety of gene defects that share a common clinical manifestation. Symptoms most often present in the 1st or 2nd decade, and a family history is typical. Patients demonstrate progressive distal ascending weakness manifesting as foot drop and pes cavus (high-arched feet). The classic "stork leg" deformity results from distal calf muscle atrophy. Deep tendon reflexes are lost. Sensory symptoms are often present but tend to be less prominent. As the disease progresses, upper extremities are involved eventually. Treatment is supportive. Orthotics are used to help give the ankle support. Foot surgery usually is required by the time the patient reaches adolescence.

BOTULISM

Botulism is due to the effects of *Clostridium botulinum* toxin. The toxin affects the presynaptic mechanisms that release acetylcholine in response to nerve stimulation; total paralysis of nicotinic and muscarinic cholinergic transmission occurs. The toxin is produced by spores of *C. botulinum* and can contaminate soil-grown foods and fish. In the past, **foodborne botulism** outbreaks occurred in infants given honey at very young ages, leading to the recommendation to not give honey to infants (< 1 year of age). Outbreaks have appeared in individuals who consumed commercial carrot juice and cheese sauce. The highest rates in the U.S. occur in Alaska and are due to ingestion of fermented fish. In infants, most cases in the U.S. probably occur because of the ingestion of environmental dust contaminated with *C. botulinum* spores. **Wound botulism** happens with increased frequency in those who inject "black tar" heroin subcutaneously or intramuscularly (not intravenously).

Infant botulism is characterized by constipation (usually the earliest symptom), generalized weakness (descending paralysis begins with cranial nerve weakness, manifested by dysphonia, dysphagia, diplopia, and blurred vision, which then is followed by extremity weakness and respiratory insufficiency), hypotonia, decreased ability to suck, poor gag reflexes, absence of deep tendon reflexes, facial diplegia, ptosis, and drooling (or pooling) of saliva. Of note, botulism may not cause lack of reflexes until the affected muscle group is completely paralyzed (contrast with Guillain-Barré syndrome where areflexia often is present). Figure 12-20 shows an infant with botulism; note the complete lack of muscle tone and head control. On an exam, look for a child with these findings and especially an alert but weak infant with symmetrical findings ptosis, weak gag, dysconjugate gaze, drooling, and lack of

pupillary response to light (in contrast to spinal muscular atrophy [SMA], in which pupils are typically unaffected and the tongue has fasciculations). Electrophysiologic testing shows an initial, very small, evoked-muscle action potential; however, at high rates (20–50 Hz), the evoked response is potentiated > 400%! For infants, look for the presence of *C. botulinum* spores in stool samples, and confirm the diagnosis by identifying the toxin in stool. Older children with foodborne botulism are likely to have the toxin identified in the blood as well.

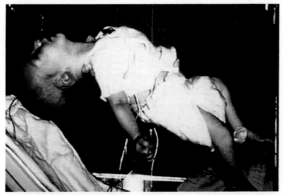

Figure 12-20: Botulism poisoning with generalized weakness and hypotonia

Older children with botulism have dryness and soreness of the mouth, blurry vision, double vision, nausea, and vomiting. They also have anhidrosis (lack of sweating); ophthalmoplegia; and symmetrical facial, bulbar, and limb abnormalities. The pupils frequently are paralyzed as well.

In wound botulism, the presentation is similar except for the lack of GI prodromal symptoms. Also, patients with wound botulism typically have fever. Isolation of the organism from the site is diagnostic. Tissue or pus specimens are best, but a wound swab can be sent if necessary.

Admit all affected children to an ICU and carefully monitor them for respiratory failure. Intubation often is required. Give antitoxin: Treat patients > 1 year of age with equine serum botulism antitoxin; human-derived botulism immunoglobulin can be used for patients < 1 year of age. Antibiotic therapy does not affect the course of the disease and may acutely worsen symptoms as the toxin is released into the intestinal lumen following cell lysis. Antibiotics only are recommended in wound botulism after antitoxin has been administered; use a broad spectrum agent, given the polymicrobial nature of these infections. Avoid aminoglycosides for infant botulism because studies show that these agents potentiate the paralytic effects of the toxin at the neuromuscular junction.

TRANSVERSE MYELITIS

Transverse myelitis is an acute-onset, quickly advancing inflammatory condition that affects both sides of the spinal cord (i.e., "transverse"). It usually involves 3 or 4 segments of the spinal cord and presents with both motor and sensory abnormalities at and below the level of the lesion. Most lesions occur at the thoracic cord level. It usually occurs after nonspecific viral infections. It is a rare disease with < 4 new cases/year per 1 million people.

The illness begins with severe back pain that radiates around to the front. This is followed by rapidly progressive paraparesis, loss of sphincter tone, and sensory loss and numbness at and below the level of the lesion. Urinary dysfunction is common, and depending on where the lesion is in the spinal cord, respiratory symptoms also may occur.

Diagnosis is made by demonstration of inflammation with gadolinium-enhanced MRI and lumbar puncture (after compressive etiology is ruled out). MRI frequently shows an intramedullary signal change (Figure 12-21). Cerebrospinal fluid (CSF) is generally normal or reveals mild pleocytosis and mild elevation in CSF protein.

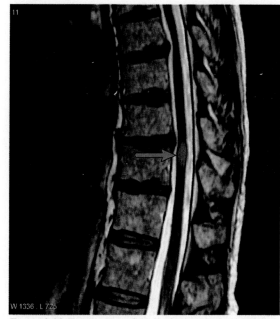

Figure 12-21: Transverse myelitis. Single segment intramedullary hyperintensity in the thoracic spinal cord (arrow)

Prognosis is fairly good, with 60% having return of functional abilities and only 10–15% having permanent, severe damage. High-dose IV corticosteroid therapy is generally used despite the absence of controlled studies in the pediatric population.

MULTIPLE SCLEROSIS (MS)

MS is an immune-mediated multifocal demyelinating disease and is rare in childhood; only about 5% of patients with MS have their disease begin at < 10 years of age. Most are affected in adolescence.

Symptoms are similar to those in adults, with vision abnormalities, oculomotor disturbance, incoordination, and sensory deficits. Watch for the adolescent presenting with optic neuritis (e.g., eye pain, vision changes)! All of the symptoms tend to remit and recur. CSF IgG or oligoclonal bands are increased in 75% of patients, but this finding is nonspecific.

MRI is helpful in diagnosis and shows evidence of demyelination. Diagnosis is made by establishing occurrence of repeated episodes of demyelination either clinically or radiologically. In patients with their 1st presentation, lesions seen on the MRI that are disseminated in space (presence in different locations) and time (old and new lesions) help in diagnosis.

Treat acute exacerbations with short-term, high-dose, pulse IV steroids for 3–5 days. The disease course is extremely variable.

ATAXIA

PREVIEW | REVIEW
- What is acute cerebellar ataxia of childhood?
- What are the symptoms of Friedreich ataxia?

OVERVIEW

The differential diagnosis of acute onset ataxia is varied. The 3 most common causes, in order, are acute cerebellar ataxia of childhood, ingestions, and Guillain-Barré syndrome. Antiseizure medications, such as phenytoin (Dilantin, Phenytek) and carbamazepine, sometimes cause significant ataxia, as do other groups of drugs such as benzodiazepines, antihypertensives, and antihistamines. Other etiologies that can cause ataxia include infectious disorders (e.g., viral meningitis/encephalitis), postinfectious conditions (e.g., acute disseminated encephalomyelitis, postinfectious cerebellitis), tumors, migraine variants, vascular causes (e.g., stroke, cerebellar hemorrhage), nutritional deficiencies (B_1, B_7, and B_{12}), and trauma (e.g., postconcussion, hematoma). In an older child, conversion reaction also may present with ataxia.

Assess with a detailed history and exam. Helpful findings on exam include (Figure 12-22):

- Vital signs: bradycardia, abnormal respiratory pattern, and hypertension (increased intracranial pressure); fever
- Bulging of the anterior fontanelle (increased intracranial pressure)
- Ipsilateral head tilt (posterior fossa tumor)
- Papilledema (increased intracranial pressure)
- Nystagmus (vestibular, cerebellar, or brainstem disorder)
- Opsoclonus (neuroblastoma)
- Otitis media
- Meningismus (CNS infection)
- Rash or viral exanthem
- Examine thoroughly for the presence of a tick

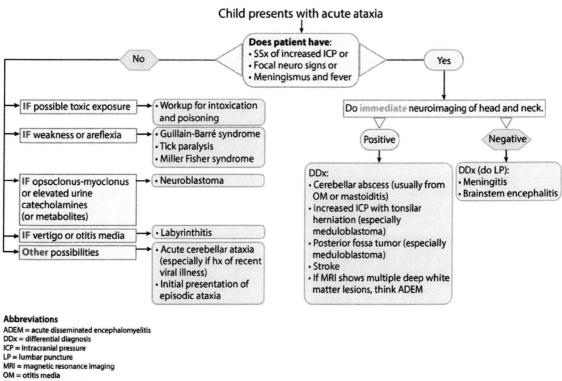

Child presents with acute ataxia

Does patient have:
- SSx of increased ICP or
- Focal neuro signs or
- Meningismus and fever

No / Yes

IF possible toxic exposure → Workup for intoxication and poisoning

IF weakness or areflexia →
- Guillain-Barré syndrome
- Tick paralysis
- Miller Fisher syndrome

IF opsoclonus-myoclonus or elevated urine catecholamines (or metabolites) → Neuroblastoma

IF vertigo or otitis media → Labyrinthitis

Other possibilities →
- Acute cerebellar ataxia (especially if hx of recent viral illness)
- Initial presentation of episodic ataxia

Do immediate neuroimaging of head and neck.

Positive / Negative

DDx:
- Cerebellar abscess (usually from OM or mastoiditis)
- Increased ICP with tonsilar herniation (especially medulloblastoma)
- Posterior fossa tumor (especially medulloblastoma)
- Stroke
- If MRI shows multiple deep white matter lesions, think ADEM

DDx (do LP):
- Meningitis
- Brainstem encephalitis

Abbreviations
ADEM = acute disseminated encephalomyelitis
DDx = differential diagnosis
ICP = intracranial pressure
LP = lumbar puncture
MRI = magnetic resonance imaging
OM = otitis media
SSx = signs and symptoms

Figure 12-22: Evaluation of acute ataxia in the child

Consider the following laboratory and imaging studies:

- Toxicology screen
- CBC
- Blood glucose
- Metabolic exam to include liver function tests, blood pH, amino acid determinations of blood and urine, serum lactate, pyruvate and ammonia levels, and urine organic acids
- Urine catecholamines
- CSF examination
- MRI (preferred) or CT (life-threatening situation) with altered levels of consciousness or awareness, focal neurologic signs, cranial neuropathies, concern for a mass lesion, history of trauma, or hydrocephalus

ACUTE CEREBELLAR ATAXIA OF CHILDHOOD

Acute cerebellar ataxia of childhood (a.k.a. acute cerebellitis) is the most common cause of childhood ataxia. Acute cerebellar ataxia of childhood typically is seen among young children between 1 and 3 years of age (although it can also be seen up to ~ 6 years of age). Its onset is abrupt, and about 50% of those affected have a history of prior upper respiratory infection or viral GI illness. These viruses can include varicella, rubeola, mumps, rubella, echoviruses, EBV, and influenza. Some bacterial infections, such as group A strep and *Salmonella*, also have been implicated.

The ataxia can be mild or severe. Frequent findings include:

- Hypotonia
- Tremor
- Horizontal nystagmus
- Dysarthria

The child is irritable and has nausea/vomiting. The sensory exam is normal, as are the deep tendon reflexes. CSF is normal, except for an occasional increased WBC to 30 lymphocytes/µL. CT and MRI of the head are normal.

Around 90% recover in 6–8 weeks without specific therapy. Steroids are not indicated.

FRIEDREICH ATAXIA

Friedreich ataxia is transmitted as an AR disorder and maps to chromosome 9. It occurs in about 1/30,000 to 1/50,000 in the Caucasian population. These patients do not make enough frataxin, a protein required for proper mitochondrial function. This causes degeneration of cells that are highly dependent on cellular energy production (i.e., nerve and heart cells).

NEUROLOGY

Symptoms of Friedreich ataxia include:

- Hypoactive or absent deep tendon reflexes
- Ataxia
- Corticospinal tract dysfunction (bilateral upgoing toes—positive Babinski sign)
- Impaired vibratory and proprioceptive function
- Hypertrophic cardiomyopathy
- Diabetes mellitus

Genetic testing confirms the diagnosis in a patient with suggestive physical findings.

There is no specific therapy, and the disease requires a multidisciplinary approach including neurology, cardiology, endocrinology, orthopedics, and occupational/physical therapy.

Rate of progression of the disease is variable. Most patients require a wheelchair within 10–20 years from onset of symptoms. Death occurs between 30 and 40 years of age and typically is due to the cardiomyopathy.

ATAXIA TELANGIECTASIA

Ataxia telangiectasia is an AR disease. The ataxia usually presents before 5 years of age. Typically the telangiectasias are not present when the ataxia first manifests. These patients also have immune disorders. See the Allergy & Immunology section for more on this topic.

OTHER DISEASES OF THE CENTRAL NERVOUS SYSTEM (CNS)

The infectious diseases affecting the CNS (e.g., meningitis, encephalitis) are discussed in the Infectious Disease section. The neurometabolic diseases are discussed in the Metabolic Disorders section and the neurogenetic diseases are discussed in the Genetics section.

THE MEDSTUDY HUB: YOUR GUIDELINES AND REVIEW ARTICLES RESOURCE

For both review articles and current pediatrics practice guidelines, visit the MedStudy Hub at

medstudy.com/hub

The Hub contains the only online consolidated list of all current guidelines focused on pediatrics. Guidelines on the Hub are easy to find, continually updated, and linked to the published source. MedStudy maintains the Hub as a service to the medical community and makes it available to anyone and everyone at no cost to users.

FIGURE SOURCES

Figure 12-1: MedStudy illustration
Figure 12-3: CDC
Figure 12-4: MedStudy illustration
Figure 12-6: MedStudy illustration
Figure 12-7: Rajkumar L. Agarwal, MD
Figure 12-13: Rajkumar L. Agarwal, MD
Figure 12-14: Rajkumar L. Agarwal, MD
Figure 12-15: D'Souza, D., Hurrell, M.
Figure 12-16: MedStudy illustration
Figure 12-19: MedStudy illustration
Figure 12-20: CDC
Figure 12-21: Frank Gaillard, CC BY-SA 3.0
Figure 12-22: MedStudy illustration
The remaining figures are from the MedStudy archives.

NEUROLOGY